PRINCE ADAM CZARTORYSKI.

MEMOIRS

PRINCE ADAM

CZARTORYSKI

AND HIS

Correspondence with Alexander I.

WITH

DOCUMENTS RELATIVE TO THE PRINCE'S NEGOTIATIONS WITH PITT,
FOX, AND BROUGHAM, AND AN ACCOUNT OF HIS CONVERSA-
TIONS WITH LORD PALMERSTON AND OTHER ENGLISH
STATESMEN IN LONDON IN 1832

EDITED BY

ADAM GIELGUD

TWO VOLUMES
WITH PORTRAITS

VOL. I

ACADEMIC INTERNATIONAL / orbis academicus

1968

.THE RUSSIAN SERIES / Volume 8

MEMOIRS OF PRINCE ADAM CZARTORYSKI
AND HIS CORRESPONDANCE WITH ALEXANDER I.

Reprinted from the edition of 1888.

Library of Congress Catalog Number: 68-57803

Printed in the United States of America

Orders should be addressed directly to

ACADEMIC INTERNATIONAL / orbis academicus

Orono, Maine 04473

Contents

CHAPTER I

CHAPTER II

1776-1782

CHAPTER III

1783

CHAPTER IV

1784-1787

CHAPTER V

1786

CHAPTER VI

1794-1795

CHAPTER VII

1796

CHAPTER VIII

1796

CHAPTER IX

1796-1798

CHAPTER X

1798-9

CHAPTER XI

1801

CHAPTER XII

1801-2

CONTENTS

CHAPTER XIII

1803-4

PREFACE

PRINCE ADAM CZARTORYSKI has long been known, and
is perhaps still remembered, in England as the friend
of Earl Grey, Lord Brougham, and other leading
English statesmen of the time of the first Reform Bill,
and as the representative and champion of his unhappy
country during the thirty years which he passed in
exile. His Memoirs,* the greater part of which were
written from his dictation in occasional hours of leisure
in Paris, end at the battle of Austerlitz; they give
vivid pictures of the life of the Polish aristocracy during the latter part of the eighteenth century, of the
Court of the Empress Catherine, of the assassination of
the Emperor Paul, and of the character of Alexander I,

* A French edition, with a preface by M. Charles de Mazade, of the French
Academy, was published in Paris in May, 1887 by M. M. Plon, Nourrit, & Co.

who had made Prince Adam his Minister and confidential friend. Of the remainder of his busy and eventful life no detailed history has yet appeared. It is not attempted in the present work to furnish such a history, but only to supplement the Memoirs by diplomatic papers, and other matter hitherto unpublished, which are of especial interest to an English reader. The documents and extracts from private letters and diaries have been copied or translated from the originals in the archives of the Czartoryski family, the introductory chapter is based on facts taken from the late M. B. Zaleski's excellent biography of the Prince, unfortunately unfinished, and the account of his stay in England after the collapse of the Polish Revolution of 1830-1 is derived from a manuscript work now in preparation, which has been kindly placed at my disposal by M. L. de Gadon, secretary to Prince Ladislas Czartoryski, the son of Prince Adam and the present head of the family. In order to elucidate the text, the Memoirs and other papers have been arranged in order of date, and are connected by a brief narrative of the incidents to which they refer, thus presenting, it is hoped, a clear, if incomplete, survey of the career of a statesman whose distinguished abilities, lofty virtue, and ever-fervent patriotism mark him out as one of the noblest and most striking figures of the century.

A. G.

Memoirs of Prince Adam Czartoryski

—◦◦◦—

CHAPTER I

INTRODUCTORY TO THE MEMOIRS.

THE Czartoryskis come of an old Lithuanian family, related to the royal dynasty of the Jagiellons. In 1569, John and Alexander Czartoryski took a prominent part in bringing about the union of Poland with Lithuania, and during the seventeenth century various other members of the family distinguished themselves by their valour in battle and their ability as politicians and churchmen, but it did not attain the height of its celebrity until the middle of the eighteenth century, when, in the words of Mickiewicz, it became the only private family in Europe that had a political history. The heads of the house were at that time the Princes Michael and Augustus. Michael, the eldest, a man of remarkable talents and energy, received an excellent training in statesmanship under his friend Count Fleming, the Minister of King Augustus II, and

A

rapidly rose to a position of almost unexampled influence among his countrymen. Augustus, his brother, proud and reserved in character, but ambitious and passionate, chose the military career. He became a Knight of Malta, and took part in the capture of Belgrade under Prince Eugene, who presented him with a sword of honour in recognition of his bravery on the occasion. In 1729, he became a Major-General in the Polish army, and in 1731, after a duel with one of his rivals for the hand of Madame Denhoff, a lady of rare intelligence and immense wealth, she selected him out of a crowd of suitors, among whom were various foreign princes, such as the Duke of Braganza, the Prince of Charolais, and the Duke of Holstein. Prince Augustus thus became one of the wealthiest men in Europe, and by good management he not only paid the debts on his wife's estates, but doubled her income. At the end of the first year after their marriage, he sent to her a number of boxes full of gold pieces, representing the revenue from her estates, which she at once ordered to be returned to him; and this ceremony was repeated annually during the forty years of their married life.

When Augustus III was called to the Polish throne in 1741, Poland was enjoying the blessings of peace, while the surrounding countries were desolated with the conflicts of hostile armies; and her people presented all the outward signs of prosperity. But as a State she was powerless. In some countries it is a frequent subject of complaint that the people do not take sufficient interest or part in politics, and that the Government consequently falls into the hands of professional politicians. In Poland, not to take part in public life was regarded almost as a crime. Nearly every voter* was an active politician; but this produced an exaggerated sense of the importance of individuals in the State. Each man had his own opinions, and refused to be bound by those of others; the *liberum veto*, originating in times when the principle of government by majority had not yet been discovered, was regarded as a palladium of liberty. Under such circumstances government was impossible.† The Diets had repeatedly to be dissolved without passing the measures necessary for administration, and a wide field was opened for the intrigues of foreign powers and ambitious magnates, especially as the old principle of elective monarchy was still retained. The two Czartoryski princes set themselves to the task of restoring order in this chaos, of combining and directing the national forces which were dissipating themselves in futile individual effort, and of enabling Poland to resume her position among the independent States of Europe. But the difficulty of the task was greatly increased by the fact that the Poles did not see their

* It is a common mistake among Englishmen to talk of Poland as 'an aristocratic republic.' The so-called nobles did not form an aristocracy in our sense of the term, but consisted of all those who had political privileges. In the eighteenth century they numbered one-fifth of the population—a proportion considerably greater than that of the electorate to the population in England, even after the first Reform Bill.

† Another cause of the weakness of Poland as a State is thus indicated by Mr Lecky (History of England in the Eighteenth Century, vol. vi. chap. xxii. p. 104):— 'The objects of Governments are not only various, but in some measure incompatible, and the Dutch constitution, like the old constitutions of Poland, being mainly constructed with the object of opposing obstacles to the encroachments of the central power, had left the country wholly incapable of prompt and energetic action in times of public danger. No augmentation of the military or naval forces, no serious measure of defence, could be effected without the separate assent of all the provinces, and the forms that were required by law were so numerous and so cumbrous that it was probably chiefly its more favourable geographical position that saved the United Provinces from the fate of Poland.'

danger and did nothing to second the efforts which were made to save them.

The princes began by associating with them in the execution of their plan some of the younger and more active members of the great Polish families—the Oginskis, the Poniatowskis, and the Zamoyskis. They thus formed a strong party in the country, which by its wealth and influence was able to give effective support to the Government and to check the flood of anarchy which was rapidly undermining the State. In the midst of the general indolence and disorganisation, people looked up with respectful awe to these self-denying patriots who, in the midst of wealth and luxury, devoted their days and nights to the improvement of the administration and the strengthening of the position of their country with regard to foreign powers. Not content with being themselves hard workers in the cause, the two princes selected a number of intelligent and able young men whom they trained at their own expense, both at home and abroad, for the various branches of the public service. Their object was, above all things, to establish a strong and orderly government in Poland, and their own conduct of affairs was a model on a small scale of such a government. With their immense wealth and extensive social relations all over the country, they constantly stepped in to remedy the defects of the existing system, protecting the poor and weak against the rich, coming forward as the champions of order in the midst of the incessant conflict of opinion in the Diets, and setting an example of steady work and high political aims. This naturally excited the jealousy and alarm of other great Polish families, such as the Potockis and the Radziwills; but they persistently carried out their scheme of action in the face of all obstacles.

Foreign alliances at that time took a very different shape from what they do at present. In 1746 England, Austria and Russia were combined against Frederick the Great, who was supported by France and Turkey. The Czartoryskis sided with the former powers, the Potockis with the latter. Poland had sunk into such a state of anarchy that no Polish statesman could gain any great influence among his countrymen unless he had the support of some foreign ambassador, and it was therefore necessary for the Czartoryskis to declare themselves openly as the partisans of one of the great powers which struggled with each other for leadership in the moribund Polish State, especially as the King himself, alarmed at their steadfast and uncompromising honesty, had gone over to the side of Prussia and France. This was the beginning of the alliance of the Czartoryskis with Russia—an alliance into which they entered with the best of motives, but which had the most disastrous consequences. The first fruit of the alliance was the mission of Stanislas Augustus Poniatowski, the nephew of the Czartoryski princes, to the Russian Court in the capacity of secretary to Sir Hanbury Williams, the British Ambassador. Poniatowski, young, handsome, and with all the accomplishments of a courtier, speedily gained the favour of the Grand-Duchess, afterwards Empress, Catherine, and this greatly strengthened the position of the Czartoryskis

at the Russian Court. Finding themselves abandoned
by the King, they looked more and more to St
Petersburg for support, and the accession to the
Russian throne of the Empress Catherine in 1762
seemed at length to hold out a prospect of the realisation of their hopes. In a long letter announcing the
event to Poniatowski, she informed him that she
would at once send Count Keyserling to Warsaw to
make Poniatowski King after the death of the reigning
sovereign ; or, if this should not be possible, to endeavour to obtain the election to the throne of Prince
Adam Casimir Czartoryski, the son of Prince Augustus
and the father of the writer of the following Memoirs.*

Catherine was thought at that time to be a
sovereign of liberal ideas, who would give her people
a constitution, and would introduce a new era of
freedom and universal justice. These illusions were
so general that even such experienced and sagacious
politicians as the Czartoryski princes were deceived by
them ; they thought that the regeneration of Poland,
for which they had worked thirty years, was at hand.
But King Augustus's favourite Minister, Brühl, did
his utmost to foil their plans. The chief dignities
in the country were taken from the Czartoryskis and
their adherents and given to their adversaries, and
scandalous scenes were got up in the Diets with the
object of decrying them in the eyes of the public.†

---

* ' J'envoie incessamment le Comte Keyserling ambassadeur en Pologne pour vous
faire roi, après le décès de celui-ci, et en cas qu'il ne puisse réussir pour vous, que ce
soit le Prince Adam.' Mémoires de Stanislas Auguste Poniatowski et sa correspondance avec Catherine II. Posen, 1862.

† The following letter, of which there is a copy in the Czartoryski archives, was
addressed on this subject by the Empress Catherine to her ambassador Count
Keyserling : ' M. le Comte de Keyserling : Je viens d'apprendre que la diète en
Pologne est rompue et que vos amis ont pensé être massacrés. Je vous recommande

This brought matters to a crisis. The two heads of the Czartoryski family were growing old, and Catherine was showing an inclination to conclude an alliance with Frederick the Great ; it seemed to them that if they did not at once take decisive action, all the fruit of their life-labour might be lost. The occasion was afforded by the candidature of Prince Charles of Saxony, the favourite son of the King of Poland, for the dukedom of Courland. The Russian candidate, Biron, was supported by the Czartoryskis, but the majority of the senate declared itself in favour of Prince Charles, and a note asserting his claims and intimating doubts as to the legitimacy of Catherine was addressed by the Ministry to the Russian ambassador. This was equivalent to a rupture with Russia, and the Czartoryskis proposed to Catherine that they should form an armed confederacy, not against the King of Poland, but against his Minister Brühl, recalling the words of the Duc de Gramont to Louis XIV : ' We make war against Cardinal Mazarin, but we serve your Majesty.' The confederacy was to take the government of the country into its own hands, restore order and reform abuses, and after the death of Augustus III give up the throne to a prince whose election should be agreeable to Russia. In order to avoid a civil war, the Czartoryskis asked that Russia should send an overwhelming force into the country to support them, and in return they promised to recognise Catherine as Empress of Russia,

d'offrir tout mon appui aux princes Czartoryski et à leurs amis et de ne rien négliger en tout ce qui leur peut procurer sûreté, appui, et profit. Je vous fais cette lettre à ce sujet, vous assurant d'ailleurs de mon affection. Moscou, ce 13 Octob. 1762. Catherine.'

and Biron as Duke of Courland; to regulate the frontier between Poland and Russia; and to give the Empress satisfaction for the insult which had been inflicted upon her. That the Czartoryskis, mistaken and disastrous as their policy has proved, were sincere in their professions of disinterestedness and wished only for the good of their country, was universally acknowledged at the time, and even Herr Benoit, the Prussian Ambassador, wrote to Frederick the Great that 'they were too patriotic to seek the throne for themselves so long as Augustus III was alive, and only thought of the regeneration of their country.' Their only object was to establish a strong and orderly system of government in Poland; and finding that they could not obtain sufficient support for carrying out this object among their own countrymen, they unhappily trusted in the apparent liberalism and justice of the young Empress of Russia.

The hesitation of Catherine, and the death of Augustus III in 1763, necessarily postponed the execution of their projects. The Empress, who had been gradually entering into friendly relations with Frederick the Great, wrote to him that she agreed in his opinion that the crown of Poland should not be retained by the House of Saxony, and that it should be given to a Pole; and she suggested that Poniatowski should be elected king, as having the least right to the crown, he would be most under obligation to the two powers that helped him to it. Frederick readily consented, and a treaty was accordingly concluded between the two sovereigns binding them to joint action with regard to Poland. This alliance opened the eyes of the Czartoryskis to the danger which threatened their country : their nephew Poniatowski was fully aware of their plans and had so far supported them, but he was totally unfitted to occupy the throne of Poland at so critical a period of her fortunes, and it seemed only too evident that Russia and Prussia intended to use him merely as a tool for establishing their influence in Poland and perhaps destroying her independence. What they most dreaded, however, was a civil war, which they were convinced could only precipitate the dangers by which Poland was threatened ; and they accordingly persisted in the course of policy on which they had started. When the Diet was convoked they came supported by a large Russian force ; their opponents protested, and left the House ; and the Czartoryskis at once took the opportunity of introducing the reforms for which they had laboured so long. The system under which the high State dignitaries were indepen- dent of each other and of the King, which was one of the chief causes of the anarchy into which Poland had fallen, was abolished, and replaced by an organisation of Ministers appointed by the sovereign and responsible to the Diet ; all classes of the population were made equal before the law ; and a multitude of smaller reforms, all in the same spirit of liberty and order, became part of the Polish constitution. Rulhière, the historian of the Saxon party, could not restrain his admiration at the Czartoryskis having 'in six weeks carried out reforms which the French kings had only executed in six centuries.'*

* Histoire de l'Anarchie de Pologne, vol. ii. p. 229.

The triumph of the Czartoryskis now seemed assured. Even their adversaries, seeing the wise measures of which they were the authors, and the benefits which these measures were already conferring on the country, abandoned their attitude of passive resistance, and Poniatowski was elected king without opposition (1764), after which the Diet passed a resolution directing that statues of the Princes Michael and Augustus should be erected at Warsaw and Wilna 'in memory of the national gratitude.' The princes did not, however, possess the qualities which ensure popularity : their strict, almost harsh, sense of justice, their aversion to compromise and conciliation, revived the dormant hostility of their adversaries and alienated many of their supporters. Yet the Poles had never enjoyed such security at home, or greater respect abroad than in the first years of the reign of their new king, when the Czartoryskis were the virtual rulers of the country. 'Every citizen,' it was said, 'at length felt that his life, his honour, and his property were safe,' and for the first time for many years Russia and the other neighbouring powers abstained from interference in Polish affairs. Unfortunately the influence of the Czartoryskis did not last long enough to produce a permanent improvement in the administration. Both the King and the people grew restive at the dictation of these two rigid old men, who were so much their superiors in wisdom and self-control, who despised popularity, and sought no approval but that of their own consciences. Moreover, the reforms which were gradually and quietly being introduced by them began to inspire anxiety in the neighbouring States.

Frederick the Great, with his usual sagacity, saw that the effect of these reforms must ultimately be to make Poland entirely independent of her neighbours, and his correspondence with the Empress Catherine and the Prussian Ambassadors at Warsaw shows how eager he was to throw every possible impediment in the way of the Czartoryskis, and especially to prevent the abolition in the Great Diet or Parliament of the *liberum veto*, to which the Poles still blindly clung as one of the pillars of their freedom. At length the Russian and Prussian Ambassadors openly declared themselves against the Czartoryskis, and taking advantage of their unpopularity, secured a majority against them in the first Parliament convoked under the new reign (1766). The Czartoryskis accepted this defeat with characteristic stoicism : the project for the abolition of the *liberum veto* was deferred for a more favourable opportunity, but they remained in office and silently but steadily pursued their work of reform. This, however, did not at all suit the views of the Russian Government, which, now thoroughly alarmed, determined to come forward in active opposition to the Czartoryskis and the King, whom it regarded as their tool. A pretext was ready to hand in the position of the dissenters, who were under the same disabilities as the Catholics then were in England, and whom Catherine had always affected to protect, thereby gaining the applause of her friends the encyclopædists, and making a display of liberalism which cost her nothing and was very convenient for her policy. The Russian Ambassador, Repnin, who had been one of the warmest of the supporters of the Czartoryskis, was instructed to demand that the disabilities of the dissenters should be removed. The princes replied that in the then existing state of public opinion it would be impossible to carry such a measure in the Polish Parliament, upon which Catherine sent her troops into the country to ravage the estates of the Czartoryskis and the King, and issued a proclamation condemning the new policy of reform and promising that the Empress would take all those who had grievances under her special protection. The Czartoryskis, in no way cowed by these barbarous reprisals, undauntedly stood their ground, and when Repnin called upon them to resign office, replied that they did not hold their posts from the Empress of Russia, but from the King of Poland.* Their steadfastness and the abuses committed by the Russian soldiery produced such a reaction in their favour that Repnin, hoping thereby to paralyse the growing opposition to his plans, caused some of the principal senators to be arrested and sent into the interior of Russia. Those who remained, threatened with a similar fate, passed all the measures that Repnin proposed to them. The disabilities of the dissenters were abolished, and a treaty was concluded with Russia assigning to that Power the right of protecting and controlling the Polish administration. But the great majority of the Polish nation indignantly refused to ratify the decisions of its intimidated representatives. On the 29th

---

* 'Je n'ai pas reçu mon emploi de S. M. Impériale, ainsi elle me pardonnera si je ne veux pas m'en défaire à sa requête. Je suis vieux, très-vieux ; elle me fera très-peu de mal en m'ôtant le peu de jours qui me restent. Mais. j'ai trop soin de ma gloire pour ternir la fin d'une vie qui, j'ose le dire, a été passée sans tache au service de ma patrie, par un acte que le monde avec raison condamnerait comme lâche et intéressé.'

of February, 1768, an armed confederation was formed at Bar to rid the country of its Russian aggressors. Russia, hampered by her war with Turkey, strove in vain to induce the King to declare himself against the confederates, and the Czartoryskis entered into communication with them in order to extend the movement over the whole country, and enable Poland to present a united front against her northern neighbour. These efforts failed through the unpopularity of the King and the jealousy of the other great aristocratic families. Yet the confederation stood its ground; its principal founder, Joseph Pulaski, was an old retainer of the Czartoryski family; and Repnin's successor in the embassy, Prince Wolkonski, reported to Catherine that ' nothing could be done so long as the Czartoryskis remained in Warsaw.' The Russian Government then confiscated their property. They persisted, however, in their patriotic attitude, declaring that whatever happened they would remain faithful to their country; and the King, feeling that they were his only support and that he had neither the ability nor the character which alone could in such a crisis enable him to maintain himself, refused to abandon them.

Even Catherine was impressed by this noble courage and perseverance. She restored to the Czartoryskis their confiscated estates, and appointed a new ambassador to Warsaw, Count Saldern, who treated the King and his Ministers in a conciliatory spirit very different from that of his predecessors. But Prussia, alarmed at the apparent reconciliation between Russia and the King, now sent her troops into Poland. The confederation of Bar was crushed, and the first partition was arranged with Russia and Austria by Frederick the Great.

Michael and Augustus Czartoryski did not long survive the fall of their country, for which they had laboured so much and so well. The former died on the 13th of August 1775 ; the latter, on the 4th of April 1782, leaving an only son, Adam Casimir, to whom Catherine had assigned the throne of Poland in the event of its not being accepted by Poniatowski. Like the rest of his family, Prince Adam Casimir maintained frequent relations with England, and he studied English institutions when a young man in the house of his father's friend, Lord Mansfield, then Lord Chief Justice. His amiable character, wit, and accomplishments made him universally popular, and he would certainly have been elected King, and perhaps have averted some of the misfortunes of his country, if Catherine had not supported the candidature of his cousin Poniatowski. The Prince de Ligne, a man well acquainted with the various European courts, calls him in his Memoirs 'the most distinguished man of the four quarters of the world.' Joseph II of Austria frequently corresponded with him, and Frederick the Great was the first promoter of the negotiations which resulted in the marriage of his relative, Prince Louis of Würtemberg, with Prince Adam Casimir's second daughter Marie. As Commandant of the Lithuanian Guard and of the Corps of Cadets, the Prince showed remarkable ability and zeal, and some of the most eminent Polish patriots, including Kosciuszko, were trained under his immediate superintendence. His services in the promotion of national education were equally valuable and untiring. As a judge, his impartiality was such that he sentenced some of the most powerful dignitaries in the country, including his own father, for acts of oppression committed by their stewards on their poorer tenants.

Prince Adam Casimir married on the 19th September 1761, the Countess Elizabeth Fleming, daughter of the celebrated minister of Augustus II; they had five children, two boys and three girls. The eldest son, Adam George, the author of the following Memoirs, was born at Warsaw on the 14th of January 1770, and it will be seen that he describes his impressions from a very early age. His mother, who in later years was looked up to with attachment and respect by the whole Polish nation, is frequently referred to by him in terms of warm affection, and before proceeding to the perusal of his Memoirs the reader may be interested in the following description of her appearance and character taken from her 'portrait,' written by herself in her thirty-seventh year :—

'I was never handsome, but I have often been pretty; I have beautiful eyes, and as all my feelings are reflected in them, the expression on my face is often interesting. My complexion is white enough to be almost brilliant when I blush; a smooth forehead does not make my face ugly, and my nose completes the symmetry of my features. My mouth is large, my teeth white, my smile amiable, and the shape of my face a graceful oval. I have enough hair to make an easy and becoming head-dress ; it is dark, like my eyebrows.   I am rather tall than short : my figure is elegant, my bust perhaps too thin, my hands ugly, but my feet charming ; and there is much grace in my movements.   I have an extreme desire to please, and am skilful in showing both my physical and my mental qualities to the best advantage.   Though vain and ill-tempered, I am endowed with such tact that I very seldom do anything which does not either give pleasure or inspire lively interest.   I am most warm and constant in my friendships ; nothing can abate my confidence in those I love, and I always look up to them as superior to myself.   My predominent passion is the love of my country.   This is a sort of religion with which all my future is bound up, and which my husband and children and my own disposition have made the dearest and most indispensable sentiment of my life.'

(*The Memoirs of Prince Adam Czartoryski, with some notes and other supplementary matter illustrative of the text which have been added by the Editor, begin in the next Chapter.*)

CHAPTER II

1776-1782

EARLY YOUTH.—FAMILY RECOLLECTIONS.—LIFE IN A POLISH COUNTRY-
HOUSE.—PRINCES AND PRINCESSES ON THE STAGE.—A CRIMINAL·
PRIEST.—THE POLISH DIET.

MY recollections of the days of my childhood pass
before my eyes like a landscape in which some objects
stand out here and there in clear and definite forms,
while others disappear in a mist or in the distance.

The first place of which I have any precise remembrance is Rozanka, on the river Bug, where there was
an old stone mansion, with numerous underground
cellars containing excellent old wines.

This was in the year 1776. My father, then commander of a regiment of the Lithuanian Guard, had
taken his detachment to Rozanka during the summer
in order to train his troops in some military manœuvres which he wished to introduce into Poland.
He obtained some good soldiers from Prussia, and
sent young Poles there to learn the Prussian system
of drill.

I well remember the tents which were pitched on
the green meadow, and the officers of the Guard who
used to assemble there for dinner, with a monk of St

Bernard, who was the almoner of the regiment—a tall, stout man, very popular with the officers on account of his merry conversation.

I also recollect the hetman Branicki, who was for many years my father's intimate friend, coming to Rozanka. At that time the hetmans had entirely recovered their former authority, and M. Branicki was accordingly received with all the official honours as well as with the hospitality always accorded to a guest. The whole regiment was in parade uniform, and seemed to me a large army, though it was only composed of two battalions. My father's man-servant was at that time in attendance upon me. He was a Frenchman named Boissy, a native of Pontoise, near Paris; a worthy and intelligent man, who by his democratic spirit had preserved me from the influence of the habits of grandeur which at that time were pretty generally prevalent in Poland. His example induced me to develop from my earliest youth a spirit of activity and independence.

At this time my parents were in the habit of passing the summer at Woloczyn, some miles from Rozanka, and my later recollections are connected with the vast palace of Woloczyn, which was then occupied by the Chancellor Michael Prince Czartoryski, my father's uncle. It was there that my mother was educated under the supervision of the Chancellor's wife, and she was also married there to her maternal uncle, the son of my grandfather Augustus.

The two old princes were very favourable to the match, but it was vehemently opposed by the Princess

Lubomirska, my father's sister. The chief reason of her opposition was this. Shortly before her marriage, my mother went to see one of the peasants on the estate, and found in the cottage a child suffering from a very severe attack of smallpox. This gave her a great shock, as she had lost several of her sisters from the same illness; and she caught the infection so dangerously that her life was despaired of. Directly she recovered, her parents hastened the marriage, and she came to the altar with her face covered with marks of the disease and a wig on her head, as she had lost all her hair. The Princess Lubomirska was much grieved to see so ugly a woman given in marriage to her brother; but though she used all her influence with her father against the match, she could not prevent it, as it was considered a very advantageous one. Some time after, my mother entirely recovered her health, and soon became celebrated for her beauty.

The main building at Woloczyn was of wood, and the outbuildings of stone. I remember the portraits of Charles XII, Augustus II, and Poniatowski, the King's father; there was a large garden crossed by a long and wide canal, at the end of which was a statue of Neptune and his attendants, in the French style then in fashion, imitated from the statues in the gardens of Versailles.

There were some brilliant fêtes at Woloczyn, at which the guests were amused by music and theatricals. Once there was a swimming race, in which the swimmers were dressed as tritons, and among them the one who was most remarked was General Count Brühl.

My mother taught me French. One day she told me to learn by heart some verses of Racine which we had read together, and in which Mithridates discloses to his children his plans against the Romans. I have never forgotten these verses, as I was punished for not having learnt them by being obliged to stop at home, while the other people at the palace went on an excursion to a neighbouring village with a spring, in a very picturesque spot, which my mother had decorated with flowers. These expeditions were very merry and noisy, and I was bitterly disappointed at not being allowed to go.

My first recollections of Warsaw are very vague. One of the incidents which struck me the most was the general mourning which followed the death of my father's uncle, Prince Michael ;* all the inhabitants of the 'blue palace 't were dressed in black.

I also recollect the shame and grief which I felt one day when I cast the blame of some fault I had committed upon one of the running footmen employed in the palace. This man's name was Anthony, and he was so stout that his place was practically a sinecure. He came dressed as for a journey, with a sheepskin coat on, and reproached me with having been the cause of his dismissal, upon which I at once admitted that I was the culprit. I learnt afterwards that the story of his dismissal was an invention ; but it produced a salutary effect.

Shortly after, I became seriously ill. There were several physicians at my grandfather's, including one

* On the 13th of August, 1775, when the author of the Memoirs was five years old. (See preceding Chapter).

† The residence of the Czartoryskis at Warsaw.

named Bart; they all arrived at the conclusion that my recovery was hopeless. My mother begged them to remain in attendance upon me, but none of them would take the responsibility. A friend of my parents then brought Dr Bekler, physician to King Stanislas Augustus, and he restored me to health.

From this date I began a new life. Colonel Ciesielski was appointed my tutor; great care was taken of my health, and I resided sometimes at Powonzki,* sometimes at Warsaw. Impromptu fêtes, in which I and my two sisters took part, used at that time to be given in the 'blue palace,' and there were several Frenchmen who contributed in a material degree to these entertainments. M. Dorigny, a very efficient dancing master, formerly attached to the opera in Paris, and ballet-master at Stuttgart, where the Duke of Würtemberg ruined himself in theatrical performances, presided over the dancing; M. Patonar directed the music, and M. Norblin designed the costumes and the scenery.

One day a fire broke out after one of these fêtes, just as the last guest had gone. It began in the wing of the building where my sisters lived. The actors, who still had their costumes on, were the first to help. One of them had red silk stockings, and while he was occupied in extinguishing the flames, a servant threw a large pailful of water on his legs, thinking they were on fire. My sisters and their governess, Mademoiselle Petit, had to escape to the other side of the building with their friends, the Miss Narbutts.

Meanwhile the flames continued to spread, and

* A villa near Warsaw.

had covered the whole of the wing. The fire did not, however, penetrate the main body of the building, and my sisters established themselves there. A third sister, Sophia, was born at this time. My health was still delicate, and it was thought necessary to teach me riding, which gave me great pleasure.

My rides were usually taken in the direction of Powoňzki; and the time I passed there was the happiest in my life. The estate was a sort of green oasis, whose verdure was the more attractive as it was surrounded by a sea of sand. Each of the children had a cottage and a garden, and in the centre, on a hillock, was a larger house inhabited by my mother, with a wood on each side of it, and looking down on a little lake, whose waters flowed into a stream that bathed all the plantations of the estate. My mother also had some artificial ruins erected, after the fashion of the time, to complete the attractions of the place. There were an island in the lake, a mill, a grotto on the island, stables in the shape of a classical amphitheatre, and a large courtyard with a great many hens and pigeons which we used to feed.

We seldom received strangers ; but living as we did for each other—our mother for her children and we for her—our life was a very happy one. It was like an eclogue—a true picture of rustic poetry.

Each of the cottages in our colony had its particular emblem. My sister Marie had a chaffinch with the motto, 'Gaieté.' My device was a branch of oak with the word 'Fermeté' inscribed upon it. At the top of my mother's house was a hen with her chickens ; on that of my sister Teresa, a basket of white roses, with the inscription 'Bonté;' on that of the steward, a swarm of bees, and below the word 'Activité.' The Miss Narbutts also had their cottages at Powonzki; and the whole organisation of the place had been devised and carried out by my mother.

We got up early, breakfasted either at my mother's or with the steward's wife, who gave us some excellent coffee, and then went to work in the gardens. At dinner-time one of our servants named Martin used to come from Warsaw, leading a donkey which carried our food in two panniers, and which was always received with joy and expected with impatience. Dinner was laid sometimes in one place, sometimes in another, and was announced by a gong.

We often went out on donkeys, and on Sundays we used to go to Mass, some riding and others on foot.

Occasionally there were grand fêtes, at which the King was sometimes present. One day the signing of the peace of Chocim* was represented in the middle of a little wood of elder trees, in a grove generally used for theatrical performances. Lubomirski, who had succeeded Chodkiewicz in the command of the army, and a Turkish Pasha, advanced towards each other with their respective escorts. These grand ceremonies were the things that gave me the least pleasure.

Meanwhile the question of my education was being seriously considered at the 'blue palace,' and my tutor sometimes objected to my going so often to Powonzki; but the attractions of the place were so irresistible

---

* In 1621, when Sigismund III was King of Poland.

that, yielding to the wish of my mother, he pitched his tent next to my cottage.

Those happy times lasted for a few years and were interrupted by a great misfortune. We lost my eldest sister through a terrible accident. We looked upon her as a second mother, and were very fond of her, for she was devoted to her younger brothers and sisters. One day, as she was standing before the chimney-piece, her dress took fire. She fled in terror ; Mademoiselle Constance Narbutt tried to hold her back and extinguish the flames, but could not stop her. In the next room was the governess, Mademoiselle Petit, who as usual was playing piquet with M. Norblin. The latter, hearing the screams of the children, ran out and wrapped my unfortunate sister in a cloak, thereby extinguishing the flames. She was, however, severely burnt ; for some days it was hoped that she might recover, but she was too delicate to bear the shock, and she died shortly afterwards.*

My mother was at this time confined to her bed, and gave birth to a little girl, my sister Gabrielle, who only lived a few days.

It was necessary to conceal from my mother the death of my eldest sister ; she was always asking to see her, but Dr John, who was her physician, did not allow her to leave her bed. Every day she wrote to her daughter and insisted on her being allowed to come into her room, so that at length Dr John was obliged to tell her the truth. The news brought on

* In the Czartoryski Museum at Cracow there is a little book of 24 pages containing a poem on the death of this princess, entitled 'Therèse Czartoryska,' by J K. L. (supposed to be Lavater), and published at Zurich on the 22nd of September, 1780.

an attack of paralysis of the side, and for a long time
afterwards my mother had to walk with crutches. It
was only by the application of electricity that she recovered the use of her leg.

I also was recovering from a serious illness which
caused much anxiety. For some time my sister's
death was concealed from me, and my man-servant,
who pretended to ask for news of my sister, told me
that she continued in the same state. I was deeply
attached to her, and when I learnt the truth I for the
first time shed tears of real grief. I still often think
of her, so good, so amiable, and with so fine a soul
that her parents and the younger members of the
family were deeply attached to her.

My father was at this time at Wilna, where he
was President of the Judicial Court. When he came
back to Warsaw for the holidays he did not know
anything of what had happened. As he was crossing
the Vistula on the ferry-boat between Praga and
Warsaw, he asked the ferryman for the news, and was
told of my sister's death. My father refused to believe
him, but was convinced when further details were
given him by my grandfather Augustus. He nearly
fainted, leaning for support against the wall of the
room; and I saw a flood of tears flow from his
eyes.

My sister's cottage was moved into the wood, and
was kept there in remembrance of her. Each Thursday, the day of her death, was for a long time given
up to mourning and pious meditation, and my mother
consecrated it by a good action.

The Princess Anna Sanguszko, daughter of the

Princess Sapieha, *Chancelière* of Lithuania, also belonged to the colony at Powonzki, and later on it was
joined by Madame Sewerin Potocka. My mother
often went into their house, where there were amusements of all kinds. There was a performance of an
opera called *Zémire et Azor*, in which two of my
sisters and Mademoiselle Narbutt appeared in an
enchanted palace, striving to calm the grief of Zémire.
After my sister's death this opera was performed at
the Warsaw theatre ; my mother wished to be present,
but she was so affected at the scene above described
that she had to quit the theatre in a fit of despair, in
spite of the efforts of the Princess Sanguszko to
console her. I was a witness of this painful incident.

After a time everything resumed its usual course,
as generally happens in this world ; the fêtes were
revived and new members were admitted into the
colony. A great friend of my mother's, the Countess
Tyszkiewicz, *née* Kinska, daughter of the Princess
Poniatowska, and niece to the King, was received
with great ceremony. She had lost an eye through an
illness in early youth, and had replaced it by one of
glass ; still she was very pretty, and was fond of
active sports, such as hunting and riding.

Being desirous of returning my mother's politeness, the Countess Tyszkiewicz had a comedy played
in her house under the title of '*L'amoureux de Quinze
Ans.*' She herself took the part, dressed in man's
costume, of the lover, and my second sister played
the heroine. The theatre was in the sheepfold, and
the Countess went to it on horseback, in the costume

in which she was to act. After the play there was a collation.

There were also theatrical representations in the house of the *Chancelière* Princess Sapieha. One of the pieces that were played there was an opera, '*La Colonie*,' in which the performers were the Princess Radziwill, *née* Przezdiecka, who often came to Powonzki and had a fine voice; my mother; M. Wojna, who was afterwards ambassador at Rome; and General Brühl, of the artillery.

On another occasion they played '*Andromaque*.' The leading part was taken by the young Princess Sanguszko, who had just married; she was very pleasant and good-natured, but a little frivolous, and she had taken lessons of a celebrated tragic actress from Paris. The part of Hermione was played by another Princess Sanguszko, who was afterwards Princess of Nassau; that of Orestes, by Prince Casimir Sapieha; that of Pyrrhus, by a Swiss named Glaize; and that of his confidant, by Prince Calixtus Poninski. This tragedy did not produce any impression upon me; I only recollect that Prince Sapieha was dressed in a Greek costume, and M. Glaize in a Roman one.

When we were at Warsaw I was often sent, according to the custom of that time, to assist at my grandfather's toilet. When I went to him they had to put pomatum on my hair, and to powder and curl it, which was very unpleasant to my mother, who did not like to see me thus disfigured. On one of these visits it was Corpus Christi day, and there was an altar in the courtyard. The Bishop, a *protégé* of my

grandfather's, was under the canopy, and my grandfather assisted at the mass. Shortly after my grandfather died,* and all amusements ceased. He
was buried in the church of the Holy Cross, and
his death caused general regret—especially to his
daughter, the Princess Lubomirska, who was at
Warsaw at the time, and did not leave him until the
last moment.

He died simply and naturally, without the least
desire to attract remark. Every day after dinner he
used to play at a game called 'tryset,' which was very
like whist, and was played by four people; the Pope's
Nuncio generally joined in the game. The Prince
kept up this habit to the last, and although he was
very weak, he had himself dressed to go to the card-
table. On the very day of his death he came as
usual, bowed to the Bishop Archetti (who afterwards
became a cardinal), and apologised for coming a little
late. As his sight was failing, he asked why they
had not lit the candles, although the room was lighted
up as usual. Meanwhile the Princess Lubomirska
was in her apartments in deep grief, and could not
come down into the room, where my mother was with
the whole family. All the people of the house, down
to the lowest servant, were assembled in profound
silence. The Prince, who was in an invalid chair,
turned to Dr Bart, who never left him, and asked
him in German: 'Wie lange wird's dauern' (How
long will it last)? The doctor felt his pulse, and
replied: 'Another half-hour, I think.' The Prince
then apologised for not being able to play any longer

---

* On the 4th of April, 1782. (See preceding Chapter).

with the Nuncio, and had himself taken into the bedroom; the prelate followed him, and began to read the psalms for the dying. While he was reading he held the Prince's hand, and as he spoke the words of the Psalmist: 'My God, I give up my soul to Thee,' the Prince pressed his hand and gave up his last breath. The crowd which had penetrated into the palace, hitherto respectfully silent, then burst into tears and sobs.

At the time of my grandfather's death, my father was still at Wilna, where he was for the second time President of the Chief Tribunal of Lithuania. He entirely devoted himself to his functions in this capacity. Several magistrates were accused of having done injustice to individuals either through indulgence for others, or from motives of personal revenge. I heard people say that while my father was in office, an action was brought against my grandfather by a gentleman who had a claim on his estate, and that my grandfather was condemned in costs.

There was much talk at this period about a crime which had been committed some years earlier, but the author of which could not be discovered. By a singular accident the first trace of the criminal was found in 1781, and it drew suspicion upon a man named Ogonowski, who had become a priest and was protected by the Bishop of Wilna, Massalski, well known for his dissolute life. My father, who was then President of the Court, used all his influence to have the culprit brought to trial.

The Abbé Ogonowski, who had rapidly passed

the various ecclesiastical grades which lead to final ordination as a priest, hearing that he was in danger, took refuge in a convent, under the protection of Bishop Massalski. A detachment of troops belonging to the Lithuanian Guard, of which my father was in chief command, was ordered to surround the convent during the night, and succeeded in getting the doors opened, notwithstanding the resistance of the priests. Ogonowski was found with some difficulty in a cell, and taken to prison in spite of his protests and those of the clergy. He was convicted of murder and other offences, after a very long and careful trial, and was condemned to death and executed.

Several old cases were settled while my father was in office, and the procedure became much more regular than had previously been the case. He finally withdrew from his post in 1782, and hastened to return to Warsaw to take part in the Diet which had been opened under the presidency of Colonel Krasinski. This was the first meeting of the Diet at which I was present. My tutor and myself frequently went both to the senate and to the Chamber of Deputies. I was struck by the grave and imposing presence of Prince Lubomirski, Marshal of the Crown, who, as I have heard other people say, was eminently fitted to keep order at the meetings of both Houses.

The most important matter that was considered at this Diet was the withdrawal by the chapter of the Cathedral at Cracow (with the support of Prince Poniatowski, Bishop of Plock) of Monsignor Soltyk,

Bishop of Cracow, from the adminstration of that diocese, on the pretext of mental incapacity.

The anti-Russian party defended the bishop, who had been one of the most valiant members of the Confederation of Bar.* The party of the King and of Russia strove to maintain and justify the act of violence committed against Monsignor Soltyk, and being the most numerous, succeeded in obtaining a majority in favour of the measure.

The opposing parties spoke with much passion, endeavouring to prove on the one hand that the Bishop of Cracow was perfectly sane, and on the other that he was mad. One of the most moving and eloquent of the speeches was that of the Castellan Ankwicz, who was at that time regarded as an exemplary patriot, but afterwards passed over to the Muscovite party. He was one of the victims of Kosciuszko's revolution; the people of Warsaw themselves executed the sentence which had been pronounced against him.

During his year's residence in Lithuania, my father had gained the sympathies of the citizens of that province, and he thought that he would have the majority of the Lithuanian votes at the Diet in favour of the party of which he was one of the chiefs; but the fear of Russia and the King's presents decided otherwise. Many of the Deputies found reasons to avoid the inconvenient results which

---

* The originators of the Confederation of Bar were two bishops, Soltyk and Krasinski. The object of the Confederation, which was formed by Casimir Pulaski on the 29th of February, 1768, was to deliver Poland from the domination of Russia. The confederates maintained their ground by extraordinary feats of arms against the Russian troops for five years, and were finally crushed by Souvaroff in 1772, a few months before the first partition of Poland. (See the previous Chapter).

would ensue from an open rupture with the King
and the Russians.

The Diet having thus come to a close in so
unfavourable a way for our party, my father determined to visit the estates which he had inherited
in Volhynia and Podolia.

CHAPTER III

1783

JOURNEY TO VOLHYNIA AND PODOLIA.——INTERVIEW WITH FREDERICK THE GREAT.

BEFORE leaving for Volhynia, I went with my tutor to pay a visit to Prince Lubomirski. This was the last time that I saw him; he did not long enjoy the fortune which his wife had inherited, and died in the same year, universally regretted. He lived in the palace which afterwards became that of the Tarnowskis, and belonged by right to the Czartoryskis. The Princess and her husband were very sensible people, but as often happens in the marriages of great families, their characters were not suited to each other. The Prince left heavy debts which his widow admitted and scrupulously paid. His sallies and repartees were characteristically Polish. My mother esteemed him greatly, and he was a true friend to her. I do not know on what occasion he once said to her that he would come to see her after his death, and for a long time she feared he would keep his word. These apprehensions recurred nightly, when everybody was asleep; the slightest noise recalled to her the promise of her deceased friend.

We left for the estates in Podolia with a large suite. My father at that time had a very numerous court, chiefly composed of noblemen's sons, many of whom came even from Lithuania. The rendezvous was at Pulawy, from which place we started. Dozens of carriages followed each other in line, and we travelled at the rate of not more than six miles* a day. After breakfast we proceeded to the next stage, where we dined ; the food and wine always preceded us. There were a great many led horses, and we often mounted them to get over a stage more quickly. One of the principal officials of the court always went on beforehand to get our quarters ready. We were accompanied by several young pages dressed after the Polish fashion ; and before we left Warsaw, the major-domo thought proper, as a prudential measure, to administer some corporal discipline to them. My father, as he was coming out of the house, perceived traces of tears and vexation on their faces, and asked what was the matter. 'See how the major-domo has punished us,' they answered. My father then asked the major-domo what they had done, to which the latter rejoined that it was a good thing to prepare them in this way for their journey.

We stopped on our way at the houses of several landowners, many of whom joined our party, which increased the number of our led horses and carriages ; we had also brought some camels with us, as my father wished to introduce them into general use. The caravan stopped at Klewan, the first of my father's estates in Volhynia. We next arrived on the property

* A Polish mile is equal to five English miles.

of Prince Sapieha, who received us with the amplest
hospitality. The Prince suffered much from gout, and
this was attributed to the custom, which at that time
was very general, of always drinking with a visitor.
Prince Sapieha came every evening leaning on a cane
to look at the brilliant illuminations in the garden.
Our next halting-place was Mikolajew, in Podolia.
There were not enough rooms here for the whole of
our party, which had become very numerous, and
many of us slept in tents.

Among the many friends who accompanied us on
this journey was Niemcewicz,* my father's aide-de-
camp. Opportunities were frequently taken of em-
barking on various love adventures, in allusion to
which one of the poets of our party wrote a song of
which the first couplet was as follows :

'Beautiful Tomira, this is probably the last of our
pleasant evenings ; I am with you to day to morrow
I shall be alone, and woods and streams will separate
us. But when I shall no longer be there, remember I
was the first to love you.'

Niemcewicz was very assiduous in his attentions
to the sex. One of the houses where we stayed the
longest was that of M. Onufry Morski. This gentleman had a very important position in Podolia, and
was a friend of my father's, for whom he had a
great liking. He had a very handsome wife, of whom
he was jealous, and he did not trust the friendship of
Niemcewicz. One day the comedy of ' *Le Joueur,*'
which my father had translated from the French, was

---

* An eminent Polish writer, best known for his ' Historical Songs ' and his
excellent translations from various English poets. He was born in 1757, and died
n exile at Paris in 1841.

performed at his house, and his wife took a part in it. He himself played the hero, and had to address her in a speech full of ardent love, to which she listened with the greatest coldness, as I remarked at each performance. Morski's younger brother was afterwards the ambassador of the King of Saxony and Grand-Duke of Warsaw at Madrid. His elder brother, the canon, was passionately fond of dancing; I still remember with what *entrain* he danced the mazurka at a masked ball at Siedlce, and he was not a man of very rigid morals.

Among the more intimate guests at my father's house was Colonel Molski, a wag fond of bon-mots and good eating. He once made a bet that he would eat an enormous dish of *pirogi** alone, without hurting himself. He gained his bet, and drank some punch to wash the *pirogi* down.

At Miendzyboz we met a large detachment of Cossacks, which gave us the idea of constructing a sort of fortress and feigning attacks upon it. My tutor shut himself up in the fortress with my brother; the besiegers were under the command of Colonel Molski, to whom I acted as aide-de-camp. When the day for the attack came, there was much noise and fighting on horseback. M. Siehen, mounted on a very spirited horse and riding at full gallop, encountered one of the Cossacks, and the shock was so violent that Siehen fell from his horse and became insensible. When he recovered consciousness, he had completely lost his memory, and he did not recollect what had happened until several days afterwards. The Cossack

* Small meat puddings.

escaped with a few contusions. Soon after there was almost a real battle between the Cossacks and the inhabitants of the village, a detachment of whom were in the fortress where we were to breakfast. The besieged at last ate the food that had been prepared for us, and an arrangement was then made to prevent further accidents. I assisted at this fight on horseback, and it greatly interested me.

From Miendzyboz we went to Kamieniec, where was M. Witt, the father of General Witt, whose wife was the beautiful Greek that afterwards married Felix Potocki. At that time she was in all the freshness of her beauty, and shortly after she travelled all over Europe, her charms attracting universal admiration. She did us the honours of her house at Kamieniec, surrounded by people distinguished by their youth, their birth, or their talents. All paid her implicit obedience, and besides her beauty she attracted by a sort of originality proceeding either from a feigned naïveté or from ignorance of the language. I was told that when people admired her beautiful eyes, or when she spoke of them herself, she used to say in French: 'mes beaux yeux,' thinking that this was a single word.

M. Witt took me and my tutor over the ramparts of the fortress to show us that it was impregnable. The rock on which it is built is surrounded by a moat, on the other side of which is another rock, containing vast casemates to hold troops for the defence of the place. The only channel by which the inner rock communicates with the outer one is very narrow, and is provided with very solid ramparts.

From Kamieniec we went to Chocim, which at that time belonged to Turkey, and where the officer in command was a pasha who displayed much luxury and politeness in receiving my father as general of the Podolian territories. After handing round chibouks and coffee, the pasha's son, a tall young man, approached me and my brother and invited us to visit the harem with his father's permission. We followed him, a *portière* was raised and then drawn down behind us, and we entered the seraglio.

I saw through the doors of the rooms looking into a passage some women, who seemed much astonished and alarmed at our presence. We went to a place where was the young man's mother, the pasha's wife, surrounded by several female attendants; this was a sort of kiosk erected in a corner of a rectangular garden. We did not like these women, and thought them very untidily dressed. They received us very amiably, examined us with much curiosity, and asked us some questions; but the conversation was neither long nor animated.

We returned to Miendzyboz, which was the last stage of our journey, for to my great regret we did not go as far as Cracow.

We travelled through Galicia, and after stopping at Oleszyce, Sieniawa, and Jaroslaw, we arrived at Pulawy, where we finally took up our residence.

[On the 27th of October, 1784, Prince Adam's sister Marie was married to Prince Louis of Würtemberg, the brother of the wife of the Grand-Duke Paul of Russia (afterwards the Emperor Paul) and a relative of Frederick the Great. The newly-married

pair went to Berlin, and soon after Prince Adam's
mother paid them a visit. Here she had an interview with Frederick, which she thus graphically
describes in a manuscript diary preserved in the
Czartoryski archives :—

'The King of Prussia always lived at Potsdam,
and only received on certain days which were fixed
beforehand. It was not without a certain degree of
fear that I made myself ready to visit him. Having
from my childhood constantly been told of his genius
and great deeds, I had formed in my mind so high an
idea of him that I felt timid. I hoped I would be
admitted to his presence with many others, and be
lost in the crowd ; but Madame Voss, the Queen's
lady-in-waiting, took me alone into the drawing-room,
and directly I entered, the door opposite me opened,
and the King came in also alone. Madame Voss
merely mentioned my name and withdrew. I thus
remained *tête-à-tête* with a man who filled me with
fear, and whom I believed to far exceed in genius and
learning all those whom I had yet seen. I was so
dazed that if I had at once left the room, I could
have sworn that Frederick was at least six feet high.
He took my hand kindly, and said: "I am old, and
my sight is bad ; allow me, Princess, to take you to
the window, so that I may have a good look at you."
This completed my confusion ; tears were in my eyes,
and I trembled like a leaf. The King, no doubt
to give me courage, then himself began the conversation, still holding my hand. "You have given us
an angel, Princess," he said. "I saw her yesterday,
and she inspires me with the greatest interest." I

then ventured to look at the man who had called
my daughter an angel. To my surprise I saw not a
giant, but a little man, shorter than myself, rather
crooked, and in a shabby uniform covered with snuff.
He had beautiful blue eyes, a mild but penetrating
glance, and a manner which inspired confidence.
Seeing that I was looking at him, but that I did not
yet venture to open my lips, he continued : " Your
angel will always find in me a friend. She has
married my nephew, but I must plainly tell you that
they are not made for each other, she is an angel and
he*—" The King did not finish the phrase, but added,
" Anyhow you know him and will do him justice ; all
I will say now is that this cannot last, but let
her boldly come to me whenever she finds it
necessary." These words calmed my anxiety, and
there remained only a feeling of gratitude which it was
easy for a mother to express when speaking of her
daughter. The interview lasted over an hour.
Frederick II afterwards spoke of many other things.
He asked me about Poland and our King. This
was a very delicate subject, as he had only recently
plundered our King with the help of his allies, who
had shared in the spoil. Among the questions he
addressed to me I remember his asking whether
Stanislas Augustus wore a military uniform. I felt
the irony of this question, as our army had at
that time been so reduced that we hardly had any
troops at all. I answered, as was the fact, that
the King wears the uniform of the School of Cadets.

* Prince Louis of Würtemberg was afterwards deprived of his command in the
Polish army for declining to fight against Russia, and his wife, the Princess Marie,
then refused to live with him.

"He is right," observed Frederick; "*c'est vraiment un roi à l'école.*" I felt indignant at this remark, which seemed to me quite uncalled for. I turned red, the tears again rose to my eyes, and I exclaimed without thinking: "*Sire, vous lui avez donné une leçon cruelle et peu méritée.*" When I came in I did not dare to raise my eyes to him; afterwards, when he began to speak of my daughter, I felt bolder, and I was thoroughly roused when he spoke slightingly of my unhappy country and King, whom he had humiliated after plundering him. After I had spoken I felt frightened, but Frederick thus went on, as if he had not heard what I said: "I have often remarked that in Poland women should govern; if they did, everything would be better there, and our conversation to-day has confirmed me in that belief." He then bowed to me politely and respectfully, again saying that my daughter could always reckon on his protection; and with this our first interview ended.'|

CHAPTER IV

PULAWY.—EDUCATION AND STUDIES.

At Pulawy we* began an existence which was entirely new to us, and we entered on our studies seriously and regularly.

Up to that time we had only been taught elementary knowledge, and our lessons were frequently interrupted, while now they became almost our sole occupation. M. Lhuillier taught us mathematics and universal history; Colonel Ciesielski, the history of Poland; Kniaznin, literature and Latin. Our classical master was at first a Dane named Schow, and afterwards Groddeck, who subsequently became a professor at the University of Wilna.

I do not quite remember whether it was then or later on that my father appointed as our tutor M. Dupont de Nemours, a member of the National Assembly, who was much esteemed in France for his ability and character. He had with him a secretary named Noyer, a very importunate man who paid

---

* The author and his brother Constantine. The Bohemian traveller Tanner, writing in 1678, says of this magnificent country seat of the Czartoryski family :—
' Prospeximus hic a dextra fluminis parte Pulavii castrum splendidum, et a circumjacentium hortorum amænitate deliciosum.'

marked attention to Madame Petit. One day he knocked at her door, and not knowing any other way to get rid of him, she told him she was not at home. M. Dupont did not stay long with us; he returned to France, and I saw him in Paris at the time of the Restoration. He introduced himself to me as my old tutor, but I had entirely forgotten him.

There was a fencing-master at Pulawy who gave us a lesson every morning in the garden after we got up, which was very early, and then we passed to other studies. The company used to be very large at dinner, as all the persons in the service of the family were present.

Besides our studies, we had various pleasures, such as hunting, excursions to the house of M. and Madame Filipowicz, the steward of the Pulawy estates at Konska Wola, country rides, and especially coursing. I was very fond of this pastime; in a wood in the vicinity there were hares on the hills, and a brood of foxes which we amused ourselves by driving out of their holes with dogs.

This was for us children what I may call 'the Pulawy period.' My father's stay in Lithuania attracted to our house a great number of citizens of that province; several young men also came from Lithuania to be educated at our house, and they amused the company during the hours which were not given up to study.

Our daily fencing-lessons took place in the garden during the summer. Although accustomed to the use of the foil at the school of Cadets, Rembilinski, one of our tutors, was once hit in the eye, and on another occasion, as he was fencing with me, my foil pierced his mask and wounded him in the mouth. He was much frightened, and his first thought was to ascertain whether his second eye had not been hurt. I was profuse in my apologies, and thanked God that my awkwardness had not had any more serious consequences.

We used to hold meetings like those of the Diets, at which we discussed public questions. I recollect that at one of these meetings the question discussed was, which was the best government, one in which political power was distributed among the people, or a government in which all power proceeded from a central authority. I advocated the greatest possible liberty, while to my great surprise Rembilinski declared himself in favour of a central and paternal government. His speech was so eloquent that I could not find words to answer him, which greatly dissatisfied me. I was beaten, but not convinced.

CHAPTER V

1786

IN 1786, I first went to travel abroad ; I was accompanied by my tutor, who had been ordered to take the waters at Carlsbad. Madame Oginska, the hetman's wife, my father's cousin and my mother's aunt, started for Carlsbad at the same time as we did, accompanied by a numerous suite, as was then the custom. We visited several German towns where I came into contact with many eminent men. I cannot say that I made their acquaintance, for my mind was as yet not sufficiently developed; but I still remember having met them.

My father had invited to Pulawy a professor of Latin and Greek who had been recommended to him by Steine, the celebrated professor of Göttingen. He was a young Dane and an enthusiastic admirer of the beauties of ancient literature, like all who came from that university. I shared this enthusiasm —a little childishly, but very sincerely—under the influence of Kniaznin, who taught us Polish and

Latin literature. I neglected the tedious though indispensable study of grammar, and tried to understand the classic poets, which gave me the appearance of knowing much more than I did in reality; and I paraded my knowledge in the presence of the German *savants* whom I met on my travels. At Prague I made the acquaintance of Meissner, professor of Greek literature and author of several German works. His reputation, which at that time was very great, did not survive him. I recollect with pleasure the conversations I had with him, and I was much astonished to find that I was able to quote to him from memory some verses from the Greek poets.

We passed through Gotha, where, thanks to a letter of introduction from my father, we made the acquaintance of Baron Frankenburg, Minister to the Duke of Gotha. He was an intelligent, amiable, and cultivated man, and he placed us in relations with other celebrated and interesting persons. He gave us letters with which we went to Weimar, already known as the German Athens, where I saw Wieland and Herder, with whom my father kept up a correspondence.

Wieland's appearance was anything but poetical; he was short, rather stout, somewhat advanced in years, wrinkled, and wearing a sort of nightcap which he seldom took off.

Baron Frankenburg also enabled us to make the acquaintance of Goethe, and I was admitted with my tutor to a private house where the poet read to some friends his play of 'Iphigenia in Tauris,' which he had just finished. I listened with great enthusiasm. Goethe was then in the brightest period of his youth ; he was tall, and his face was handsome and imposing, with a piercing look, sometimes a little disdainful, as if he were looking down upon the horizon of humanity. This slight tinge of arrogance was also visible in the smile on his beautiful mouth. He hardly remarked the admiration of a youth like myself, for this was a homage to which he was accustomed. When he afterwards became Minister to the Grand-Duke of Weimar he no longer showed the same disregard of official favours and decorations ; but he always retained in his face and demeanour a sort of grandeur which made people compare him to Phidias's statue of the Olympian Jove.

At length we arrived at Carlsbad, where we found Madame Oginska, whose presence greatly contributed to our pleasure. She had with her several young ladies, the daughters of her major-domo Siedlecki, and also Dr Kittel, who was young and very handsome, and was consequently much in request with ládies whose health required, or seemed to them to require, a doctor's care.

There was at that time at Carlsbad a very brilliant casino, where the whole society of the place assembled, and where there was dancing almost every evening. One of the ladies was said to be much admired by the Archduke Leopold, whose weakness for the sex was notorious, and who ascended the throne some years later. I was struck by the beauty of the features of this lady, and especially by the extraordinary vivacity of her movements.

We returned home in the autumn, and the winter

of 1786 to 1787 was passed partly at Pulawy, partly at Siedlce. We continued our studies at Pulawy without much regularity, but with great interest and diligence, and passed the carnival at Siedlce, where there was a numerous and brilliant gathering of visitors. Madame Oginska, who held her Court there, was very pious, but her sole anxiety was to amuse her guests and make them merry. She had in her house a great many charming young ladies belonging to noble families. When her toilet was over, her guests were admitted into her apartments, and these young ladies were to be seen taking to her some article of dress—a flower, a ribbon, a veil, or a bonnet—which was to be worn in the course of the day. Afterwards everybody went into the drawing-rooms, where amusements of all kinds were constantly going on.

Madame Oginska was very fond of playing at cards, and invited the best players to Siedlce. This was not perhaps very praiseworthy, but it contributed to our amusement for part of the day. In the evening there was dancing and drawing-room games; in the summer we walked about in a large garden which was called Alexandria, and which Madame Oginska had decorated in the English fashion; in the autumn we went out shooting, and she used to join our party, firing from her place at the birds as they flew by.

It was difficult to suffer from *ennui* at Siedlce, and the natural consequence was that romantic adventures frequently occurred, in which I sometimes played a part. I had found some books which fired my imagination; I read them during several nights, when I should have done better to devote the time to study. One of the young ladies at Siedlce, Mademoiselle Marie Niezabitowska, became the object of my 'sighs,' which I did not venture to communicate to her without great hesitation. To enter into the young ladies' room was beyond my power, and often I used to stand near the door, fearing to cross the threshold. At length I got over my timidity, and my usual place was on a box in the young ladies' room.

To make love or fall in love was the lot of every young man at Siedlce, and I had some rivals, among whom was Niemcewicz. Mademoiselle Niezabitowska was one of the prettiest of the young ladies there, and she was also endowed with other qualities by Nature which distinguished her from other women during her long life. Poets wrote verses to her, and I remember that one of these effusions ended by deploring her severity to those who surrounded her. It was indeed difficult to secure her good graces, and she treated her admirers with much rigour.

Some cases of scarlet fever having broken out in the ladies' apartments, my mother recalled me to Pulawy.

* * * * * * *

[Here there is a break in the Memoirs, which are not resumed until the year 1795, when Prince Adam Czartoryski proceeded with his brother Constantine to St Petersburg. In 1789, when he was nineteen years of age, he went with his mother to Paris and then to London, where he stayed for some weeks with Lord Mansfield, to complete his political education by studying the English constitution. During this time he witnessed the trial of Warren Hastings; and afterwards he visited Scotland and the principal manufacturing towns in England. One of his English acquaintances of that period, Dr Currie of Liverpool, thus describes, in a letter to Mr F. Creevy, M.P., dated the 31st of October, 1803, his impressions of the Prince in 1790:—'I dined yesterday by special invitation with Prince William of Gloucester. There was a good deal of talk about the Northern coasts, where the Prince and several of his suite were last year, and I was a good deal interested to hear that the politics of Russia were led by Prince Adam Czartoryski, the Secretary of State. The Prince said that he was a most agreeable, accomplished man, but decidedly in the French interest, a Jacobin, etc. etc., and that his influence was the great bar to England resuming her proper weight at the Court of St Petersburg. Now you must know this Czartoryski is an old acquaintance of mine—was a correspondent, and might have been so yet, but for my own neglect, for he wrote me several letters since I ceased to write to him. He made the tour of the island along with his mother in grand style, some time in the earlier and better stages of the French Revolution. He was then about twenty or twenty-one, and a very fine young man indeed, full of great expectations of happy changes in society; full of ardour, benevolence, and adventure. He had passed the preceding winter at Paris, in close attendance on the National Assembly in the most brilliant days of

Mirabeau. He had afterwards been a close attendant
on the debates in our own Parliament, at that time
so interesting. He seemed to me extremely capable
of appreciating the great talents then displayed on
the theatres of both nations, and was very fond of
comparing the statesmen and orators of France and
England. Mirabeau and Fox were his heroes—but
he preferred the latter. He was absolutely as great
an idolater of Fox as you are of the General [Sir
John Moore], and seemed to me to have that simplicity and elevation of soul which is necessary to
appreciate our incomparable Charley. I took to
Czartoryski extremely, and he used to ride out with
me and walk with me during the fortnight he stayed
here, as you do. He is an English-looking man, a
black fellow, very tall and handsome—spoke our
language and loved our country. I had several
letters from him during his tour in Scotland (where I
introduced him) and mean to have a search for them.
He was very deeply interested in the Revolution in
Poland, in which I think his mother played a principal part. She was with him, and took the direction
of him—a woman then still handsome, and said to be
of great address of every kind, but perfectly intelligible and feminine. When I revolve all these things,
Sheridan's scheme of sending Fox to St Petersburg
struck me as a noble thought. Depend upon it, if it
could be accomplished, that his influence there would
be speedily felt. For this Czartoryski is a virtuous
man, and, if we knew how to approach him, neither is
nor can be the tool of Bonaparte.'

Prince Adam returned to Poland in 1791, and

entered the army under the command of his brother-in-law, the Prince of Würtemberg. It was in this year that the famous Reformed Constitution of the 3rd of May, which was afterwards made by Russia and Prussia the pretext for a second partition of the country, was passed by the Grand Diet (known as 'the Four Years' Diet') at Warsaw.* This Constitution was regarded

* 'It was the deliberate and systematic policy of Russia and Prussia to maintain anarchy in Poland, in order that it might never rise to prosperity or power or independence. With this object they agreed, at the beginning of the reign of Stanislas Poniatowski, that they would maintain by force the existing Constitution, and oppose any attempt to abolish the *Liberum Veto*, or to make the monarchy hereditary. A strong and earnest effort was, notwithstanding, made to effect the former object, and the reform was so powerfully supported that it would have undoubtedly succeeded had not Russia again interfered, and re-established, with the concurrence of Prussia, *Liberum Veto* in its full stringency. The jealousy of three great powers alone for a time saved Poland. At last they agreed upon their share of the spoil. In 1772 they signed 'in the name of the Holy Trinity,' treaties for the plunder of Poland, and in a few months the first partition was easily effected. It was justified at the time, and has been defended by some later historians on the ground of that very anarchy which it had been for many years a main object of two of the plundering powers to foment and to perpetuate. Prussia solemnly guaranteed the integrity of Poland. She promised to assist her against all hostile attacks, and all interference with her internal concerns. The King of Prussia not only fully recognised the right of the Polish people as an independent nation to revise their Constitution, but he also strongly urged them to do so.

'The Prussian policy of detaching Poland from Russia was, however, perfectly successful, and, relying on Prussian support, the Polish Diet, which first met in September 1788, and which was confederated for the emergency, carried a series of reforms which totally changed the constitution and condition of Poland. It was decreed that the army should be raised from 20,000 to 100,000 men. The system of taxation was thoroughly revised. A considerable representation was given to the trading towns. The excessive powers of the Dietines were abolished. The *Liberum Veto* was swept away, and finally on May 3, 1791, a new Constitution was voted, in which, after the reigning King, the crown was offered to the Elector of Saxony, and to his heirs for ever. It was certain that Russia would resist bitterly what was done, and she early announced to the Diet that she would permit no change whatever in the Constitution of 1775. The King of Prussia expressed his satisfaction at what had occurred, to the Polish Minister at his Court, to the King of Poland, and the Elector of Saxony. He urged the Elector to accept the Polish crown: he offered him his warm alliance, and he professed himself fully determined to fulfil his own treaty obligations.

'As for the policy of Russia towards Poland, it was one of cynical, undisguised rapacity. The course of events depended largely on the King of Prussia. That sovereign, as we have seen, had first induced the Poles to assert their independence of Russia. He had himself urged them to amend their constitution. He had been the first to congratulate them on the constitutional reform of May 1791. He had bound himself before God and man, by two solemn and recent treaties, to respect the integrity of Poland ; to defend the integrity of Poland against all enemies ; to oppose by force any attempt to interfere with her internal affairs. Yet, as we have

by the greatest statesmen and political writers of the
time as the highest step yet attained in the science
of government. Burke said that it was 'a glory to
humanity' and 'the noblest and greatest benefit shed
upon the human race.' Fox described it as 'a work to
which all the friends of freedom should be sincerely
attached,' and Volney remarked that Poland was the
only country of Northern Europe which had amelio-
rated the hard lot of its peasantry.

In 1792, Prince Adam took part in the campaign
against the Russians, who had invaded Poland in consequence of the issue of the new constitution; he
fought in the battle of Granno, and was decorated by
the King for his bravery.

In 1793, he again went to England, and entered
into close relations with nearly all the politicians of
note in that country.* It was while he was still
staying there in 1794 that the Kosciuszko insurrection
broke out. Directly he heard the news, he hurried
back to join the insurgents, but was stopped at
Brussels and put in arrest under orders from the
Austrian Government. Meanwhile the insurrection
was suppressed, and the third partition of Poland took
place. Soon after the Prince rejoined his parents at
Vienna, where the Emperor Francis intervened with
the Empress Catherine of Russia to cancel the confis-

---

also seen, he had resolved as early as March 1792, not only to break his word and to
betray his trust, but also to take an active part in the partition of the defenceless
country which he had bound himself in honour to protect.' (Lecky, *History of
England in the Eighteenth Century*, Vols V and VI.)

* There are in the Czartoryski archives several bulky manuscripts written by the
Prince during his stay in England at this time. Two of these, in the English
language, are treatises on English law and on the system of police and civil
administration generally; a third, in Polish, is on the judicial administration in
England.

cation of the estates of the Czartoryski family, ordered by her in consequence of their participation in the insurrection. The Empress insisted, as a condition of her entering into negotiations on this subject, that the two young princes should go to St Petersburg to enter the Russian service, and after much deliberation at a family council this condition was accepted.]

CHAPTER VI

1794-1795

IT was the 12th of May 1795, when my brother and I
arrived at St Petersburg. In order to form an idea
of our feelings on entering that city, it is necessary to
know the principles in which we were brought up.
Our education had been entirely Polish and Republican.
The study of ancient history and literature, and of the
history and literature of our country, had occupied
the years of our adolescence. Our minds were full of
Greeks and Romans, and, following the example of
our ancestors, we thought only of perpetuating the
ancient virtues on the soil of our fatherland. With
regard to political liberty, more recent examples,
taken from the history of England and France, had
up to a certain point rectified our ideas, without in
any way diminishing their energy. The love of our
country, of its glories, its institutions, and its liberties
had been inculcated into us by our studies, and by
everything we had seen or heard around us. I should

add that this feeling, which penetrated the whole of our moral nature, was accompanied by an invincible aversion to all who had contributed to the ruin of the fatherland which we so much loved.

This two-fold sentiment of love and hatred dominated me so entirely, that I could not meet a Russian either in Poland or elsewhere without feeling a rush of blood to the head—without blushing or turning white with anger—for every Russian seemed to me an author of the misfortunes of my country.

My first task was promptly to replace on a satisfactory footing the affairs of my father. Threefourths of his fortune, all consisting of land situated in the provinces seized by Russia, had been sequestrated. These estates were mortgaged to a considerable extent, so that not only my father's own property, but also that of a great number of our countrymen, was in question. The representations made in my father's favour by the Court of Vienna had had no result. Catherine was provoked by the patriotism of my father and mother, and their sympathy with the Kosciuszko insurrection. 'Let their two sons come to me,' she said, 'and then we will see.' She wished to keep us as hostages.

Our departure for St Petersburg was thus indispensable. Our father, kind and considerate as ever, did not venture to demand this sacrifice from us; and it was the fact of our knowing this that prevailed over every other consideration. Our fatherland was lost: were we also to condemn our parents to want, and make it impossible for them to discharge their debts? We did not hesitate an instant. At the same time we knew well that to go to St Petersburg, far from all our connections—to give ourselves up as prisoners, so to say, into the hands of the most detested of our enemies, of the executioners of our country—was in our situation the most painful sacrifice we could make to paternal affection ; for to do this it was necessary to act in opposition to all our sentiments, all our convictions, all our plans—to everything that was nearest to our hearts and minds.

I described with all the ardour of a youthful poet my state of mind at this time, in some verses entitled ' The Song of the Bard,' which I composed during my stay at Grodno. When I left that town I sent the manuscript to our friend Kniaznin, and it was often read with tears of sympathy by my family.

We bade adieu to our parents (who at that time were residing at Vienna), in the month of December 1794. After sadly passing a few days at Sieniawa,* we proceeded on our journey at the beginning of January, and stopped at Grodno (where the King Stanislas Augustus then lived under the surveillance of Prince Repnin), until we received permission, which did not arrive till the following spring, to go on to St Petersburg. The Empress at first refused to give this permission, and we were shown a note in her own hand in which she stated as the reason of her refusal that my mother had, as in the story of Hamilcar and Hannibal, made us swear eternal hatred to Russia and her sovereign. While at Grodno we often went to see the King, and we were witnesses of his grief and bitter self-reproaches at not being able

* In Galicia, now the country residence of Prince Ladislas Czartoryski.

either to save his country or to perish in fighting for her.

Since my first arrival at St Petersburg my feelings have never changed, but their outward expression has necessarily been modified by events. The same juvenile ardour which made us regard our departure as a heroic sacrifice to paternal affection, made the detested position in which we were placed more tolerable. When one is young, there are few things that cannot be borne; one is strong enough to contend with every kind of adversity and even of misfortune. New scenes, new impressions, though painful, yet hitherto unknown, always distract the mind in the end even if they do not change it.

We were received in St Petersburg society with much consideration and good-will. Our father, who had lived in the Russian capital at the time of Elizabeth, of Peter II, and of the accession of Catherine, was well known and respected there by the older inhabitants. His letters, which we brought with us, procured us a favourable reception. The injustice with which we had been treated by the Cabinet, elicited a sympathy in our favour which was not entirely barren, as it was openly and fearlessly expressed. I have no doubt, remembering the compliments which were paid to us, that the courtiers of whom St Petersburg society was at that time almost entirely composed, knew beforehand that their politeness to the disinherited of Poland—the foster-children of liberty—could not compromise them at Court. Perhaps they had even received a hint that this conduct on their part would be pleasing to the

Empress. After a few weeks we had made many acquaintances, and we received invitations every day from the members of the aristocracy. Dinners, balls, concerts, soirées, private theatricals, succeeded each other without intermission.

We were everywhere accompanied by M. James Gorski, who had been requested by our father to be our friend and guide, and to assist us by his advice. No better mentor could have been selected. Easygoing, merry, tolerant, a genial and witty companion, and at the same time scrupulously honourable and never hesitating to tell an unpleasant truth, he was the very man to keep us in the right way without alienating us by excessive severity. We were very happy in the society of this excellent friend, and I only satisfy the demands of my conscience in here expressing our gratitude to him and our grief at his unexpected loss. He encouraged us to take advantage of the friendly reception given to us, by entering into relations with the persons who were ultimately to bring about the restitution of our fortune. Gorski spoke French with a strong Polish accent, but this did not in any way disconcert him. All he said and did was marked by a laconic precision which was thoroughly in accordance with his character and appearance. He held his head high, and had a proud manner and a brief and decided way of speaking, always, however, within the limits of politeness. Although he did not much esteem the majority of his acquaintances, they were devoted to him. He was very fond of pleasure and good living, and persuaded us to go into society, which perhaps our melancholy, and also a little natural indolence, would otherwise have prevented us from doing. He never lost sight of the object of the journey we had undertaken, and he never neglected any means calculated to achieve it. He always urged us to pay visits and take steps which were inexpressibly disagreeable to us, and it was to his persistence in this respect that our success was mainly due.

This period of our youth was a decisive one for the rest of our career : for, thus suddenly introduced into a state of things entirely foreign to us and contrary to our ideas, we saw all our plans disappear and our future changed and broken in opposition to our wishes and our convictions. As regards myself this phase of my life ·produced deep and painful results. The misfortunes of my country, of my parents, and of many others of my countrymen, the defeat of justice and the triumph of violence and crime, had unhinged my mind. I began to doubt the ways of Providence. I saw only contradictions and aimless struggles ; nothing seemed to me to deserve any serious attention ; I was absorbed by a feeling of scepticism, of cold and despairing indifference. I have since more than once relapsed into these attacks of despair. But although, seeing nowhere any solid basis of action, and suspecting everybody, I looked upon men and things with contempt, an interior voice suggested to my reason that virtue and charity were indubitable realities that were worth living for, and that even if this were not the case, they were to be preferred to anything else. This debate of my conscience alone saved me from the fatal effects of universal doubt. The first germs of belief, though weakened, still remained in my soul.

Compliments and pleasures always produce their effect on a youthful mind, though they do not prevent, and indeed sometimes promote, a feeling of scepticism. Our souls retained their wounds, but we felt some change on the surface. We found that, according to the proverb, the devil is not so black as he is painted, especially if he makes himself amiable ; that it was not just, notwithstanding the outrages that had been committed on our country, to accuse the whole Russian nation of them—to include in our detestation of the Government, individuals who had nothing in common with it ; that the appearances of things change according to the condition and status of persons, and that to arrive at a sound judgment of their private, and still more of their public, conduct, one should put one's self in their place and have regard to the circumstances by which they are surrounded. By degrees we came to the conviction that these Russians, whom we had instinctively learnt to hate— whom we indiscriminately classed as malignant and sanguinary beings, with whom we were to avoid every contact, and whom we could not even meet without disgust—that these Russians were much like other people ; that there were among them young men who were witty and courteous, and even kind, so far at least as could be judged from their words ; that Russian ladies were very amiable ; that, in a word, one could live among Russians without repulsion, and even sometimes feel obliged to give them one's friendship and gratitude.

I only make these self-evident remarks to show that we were in no way prepared for the transition, and that, passing so suddenly from one extreme to the other, we felt as if we had been cast from a precipice on a sea where, not being able to land, we were obliged to direct our course as best we could. We were young, and we met with dangerous and insidious acquaintances and amusements. The society of St Petersburg was on the whole brilliant, animated, and full of variety. Many houses of different kinds were open to us, and strangers were everywhere received with eagerness.

The salons of the Princess Basil Dolgoroukoff and those of the Princess Michael Galitzin, both of whom have since become well known in Paris, were distinguished by their elegance. These two ladies rivalled each other in wit, beauty, and amiability. It was said that both had been admired by Prince Potemkin. The unfortunate adorer of the Princess Dolgoroukoff was at that time Count de Cobentzel, the Austrian ambassador, while the Princess Galitzin had enchained Count de Choiseul-Gouffier, known by his mission to Constantinople and the narrative of his travels in Greece. He had converted the Princess's palace into a sort of art museum, though she herself did not much care for art.

The Narishkin palace was of quite a different kind. With all its anachronisms, it was a true Russian building of the Asiatic type, and the young ladies there, who were less looked after than they usually are in Russia, were said to have been also distinguished by Prince Potemkin. The doors were open to everybody, and Cossacks, Tartars, Circassians, and other Asiatics were among the guests. The owner, Leo Narishkin, gay, affable, good-natured, an old favourite of Peter III, and after wards a courtier of the Empress Catherine, always ready to please her favourites, with all of whom he was on good terms, spent enormous sums as Grand Equerry in balls and receptions, and yet, though he had been doing this for ten years, did not manage to get through his fortune. I do not know if his heirs, who had the same taste for lavish expenditure, have been more successful.

At the Golowin palace there were not daily soirées, as elsewhere, but little coteries like those got up in Paris, to perpetuate the ancient traditions of Versailles. The mistress of the house, whose two daughters have since married MM. Fredro and Potocki, was very witty, talented, sentimental, and fond of art.

Another house which had a peculiar character of its own was the palace of Count Strogonoff. The Count had lived for a long time in Paris, and had contracted habits there which were in singular contrast to the old Muscovite customs. He and his friends talked of Voltaire, of Diderot, of the Parisian stage, and discussed the merits of the pictures of the old masters, of which the Count had a rich collection; and while this conversation was going on, a huge table was laid, with a barbaric disorder betraying the origin of his Siberian riches, at which people dined without being invited and were waited upon by a crowd of serfs.

I will not sketch in detail the society of St Petersburg ; I have to speak of more serious subjects.   I
will only add that Russian society was at that time,
as it probably is still, only a reflection of the Court.
It might be compared to the vestibule of a temple,
where no one has eyes or ears for anything but the
divinity within.   Every conversation, I had almost
said every phrase, always ended in a reference or
question relating to the Court—what was said or done
there, or what was intended to be done.   Every
important impulse came from the Court ; this deprived society, it is true, of any distinctive character,
yet it seemed to be animated and gay.

The Empress Catherine, the immediate author of
the ruin of Poland, whose very name inspired us with
horror, and who was cursed by everyone with the
heart of a Pole—who, in the opinion of people outside
her capital, neither had virtue nor even womanly
decency—had nevertheless succeeded in gaining the
veneration and even the love of her servants and
subjects.   During the long years of her reign the
army, the privileged classes, and the administrators
had their days of prosperity and lustre.   There can
be no doubt that since her accession the Russian
Empire had gained in prestige abroad and in order at
home far more than during the preceding reigns of
Anne and Elizabeth.   People's minds were still full
of the ancient fanaticism and of a servile feeling of
adoration for autocrats.   The prosperous reign of
Catherine had confirmed the Russians in their servility,
though some gleams of European civilisation had
already penetrated among them.   Thus the people,

great and small, were not in the least shocked at the
depraved tastes of their sovereign or the murders and
other crimes which she committed. Everything was
allowed to her. Her luxuriousness was a sacred thing,
and no one dreamt of condemning her debaucheries;
it was like the pagans respecting the crimes and the
obscenities of the gods of Olympus and the Cæsars of
Rome.

The Muscovite Olympus had three stages. The
first was the so-called 'young court,' occupied by the
young princes and princesses, all of whom were graceful and cultivated, and promised well for the future.
The second was held solely by the Grand-Duke Paul,
whose sombre character and fantastic humour inspired
terror, and sometimes contempt. At the top of the
edifice was Catherine, with all the prestige of her
victories, of her prosperity, and of her confidence in
the love of her subjects, whom she could always lead
according to her caprices.

All the hopes that could be based on the 'young
court' belonged only to a distant future, and did not
in any way diminish the general affection for the
supreme authority of the Czarina, especially as the
'young court' was regarded only as a creation of the
ruling power. Catherine reserved to herself exclusively the care of the education of her grandchildren;
and their parents were forbidden to exercise any
influence in this respect. Directly they were born
the princes and princesses were taken away from their
parents, and they grew up under the eyes of the
Empress, to whom alone they seemed to belong.

The Grand-Duke Paul was the shadow in the

picture, and augmented its effect. The terror which he inspired greatly strengthened the general attachment for the rule of Catherine. Everyone wished that the reins of government should long remain in her strong hands; and as all feared Paul, they admired the more the power and the great abilities of his mother, who held him in dependence, far from a throne which by right belonged to him.

This rapid sketch will explain the idolatry of the inhabitants of St Petersburg for their female Jupiter. It was in some sort a reproduction of the adoration of Louis XIV before death had carried away his numerous descendants.

It would have been very difficult, if not impossible, for a stranger arriving at St Petersburg to resist impressions and prejudices so deeply rooted. Once he entered the Court atmosphere and the society which depended upon the Court, he was imperceptibly carried away by the same ideas, and generally ended by joining in the concert of praise which was continually rising around the throne. As a proof of this, illustrious travellers might be cited, such as the Prince de Ligne, the Counts de Ségur and de Choiseul, and many others. In the group of strangers and natives who slandered their acquaintances, who would sacrifice anything to a *bon mot*, and who had no reason to mistrust us, there was not one who, so far as I knew, ever ventured to make a joke at the expense of the Empress. They respected nothing and gossipped about everything; a disdainful and mocking smile often accompanied the name of the Grand-Duke Paul; but if that of Catherine was mentioned, all men's faces at once put on an air of seriousness and submission. There were no more smiles or jests; no one dared even to murmur a complaint or a reproach, as if the most unjust and outrageous actions, when committed by her, were decrees of fate, to be accepted with respectful submission.

Catherine was ambitious, spiteful, vindictive, arbitrary, and shameless; but her ambition was combined with love of glory, and although when her personal interests or passions were concerned everything had to give way, her despotism was in no way capricious. Her passions, disorderly as they were, were dominated by her reason and her abilities. Her tyranny was not the fruit of impulse, but of calculation. She did not commit crimes which were of no advantage to her. She even consented sometimes to be equitable in matters to which she was indifferent, in order that tho glory of justice might increase the splendour of her throne. Moreover, being jealous of every kind of fame, she aspired to the title of a legislator, in order to give herself, at least in the eyes of Europe and of history, a reputation for statesmanship. She knew only too well that sovereigns cannot dispense with appearing just, even if they are not so in reality. She was anxious to gain over public opinion to her side so long as it did not run contrary to her views; otherwise she disregarded it. The political crimes which she committed in Poland, she explained as necessary for the security of the State and as adding to its military glory. She seized the estates of the Poles who had shown most zeal for the independence of their country, but in distributing these estates she benefited the great Russian families, and the bait of an illicit gain induced all around her to flatter her taste for a criminal, pitiless, and conquering policy.

Much astonishment was expressed when General Fersen, the winner of the battle of Macieyovice,* refused the confiscated estates of the Czacki family, and asked as his reward some bonds of the Imperial domains. No one else would have ventured to make so legitimate a request, as every order of the Empress was received with blind submission. Her wish, even if it entailed a revolting act of injustice, was not to be discussed: to do so would have been a proof of unexampled boldness. People held that her acts were not to be judged by ordinary standards, and that even the principles of equity were subject to her decrees.

I will quote an example of this which made some noise at the time. The Princess Schakoffskoy, who had a colossal fortune, had married her daughter to the Duke of Aremberg. This had happened abroad. Catherine, indignant at her consent not having been asked, ordered the princess's goods to be confiscated. The mother and daughter came to implore the Empress's pardon, but Catherine was deaf to their prayers. She cancelled the marriage, saying that it was invalid, as it had been contracted without her permission. The mother and daughter quietly submitted, and the public took this iniquitous decision as a matter of course; at least nobody said a word about it. Some time after, the young princess was per-

---

* The battle in which Kosciuszko's insurrection was finally suppressed, and Kosciuszko himself was wounded and taken prisoner (10th of October 1794).

suaded to contract a second marriage; but being sincerely attached to her first husband, and stung by remorse, she killed herself.

There was also an analogy between the Court of the Empress Catherine and that of Louis XIV in so far that his mistresses played exactly the same part at Versailles as her favourites did at St Petersburg. As to the immorality, the license, the intrigues, and the baseness of the Court of St Petersburg, they are rather to be compared to what we read of the courts of the Byzantine Emperors; while for a parallel to the submission and the veneration of the people we must look to the fascination exercised upon the English nation by Queen Elizabeth, who, equally cruel and ambitious, was endowed with greater talents and a masculine energy.

Even the libertine spirit of Catherine, which often prompted her to improvised amours, was of service to her with the army, the Court, and the privileged classes. Every subaltern, every young man who possessed physical attractions, aspired to the favours of his sovereign; and although she descended from her Olympus only too often to visit ordinary mortals, her subjects did not the less respect her power and her authority; on the contrary, they were always admiring her discretion and cleverness. Those who approached her, of whatever sex, and who had enjoyed her benefits, were truly attached to her, and were never weary of praising her goodness and amiability.

For some time we were forbidden to see this source of favour and power, whose rays dazzled all eyes. In other words, we had not received permission to present ourselves at the Imperial Court, which as usual occupied the Tauris Palace from the beginning of spring. The only members of the Imperial family we had seen were the young princes, who were in the crowd on the day of our arrival, the 1st of May according to the Russian calendar, when nearly the whole of the population goes to the promenade of Catherinenhoff. Some time after, when we were already received in society, we were invited to assist at a fête which was to last about twenty-four hours, for it was to begin with a breakfast, to continue with a dance, walks, and the theatre, and to end with a supper. This fête was given by the Princess Galitzin in honour of the 'young court.' We had not been as yet presented ; but the Princess Galitzin, following the instructions she had received from the Countess Schouvaloff, her mother, who had been given a hint by the Empress, had invited us, and this gave us a certain position in society. It would be impossible to see a handsomer couple than the Grand-Duke Alexander, who was then eighteen, and his wife, who was only sixteen. Both beamed with youth, grace, and goodness.

The evenings were passed in the amusements I have described, but during the day, which is so long in that climate, the whole bitterness of our situation forced itself upon our minds. We had to visit, to solicit, to humble ourselves. It was hard, and we should have had much more difficulty in doing it if Gorski had not been there to keep us up to the work. He exercised all his authority over us ; he did not leave us a moment's relaxation, repeating that the effects of our neglect would fall upon our parents, and that the only object for which we were at St Petersburg was to replace them in their estates.

Plato Zuboff was at that time the most powerful of the Empress's favourites, and we had to go to him first. We came to his apartments in the Tauris Palace at the appointed hour. He had a brown coat on, and was leaning on a piece of furniture. He was under middle age, with a good figure and an agreeable countenance; his dark hair was curled and brushed up into a tuft; his voice was soft and clear. He received us with an air of benevolent protection. Gorski acted as our interpreter, and hastened to reply to the questions which Zuboff addressed to us; his French was not correct, but his mien was always imposing. Zuboff assured us that he would do all he could to help us, but added that we must not be under any illusions, that everything depended on her Majesty's favour, and that neither himself nor any one else was able to influence her decisions. He added that we would soon be admitted to her presence.

Prince Kourakin, brother to the future ambassador, who had undertaken to protect us, had taken us to Zuboff; but at the moment when we entered he disappeared, or rather stayed behind in the antechamber. He rejoined us as we were going out, and listened with a smile of curiosity to our account of what had happened. All his questions proved that he was convinced that we had just left the most powerful man in Europe.

But there was another man equally important;

this was Valerian Zuboff, Count Plato's younger
brother. His more masculine face and figure made
him more attractive than his brother, and it was
said that the Empress liked him so much that if
he had presented himself first he would have become
the favourite. As it was, the fact of his being Count
Plato's brother, and his personal qualities, gave him
great influence over the mind of the old Czarina.
We were therefore obliged to pay him a visit. By a
singular coincidence, Valerian Zuboff had been the
commander of the detachment which had sacked
Pulawy* in the previous year. The horrors which
marked the passage of the Russian troops through
Poland are well known, and though Zuboff did not
preside in person over the pillage of Pulawy, it can
hardly be credited that the most savage soldiery
would have acted in so outrageous a manner without
their commander's consent. If, as is probable, they
acted under orders from above, a man of honour would
have taken care to show that it was with reluctance
that he acquitted himself of such a mission, and would
have at least moderated the execution of it. No such
moderation, however, was shown; and we, the victims
of the pillage, had to ask the spoiler (for such we
thought him) for his protection. We were even
obliged to request his intercession to be admitted into
the presence of his brother, and it was to him that
we owed the special honour of a private reception.

In the opinion of the Russians, however, Valerian
Zuboff was a young man of loyal and noble sentiments. All that was said against him was that he

* See note on page 42.

was too fond of pleasure ; his honour was believed to be untarnished. He was at that time engaged in a love intrigue with Madame Prot Potocka, who had followed him to St Petersburg, where she lived in concealment : this, however, did not prevent him from making other *liaisons*. He had lost a leg in a skirmish, before Praga* was taken by assault, and his crutches seemed to add to his charms in the eyes of the Empress and other ladies. On examining him more closely one saw the nonchalance of a young man spoiled by fortune and by women. His rooms were always full of flatterers of all kinds. In the interest of our parents, our worthy friend Gorski took us there also, much against our will. When, by repeating our visits, our relations had developed into a sort of familiarity, we still felt them to be inexpressibly tedious ; there were no points of sympathy between us, and it was impossible to enter into any conversation. Count Valerian usually began by assuring us that he and his brother did not possess anything like the influence they were supposed to exercise over Catherine's mind, and that very often she did the very opposite to that which they wished her to do. I believe, however, that Count Valerian Zuboff was the only one who had our interests at heart. Whether as a matter of conscience, or from a desire to retrieve his reputation, he urged his brother to help us, and he pleaded warmly to the Empress in our behalf.

The principal favourite acted very differently.

* A suburb of Warsaw, captured in 1795 by Souvaroff, who put its inhabitants to the sword. This event was followed by the capitulation of Warsaw, the abdication of King Stanislas Augustus, and the third partition of Poland.

Count Plato Zuboff, as I said above, had granted us the honour of a special audience, and, like other applicants, we had to remind his Excellency of our existence in order to obtain his protection. Every day about eleven o'clock he had a levee, in the literal sense of the word. An immense crowd of petitioners and courtiers of all ranks hastened to assist at his toilet. The street was full of carriages with four or six horses, exactly as at the theatre. Sometimes, after a long period of waiting, the crowd was informed that the Count would not see them on that day, and they then dispersed to come again on the morrow. If Zuboff was disposed to see them, the folding doors were opened, and generals, high civil functionaries, Circassians, and merchants with long beards, crowded into the room. Among the applicants were many Poles who came to claim the restoration of their estates, or redress for some grievance. One of these was Prince Alexander Lubomirski, who intended to sell his estates in order to save the remains of his fortune, which had been involved in the ruin of the country. There was also the Metropolitan of the United Greeks,* named Sosnowski, who came to bow his venerable head to the favourite in order to obtain the restitution of his property and save his church, which the Russian Government had already begun cruelly to persecute. M. Oskierko, a young man of interesting appearance, came to ask for an amnesty for his father, who had been imprisoned or banished to Siberia, and whose fortune had been confiscated.

---

* The union of the Roman and Greek churches in Poland was effected in the 1434.

The number of persons who had been thus treated was immense;* the proportion of them who would be able to avail themselves of the doubtful chances of the so-called amnesty was very small. Some were in chains, others in Siberia; and it was not every one who could get permission to go to St Petersburg. All complaints were suppressed, and the Government officials, who constituted a hierarchy of fabulous extent, did not give the required permission unless they themselves derived some advantage from it. And even when all difficulties had been overcome, and the petitioner had obtained admission to the Russian Court, the usual answer was that given to the Metropolitan of the United Greeks—that the Empress's decrees, whether just or unjust, were irrevocable, that complaint was useless, and that what had been done could not be undone—especially as official avidity closed the doors to every appeal.

To return to the assemblages in the favourite's rooms. Each suitor showed in his face what he wanted. Some expressed grief and a simple desire to defend their property, their honour, and their exist-ence; others betrayed a design to seize somebody else's property, or to keep it if they had already obtained it. Thus some were led by misfortune, others by greed. Others again only came to pros-trate themselves before the rising star. It seemed almost impossible to be humiliated on finding one's self in a crowd composed of the first dignitaries of the

---

* Many of these exiles, being deprived of all means of communication with their friends and relatives in Poland, remained in Siberia for the rest of their lives. There are thousands of Polish families now in Siberia which are descended from the confederates of Bar and men who took part in subsequent Polish insurrections.

Empire, men of the most illustrious names, and generals in command of our provinces, who placed everybody in their districts under tribute and inspired universal fear, and who, after coming in all humility to bow their heads before the favourite, either went away without obtaining a look from him, or stood waiting like messengers while he changed his dress reclining on a sofa.

The following was the usual course at these receptions. When the folding-doors were opened, Zuboff slowly entered the room in a dressing-gown, with scarcely any underclothing, and after nodding slightly to the suitors and courtiers, who stood respectfully in a circle, began his toilet. The servants approached him to dress his hair and powder it. Meanwhile other applicants came in; they also were honoured by a nod when the Count perceived them; all watched carefully for an opportunity to catch his eye. We were among those who were always received with a gracious smile. Everybody remained standing, and none dared to speak. It was by his gestures, by an eloquent silence, that each person advocated his cause before the all-powerful favourite. Only those spoke to whom the Count addressed himself, and on these occasions he never talked of the subject of the application. Often he did not say a word, and I do not remember his having ever offered anybody a seat except Field Marshal Soltykoff, who was the chief personage at Court, and had, it was said, made the Zuboffs' fortune; it was through his intervention that Count Plato had succeeded Mamonoff. The despotic pro-consul Toutoulmin, who at that time was the terror of Podolia and Volhynia, having been invited

by one of the servants to take a seat, only ventured
to sit on the edge of a chair and got up directly
afterwards.

While the favourite was having his hair dressed,
his secretary, Gribovsky, usually brought him papers
to sign. The applicants used to whisper to each
other the sum that was to be paid to induce him to
get his master to look favourably on their requests,
and he took these presents with as much pride as Gil
Blas. When the hair-dressing was over and the
papers were signed, the Count put on his uniform or
his coat and withdrew into his apartments. All this
was done with a nonchalance which he tried to pass
off as gravity and dignity; but there was too much
artifice in it. When the Count had disappeared, all
went to their carriages, more or less discontented at
their reception.

We did not plead our case before any Minister, as
in Gorski's opinion it was better to rely on the protection of Zuboff alone. We were introduced, however,
to several other eminent persons. One of the most
important of these was Count Bezborodko. He was
a native of Little Russia, and had begun his career
under the orders of Marshal Romantzoff. Having
been recommended to the Empress by his chief, he
soon obtained by his talents, his great aptitude for
work, and his extraordinary memory, rapid promotion
both as regards fortune and dignities. He was
appointed a member of the Committee of Foreign
Affairs, and was employed by Catherine in the most
secret negotiations. With the outward appearance of
a bear, he had a keen wit, a lucid intelligence, and a

rare power of mastering a subject. Lazy to a degree,
and given up to pleasure, he never set to work till the
last moment : but then he worked very rapidly and
without stopping.   This gained him the esteem of the
Empress, who loaded him with rewards.   He was the
only man of any distinction at Court who did not
flatter the Zuboffs ; he did not even visit them.   All
admired his courage ; but no one imitated it.

The old Count Osterman, Vice-Chancellor and
senior member of the Committee of Foreign Affairs,
looked like a figure in a piece of old tapestry.   Long,
thin, pale, dressed in the ancient fashion with cloth
boots, a brown coat, gold buttons, and a black
ribbon round his neck, he represented the period of
the Empress Elizabeth.   He was quoted as an example of honesty, a rare quality in those days ; he
was grave in manner, and without saying a word
he would wave his visitors to their seats with his
long arm.   He now only appeared at solemn dinners
on great occasions, when there was a question of a
final despatch or declaration to which his name was
to be signed at the head of those of the other
members of the Committee.   Though advanced in
years and of moderate capacity, Count Osterman was
valued for his high principle, his good sense, and his
great experience.   He was the only member of the
Council that had opposed the partition of Poland ; he
represented that such an event would rather be of
advantage to Austria and Prussia than to Russia.
His advice was not taken, but he should have the
credit of it.   Since then his influence declined daily,
and although still the titular head of the department

of Foreign Affairs, he was really shelved; this, however, did not prevent Catherine from treating him
with every consideration.

At the time of the accession of the Emperor
Paul, Osterman retired to Moscow, with the title
of Chancellor of the Empire. His elder brother,
the Senator, known for his absence of mind, also
lived there. These two old men were still in existence at the time of the coronation of the Emperor
Alexander. As they did not leave any direct heir,
they adopted as their successor Count Tolstoï, who
assumed the name of Tolstoï-Osterman, and afterwards distinguished himself by his bravery at the
battle of Culm, where he lost a leg.

Count Samoïloff, Procurator-General (an office
which at that time comprised the direction of the
Ministries of the Interior, of Justice, and of Finance),
although he was a nephew of Potemkin, was one of
the most assiduous of the flatterers of the Zuboffs,
who, as everybody knew, were declared adversaries
of his late uncle. Samoïloff was not remarkable for
ability, and indeed he made himself ridiculous by his
foolish pride. He was not ill-natured, but, as was
well said by Niemcewicz, he committed evil actions
by his want of discernment, his meanness, and his
pusillanimity, rather than by inherent wickedness.
In making use of him, Catherine wished to prove to
the world that she could govern her immense empire
even with an incapable minister. She took a pride
in showing that she was thoroughly acquainted with
legislation in everything that related to the conduct
of the affairs of the country, and one must in justice

admit that its internal organisation was visibly improved under her reign.   Samoïloff, however, had really no preponderant position in the Government, and any one who had to do business with him generally found reason to regret it—not because he wished to do harm, but because he was incapable of understanding anything clearly, and was at the same time too vain to admit it.   Prince Alexander Lubomirski, who negotiated with him for the purchase of his estates, and our unfortunate fellow-countrymen who were locked up in prison, had only too much reason to know this.

Days and weeks thus passed in constant movement—various scenes, sometimes disagreeable, sometimes unimportant, succeeding each other and at least giving variety to our lives.   But neither our constant anxiety as to the recovery of our parents' fortune, nor the splendour of the society into which we were thrown, effected any change in the deeper sentiments of our hearts.   When we returned to our rooms we always thought of our parents, our sisters, our country, and of the sad position in which we were placed. What we felt most bitterly was that, at the moment when we were passing our time at balls and entertainments, the most heroic of our countrymen were in prison.   It was very difficult and dangerous to get news of them ; but fortune favoured us in this respect. After the second partition, when part of the Polish army in Podolia and the Ukraine was forced to enter the Russian service, two young men put on the Russian uniform and managed to obtain places in the service of Plato Zuboff.   One of these was Komar, afterwards the possessor of millions in Podolia, who was not unknown to us, as his father had been employed by my grandfather to manage his affairs ; the other was Poradowski, afterwards a valiant general, killed in the war of 1812.

Poradowski had been an officer in the regiment of my brother-in-law, the Prince of Würtemberg ; we were thus old acquaintances. These two gentlemen, Poradowski especially, found means of obtaining some news for us about the prisoners. We learnt in this way that Niemcewicz, Konopka, and Kilinski were shut up in the casemates of the fortress; that Kosciuszko had been removed from them and confined somewhere else, and that he was treated with every consideration and generally respected. He was placed in charge of Major Titoff, who was much attached to him and related various anecdotes of him which were very insignificant (the Major was very rough and ignorant), but, being about such a man as Kosciuszko, were repeated from mouth to mouth. Potocki, Zakrzewski, Mostowski, and Sokolnicki were confined in a house in Liteïna Street. Not being able to do anything for them, we at least gave ourselves the pleasure of often going through this street, either in a carriage or on foot, in the hope of seeing them. Sometimes we succeeded in catching a glimpse of them passing like shadows before our eyes ; but they probably never perceived us, as the house was very strictly guarded both within and without. Our hearts beat fast, however, when we raised our eyes to the windows behind which the prisoners were confined. Except Marshal Potocki, they were not personally known to us; but they had become dear to the heart of every good Pole by the great deeds which they were being made to expiate by sufferings equally cruel and unjust.

When we came back in the evening we used to talk of the impressions of the day. Our worthy friend Gorski did not spare his epithets with regard to those whom he had been obliged to treat with consideration in public. Whenever the name of any of these people (except a few whom he really respected) was pronounced, he immediately added: 'Yes, he is a villain, a rascal,' and so on. These expressions he used particularly with regard to Poles of an equivocal or tarnished reputation. People unfortunately were to be found daily, who thought that their indifference to the fate of their country and their treasonable practices would gain them the favour of the Ministers and the Court. If their former services did not seem to them to have been sufficiently rewarded, they tried to show themselves more base in order to get a larger reward. We had more than once to blush at this disgraceful conduct on the part of some of our countrymen. We were not, however, confounded with them; the Poles at St Petersburg were divided into two classes, entirely distinct by their qualities, their manners, and their sentiments.

There was no Pole whose society we enjoyed more than that of Prince Alexander Lubomirski. He was a good patriot and a wise and worthy man; the turn of his mind was both tranquil and gay, so that he sometimes evoked merriment out of the saddest events. He often went with us on our visits.

Between one visit and another we gave free course to our observations and criticisms, as sometimes happens when men who are tired of concealing their thoughts, and of feigning to agree by a gesture to what thcy do not approve, can afterwards, when they are in the society of people with whom they are intimate, freely express their true opinions, and thereby compensate themselves for the constraint and humiliations they have been obliged to suffer.

Notwithstanding these moments of confidential talk, the sad necessity of concealing our sentiments and our sufferings, of dissimulating our thoughts, the impossibility of declaring aloud what we felt— were most painful to us; and they influenced my character and my intellectual faculties in the most disastrous manner. This clog on my frankness made me sombre, extremely silent, and reserved, and I seldom made any remark except to myself. It may be that I was by nature inclined to reticence, but more propitious circumstances would perhaps have made this inclination disappear or might have diminished it, while my position at St Petersburg only aggravated it. During the whole of my life I have not been able to master this tendency, imposed on my youth by an inevitable fate.

At length, after waiting for several months, we were informed that we were to be presented to the Empress at Tsarskoe-Selo, the summer residence of the Court. This was a decisive moment for us, for until that time we had not had the slightest idea of what was to be the result of my father's memorial announcing that he had sent us to St Petersburg and asking for the restitution of his estates. We were advised to come early : the presentation was to take place after church. Meanwhile we went to General Branicki, who was married to a niece of Potemkin's, and had rendered great service to Catherine in the affairs of Poland ; he was still in high favour with her, and an apartment was reserved for him in all the Imperial Palaces. It was very unfortunate that he should have degraded himself by assisting in the ruin of his country. A courtier stained with misdeeds, ambitious, unprincipled, and greedy of wealth, he yet felt himself a Pole at heart, notwithstanding his family relations with the Russians ; and he would have preferred to satisfy his tastes and his ambition in Poland rather than in any other country. He was still proud of the Poland he had lost ; he regretted her and suffered at her humiliation. He detested the Russians, whom he knew well, and he revenged himself upon them by silent contempt and mockery of their faults. On the other hand, his heart was open to some old friends to whom he could speak without fear. His lively, essentially Polish mind and his witty remarks made his conversation gay and interesting. Though very fond of describing his experiences, he avoided all allusion to the fatal league of Targowitza.* He also liked to talk of old times, and then he assumed a *grand seigneur* air which entirely disappeared when he was in the crowd of courtiers whose nothingness he felt, or in the presence of Catherine, who often invited him to play cards with her.

* This League, formed by Branicki and others at the instigation of the Empress Catherine, was the precursor of the second partition of Poland.

He seemed really attached to our parents, with whom he had passed many long and eventful years; but he could only help us by advice, which might be expressed in the words 'patience and submission.' He told us of all that passed, and offered us a room at Court on the audience-days, when people had to wait a long time. We accordingly went to him on arriving at Tsarskoe-Selo to wait for the hour when we should be presented. He gave us his instructions, and when we asked whether we were to kiss the Empress's hand, he replied, ' Kiss her where she likes, so long as she gives you back your fortune.' He also showed us how to bend the knee.

The Empress was still in the chapel when those who were to be presented to her went to the reception room. We were first presented to Count Schouvaloff, Grand-Chamberlain, formerly the favourite of the Empress Elizabeth ; he was at that time all-powerful, and was known for his correspondence with D'Alembert, Diderot, Voltaire, and other eminent writers who solicited his favour. It seems that it was by Elizabeth's orders that he engaged Voltaire to write the life of her father Peter, and Catherine, who was then young, also strove to gain his good-will. Count Schouvaloff was now old, but still vigorous, and insisted on performing the functions of his office. We were placed by him in a line near the door through which the Empress was to come. The mass being over, the procession passed two abreast. First came the gentlemen of the chamber, the chamberlains, and the great dignitaries ; then the Empress herself, accompanied by the princes, the princesses, and the ladies of

the Court.   We had no time to look at her closely, for
it was necessary to bend the knee while she pronounced
our names.   Then we stood in a circle with the ladies
and other Court personages, and the Empress walked
round addressing a few words to each person.

She was well advanced in years, but still fresh,
rather short than tall, and very stout.   Her gait, her
demeanour, and the whole of her person were marked
by dignity and grace.   None of her movements were
quick ; all in her was grave and noble ; but she was
like a mountain stream which carries everything with
it in its irresistible current.   Her face, already wrinkled,
but full of expression, showed haughtiness and the
spirit of domination.   On her lips was a perpetual
smile, but to those who remembered her actions, this
studied calm hid the most violent passions and an
inexorable will.   In coming towards us her face
assumed a gentler expression, and with that sweet
look which has been so much praised, she said : ' Your
age reminds me of that of your father when I saw
him for the first time.   I hope this country suits you.'
These few words sufficed to attract to our side a
crowd of courtiers, who began to lavish upon us
compliments even more flattering than those we had
previously received.   We were invited to occupy seats
at the table under the colonnade ; this was a particular honour, as the Empress never gave such invitations but to her private friends.

Our reception by the Empress and the society of
St Petersburg was, considering our age and position,
evidently only the last echo of old traditions relative
to Poland—of the high opinion still held by the

Muscovites as to our leading men. Our family especially, which during the previous century had unfortunately been forced into frequent relations with Russia, was better known than the others. My grandfather and my father were generally respected in Russia, and we met at St Petersburg the two Narischkins and their wives, who had known my father when he was in great favour with Peter III, and with Catherine at the time of her accession.

We were presented on the same day to the Grand-Dukes. Paul received us coldly, but with dignity; his wife, the Grand-Duchess Maria, showed us much consideration, chiefly on account of her brother, whom she wished to reconcile with our sister.* The younger Grand-Dukes received us frankly and graciously.

The wealthier classes at St Petersburg pass the summer in country-houses in the vicinity. Every great nobleman has one, and lives in it as luxuriously as in the capital. As the fine season is short, every one tries to use it to the best advantage, so that for some months the town is deserted. Our visits consequently had to be paid in the country, and as we were always travelling we often returned to town very late. There is scarcely any night in the summer, and the recollection of our moonlight nights in Poland made us sad. Gorski allowed us no breathing time; we had to renew our journeys daily, and neglect no opportunity of multiplying our relations. This was, indeed, the only means of attaining our object, for in spite of our flattering reception at Court, and the repeated recommendations of people

* See note on page 40.

in power, our business was still in suspense.   Catherine, who was well informed as to everything that was going on, knew that we were popular in the capital, and the praise that was lavished upon us could not fail to produce a good impression upon her.

Besides our journeys to the country villas, which were in themselves very fatiguing, we had to go every other Tuesday and on each holiday to Tsarskoe-Selo to assist at Zuboff's toilet.   Having been presented, we were also qualified to go to the Palace, and on these occasions we were usually invited to dine at the principal table.   At the head of this table sat the Empress and the Imperial family, but people of all the higher classes were admitted to it.   We were also advised to take part in the evening entertainments, which in fine weather took place in the garden. The Empress walked there with the whole of her Court, or sat on a bench surrounded by the older courtiers, while the young Grand-Dukes and Grand-Duchesses, with the younger ladies and gentlemen of the Court, played at various games before her on the grass.   The Grand-Duke Paul never took part in these amusements, for when divine service or dinner was over he went to his residence at Pavlovsk. While playing at these games we became more closely acquainted with the Grand-Dukes, who were most amiable to us.

It was the custom for certain of the elect, ourselves included, to go after dinner to Zuboff's rooms. This was not a ceremonious visit; one was supposed to be admitted to a certain familiarity, and to form part of a friendly meeting.   The favourite used to wear a loose coat, and was more nonchalant than ever; he would ask his visitors, who usually were not numerous, to sit down, and would then stretch himself at full length on a sofa. The conversation was characteristic of the host: it was sometimes brightened by Count Cobentzel, the Austrian Ambassador, or by Count Valentine Esterhazy, afterwards master of the ceremonies at Vienna. The latter was a welcome guest at Tsarskoe-Selo, having by his good stories, and a bluntness of manner which is best suited to every kind of flattery, insinuated himself so far into the good graces of Zuboff and the Empress that he obtained some considerable estates in Volhynia. Neither Count Esterhazy nor his wife had any nobility of character or appearance, yet the latter was on a very intimate footing with Catherine. Their scapegrace of a son, a spoilt child brought up in the palace with a Calmouk girl, and amusing by his tricks, greatly contributed to the good fortune of his parents.

It was whispered at the Court that while Count Plato Zuboff was being loaded with favours by his septuagenarian mistress, he paid court to the Princess Elizabeth, the wife of the Grand-Duke Alexander, who was at that time only sixteen. This aspiring and chimerical pretension covered him with ridicule; people were surprised at his having dared to nourish such a thought under the very eyes of Catherine. As for the young Grand-Duchess, she took no notice of him whatever. It seems that he was seized with a love-fit generally after dinner, and he then did nothing but sigh, lie on a sofa with a sad air, and look as if he were oppressed by a heavy burthen on his heart. Nothing would please him but the melancholy and voluptuous sounds of the flute, and he had all the appearance of a man seriously in love. It is said that he had imparted the secret to some of his confidants, who professed to sympathise with his sorrows without appearing to have guessed their cause. His servants alleged that whenever he returned to his rooms after a visit to the Empress, he was prostrate with fatigue and pitiably sad ; he then used to pour scent on his handkerchief and receive intimate visitors with an air of depression which was the subject of general remark. Yet he refused to take any rest, alleging that sleep deprives us of some of the most beautiful moments of our lives.

In this manner the summer season of 1795 passed away. In the autumn the Court returned to the Tauris Palace, and our morning visits to the favourite recommenced with more frequency than ever, as the day was approaching when our case was to be decided. The Zuboffs constantly repeated to us that their good-will was not sufficient, and that they could not do all they wished. No good augury was to be discovered in these words. Meanwhile, the suitors became more and more pressing : some sought to recover their estates, while many others set every engine in motion to obtain part of the sequestrated estates for themselves. From the highest to the lowest, each wished for a share of the spoil : for Catherine had not yet said anything as to what she would do with the immense private estates, crown domains, and church property, which she had seized.

The crisis was very interesting, and its solution was looked forward to on all sides with anxiety. How many Russians founded upon it their hopes of enlarging their estates and increasing the number of their serfs or ' souls,'* as they called them ! This gave a new stimulus to sycophancy, not only with regard to the favourite, but to his secretaries, who aped his ridiculous morning receptions, and rehearsed his arrogance before the stupid mob that crowded their ante-chambers. Among the speculators who, like pillagers on a battlefield, sought to enrich themselves at the expense of the vanquished, there were unfortunately some Poles unworthy of the name they bore. Appealing to their services, to their treason to the fatherland, they chose their victims among those who had been convicted or even suspected of patriotism. The more they increased the number of these victims, the greater were their chances of plunder.

Our parents, pressed by their creditors, and anxious about their fate, were still more so for us, as at the time when we were informing them of the friendly receptions we had met with at St Petersburg my mother had received an anonymous letter, written in excellent French, describing in exaggerated language the effect we had produced in society and our favourable reception at Court, but adding that what was most to our credit was that, insensible to all cajoleries, we remained steadfast in our love for our country and our hatred for the Empress Catherine. As it was known that all letters to my family were opened at

---

* Serfage properly so called, *i.e.*, the right of selling a peasant as part of one's property, never existed in Poland ; it was a purely Russian institution.

the post-office, my mother's distress on receiving this communication may easily be imagined. It was evident that the anonymous letter had only been written with the intention of awakening Catherine's suspicions, and preventing the restitution of my father's estates. It will be recollected that during our stay at Grodno, Prince Repnin had shown us the autograph of a note from Catherine, with regard to an oath of hatred to Russia and the Empress which I was supposed to have taken before my mother. This story was probably also manufactured by one of our countrymen; it was absurd to suppose that such a theatrical demonstration should be necessary to inspire us with hatred for such enemies.

The only means left to us for obtaining the recovery of our parents' estates was to resign ourselves to entering the Russian service. This was the *sine quâ non*, the completion of our sacrifice, the inevitable consequence of our journey to St Petersburg. At one of our evening visits to Tsarskoe-Selo, Zuboff had told us that the Empress intended to give us commissions as officers of her guard; and that it was the greatest piece of good fortune that could happen to us that we should thus become part of a glorious and irresistible army, which was strong enough to march across the world without being stopped by any obstacle. This was indeed the prevalent idea among the officers in the Russian army, and they could not as yet rid themselves of it. Although we were prepared for the proposal, our hearts failed us when it was made officially. It was impossible, however, to refuse it, and moreover, having once determined to give ourselves up to the Russians, the form which the sacrifice should take was a matter of very little importance. We considered that it would be unworthy of us to propose the slightest compromise, or to show the least anxiety to obtain any higher position. The highest rank would be as insupportable to us as the lowest; any discussion on this point would show that we attached importance to the proposal, while the fact was that it was to us a matter of perfect indifference.

With bowed heads, feeling like victims, we were ready to accept any suggestion that might be made to us, without enquiry into its consequences. A traveller suddenly placed by some chance in Central Africa, would not attach the least importance to the forms, distinctions, or honours used among the savages, and this was precisely our case. Thrown out of our natural sphere by misfortune, surrounded by violence and compulsion, filled with disgust and despair, we thought it our duty not to express any wish whatever : it was not worth while.

At length came the long-expected ukase announcing the decision of the Government as to the confiscated estates. Catherine distributed a whole mass of them among her favourites, her Ministers, her generals, governors of provinces, and even subaltern officials; also among some Poles who were traitors to their country. She did not restore my parents' estates, but without mentioning them she made a present of their fortune (amounting, according to the Russian mode of calculation, to 42,000 souls) to my brother and myself. The estates of Latyczew and Kamieniec, which

formerly belonged to my father, fell to the lot of
Count Markoff. The ukase did not mention my
sisters; but this arbitrary and illegal act having
always been regarded by my family as invalid, it
remained without result both with regard to my
sisters and my parents. The property really went
back to them, as all we had to do was to send my
father full power to dispose unconditionally of the
fortune which had been ceded to us.

There had been so much uncertainty as to
Catherine's final decision in this matter, that the
result was received in society with general satisfaction. We were told that the loss of Latyczew and
Kamieniec should be regarded as a fine, and that
we had no reason to complain. We thanked Catherine
with one knee on the ground, as required by the
etiquette of the Court, and almost immediately after
we had our uniforms on. Mine was that of the
cavalry of the guard; my brother's, that of the
Ismaïloff regiment of infantry.

It would not have been proper abruptly to cease
our visits to the favourite, and Gorski was too much
a man of the world to allow it. We also received
several invitations to the concerts in the Tauris
Palace, which was regarded as an extraordinary favour
for officers of the guard who do not form part of the
Court. These were further signs of the Empress's
good-will; but they all ceased directly the Court
moved to the Winter Palace. We were then classed
as officers of the guard, who only go to the palace
on Sundays and holidays, when they have to stand
at a door next to the diplomatic corps as the Empress

goes by. She merely gratified us with a look as she went to the chapel and returned from it. The Grand-Dukes always bowed to us with much grace.

It was for these dress receptions, which were repeated on every Sunday and holiday, that the dandies of the barracks put on their best uniforms, tightened their waists, put pomatum on their hair, and placed themselves in line with the hope of attracting the eyes of the Empress and fascinating her with their tall stature and broad shoulders. It is said that some of them used in days gone by to be promoted to her favour on these occasions; but she was now too old to indulge in such fancies.

The military service in the Guards' regiments was at that time much neglected, but it was necessary to attend drill at least once a year. Some officers really liked the service and performed it, but this was because they chose to do so, and their zeal was thought rather ridiculous by young men of fashion. The generals who commanded us did not take any pains to make us work. We were seldom on guard in the palace, and my turn only came once. As to my brother, being an infantry officer, he was on duty with a detachment of his regiment, which always had to guard the castle at night. The Empress having perceived him, said that now he was on guard she would sleep in peace.

An amusing adventure happened at this time to my friend Gorski. The ukase relating to my father's family had been published, but the order for handing over the property to us had not yet appeared. Plato

Zuboff was entrusted with the task of communicating
the order to the Governor-General Toutoulmin, who
was then at St Petersburg, hoping to participate in
the act of spoliation and to derive illicit advantages
from it; but Zuboff did not hurry. We were therefore obliged to continue to assist at his toilet. One
day the favourite, who had on his shoulders a white
towel, beckoned to Gorski to come to him. The
latter came up at once, and listened with such
attention to Zuboff that he allowed some snuff to drop
from his nose and stain the favourite's towel. The
audience expected some tragical *dénoûment*, but
Gorski, who never lost his presence of mind, finished
what he had to say and returned to his place as if
nothing had happened.

On New Year's Day we were appointed Gentlemen of the Chamber. Court appointments were at
that time held in much higher estimation than they
are now. Ranks at Court stood on the same footing
as corresponding ranks in the army, and took preced-
ence of ranks in the civil service; the consequence
was that families with a great name, or with great
interest, always placed their sons in the Guards, and
tried at the same time to obtain for them an appointment at Court. Being thus raised in the hierarchy
of the *tchin*, they afterwards passed into the civil or
military service with the rank to which they had
been promoted.

Catherine wished the Grand-Duke Constantine to
marry while she was still living, and all preliminary
preparations were made for the establishment of his
household. People intrigued for places either for

themselves or for others, and lists were formed of the gentlemen of the chamber and the chamberlains, the former with the rank of brigadier, and the latter with that of major-general. The Duchess of Saxe-Coburg, accompanied by her three children, had just appeared at St Petersburg, and it is from that time that the elevation of this princely family began. Whenever a princess was wanted at Moscow, a diplomatic agent was sent to the capitals of the small German princes who had pretty daughters to marry, and made a detailed report on the qualities of these princesses, and the moral character and blood-relations of their parents. After reading these reports, the Empress designated the princesses whom she wished to see at St Petersburg, in order to make her selection. She had in her time herself undergone an examination of this kind, and did not think that she was inflicting any humiliation on these ladies by subjecting them to the same ordeal. Indeed all the German princesses were very glad to get a summons of this kind for any of their daughters, and felt very flattered when one of them was chosen as the bride of a Grand-Duke. During the past century Russia had perhaps more prestige—in Germany at least—than she has now, and the young princesses who were destined for that country looked forward to a life the prospect of which singularly pleased their old mothers. They were like the Circassian women who think their fortunes made when they are taken as slaves to inhabit the harems of Turkish pashas. The mothers looked upon the brilliant position of Catherine as a presage for their daughters, and were not repelled by any thought of possible sacrifices, or else only looked upon them as difficulties from which the young Grand-Duchesses could easily extricate themselves, and which therefore need not cause them any anxiety. It was Baron Budberg, then a diplomatic agent, and afterwards Minister of Foreign Affairs, who procured for the Duchess of Saxe-Coburg the happiness of bringing her three daughters to St Petersburg.

The Duchess was very clever, and her daughters were all pretty. It was painful to see this mother offering her daughters like goods for sale, and watching anxiously to discover on which of them would fall the eye of the Empress and the handkerchief of the Grand-Duke Constantine. There was something so humiliating in this conduct that we tried not to notice it, especially as the Duchess and her daughters were in all other points very amiable and worthy of respect. Various anecdotes about the Grand-Duke Constantine were current which were far from confirming the hope that the match would be a happy one. These stories ought to have opened the eyes of the daughters and their mother, but perhaps they thought that as they had come from so far it was too late to go back, or maybe their eyes, fascinated by the splendour of greatness, did not see things in their right light.

Catherine had received the mother and her daughters with open arms; she was continually with them, and while she talked with the mother, her grandsons had plenty of opportunities of becoming acquainted with the daughters, as there were fêtes, soirées, balls, and promenades every day. The Grand-Duke Constantine had received orders from his grandmother to marry one of these princesses; he was only allowed to choose from among the three. Constantine was then seventeen years old. When he was older, and indeed during the whole of his career, he always proved by his conduct that his passions were independent both of his will and his reason. It was not therefore probable that at so early an age he should have consulted either; he simply obeyed the orders of his all-powerful grandmother.

It was thought in the capital (we did not yet belong to the Court) that the Grand-Duke would select the youngest of the three sisters. The eldest had managed to withdraw by frankly declaring that her heart was not free; and she was the only one who could congratulate herself on her courage. She had accepted the addresses of a young Austrian officer (afterwards a general); her parents, not wishing to oppose her inclinations, finally gave their consent, and she alone of the three sisters was happy.

The appointments of officers of the Guards and of Gentlemen of the Chamber were both sinecures. At the same time this combination of military rank in the Guards regiments, to which no duty was attached, and of honorary rank in the Court, was not without its advantages. It furnished a career of adventure and emotion to young men who were ambitious, rich, and fond of pleasure. They were admitted to the games, dances, soirées, and theatrical performances of the Court—into the interior of that sanctuary in the midst of which people who had real duties to perform could not penetrate unless they had attained the highest ranks. It seemed strange that men without any personal merit should find the gates of the palace open to them, while generals of long service mixed with the crowd in the ante-chambers. We had at least some satisfaction in seeing the terrible Governor-General of a province totally eclipsed in the capital, barely obtaining a look from the favourite, and not daring to show himself in any distinguished society. There was some sweetness in this little revenge ; but, the sentiment of social superiority apart, all other relations remained the same; for this governor, who was treated with contempt in the capital, indulged in the same tyranny as before directly he returned to his province : he compensated himself over and over again for the humiliations he had had to put up with, and, sure of impunity, inflicted rapine and persecution on the members of families which he dared not visit at St Petersburg. It was difficult, if not impossible, to obtain justice with regard to the permanent abuses of discretionary power, so long as these abuses were not too revolting—revolting in a country where nothing shocks !—and were covered by certain forms. In the provinces everything was done by officials and secretaries who had no access to society, still less to the Court, and who decided every case in the name of their chiefs, most of whom were either indolent or stupid. To have on one's side the clerks was a sure way of success, for the provincial oppressors and pillagers kept up so close an understanding with the underlings of the senate and the ministerial departments that the truth could not come out any where.

Our appointment as Gentlemen of the Chamber

initiated us into the private habits of the Court, and enabled us to make a closer acquaintance with several high dignitaries and with some young men whom we met in the salons and who became our comrades. It also had the effect of bringing us nearer to the Grand-Dukes.

I will first speak of the ceremonies which attended the marriage of the Grand-Duke Constantine. His choice was well known to the public. The young Princess Julia, who, as the future Grand-Duchess, was to assume the name of Anna, was already being taught the Russian catechism, and was preparing to change her religion. It is said that German princesses who had any chance of marrying a Russian Prince, did not receive any special or profound instruction as to the dogmas which mark the line of distinction between the various Christian religions. This precaution was taken by the prudent parents so that the princesses might change their religion without much conscientious scruple. Be this as it may, the facility with which they adopted the Russian faith certainly gave the statement a colour of truth. They were mostly quite indifferent to religious dogmas, or if not, they adhered secretly to the religion which they had publicly disowned.

The day of renunciation and baptism—for even if you are a Christian you have to be baptised over again when you embrace the Russian religion—came first. The Imperial family and all the courtiers proceeded in splendid dresses to the chapel, which was already occupied by the bishops and the clergy. It was painful to see the young princess advancing in a dress of cloth of gold laden with diamonds, like a victim crowned with flowers, to bow her head to images which were in no way sacred to her, to submit to the exigencies of a ceremony which was opposed to her convictions and her sentiments. It was evident that she did this simply out of deference, knowing opposition was useless, and without attaching the slightest importance to the ceremony.

The Russian rite reminds one rather of pagan than of Christian observances. The bishops and popes, all with long beards, involuntarily recall to one's mind the high priests of antiquity. Everything is calculated for external pomp and to appeal to the senses ; there is no provision for that religion of the heart, lifting up the soul to the Creator, which demands tranquillity and reflection. Preaching is a mere form; I have never heard a good sermon in a Russian church either at Court or elsewhere. Moreover, the clergy never preach except on grand occasions. Their sermons are, both by habit and obligation, borrowed to a great extent from the writings of the primitive Slavonic church ; this always makes their eloquence subtle and pompous rather than instructive or convincing. Hymns and ceremonial take up the whole time of the service, so that there is none left for doctrine. The services are, in fact, theatrical representations copied direct from those of idolaters. The chalices carried on the acolytes' heads, the opening and closing doors of the sanctuary, the worship before images, the censers constantly in motion, present a scene very like those we read of in connection with pagan sacrifices. One would look in vain for the simplicity and instruction to be found in Protestantism, or the devotion and the tender aspirations of Catholicism; these bear the stamp of civilization, while the Russian rite is Asiatic and barbarous. There is something strange even in its manifestations of devotion. Thus everybody—young or old, elegant or shabby—takes the sacrament. People who belong to the churches of Western Europe often do not wish or do not dare to approach the holy table, yet they often have more faith and true piety; their abstention from the sacrament, though sometimes blameable, is accompanied by respect for their religion, and may be merely a consequence of it. In Russia, on the other hand, religious ceremonies are often performed not in satisfaction of one's moral aspirations, but merely as a matter of custom, and the people who go to church turn the hymns and prayers sung by the popes into ridicule. At confession the priest reads to the penitent or penitents (for sometimes several confess their sins at the same time) a list of sins, and the penitent usually does not answer aloud, but when some sin is mentioned of which he is guilty, he murmurs long prayers, often without seeming to pay attention to them, and then goes to take the sacrament.

These reflections occurred to me when I saw the young princess, endowed by nature with gaiety and charm, accepting the new religion without foreseeing her destiny—which, however, it was easy to guess at; while those of her family who were present seemed to beam with happiness.

Some days afterwards the marriage took place. The princess was given to a youth barely entering manhood, but with a violent temper and savage caprices which had already furnished many a topic of conversation. The ceremonious dinners, balls, entertainments of all kinds, and fireworks lasted for several weeks; but as usual all these noisy diversions, splendid as they were, did not inspire mirth. The marriage ceremony always has a tinge of melancholy; it is a solemn moment which decides the whole future of the persons who are united by it, and those who witness it cannot help reflecting on the fact that at that moment the happiness of two human beings is at stake. This was especially the case at the marriage of the Grand-Duke Constantine; a sinister veil of sadness hovered over the ceremony and the fêtes which followed it. It was a mournful spectacle, this handsome young princess, come from so far to adopt a foreign religion on a foreign soil, to be delivered up to the capricious will of a man who it was evident would never care for her happiness. These fatal presentiments were soon confirmed by the confidential avowals of the Grand-Duke himself. What he related to those with whom he was intimate about his honeymoon was marked by an unexampled want of delicacy towards his wife. She and the wife of the Grand-Duke Alexander became friends. Being both German and both far from their respective families, they were naturally inclined to a mutual confidence which might be their consolation in case of adversity, and might double their happiness if their marriages should prove a success. The Grand-Duchess Elizabeth, who was destined to a more elevated position, and was incomparably more fortunate in the character of her husband, seemed to be the supporter and protectress of her sister-in-law, and a substitute for her mother and sisters, who were soon to leave St Petersburg. The inequality of their respective positions drew the bonds between them still closer.

When the fêtes were over, and the Coburg family had gone, the Court resumed its normal life. Sledging parties were organized; the Empress sometimes wished them to take place in the morning, and the Gentlemen of the Chamber who were on duty were then called to accompany her. On one of these occasions I saw Catherine in a morning négligé and Zuboff coming familiarly out of her room in a pelisse and kid boots—which did not disconcert either the Empress, her favourite, or the bystanders.

In the Winter Palace, so called because the Court inhabited it at that season, the evening assemblies used to take place in a room known as the *salle des diamants*, because the crown jewels were kept in it in glass cupboards. This room communicated on one side with the bedroom and other private rooms of the Empress, and on the other with the rooms allotted to her servants. The throne-room, which was regarded as belonging to the private apartments, separated the servants' rooms from the drawing-rooms beyond. The *chevaliers-gardes*, a detachment of officers selected for their stature and merit, used to sit at the entrance to the throne-room. They were the direct descendants of the famous company of grenadiers who had placed the Empress Elizabeth on the throne, and had been rewarded for this service by all of them who were soldiers being promoted to the rank of officer and made her private guard. This guard was maintained on the same footing until Catherine's death, and it always kept its rich costume.

The ordinary Court assemblies used to take place in the *salle des diamants;* one only saw there people who were on intimate terms with the Imperial family and officers on duty. The Empress used to play cards with Zuboff and other dignitaries. It was remarked that the favourite did not pay much attention either to his sovereign or to the game; he was often absent-minded, and his eyes were constantly turned to the table where the two Grand-Duchesses were with their husbands. It was surprising that the Empress did not notice what was evident to every one else. These evenings would have been terribly dull in any other place, and even in the Empress's salon people were glad they were so short. The Empress did not wait for supper, but used to leave early and withdraw into her room. She bowed with dignity to the princesses and the members of the Court, the folding-doors of her room opened, and then Zuboff, bowing like the Empress, used to go in with her and the doors were shut. The Grand-Dukes and Grand-Duchesses withdrew at the same time as the Empress.

Two snow hills were sometimes erected in the vicinity of the Tauris Palace. The princesses and the whole *personnel* of the Court used to go there to descend in sledges according to the Russian custom. People were very merry at these entertainments, the young men having young and pretty ladies as their

partners. One day young Strogonoff gave the officer
of police, who wished to prevent his passing, a box
on the ear. Strogonoff was reprimanded, and there
was an end of the matter. Some excellent concerts
were given in the Grand-Duchess's apartments, and
at the Hermitage Palace French plays and Italian
operas were admirably performed. The Austrian
Ambassador, Count de Cobentzel, usually conversed
with the Empress; besides these the only persons
present were the Grand-Dukes and Grand-Duchesses
and people belonging to the Court. These performances took place twice a week, and were very pleasant
as there was no constraint of any kind. I still see the
audience as it then appeared to me. In front of the
stage was the Empress, occupying a double seat owing
to her size; next to her was the Count de Cobentzel,
with his squint, and his bald head covered with a
thick coat of powder, approving everything she said.
On either side were the Imperial family, all fresh
and pretty faces, except that of the Grand-Duke
Constantine; and the rest of the society occupied
seats raised in the shape of an amphitheatre.

The Empress was quite satisfied at her second
grandson's marriage, and she seemed to revel in the
leisure which was given her by the favourable turn
in foreign politics. Everything went smoothly: the
affairs of unfortunate Poland had been settled according to her wish, the King of Prussia was about to
cede the city of Cracow to Austria in compliance
with her orders, and all the European monarchies
were at her feet, approving and flattering her plans.
This was because England and Austria wished to

procure her active assistance against France, while Naples, Rome, and Sardinia, fearing the republican movement, sought the same object. The King of Prussia took care not to oppose her in anything. But while Catherine issued the most vehement diplomatic notes against the Revolution and the French Republic, and fomented the whole of Europe against them, she prudently avoided war, observing the vicissitudes of the fortunes of the allies, and taking care not to allow her troops to intervene. While the others were exhausting themselves in sanguinary battles, she twice * robbed Poland of territory and distributed fragments of the booty among her accomplices ; she was supreme over the whole of Northern Europe, the terror of the Turks, and proud of the universal homage paid to her. Tranquil at home, she sent troops to Persia under the orders of Valerian Zuboff, for her feminine instincts were always mixed up with the masculine, or rather Macchiavellian, enterprises of her policy. These were the last of her happy days. The victories of Buonaparte in Italy and the conduct of the young King of Sweden were soon to fill with bitterness the last year of her life.

* In the partitions of 1773 and 1792.

CHAPTER VII

1796

CONVERSATIONS WITH ALEXANDER.—STAY AT TSARSKOE-SELO.—
RELATIONS BETWEEN THE GRAND-DUKE PAUL AND HIS SONS.—
BIRTH OF NICHOLAS.

BEFORE the break-up of the ice on Lake Ladoga,
which generally occurs towards the end of April, St
Petersburg usually has a few days of fine weather,
with bright sun and a moderate temperature ; and the
quays are then full of gaily dressed people walking
and driving. The Grand-Duke Alexander was often
there either alone or with his wife ; and this was an
additional incentive for high society to assemble. I
used also to come with my brother, and whenever the
Grand-Duke met one of us, he stopped to talk, and
showed us particular attention.

These morning meetings were, so to say, a continuation of the Court soirées, and our relations with
the Prince daily became more intimate. In the spring
the Court moved as usual to the Tauris Palace, where
the Empress Catherine professed to live in greater
retirement, and only admitted very select company in
the evening. The Grand-Duke still came occasionally
to the quay ; he told me he was sorry to see me so

seldom, and asked me to come to him to the Tauris Palace for a walk in the garden, which he wished to show me. Spring had already begun, and as generally happens in this climate, nature had made up for lost time, and vegetation had rapidly developed itself in a few days; the trees and fields were green and covered with flowers. I went on the day and hour fixed by the Prince. I am sorry I did not take note of the exact date, for that day had a decisive influence on a great part of my life and on the destinies of my country. Thenceforward I became devoted to the Grand-Duke, and I may say that our conversation then led to a mutual friendship, followed by a series of fortunate and unfortunate events, whose results still make themselves felt and will be perceived for many years to come.

As soon as I came in, the Grand-Duke took me by the hand, and proposed that we should go into the garden, in order, he said, that he might enable me to judge of the skill of his English gardener. We walked about in every direction for three hours, keeping up an animated conversation all the time. The Grand-Duke told me that my conduct and that of my brother, the resignation we showed in a position which must be painful to us, and the calm indifference with which we had received both the smiles and the frowns of fortune, had gained us his esteem and confidence; that he divined and approved our sentiments; that he had felt it necessary to let us know what he really thought, and that he could not bear the idea that we should judge him otherwise than as he really was. He added that he did not in any way share the ideas and doctrines of the Cabinet and the Court; and that he was far from approving the policy and conduct of his grandmother, whose principles he condemned. He had wished for the success of Poland in her glorious struggle and had deplored her fall. Kosciuszko, he said, was in his eyes a man who was great by his virtues and the cause which he had defended, which was the cause of humanity and of justice. He added that he detested despotism everywhere, no matter in what way it was exercised; that he loved liberty, to which all men had a right; that he had taken the strongest interest in the French Revolution, and that while condemning its terrible excesses, he wished the French Republic success and rejoiced at its establishment. He spoke to me with veneration of his tutor, M. de la Harpe, as a man of great virtue, of true wisdom, of strict principles, and of energetic character. He owed to him all he knew and any good qualities he might possess—especially those principles of truth and justice which he was happy to bear in his heart and with which M. de la Harpe had inculcated him.

While we were walking about in the garden we several times met the Grand-Duchess, who also was taking a walk. The Grand-Duke told me that he confided his thoughts to his wife, that she alone knew and shared his sentiments, and that I was the only person besides herself to whom he had dared to speak of them since his tutor had gone; that he could not mention them to any Russian, as none were as yet capable even of understanding them; and that I must therefore feel how great a pleasure it would be for him to have in future some one with whom he could talk openly and in entire confidence.

This conversation was, as may be imagined, occasionally interrupted by demonstrations of friendship on his part, and of astonishment, gratitude, and devotion on mine. He bade me farewell, saying that he would try to see me as often as possible, and urging on me the greatest circumspection and secrecy, though at the same time he authorised me to communicate to my brother the subject of our conversation.

I was deeply moved, and could hardly believe my ears. That a Russian Prince, Catherine's successor, her grandson and her favourite child, whom she would have wished to see reigning after her instead of her son, and of whom it was said that he would continue her reign, should disavow and detest his grandmother's principles—should repel the odious policy of Russia—should be a passionate lover of justice and liberty—should pity Poland and wish to see her happy—seemed incredible. And that such noble ideas and great virtues should be able to grow and flourish in such an atmosphere and with such surroundings, was surely little less than a miracle.

I was young, full of exalted sentiments and ideas; extraordinary things did not long astonish me, for I readily believed in anything that seemed to me great and virtuous. I was subjugated by a charm which it is easy to understand: there was so much candour, innocence, resolution which seemed unshakeable, and elevation of soul in the words and countenance of this young prince, that he seemed to me a privileged being whom Providence had sent to this world for

the happiness of humanity and of my country. My
attachment to him was boundless, and the feeling
with which he inspired me at that moment lasted
even after the illusions which had given birth to it
successively disappeared; it resisted the attacks
which Alexander himself made upon it, and it never
died in spite of the many events and sad misunder-
standings which might have destroyed it. I told my
brother of our conversation, and after giving a free
rein to our surprise and admiration, we plunged into
reveries of a radiant future which seemed to be
opening before us. It should be remembered that at
that time so-called liberal opinions were much less
prevalent than they are now, and had not yet penetrated into all the classes of society and even into the
Cabinets of sovereigns. On the contrary, everything that had the appearance of liberalism was
anathematised in the Courts and salons of most of the
European capitals, and especially in Russia and at St
Petersburg, where all the convictions of the old
French régime were grafted in an exaggerated form
on Russian despotism and servility.

It was assuredly a most fortunate and important
incident that in the midst of these elements there
should be a prince, the future ruler of Russia, who
would necessarily exercise immense influence in
Europe, holding such decided and generous opinions
entirely opposed to the existing state of things. Now
that I look back, forty years afterwards, upon the
events which have taken place since that conversation,
I see only too well how little they have realised the
picture that our youthful imaginations had drawn.

Liberal ideas were at that time in our eyes still surrounded by an aureole which has paled since they have been tested by experience; their realisation had not yet produced the cruel deceptions which have so often disheartened us. That period, in the years 1796 and 1797, was the most brilliant one of the dawn of liberal ideas: the cycle of the French Empire had not yet chilled and dispersed the warmest partisans of the Revolution.

Our Polish sentiments, our wishes, our inexperience—our faith in the ultimate success of justice and liberty—will explain how at that moment we abandoned ourselves with joy to the most seductive illusions. For some days after this remarkable conversation we had not an opportunity of talking with the Grand-Duke; but whenever he met us we exchanged friendly words and sympathetic gestures.

Soon after, the Court left for Tsarskoe-Selo. All the cavalry officers of the guard had to go there on Sundays and holidays to attend at mass, at dinner, and in the evening; some even resided there, either in one of the very inconvenient little houses which surrounded the courtyard opposite the palace, or in the village, where the discomfort was equally great, but where the officers were less under constraint.

Alexander at first urged us to come often, and then to stay at Tsarskoe-Selo, in order, as he said, to have an opportunity of being more with him. He liked our society and wished for it, as it was only with us that he could speak unreservedly. We had a right to come into the Imperial apartments when the Empress went there in the evening, to take part in the promenades and games which took place every fine day, and to join the courtiers who met under the colonnade, a part of the palace which the Empress liked best, and which was close to her apartments. The officers did not on ordinary days dine at the Empress's table unless they were on duty. This happened to me once; I was placed opposite to Catherine and had to wait upon her, which I did with some awkwardness.

We often returned to Tsarskoe-Selo, and soon after we settled there for the season. Our relations with Alexander naturally aroused much interest: it was a kind of freemasonry, but the Grand-Duchess was let into the secret. An intimacy whose object was at that time so recent and so ardently discussed furnished material for conversations which were suspended only to be resumed on the next opportunity. Political opinions which now seem trite and hackneyed were at that time startling on account of their novelty, and the mystery we had to preserve, the idea that we were expressing these opinions under the eyes of a Court encrusted with the prejudices of absolutism and of Ministers puffed up with their supposed infallibility, added interest and piquancy to these relations, which grew more frequent and intimate every day.

The Empress Catherine looked favourably upon the connection which was establishing itself between her grandson and ourselves; she approved it, of course without guessing at its true motive or at its probable consequences. Probably, with her old ideas as to the splendour of the Polish aristocracy, she thought it would be useful to attach an influential family to her grandson. She in no way suspected that this friendship would confirm him in the opinions which she detested and feared—that it would be one of the thousand causes of the progress of liberty in Europe, and of the re-appearance—only for a time, alas!—of Poland, which she had thought she had buried for ever, on the political scene. Her approval of the marked preference shown us by Alexander closed the mouths of all objectors, and encouraged us in continuing our relations, which were so attractive to us in all respects.

The Grand-Duke Constantine, from a spirit of imitation, and seeing that his doing so pleased the Empress, now made great professions of friendship to my brother, invited him to his rooms, and admitted him to the intimacy of his family; but there was no question of politics in this connection. My brother was not in this respect as fortunate as I was; none of the motives which had bound us to Alexander existed in the case of Constantine, and his capricious and violent character, not admitting any impression but that of fear, rendered all intimacy with him undesirable. Alexander, however, requested my brother to take Constantine's overtures in good part, at the same time charging him not to reveal the secret of our political conversations.

At first Alexander was quartered in the palace, and did not yet live in the separate building in the park which the Empress had ordered to be built for him, and which had just been completed. We used to go there for our afternoon walks until

Alexander established himself in the new building, when he was much more free to see us. He often had either my brother or myself to dinner, and a day seldom passed but one of us supped with him also, when the rooms at the palace were quite finished. In the morning we used to take long walks together ; the Grand-Duke was very fond of walking and of visiting the villages in the neighbourhood, and it was especially on these occasions that he used to talk of his favourite subjects. He was under the charm of early youth, which creates images and dwells upon them without being checked by impossibilities, and which makes endless projects for a future which seems to it eternal.

His opinions were those of one brought up in the ideas of 1789, who wishes to see republics everywhere, and looks upon that form of government as the only one in conformity with the wishes and the rights of humanity. Although I was myself at that time very enthusiastic—although born and brought up in a Republic where the principles of the French Revolution had been accepted with ardour—yet I had constantly to moderate the extreme opinions expressed by Alexander. He held, among other things, that hereditary monarchy was an unjust and absurd institution, and that the supreme authority should be granted not through the accident of birth but by the votes of the nation, which would best know who is most capable of governing it. I represented to him the arguments against this view, the difficulty and the risks of an election, what Poland had suffered from such an institution, and how little

Russia was adapted to or prepared for it. I added that now at any rate Russia would not gain anything by the change, as she would lose the man who by his benevolent and pure intentions was most worthy of acceding to the throne. We had incessant discussions on this point. Sometimes during our long walks we talked of other matters. We turned from politics to nature, of whose beauties the young Grand-Duke was an enthusiastic admirer. One had to be a great lover of nature to discover its beauties in the country we walked in; but everything is relative in this world, and the Grand-Duke flew into ecstasies about a flower, the greenness of a tree, or the view over an undulating plain. There is nothing uglier or less picturesque than the neighbourhood of St Petersburg. Alexander loved gardens and fields, and was fond of agriculture and the rustic beauty of village girls; the occupations and labours of the country, a simple, quiet, and retired life in some pretty farm, in a wide and smiling landscape—such was the dream he would have liked to realise, and to which he was always returning with a sigh.

I knew well that this was not the thing best suited to him; that for so high a destiny more elevation, force, ardour, and self-confidence were necessary than Alexander seemed to possess; that it was not right for a man in his position to wish to rid himself of the enormous burthen which was reserved for him, and to yearn for the pleasures of a quiet life. It was not enough to perceive and feel the difficulties of his position; he should have been filled with a passionate desire to surmount them. These reflections occasionally presented themselves to my mind, and even when I felt their truth, they did not diminish my feelings of admiration and devotion for Alexander. His sincerity, his frankness, his self-abandonment to the beautiful illusions that fascinated him, had a charm which it was impossible to resist. Moreover, he was still so young that his character might yet gain the qualities in which it was defective; circumstances and necessities might develop faculties which had not the time or the means of showing themselves; and although he was afterwards much changed, he retained to the last a portion of the tastes and opinions of his youth.

Many people—my countrymen especially—in later years reproached me for having placed too much confidence in Alexander's assurances. I have often maintained against his detractors that his opinions were sincere. The impression produced by the first years of our relations could not be effaced. Assuredly, when Alexander, at the age of eighteen, spoke to me with an effusiveness which relieved his mind, about opinions and sentiments which he concealed from everybody else, it was because he really felt them, and wished to confide them to someone. What other motive could he have had? Whom could he have wished to deceive? He certainly followed the inclination of his heart and expressed his real thoughts.

Besides our political discussions, and the ever-welcome topic of the beauties of nature, and the dream of a quiet country life after the destinies of free Russia should have been secured, Alexander had also a third object to which he ardently devoted himself, and which was not at all in accordance with the others, namely, the army, which was his hobby, as it was that of his father, the Grand-Duke Paul. This prince lived during the summer in his country-house of Pavlovsk, half-a-league from Tsarskoe-Selo. The Empress Catherine had allowed him to keep there for his amusement some battalions of marines. He was Grand-Admiral, and this honorary title gave him certain privileges. The Empress pretended not to perceive that Paul made too large a use of them, and that following the example of Peter III, his unfortunate father, he had created for himself a sort of little army, which he clothed and endeavoured to drill according to the system he had observed in Prussia when he visited Frederick the Great at Berlin. This army was, I believe, composed in all of twelve very small battalions, some cuirassiers, dragoons, and hussars, and some guns; and all promotions in this force were in the Grand-Duke's hands. The uniforms were very eccentric in cut, and were in striking contrast to the uniforms of the Russian army in this respect; they were a caricature of the uniforms of the troops of the Great Frederick. Many people of society and of the Court had obtained permission to wear these uniforms, and they were the only courtiers whom Paul allowed to attend at his country-houses. Among them was M. Rostopchin, who played an important part after Paul became Emperor, and was afterwards much talked about at the time of the fire of Moscow. These courtiers took their uniforms with them whenever they went to Pavlovsk or to Gatchina, another country-house belonging to the Grand-Duke,

or even to his soirées in the Winter Palace, for Paul
never went to his mother's in the evening. People
only appeared in this costume, however, in Paul's
apartments; everywhere else it was tabooed so long
as Catherine lived, and people laughed at it with
impunity.

The two young Grand-Dukes had commands in
Paul's army. They gave themselves up to their
duties with the zeal of young men who are for the
first time given something to do, and the Court and
the public compared them to children playing at
soldiers. This, however, produced no impression
upon them; all they thought of was to obey the
wishes and even the eccentricities of their father.

There occurred at the parades and manœuvres of
this miniature army grave events, defeats, ups and
downs of favour, misfortunes or successes, which
sometimes caused the deepest consternation, at others
the greatest joy. I heard of them from the two
brothers, who took a pleasure in relating all the
vicissitudes of the Court of Pavlovsk. To these
young princes it was an active life which gave them
importance, in a restricted circle no doubt, but where
they played a part which, while it flattered their
vanity, contented their juvenile activity without
much expenditure of thought. The regulated uniformity of their grandmother's Court, on the other
hand, where they had no serious occupation, was
often inexpressibly tedious to them. Their bodily
fatigues, the necessity of keeping out of the way of
their grandmother when they returned tired from
their drill, in a dress which they had to take off at

once—even their father's scoldings, which they greatly feared—gave attractions to this mode of life, which was very different from the one which the public of St Petersburg and the views of Catherine had marked out for them.

The Empress did not know how to appeal to the imagination of her grand-children or how to give them active and varied occupation. Their father was more successful, and this was a great evil which had unfortunate consequences. The young Grand-Dukes thought themselves, and were in reality, more a part of the army of Gatchina than of the Russian army. Gatchina was Paul's favourite Palace and his residence during the autumn; he was there at some distance from St Petersburg, and could give himself up without constraint to his hobbies. The Grand-Dukes regretted not to be able to go there, but they liked to imitate the manners of Paul's troopers, and, in speaking of what was done in his little army, to say, 'That is our way, after the fashion of Gatchina' (*Po naszemu, po Gatchinski*).

I recollect that the Empress one day thought of sending Alexander with General Kutuzoff, to inspect the fortresses on the Swedish frontier. The young Prince did not seem to like the idea, and it was consequently abandoned. The minutiæ of the military service and the habit of attaching extreme importance to it gave an unfortunate turn to Alexander's mind; he took a liking for it of which he could not afterwards rid himself, even after he had perceived its absurdity. During the whole of his reign he had a mania for parade which made him lose much precious time while he was on the throne, and prevented him during his youth from working usefully and acquiring indispensable knowledge. This was also the bond of union between Alexander and Constantine, and it often gave the latter too great an influence over his brother, for Constantine was well versed in military science so far as mere drill is concerned, and his brother could not help having a great idea of him in this respect. It was the constant subject of their most animated conversations.

The Empress Catherine saw the understanding between Paul and his sons with displeasure, though she did not foresee all its consequences, for if she had, she would probably have prohibited it. Alexander said to me one day as he was returning from Pavlovsk: 'They do us the honour of fearing us,' meaning that Catherine was beginning to be anxious at the maintenance of the troops at Pavlovsk, and at the sort of concert which had been established between Paul and his sons. Alexander was flattered at the thought of having inspired some fear in the Empress; but I doubt whether she really felt any such sentiment; if she did so it was very occasionally and to a very slight extent. Catherine knew too well the cowardly spirit of her son, the ridiculous appearance of his troops, and the disfavour with which they were regarded by the public and the rest of the army, to trouble herself by fearing them. She remained in peace under the protection of a single company of Grenadiers, while Paul was manœuvring with his little army half-a-league off.

The Empress Elizabeth had done the same at Peter-hoff with Peter III, who lived at Oranienbaum, sur-rounded by a corps of devoted Holsteiners; she also knew the extreme pusillanimity of her successor, and perhaps also his kind heart. Various rumours have been current as to the legitimacy of Paul I; but those who saw the extreme resemblance of character and conduct between him and Peter III, could have no doubt that he was really Peter's son.

During this year an event occurred which had vast consequences for Europe and terrible ones for Poland. The Grand-Duchess Maria gave birth to a son. The baptismal ceremony took place in the chapel of Tsarskoe-Selo; the whole Court attended in full dress in the spacious hall which precedes the chapel. The ceremony, as was to be expected, was a most sumptuous one. The ambassadors were present, and some of them held the child at the baptismal font as the representatives of their respec-tive sovereigns. He was named Nicholas! Looking at him then in his swaddling clothes as he moved about impatiently while the long baptismal ceremony of the Russian Church was being performed, I little thought that this weak and pretty child would one day become the scourge of my country.

Among the motives which attracted the young Grand-Dukes to their father was one that was more noble and sensible than those above mentioned. They were painfully impressed by the cruelty of Catherine in not allowing her sons and their wives to enjoy the company of their children even in ex-treme youth. As soon as the Grand-Duchess Maria could leave her bed, her child was taken away from her to be brought up with his brothers and sisters under the eyes of their grandmother. Not one of them was, so long as Catherine lived, left to the care of its parents or remained with them. Such injustice revolted the young princes and alienated them from the Empress. Moreover, Alexander's views as to his grandmother's policy did not make him disposed to follow her wishes when he could do otherwise. He always found some objection to raise, and showed nothing but *ennui* and indifference when he was called upon to take part, however little, in a government which was not at that time at all in accordance with his opinions. Constantine, who did not share his brother's liberal views, yet agreed with him in his disapproval of the manners and character of Catherine. I have heard him more than once speak about his grandmother, even after she was dead, with outrageous rudeness and in the coarsest terms.

The stay of the Court at Tsarskoe-Selo was drawing to a close. This gave us a feeling of sadness : we regretted our unceremonious meetings, our daily conversations, our long walks in the gardens and in the country. We had gathered the first flower of youthful and confiding affection—we had enjoyed the dreams with which it is soothed. Whatever we may do, we do not again find sensations so strong and fresh; as we advance in life they become more and more rare.

The Court proceeded as usual to the Tauris Palace for the season which precedes the winter. Alexander was not so often visible, and could not have us so often with him at his meals. Yet our relations, the partial interruption of which caused us much regret, continued to be the object of our constant pre-occupations.

CHAPTER VIII

1796

THE FATE OF THE PRISONERS.—REFLECTIONS ON ALEXANDER'S EDU-
CATION.—ARRIVAL OF THE KING OF SWEDEN.—FAILURE OF THE
NEGOTIATIONS FOR HIS MARRIAGE WITH THE GRAND-DUCHESS
ALEXANDRA.—DEATH OF CATHERINE.

OUR friendship with Alexander had not helped us to
improve the condition of our countrymen who were
imprisoned in the town or the casemates of the fortress.
We often talked of them and of Kosciuszko; Alexander
always spoke with enthusiasm of the devotion and
the great deeds of these martyrs of patriotism, and
was indignant at the unjust tyranny of which they
were the victims. But, bound by his position, and
timid from a consciousness of his youth and inexperience, he took no part in affairs of State, and did
not even think he ought to seek to interfere in them.
He accordingly had no influence or even contact with
those who had the management of affairs.

It is certainly astonishing that Catherine, who
took pleasure in the thought that Alexander would
continue her reign and her glory, did not think of
preparing him for this task by familiarising him in
his early youth with the various branches of govern-

ment.   Nothing of the sort was attempted.   Perhaps
he would not have acquired very correct information
on many things, but he would have been saved from
the want of occupation.   Yet it would seem that either
the Empress and her council had no such idea, or that
the former did not at least insist upon its being carried
out.   Alexander's education remained incomplete at the
time of his marriage, in consequence of the departure
of M. de la Harpe.   He was then eighteen years old ;
he had no regular occupation, he was not even advised
to work, and in the absence of any more practical
task he was not given any plan of reading which
might have helped him in the difficult career for which
he was destined.   I   often spoke to him on this
subject, both then and later.   I proposed that he
should read various books on history, legislation, and
politics.   He saw that they would do him good, and
really wished to read them ; but a Court life makes
any continued occupation impossible.   While he was
Grand-Duke, Alexander did not read to the end a
single serious book.   I do not think he could have
done so when he became Emperor, and the whole
burthen of a despotic government was cast upon him.
The life of a Court is fatiguing and yet idle.   It
furnishes a thousand excuses for indolence, and one
is constantly busy in doing nothing.   When Alexander
came to his rooms it was to take rest and not to
work.   He read by fits and starts, without ardour
or zeal.   The passion of acquiring knowledge was not
sufficiently strong in him ; he was married too young,
and he did not perceive that he still knew very little.
Yet he felt the importance of useful study, and

wished to enter upon it; but his will was not sufficiently strong to overcome the daily obstacles presented by the duties and unpleasantnesses of life. The few years of his early youth thus passed away, and he lost precious opportunities which he had in abundance so long as Catherine was alive, and of which he might have recovered a part even under the Emperor Paul.

While he was Grand-Duke, and even during the first years of his reign, Alexander remained what his education had made him, and was very different from what he became later on when he followed his natural propensities. It must be concluded that nature had endowed him with rare qualities, as notwithstanding the education he had received he became the most amiable sovereign of his age and the cause of Napoleon's fall. After having reigned for some years, and acquired the experience entailed by the necessity of at once taking the management of important affairs of State and by constant intercourse with men in office, people were surprised to find him not only an accomplished man of the world, but an able politician, with a penetrating and subtle mind, writing without assistance excellent letters on complicated and difficult subjects, and always amiable, even in the most serious conversations. What would he have become had his education been less neglected and more adapted to the duties which were to occupy his life? M. de la Harpe was the only man that can be mentioned with praise among those to whom the education of the two Grand-Dukes was entrusted. I do not know exactly who were the persons directed by Catherine to select their tutors; probably they were some encyclopædists of the clique of Grimm or the Baron d'Holbach.

M. de la Harpe does not seem to have directed Alexander into any serious course of study, though he had acquired so much influence over the Grand-Duke's mind and heart that I believe he could have made him do anything. Alexander derived from his teaching only some superficial knowledge : his information was neither positive nor complete. M. de la Harpe inspired him with the love of humanity, of justice, and even of equality and liberty for all ; he prevented the prejudices and flatteries which surrounded him from stifling his noble instincts. It was a great merit in M. de la Harpe to have inspired and developed these generous sentiments in a Russian Grand-Duke, but Alexander's mind was not penetrated by them ; it was filled with vague phrases, and M. de la Harpe did not sufficiently make him reflect on the immense difficulty of realising these ideas—on the thorny task of finding means to obtain possible results. He was, however, merely charged with Alexander's literary education ; the choice which was made of those who were to look after his moral training was extraordinary. Count Nicholas Soltykoff, who was a subaltern during the Seven Years' War and had not since seen any active service (which did not prevent him from attaining the highest rank in the army), was the superintendent of the education of the two Grand-Dukes. Short, with a large head, affected, nervous, and of health so delicate that it required constant attention (he could not wear braces, and constantly hitched up his breeches like a sailor) he had the reputation of being the most astute courtier in Russia. When Catherine discovered that her favourite Momonoff had formed intimate relations with one of her maids of honour, she ordered the culprits to come before her, had them married, and then expelled them from her Court; after which Soltykoff at once introduced to her Plato Zuboff, who speedily became Momonoff's successor. The elevation of Zuboff so angered Prince Potemkin that he declared he would go to St Petersburg to extract this tooth (*zub* means tooth in Russian); but he died before he could carry out his intention, and Soltykoff remained in high favour with the Empress. He was not only the channel by which her messages and admonitions were conveyed to the young princes; he also acted as intermediary whenever Catherine had anything to communicate to the Grand-Duke Paul. Soltykoff used to omit or soften any words which seemed too disagreeable or severe in the orders or the reproaches of his Imperial mistress, and he did the same with regard to the replies he had to convey to her. This gave satisfaction to both sides; he alone knew the truth, and took good care not to tell it. There was perhaps some merit in doing this successfully, but Count Soltykoff was certainly not the man to direct the education of the young heir to the throne, or to make a salutary impression on his character.

Besides Count Soltykoff, each of the two princes had a special director of studies with assistants. The selection of the two directors was even more extraordinary than that of the chief superintendent. The one attached to Alexander was Count Protasoff, whose only merit was to be the brother of the *demoiselle à portrait,** an old favourite of the Empress as to whose functions, though she was a good woman at heart, there were all sorts of extraordinary anecdotes. Constantine's special director was Count Sacken, a weak-minded man who was the object of incessant ridicule on the part of his pupil. Count Protasoff may justly be said to have been a complete imbecile ; Alexander did not laugh at him, but he had never the smallest esteem for him. The assistant directors were selected solely by favour, with the exception of Mouravieff, whom Alexander when he ascended the throne made his secretary for petitions, and afterwards appointed curator of the schools of the Moscow district. He was a worthy man and was said to be well-informed, but he was so timid as to be almost incapable of transacting business. I should also not omit Baron Budberg, who some years later succeeded me as Minister of Foreign affairs.

Such surroundings could only produce a bad effect on the young princes, and the qualities displayed by Alexander are the more astonishing and praiseworthy, as he developed them notwithstanding the education he had received and the examples which were before his eyes.

At the close of the stay in the Tauris Palace in 1796, the last year Catherine was there with her Court, the chief topic was the approaching arrival of

---

* A decoration which gives the rank of Field Marshal. Three ladies under Paul, and one under Nicholas, obtained this rank.

the young King of Sweden, who came to marry the eldest of the Grand-Duchesses. The Empress directed the ladies of the Court to learn the French *contre-danse*, which was then the favourite dance at the Court of Stockholm, and this was the daily occupation of all at Court who were dancers. The King of Sweden was received with exquisite politeness. He came with the Regent, his uncle, Duke of Suder-mania, and with a numerous suite. The Swedish costume, which resembled that formerly worn in Spain, produced a fine effect at the receptions, balls, and other fêtes which were given to the young King and his suite ; all the Court entertainments were for them. The Grand-Duchesses only danced with Swedes, and never did a Court show more courtesy to strangers.

While the fêtes were going on at the Winter Palace, and balls, concerts, and *montagnes Russes* were daily repeated at the Tauris Palace, the King of Sweden was admitted to the presence of the Grand-Duchess Alexandra as her future husband. She was of rare beauty and sweetness of character ; to know her was to admire her, and his daily interview with her could only add to the motives which seemed to prompt the King of Sweden to unite himself by family ties with the House of Romanoff. The Duke of Sudermania was strongly in favour of the match, and had urged his nephew to go to St Petersburg so as to leave no doubt as to his intentions. All that remained was to agree as to forms and the treaty to be drawn up between the two powers ; and this did not seem of a nature to cause any difficulty.

As both parties were said to be agreed, no negotiation seemed requisite, and the task of framing the necessary documents was entrusted to Count Markoff, whom the Zuboffs were putting forward in order to eclipse Count Bezborodko, who, though he had refused to cringe to them, yet kept his place and his credit with the Empress.

After some gay and brilliant weeks the day of the betrothal was fixed; the ceremony was to take place in the evening. The Archbishops of St Petersburg and Novgorod, with a numerous suite of clergy, went to the chapel where the ceremony was to take place. The whole of the Court, the Ministers, the Senate, and many generals were assembled in the waiting-room. We waited for several hours. It was getting late, and people observed whisperings among those who were likely to be well informed, and movements to and fro of persons proceeding to the Empress's apartments, all of whom came out at a quick pace. At length, after four hours of suspense, we were told that the ceremony would not take place. The Empress sent to apologise to the Archbishops who had come in their pontifical robes, to the ladies in panniers, and to the rest of the Court, and announced to them that the ceremony had been postponed owing to some unexpected difficulties.

Soon after it became known that the marriage was broken off. Count Markoff, frivolous through self-sufficiency, and inattentive through pride and disregard of all but himself, was persuaded that all was arranged without troubling himself to put the arrangement in writing and get it signed. It was when the signature was required that difficulties arose. King Gustavus IV wished to limit the liberty which the Russian princess who was to be his queen should enjoy in following the rites of her religion. The Swedes, who are staunch Protestants, had made objections on this subject, but Count Markoff took no notice, and proceeded to act as if the matter had already been decided, thinking that the Swedes would not dare to withdraw at the last moment, and that the Grand-Duchess's beauty would succeed where the ability of the Russian Ministers had failed. But he was wrong in his calculations. The young King was the most zealous Protestant in his kingdom, and he would never consent to his wife having a public Russian chapel at Stockholm. His Ministers, his Councillors, and the Regent himself, fearing the consequences of an affront to the Empress, pressed him to yield or to seek a compromise, but in vain. Instead of inclining to the Russian demands, Gustavus IV, in the prolonged conversations which he had with the Grand-Duchess, strove to convert her, and almost made her promise that she would adopt the religion of her husband and of the country in which she was to reside.

The King obstinately rejected all the proposals which Count Markoff made to him with the view of overcoming the difficulty; he was told in vain that he would expose himself to a war with Russia, if after having gone so far, he broke off the marriage just as it was about to be concluded. All was useless— even the fixing of the day, the presence of Catherine in her Imperial robes, and the convocation of the clergy and the whole Court, failed to move the Swedish King.

The young sovereign's obstinacy at first made the Swedes anxious, then frightened them, but finally pleased them; they were proud at their King having shown so much character. As for the Russians, all the excitement produced by the appearance of the King of Sweden in their capital was changed into a sombre silence of disappointment and vexation. The next day was the birthday of one of the little Grand-Duchesses (afterwards the Queen of Holland), and there was a Court ball in honour of the occasion. The Empress appeared with her eternal smile, but her eyes had a sombre expression of sadness and anger; people admired the impassive dignity with which she received her guests. The King of Sweden and his suite showed constraint, but not embarrassment; there was a stiffness of manner both on their part and on that of the Empress which communicated itself to the whole company. The Grand-Duke Paul expressed great irritation, though I suspect he was not really displeased at the blunder made by the Cabinet. As for Alexander, he was indignant at the insult which had been offered to his sister, but cast the blame of it on Count Markoff; and the Empress was very glad to see her grandson share her indignation.

The Swedish cloaks and plumes seemed no longer to float in the air with the same grace as before and shared in the general constraint; they were no longer the fashion. Some minuets were danced with even more gravity than usual. My brother was one of the dancers, and he acquitted himself very well.

Two days after the King left with his suite, and St Petersburg remained gloomy and silent. People were astounded at what had happened; they could not believe that a 'little kinglet' should thus dare to insult the Sovereign of all the Russias. What would she do now? It was impossible for Catherine II to pocket the affront and not take her revenge. So at least people said. As for the Court, the Grand-Duke Paul was at Gatchina, while the Empress remained in her apartments; and it was thought that she was preparing some resolute step which would make the King of Sweden repent his obstinacy. But it was Catherine herself that succumbed.

It was November; the weather was cold and foggy, and harmonised with the appearance of the Court and the Winter Palace after the fêtes which had animated them. Alexander continued his walks on the quays, and one day he met my brother. After having walked for some time, they stopped at the door of the lodgings where we lived. I had just come down and we were talking together, when a footman of the Court who was looking for Alexander came to tell him that Count Soltykoff wished to see him as soon as possible. Alexander immediately followed the man, not guessing the cause of this urgent message.

The Empress had had an apoplectic stroke. Her feet had for sometime been much swollen, and she had not done anything that her physicians had prescribed, but had taken some quack remedies which her chambermaids had recommended to her. The humiliation inflicted upon her by the King of Sweden was too hard a blow to her pride, and it may be said that Gustavus IV shortened her life by several years. She got up the same day, to all appearance in good health, and remained in her dressing-room longer than usual. The valet in waiting, not seeing her returning, went to the door, and opening it softly saw the Empress lying unconscious. When Zuboff came, she opened her eyes, placed her hand on her heart with an expression of extreme pain, and then shut them for ever. This was the only and the last sign of life and consciousness which she gave. The physicians hastened to the room and for three days used all the resources of their science, but in vain.

Next day the news of the Empress's fatal illness spread in the town. Those who had the entry to the Court went there with a feeling of terror, of anxiety, and of doubt as to the future. Both the town and the Court were in the greatest confusion. Most of those who were present in the room expressed sincere grief; the pale and distorted features of many betrayed a fear of losing the position they enjoyed and perhaps of being obliged to render an account of their administration. My brother and myself were among the spectators of this scene of regret and of terror. Zuboff, with his hair dishevelled and an air of consternation on his face, attracted all eyes. Both himself and all those whose fortunes he had made were naturally in despair. At one time he was busy burning papers which might have compromised him; at others he came to see if the remedies tried by the physicians gave any hope. All was disorder, and etiquette was abandoned.

We entered the room where the Empress was lying on the ground on mattresses, lifeless, like a machine whose movement has ceased.

When Zuboff learnt from the physicians that there was no longer any hope or possibility of her reviving, he sent his brother, after destroying a number of papers, to the Emperor Paul at Gatchina to inform him of his mother's death. Although Paul had for some time thought of the chances of this event soon occurring, he was thunderstruck, and arrived at St Petersburg much troubled with the uncertainty of what was awaiting him, and doubting whether his mother would not recover after all. So long as her body moved, although she had completely lost consciousness, Paul did not make use of the power which had already accrued to him, and remained concealed in his mother's room, or in his own apartments. He came with the whole of his family to see the lifeless body, and repeated this lugubrious visit twice a day.

CHAPTER IX

1796-1798

NEVER was there any change of scene at a theatre so
sudden and so complete as the change of affairs at
the accession of Paul I. In less than a day costumes,
manners, occupations, all were altered. Under
Catherine we had worn our collars so high as to cover
the lower part of the face ; we now had to wear them
narrow and turned down, showing thin necks and
prominent jaws which until then had remained unseen.
The hair was dressed *en pigeon* in the Parisian
fashion ; it was worn flat and long behind, with two
very stiff curls above the ears, and a pigtail, all well
pomatumed and powdered. Hitherto the dandies had
endeavoured to give a more graceful cut to their
uniforms, which they often wore unbuttoned, while
now the Prussian uniform of Frederick the Great,

already used by the troops of Gatchina, was adopted for the army generally. The military parade became the chief occupation of each day; it was then that the most important events occurred, making the Emperor either indulgent and lavish of his favours, or severe and even terrible, for the rest of the day.

Soon the little army of Gatchina made its solemn entry into St Petersburg. It was to be a model for the Guards and the whole Russian army. The Grand-Dukes were much agitated, for they had been ordered to place themselves at the head of these troops and take them to the capital. They had to appear before a public which had hitherto been ill-disposed, and, which was more difficult, to give satisfaction to the Emperor. But all went off well. The Gatchina troops were placed in battle array on the great square of the Winter Palace, in the midst of a timid crowd astounded at the sight of soldiers entirely different from those it had been accustomed to see. The troops defiled in good order before the Emperor, who expressed to his sons his satisfaction at the manner in which they had carried out this first manifestation of his rule. They were much pleased at the Emperor's words, and the new comers were at first quartered on the inhabitants, who hastened to give them a friendly reception. In the evening grenadiers with pointed hats like Prussians, whose hosts had freely treated them with wine and brandy, were to be seen staggering about dead drunk in the streets.

During the long years of his retirement Paul had

planned out everything he proposed to do directly
he should come into power. Changes and novelties
accordingly succeeded each other with extraordinary
rapidity. The men of Gatchina were divided among
the three regiments of foot guards and the regiment
of horse guards. The regiment of cavalier guards
was supplied with silver helmets and cuirasses which
were manufactured for the occasion, as these articles
of uniform had ceased to be worn in the Russian
army. The officers of Gatchina were all promoted,
and one soon saw old soldiers and courtly officers of
the Guards obliged either to retire or to obey the
commands of ill-bred braggarts, whose names they
had never mentioned except to laugh at them.

In the midst of all that was eccentric and ridiculous about the first acts of Paul's reign, there was an
element of seriousness and justice; thus the Emperor
ordered the young courtiers to choose some career
and devote themselves to it. No one was allowed to
join the Guards as an amateur; and the service became
so severe that most young men preferred a civil
career.

Scarcely had Paul come into power when his
first thought was to render a striking act of homage
to the memory of his father, and at the same time a
sort of verdict upon those who were guilty of his
death. During the first few days after the death of
the Empress and the time necessary for embalming
her body, the whole of the Court, including ladies and
high functionaries of State, were ordered to watch
by the body day and night in the Imperial apartments, and soon after the Emperor directed that his

father's remains should be exhumed and carried in
ceremony from the Nevski convent to the Winter
Palace to be deposited by the side of Catherine. There
were still living three or four of those who had been
accused of complicity in the murder of Peter III.
They were at that time privates or sub-officers in the
Guards; they were now great nobles with large
incomes. Among them was the Court-Marshal,
Prince Bariatynski, who was disliked because he was
rude, ill-bred, and ill-tempered, and Passeyk, Governor-General of White Russia, who was the Empress's
aide-de-camp. There were very few who possessed
this title, and it gave very high rank and great
privileges. When the Imperial aide-de-camp was
present he alone held a cane, commanded at the
palace, and watched over the safety of his sovereign.
Passeyk disappeared on the day of Catherine's death,
and Prince Bariatynski almost died of fear. He and
some of his accomplices were forced to watch at the
coffin of Peter III and follow his body in the funeral
procession. Count Alexis Orloff, one of the principal
assassins of the late Emperor, was the only one who
walked with a firm step and a countenance apparently
tranquil.

The Emperor Paul had the two coffins placed
together on a bier, where they were exposed (that of
Catherine was open) to the sight of the crowd. The
high functionaries and ladies of the Court continued
their service by the side of the bodies night and day
for six weeks; this gave rise to singular meetings,
and created friendly relations among people who had
previously been almost strangers. Others, after pass-

ing twenty-four hours together at a stretch, and finding each other amiable and pleasant companions, never
saw their fellow-watchers again.

The burial of Peter and Catherine took place six
weeks after; they were interred in the same vault of
the Nevski convent. All the troops of the garrison of
St Petersburg and of its neighbourhood accompanied
the procession, and all who belonged to the Court or
Government went on foot to the convent, which is
at the other end of the town. Neither the men nor
the women were allowed to wear powder, and as they
had not altered their way of dressing the hair, this
was very unbecoming. Mourning was strictly prescribed and observed; and as the funeral procession
was extremely long, the ceremony lasted a whole
day.

The Emperor kept the apartments at the Winter
Palace which he had occupied when he was Grand-
Duke. The waiting-room was usually filled by those
who were admitted to his presence. People sometimes passed the whole day there, and went as if to a
diverting entertainment. There was incessant agitation and excitement: footmen and aides-de-camp in
thick boots ran about knocking against each other,
some carrying the Emperor's orders, others looking
for some one they were sent to summon to his presence. Those who were called ran up breathless, not
knowing what was to be their fate; many entered
the room and left it immediately after with radiant
faces and a red or blue sash across their chests. One
of those whom I saw coming out of the room was
Count Nicholas Zuboff, appointed Grand-Equerry

and decorated with a blue ribbon for having been the first to bring Paul the news of his accession. Changes were occurring daily. Nearly all that had been great and distinguished under Catherine became neglected and insignificant under Paul. New persons were constantly coming forward and being advanced with extraordinary rapidity, and almost all the Ministers were changed.

Plato Zuboff, who looked like a dethroned sovereign, went to his estates in Lithuania, a vast domain which Catherine had given him (and the desire to acquire which was one of the causes of the two last partitions of Poland), sufficient to furnish him with ample means to defray the expense of his travels. He visited several towns in Germany. Some women of ready wit and easy virtue made him lose that air of languid dignity which he usually wore. He recognised the advantages of an independent existence, but soon his ambition and vanity, leading him to believe that he was destined still to play a great part, brought him back to St Petersburg, and rendered him more guilty and unfortunate than he had ever been before.

The only one of Catherine's Ministers whom Paul adopted was Count Bezborodko; this was because of his remarkable talents, his high reputation, and perhaps also because he had neglected Zuboff when he was at the height of his favour with the Empress. Paul felt that while he was still inexperienced in the art of government he needed Bezborodko's services, and he loaded him with distinctions of all kinds. He made him a prince, consulted him when he wanted to carry out some of his hobbies, and doubled his property by grants of land and of considerable sums in cash.

The Emperor's choice of his Ministers was always directed by one dominant idea—that of surrounding himself with servants on whom he could entirely rely; for from the moment of his accession he foresaw and dreaded a Palace revolution. He raised to the highest positions persons who were quite insignificant and often the least capable of performing their new duties. They were chiefly taken from among those (or their descendants or relations), whom he had employed at Gatchina, and who had given proofs of fidelity to his father. He persecuted and dismissed those who had been in favour with his mother; this alone made him suspect them. The fear of treason was continually present to his mind during the whole of his reign. He erred in the selection, and especially in the extent, of the means which he employed to save his life and his power; they only precipitated his deplorable end. Among the men whom he suspected, he persecuted some with implacable rigour, while he retained others at their posts and endeavoured to secure their fidelity by presents; this, however, only made them ungrateful. Never was there a sovereign more terrible in his severity, or more liberal when he was in a generous mood. But there was no certainty in his favour. A single word uttered intentionally or by accident in a conversation, the shadow of a suspicion, sufficed to make him persecute those whom he had protected. The greatest favourites of to-day feared to be driven

from Court on the morrow, and banished to a distant
province. Yet the Emperor wished to be just.
Notwithstanding his capricious and disorderly impulses, he had a profound feeling of equity, which
often caused him to perform praiseworthy actions.
It often happened that after he had dismissed some
one whom he had badly treated, he called him back,
embraced him, almost asked his pardon, confessed
that he was wrong, that he had unjustly suspected
him, and gave him presents to make up for his past
severities. He inspired all the officials of his empire
with the terrors which he often felt himself, and this
universal fear produced salutary effects. While at
St Petersburg and at the centre of Government the
uncertainty of the morrow tormented and agitated
people's minds, in the provinces, the civil governors,
the governors-general, and the troops, fearing lest the
abuses they committed should reach the Emperor's
ears, and they should some day be suddenly dismissed
without any form of trial and banished to Siberia,
paid more attention to their duties, treated their
subordinates with more humanity, and refrained from
abuses of a flagrant kind. In the Polish Provinces
especially the inhabitants felt the change, and the
reign of Paul is still mentioned there as a period
when there were less abuses and acts of oppression and
injustice than at any other time when Poland was
under foreign rule.

One of Paul's first and most generous thoughts
after his accession, was to liberate the Polish prisoners.
Like his father, when he visited Ivan VI in his prison,
Paul went himself to Kosciuszko and ordered him to be

treated with the greatest consideration, telling him
that if he had been on the throne at the time, he
would not have consented to the partition of Poland,
and that he regretted that so unjust and impolitic a
deed had been committed; but that it was not now
in his power to withdraw it.   At Kosciuszko's request
he liberated all the other prisoners, only requiring
them to take the oath of allegiance.   Whenever Paul
did not grant a request made by Kosciuszko on behalf
of his countrymen, he excused himself by alleging
that he was obliged to pay attention to the representations of his Ministers, who prevented him from
following his inclination in this respect.   Kosciuszko,
oppressed by a feeling of sadness, covered with wounds
which were not yet healed, and bearing on his face an
expression of despair, of touching resignation, almost
of remorse at being still alive and having failed to
save his country, greatly interested the Emperor and
did not inspire him with the least fear or suspicion.
He often used to visit Kosciuszko, accompanied by
the whole of the Imperial family, which showed real
interest and almost affection for the unfortunate
patriot.   Alexander no doubt felt these generous
sentiments more than anybody, but his duties at that
time entirely absorbed him, so that at first I could
hardly see him.   Since Paul's accession our relations
had become more rare and more difficult, and his
extreme fear of his father prevented him from
expressing on his own account to Kosciuszko what he
had long felt with regard to him.

    We were each called to the palace to sign an
assurance that Marshal Potocki would not enter on

any enterprise prejudicial to the State, and to be guarantees for his conduct at our own risk. This obligation had to be expressed clearly and precisely in writing. The meeting was a numerous one. Prince Kourakin, the new Vice-Chancellor, was present, and was directed to see that each document clearly expressed the obligations undertaken by the signer of it. My brother and I signed without hesitation; we had long felt too much esteem and family attachment for the Marshal to hesitate to give this general assurance which alone could restore him to liberty. Some raised difficulties, others went away directly they learnt the object of the meeting. Among the latter was Count Irenœus Chreptowicz, the son of the Chancellor of that name who had done the most to induce King Stanislas Augustus to join the Confederation of Targowitza,* and who soon became entirely Russian. The number of signatures, however, was sufficiently large to induce the Emperor to liberate Count Potocki.

One may imagine how happy the prisoners were to see each other again after so long and painful a confinement, though their happiness was mingled with regret. The most illustrious members of the Grand Diet of 1788-92† were assembled there : Count Potocki, Count Thaddeus Mostowski, Julian Niemcewicz; Zakrzewski, mayor of Warsaw, known by his integrity, his patriotism, and his great courage ; General Sokolnicki, who voluntarily went to prison with him, not wishing to leave him ; and Kilinski and

---

* See page 84.

† The Diet which passed the famous Constitution of the 3rd of May 1791 (see page 52).

Kapostasz, worthy citizens of Warsaw, the first a master bootmaker, and the second a money-changer, who exercised great influence over the population of that city. We saw them every day. After having had the happiness of being liberated from prison and of seeing each other, they had to disperse in different directions. The Emperor lavished presents of money on Kosciuszko to make him independent, and the latter was obliged to accept them. When he arrived in America, however, he sent them back with a letter expressing his gratitude and that of the other prisoners.

On Twelfth-day, one of the most solemn festivals of the Russian Church, there was a great military parade in the Russian fashion, and the Emperor wished the day to be celebrated with all possible pomp. The Guards and all the regiments in the neighbourhood were posted on the banks of the Neva, between the Winter Palace and the Admiralty. The Imperial family alighted there, and the Emperor took the command of the troops in person ; he liked to put himself forward on these occasions. He defiled at the head of the army together with the Grand-Dukes before the Empress and the Princesses. I thought this march past would never end. The cold was intense, and we were in Court dress, with silk stockings ; although we wore warm coats, we were almost frozen. My arms and legs were numbed, and I and several others, feeling that our lives were in danger, stamped our feet and moved our arms about to keep up the circulation. I could not stand this martyrdom, and went home, where it took me some hours to get warm. My fingers have since that day lost all feeling whenever there was the slightest cold.

Our King, Stanislas Augustus, with whom we had dined during our six months' stay at Grodno, was invited by Paul immediately after his accession to come to St Petersburg. During Paul's journey abroad (in 1785 I think) with his wife, they had passed through Southern Poland, and King Stanislas Augustus had left Warsaw to meet them. The principal reception took place in the Palace of Wisznioviec, which belonged to Count Mniszek, Grand Marshal of the Crown. This palace was a princely abode that had belonged to the Wiszniowiecki family, now extinct, whose last heir had married a Mniszek, the descendant of the one whose daughter was for some time seated on the throne of the Russian Czars.* The apartments of the palace were full of valuable historical portraits. Among them was that of the famous Marina and of Dimitri; there were also pictures representing their consecration at Moscow.

It was in this beautiful palace that the King of Poland welcomed the Grand-Duke of Russia to his kingdom. Stanislas Augustus had the gift of amiability, and Paul took a liking to him; he also made himself agreeable to the Grand-Duchess Maria. They had several confidential interviews, at which perhaps promises, or at least hopes, which were never realised, were expressed that when Paul should come into power, he would repay to his host a hundredfold the splendid reception given him in Poland. It is

* Marina Mniszek, married to 'the false' Dimitri 18 May 1605.

said that Marshal Mniszek at that time hoped that the goodwill of Catherine's successor might one day bring them even to the throne, to which he might perhaps have thought he had a claim as the heir of Wiszniowiecki* and the descendant of the father of the celebrated Czarina. The story goes that in the course of a familiar conversation with him the Grand-Duchess, showing her diamonds to make her hosts remark the beauty of a diadem in precious stones which was in her jewel-box, placed it on the head of the King's niece, and then on that of the Grand Marshal. 'I accept the augury,' said the latter, carried away by an impulse of naïveté or of empty vanity which he probably regretted immediately afterwards.

By inviting to his Court the prisoner-King from his confinement at Grodno—an invitation in which the Empress Maria heartily concurred—Paul made some return for the hospitality he had received, and gladly found an opportunity of showing himself more generous than his mother had been. The King was received at St Petersburg with all the honours due to a sovereign. On approaching the capital he was met by chamberlains and other high dignitaries, who complimented him on behalf of the Emperor and the members of the Imperial family. Paul offered him one of his palaces, furnished it magnificently, and did all he could to make the King's stay at St Petersburg agreeable. There were mutual receptions and banquets, and at first no cloud obscured the friendly relations which seemed to be a continuation of those

---

* Michael Wiszniowiecki, King of Poland from 1669 to 1675.

of Wiszniowiec ; but there was no talk of Stanislas returning to his kingdom, except perhaps that the Emperor told him, as he had done to Kosciuszko, that it was impossible to undo what had been done, however unjustly, by the Empress Catherine.

The first years of Paul's reign were marked by a curious confusion ; they were a series of moving incidents and of singular and ridiculous scenes, which seemed to foreshadow the reversal of the existing state of things and the establishment of a new one, not radically, but only in outward form.   The civil officials and generals were constantly changed, and promotion was given without any enquiry as to the capacity of those whom seniority placed in ranks to which they had never hoped to attain.

The Emperor's only consideration in the decisions he gave, was that his will, although the fruit of impulse and not of reflection, should at once be executed. The terror which he inspired ensured submission to his most unexpected and most eccentric commands. The parades daily gave rise to singular and provoking incidents.   Generals and other officers of rank received for mere trifles, degradations or distinctions which only unpardonable faults or great services to the State could have justified.

Paul had forbidden round hats, which he regarded as a sign of liberalism.   If a poor man, with an old round hat on his head, showed himself in the crowd which witnessed the parades, an aide-de-camp immediately pursued the culprit, who fled to avoid being bastinadoed at the first guard-house.   The chase was often continued in the streets, to the great amusement of the people, who hoped the unhappy man would succeed in making his escape.

Lord Whitworth, the British Ambassador, was obliged to have a hat of peculiar shape made for him, so as to be able to walk about in the morning without contravening the Emperor's orders.

Paul drove through the town daily in a sledge or an open carriage, accompanied by one of his aides-de-camp. When he met a carriage it stopped, the coachman and footmen had to take off their caps, and the persons in the carriage had to alight and make a profound bow to the Emperor, who observed whether it was sufficiently respectful. Sometimes women, with their children trembling with fright, were seen descending into the snow in a hard frost, or into the mud during a thaw, to accomplish this salutation. Paul always thought that people wished to slight him as they did when he was Grand-Duke; he liked everywhere to meet with marks of fear and submission. When people went out into the streets in carriages or on foot, all took care to avoid meeting their Imperial master; they fled at his approach and went down a side street or hid under a gateway. Another dangerous person to meet was the terrible Archaroff, Grand-Master of Police, who also drove through the town to see that everything was being done according to his orders. He prohibited rapid driving in sledges, which is one of the greatest pleasures of a Russian; and when he perceived a sledge which seemed to go at a forbidden pace he at once ordered it to be seized, had the coachman flogged, and then appropriated both sledge and coachman to his own use for any period he pleased, while the occupant of the sledge had to walk home. This once happened to my brother. He had driven out in a sledge and met the Emperor, upon which he at once jumped to the ground. As he passed, Paul cried out to him, 'You might have broken your neck.' On his return, M. Archaroff sent by the Emperor's orders for my brother's horses and his sledge, and used them for a week, after which he returned them.

Both at Court and at parade the Emperor wished to establish strict exactitude in the ceremonies, in the way of approaching him and the Empress, and in the number and kind of salutations to be made. The Grand-Master of the Ceremonies, Natouyeff, treated the courtiers like recruits who do not yet know their drill and in what order they ought to march. Whenever they met the Emperor they had first to make a profound bow, and then, with one knee on the ground, apply a sounding kiss to the Emperor's hand while he kissed them on the cheek. The same genuflexion had to take place when they approached the Empress, after which they had to withdraw without turning their backs, which often caused confusion, as they trod on the toes of the other courtiers who were coming forward to perform the same ceremony. Thanks to the efforts of the Grand-Master of the Ceremonies, the courtiers at length learnt to go through this manœuvre without a hitch, and Paul, satisfied at the look of fear and submission which he saw on their faces, then made the etiquette less rigid. My brother and I had to go through this ordeal, and in doing so we nearly fell into disgrace. The

Emperor and Empress were once present at the christening of a child in the Chapel of the Palace. We were on duty together with two chamberlains, and we had to be ready to precede their Majesties as they left their apartments. We were late, and when the time for the ceremony came we were not at our posts. Paul, not seeing his escort as he came out of his room, flew into a terrible rage. We arrived breathless with haste, and found all the courtiers assembled at the closed door of the chapel, anxious to see what would happen. The door opened ; Paul came out and passed before us with a threatening look, making furious gestures and breathing hard as he generally did when he was angry and wished to inspire terror. Our punishment, however, was slight ; we were simply ordered to remain in our apartments and not leave them until further orders. Alexander interfered on our behalf, explained that we had not received our orders in time, and pleaded in our favour so effectively, with the assistance of Koutayschoff,* the Emperor's barber, that in a fortnight's time we were free. Soon after we entered the army, in conformity with the rule that every officer of the Court must take up an active career.

Our rank in the army was that of brigadier, the one usually given to gentlemen of the chamber ; and by a special favour due to the preference shown to us by the Grand-Dukes, I was appointed aide-de-camp to Alexander and my brother to Constantine. These appointments greatly pleased us, as they attached us more closely to the Grand-Dukes and relieved us of

See page 184.

the functions of the Court, for which we had no vocation. Our duties consisted in accompanying the Grand-Dukes at military parades, and in standing behind them when the Emperor passed the officers in review. He used to address his sons by the title of Monseigneur, and then returned to place himself in the midst of the officers and superintend the drill which usually preceded the regular parade.

We constantly saw the Grand-Dukes in our capacity of aides-de-camp. Both of them were absorbed by their Court, family, and military functions, and by endless details connected with their command of the two regiments of the Guards. The whole morning was taken up by these occupations, which involved more bodily fatigue than mental work, although great attention was necessary not to omit any of the minute details of the service. Alexander almost always dined with the Emperor. The afternoon was the only time when one could speak to him more freely, but he was generally too tired by his work of the morning, and he took some rest until the evening, when he had to go to the Empress.

In the beginning of the spring of 1797 the Emperor went to Moscow for his coronation. All the society of St Petersburg followed him. It was still very cold, and the *habitués* of the salons of St Petersburg were to be seen passing each other on the roads, wrapped up in furs and reclining in sledges, all hastening to the ancient capital of the Empire. Moscow had at that time a characteristic appearance, which must have greatly changed since it was burnt down and rebuilt. It was like a collection of towns

communicating with each other not only by gardens
and parks, but by vast fields.   People often had to
drive for an hour to pay a visit in another part of the
city.   Everywhere, by the side of ugly huts, were
sumptuous palaces, inhabited by the Galitzins, the
Dolgoroukis, and other families with historic names—
great noblemen who consoled themselves by the
luxury in which they lived for the vexations and dis-
appointments they had experienced at Court.   In the
midst of this vast city was the Kremlin, a sort of
fortress surrounded by a crenelated wall, outside
which the tradesmen had their principal shops in a
series of bazaars.   The ancient residence of the
Muscovite Grand-Dukes, full of old associations, was
the place where the ceremony of coronation was to be
performed.   It lasted several days.   Paul had stopped
for the night outside the barriers of the town, and
made his solemn entry into the Kremlin on the following day, with an immense suite.   He first went to the
cathedral, where Plato, Archbishop of Moscow, who
was regarded as the ablest and most learned prelate of
the Russian Church, complimented the Emperor in
biblical language.   Then took place the coronation,
the return to the palace with the same solemnity, and
finally the Imperial banquet, at which the sovereigns
and their families were served on a raised platform and
under a magnificent canopy by the high officers of the
Crown.   Various minor ceremonies took place during
the following days.   The Emperor appeared in them
all; he was passionately fond of display, and was
proud of his figure and his grace.   Whenever he
appeared in public he walked with a measured step,

and tried to look tall and majestic, though he was really short; it was only when he entered his apartments that he showed the fatigue which his efforts had cost him. Each ceremony was preceded by a dress rehearsal, in order that everybody should know where to place himself and what to do. My brother and myself of course had to take part in the ceremonies as aides-de-camp to the Grand-Dukes. The Emperor was as active and busy as a stage manager, and looked after the smallest details of costume and decoration. He liked to appear to the best advantage before the ladies, and once he stood at the head of his favourite battalion of the Guard with a halbert, to do honour to the Empress, whom he had crowned with his own hand.

Paul ordered the King of Poland to follow him to Moscow, and insisted on his being present at all the solemnities of the coronation He had to join the brilliant suite which surrounded the Emperor and his family—a sad part for a King to play. During divine service and the ceremonies which preceded the coronation, and were very long and tedious, Stanislas Augustus was so tired out that he sat down in the tribune which had been assigned to him. Paul at once remarked this, and sent a messenger to tell him to stand up so long as they remained in the church; and the poor King had no alternative but to submit.

When the ceremonies were over, the Emperor and his family left the Kremlin to go to a more spacious residence, called the Petrovski Palace, in another quarter of the town. He gave up the rest of his time at Moscow to fêtes, parades, and military exercises.

There were fireworks and public banquets both at Moscow and at St Petersburg, and the nobility gave the Emperor a ball in a vast hall where they usually met. These fêtes were somewhat tedious, and did not give satisfaction either to Paul or to his hosts. Numerous deputations from all the provinces of the empire were ordered to salute the Emperor and present addresses of submission. The delegates from the Polish provinces had an air of great constraint and depression. All of them had been citizens of an independent Poland; all had distinguished themselves either in their palatinates, at the last Diet, or in appointments of State. They saw their King relegated to a side gallery, and had to pass him to kneel before a foreign prince and declare themselves his subjects. I met several of my acquaintances, but could not feel any pleasure at seeing them again under such circumstances. I was struck by the change in their appearance; they looked confused and humiliated. Among the delegates from Lithuania was Bukaty, who had for several years occupied the post of Polish Minister in England. He was a man of simple manners and great good sense, and had acquired the esteem of the English people and their Government. Several of his English friends gave as a token of their friendship their names to his children at their christening. I had often dined with him in London with my mother. He was at that time stout, in good health, and in excellent spirits. He was now thin, his face was pale and haggard, his clothes, which in England fitted tight to his body, now hung about him in loose folds; he walked with bent head and an uncertain step—he was a picture of what Poland had become. No satisfactory or consoling word came from his mouth. Soon after his return to his home at Minsk he died.

The death of Catherine and the accession of Paul, which brought Alexander nearer to the throne, had so far in no way changed the latter's political opinions; on the contrary, all that had happened since these events seemed to confirm him in his views, and the resolutions he thought he could execute. When he had a few moments of leisure after his military labours, to which he devoted himself with zeal and with a desire to carry out the wishes of his father, he always spoke of his plans and the future he wished to prepare for Russia. The despotism of his father— sometimes eccentric, terrible, and even cruel—and its immediate and probable effects, produced a lively and painful impression on Alexander's generous mind, which was full of ideas of liberty and justice. He was at the same time appalled at the extent of the diffi- culties which awaited him and were rapidly advancing upon him. The ceremonies of the coronation, which he would have to undergo some day, and which were totally opposed to his principles and his natural tastes, contributed to strengthen him in his views.

My brother and myself having obtained three months' leave to see our parents in Poland, Alexander was uneasy at the prospect of remaining without any one who could understand him or in whom he could confide. His anxiety increased as the time for our departure arrived. He asked me to leave him a draft proclamation expressing his resolutions, in case he should be called to the throne during our absence. In spite of my objections he insisted upon my doing this, and I ultimately complied to quiet him. My draft set forth the evils of the régime under which Russia had up to that time existed, and the benefits of the one which Alexander proposed to introduce ; the blessings of liberty and justice which Russia would enjoy after the obstacles to her prosperity had been removed ; and his resolution to abdicate after having accomplished this task, in order that some one more worthy than himself to be in power should be called upon to consolidate and perfect the great work which he had inaugurated.

I need not say how little all these reasonings and fine phrases, which I endeavoured to bring into connection as much as possible, were applicable to the true state of affairs. Alexander was delighted at my work, which satisfied his fancy of the moment—a very noble, but at bottom a very selfish one, as while wishing to secure his country's happiness as he then saw it, he at the same time desired to be free to withdraw from a position which he feared and disliked, and to live quietly in retirement where he would enjoy at a distance the good he had done. Alexander put the paper in his pocket with great satisfaction and thanked me effusively for my work. It reassured him as to his future. He thought that with this paper in his desk he would be prepared for the events which fate might suddenly bring : a strange and almost incredible effect of the dreams and illusions which youth cherishes even in circumstances where experience soonest chills the heart ! I do not know what became of the

paper. I believe Alexander did not show it to anybody, and he never spoke to me about it again. I
hope he burnt it, seeing how unreasonable was what
he had asked me to write—which indeed I never
doubted.

While we were talking about these chimeras a
new incident gave a more practical character to
Alexander's intentions. Since my arrival at St
Petersburg, one of the houses which I most visited
was that of Count Strogonoff. I had become, so to
say, part of his family. The friendship, indeed the
affection shown to me by the old Count has left me
recollections which will be always dear to me, and
which fill me with gratitude. I was on intimate
terms with his son Paul and his friend M. de
Novosiltzoff, said to be a distant relation of the
family, both of whom were of about the same age as
myself. The young Countess was a lady of much
distinction, good, amiable and witty; without being
exactly beautiful, she had more than beauty, the gift
of pleasing and charming all who came near her.
The old Count had long lived in Paris under Louis
XV; like most Russian noblemen, he wished his son
to be brought up by a Frenchman. He even sent
him to France with his tutor, M. Romme, a man of
ability, and, as I was assured, of high principle, but
an enthusiastic admirer of Rousseau. He proposed
to make an Emile of his pupil, a plan which did not
displease the old Count, whose generous propensities
and loving heart had inclined him to some of the
doctrines of the philosopher of Geneva. Count Paul
was accordingly placed in M. Romme's charge, and

the latter made him go on walking tours and endeavoured to give him an education in which Rousseau's precepts were followed and perhaps too closely imitated. When the French Revolution broke out, and the revolutionists boasted that they were following Rousseau's teaching, M. Romme strongly sympathised with it, and wished to combine what he regarded as his duties as a citizen with those which he had undertaken with his pupil. Frequent occasions presented themselves of showing him in practice the principles M. Romme had inculcated in theory. Both master and pupil eagerly took part in the revolutionary scenes which were then succeeding each other in France with alarming rapidity, and joined the Jacobin club, whose meetings they regularly attended. Count Strogonoff was informed of this by the Russian embassy, which had not yet left Paris, and also, I believe, by the letters of M. Romme himself, who thought he could not complete the education of Count Paul more effectively than by making him take part in a practical course of his teacher's doctrines.

M. de Novosiltzoff was then sent to Paris to withdraw his young friend from the charge of a tutor whose zeal had become so dangerous, and he acquitted himself of his commission with great skill. He managed to overcome the resistance of M. Romme, and his regret at the separation of, as he said, two friends who understood each other so well. Notwithstanding the attachment of the young Count for his tutor, he was persuaded to return to St Petersburg, where he was soon made to perceive the danger to which he had been exposed. His opinions changed entirely, but he always retained in his character and his principles of action some traits of his first education.

The general tone of conversation in Count Strogonoff's house had always been, so to say, liberal and somewhat critical ; the doings of the Court were a favourite topic. Yet the old Count was always on good terms with the Empress Catherine. She liked to see in him a man who had known her old friends the encyclopædists, and who was not a stranger to any of the doctrines or sayings of that sect. This permitted him sometimes to speak frankly even to herself or in her presence. He has often told me that being admitted to the Empress's toilet, a privilege granted only to the most distinguished noblemen of the Court, he was once there when she was preparing to give an audience to a deputation from the Confederation of Targowitza, which had come to thank her for the 'signal benefits' she had conferred upon Poland (in depriving her of the constitution of the 3rd of May,* and soon after taking her finest provinces at the second partition). When it was announced that the deputation had arrived, and that the Empress was about to enter the throne-room to listen to the false speeches which were to be addressed to her, Count Strogonoff laughed and said : 'Your Majesty will not have any difficulty in replying to the eloquent thanks of these gentlemen ; all you can say is that really they have nothing to thank you for.' This remark did not please the Empress. She took it in cold silence, and went out to receive homages

* See page 52.

the absurdity of which she probably felt. Despotic sovereigns should spare those whom they oppress the necessity of telling them falsehoods by which nobody is deceived.

The service rendered by M. de Novosiltzoff to the Strogonoff family, by bringing back the young Count to Russia, had strengthened the friendship for him both of the father and the son. He became the adviser of the family in all circumstances, and took a pride in having an independent character, in acting according to fixed principles, and in not tolerating any unjust constraint. He had been attached as aide-de-camp to the Prince of Nassau when he was charged with the command of the Russian fleet against the Swedes, and he had also accompanied him at the siege of Warsaw in 1794. He thought he had deserved the military cross, and he indignantly refused the civil cross of Vladimir with which the Empress wished to decorate him. He insisted on sending it back, and it was only with great difficulty that he was appeased on being shown the risks he would run by taking such a step. He finally consented to wear the cross, when a knot of ribbon was added to it, signifying that it was the reward of military prowess.

M. de Novosiltzoff had wit, penetration, and great aptitude for work, but an extreme love of pleasure and sensual enjoyments; this had prevented him from reading many books, and from acquiring any sound knowledge of law, of legislation, or of political economy, though he had studied all these subjects. He had a facile philosophy which strove to be free from all prejudice, but which did not seem to impair the clear and decided qualities of his mind. These qualities were reflected as in a glass in the young Count Strogonoff. The opinions and feelings of these two young men had a spirit of justice, of sincerity, of European enlightenment which at that time was scarcely ever to be found in Russia, and which was the foundation of the intimate friendship and reciprocal confidence between us of which I have spoken. They often asked me questions about Alexander; and I thought that while maintaining a certain reserve, I could without indiscretion communicate to them some of the statements he had made to me, and the generous projects which he entertained. They fully appreciated the extreme importance of what I told them.

I spoke of my two friends to Alexander; he had already remarked Count Paul, and I told him that their convictions resembled his own, that he could rely on their sentiments and their discretion, and that they wished to see him in private, to offer him their services, and to ascertain what would have to be done to carry out his noble impulses. Alexander consented to their being informed of his secret plans and associated in his designs. I spoke to them on the subject at St Petersburg, immediately after Paul's accession, but the arrangement was not finally completed until after the coronation at Moscow. It was agreed that we should meet on a certain day and hour in a retired spot, and that Alexander should join us. Novosiltzoff prepared himself for the conference by translating into Russian a fragment of a French work whose title I do not remember, which related to advice given to a young prince about to

ascend the throne, and desirous of making his country
happy and of knowing how to set about it. The
portion which Novosiltzoff translated was only the
introduction, where the subject was treated generally,
each special branch of Government being dealt with
in detail in the body of the work. He was to trans-
late the rest of the book, but he never did so. The
succinct review, however, of the obligations of the
head of a State and the labours which should occupy
him was listened to by Alexander with much attention
and satisfaction. It contained well-chosen views and
general deductions as to the foundations of national
prosperity, with a scheme of the measures necessary
for promoting it. The author had introduced some
eloquent passages which went straight to the young
prince's generous and patriotic heart. Novosiltzoff
wrote Russian with elegance ; his style was clear and
seemed to me harmonious. Alexander praised him
highly, and assured both him and Count Paul that
he adopted the principles expressed in the work,
which were indeed his own. He urged Novosiltzoff
to complete the translation and then forward it to
him, in order that he might be able more maturely
to consider its contents and some day put its theories
into practice. From that day the young Count
Strogonoff and Novosiltzoff shared in the confidence
which Alexander had bestowed upon me, and were
admitted to our understanding, so long kept a secret.
This afterwards produced serious results, and the
admission of two zealous Russian patriots to Alexander's confidence, naturally began to dissipate the
illusions of our first dreams—so attractive to me as

holding out the prospect of the independence of my country, and to Alexander as leading him to believe in the possibility of tranquil retirement from State affairs. These dreams were not, however, at once abandoned ; we adhered to them in spite of hard facts which gradually destroyed them. Alexander constantly reverted to his plans, seeking in them consolation for a near future whose approach and whose burthens he already felt. He could not make up his mind to lose the hope of another future, more distant and more in conformity with his wishes; his imagination presented it to him under such attractive colours, that it was even after the conversation which I have described that he insisted upon having the draft proclamation which I mentioned above.

Alexander's new friends perceived his inclination for a quiet life, relieved of the cares which the Crown would impose upon him ; they said with justice that this could neither promote his fame nor the happiness of his country, which should be his sole object. They took every occasion of opposing these egotistical leanings, while pretending not to know of them. I understood Alexander's views, and I could not entirely condemn them, though I did not conceal from him my belief that they were impracticable. The consequence was that his confidence in me grew stronger. It continued, after many vicissitudes, for a considerable time, and did not cease until after I had left St Petersburg.

At the conference which took place during the coronation it was decided that Novosiltzoff, who was in bad odour on account of the opinions he was supposed to hold and his known independent spirit, should leave Russia until it should be possible to recall him, and that he should pass the interval in England. Alexander obtained a passport for him through Rostopchin, the Minister for War, who was beginning to be in high favour with the Emperor. This Minister had been one of his most assiduous courtiers at Gatchina and Pavlovsk before his accession to the throne. He was, I think, the only able man who had attached himself to Paul's person before he became Emperor. Alexander, who during Catherine's reign was devoted to his father, had remarked Rostopchin, and had felt great esteem and friendship for him. These relations were afterwards converted by Court intrigues into coldness and opposition; but at that time they still existed, and Rostopchin was also on friendly terms with Novosiltzoff, for both had found fault with the Government. Although, however, he had promised Novosiltzoff a passport, he did not at once carry out his promise, and when I reminded him of it, he expressed impatience and suspicion at the political importance which he said appeared to be attached to this journey. The passport came at last, and Novosiltzoff proceeded to St Petersburg and thence to England, where he remained during the whole of the period of Paul's reign. He completed his studies there, and entered into relations with English statesmen which were afterwards very useful to him.

Our leave having been granted, my brother and myself, accompanied by Gorski, left for Pulawy, where our parents were impatiently expecting us after an absence of two years which had given them much anxiety and care. The time we passed with them, in the place where we had lived in our happy youth, was one of great joy to us, though it was somewhat marred by the prospect of having soon to go back again to St Petersburg, where we knew that fresh trials and troubles were awaiting us. We talked of nothing but Alexander's good qualities and the hopes we had of him. Our parents listened with astonishment, anxiety, and doubt. I received at Pulawy several letters from Alexander full of friendly expressions; they were brought by various persons, among others by the Archduke Palatine, who had just married the Grand-Duchess Alexandra. This obtained for me a friendly reception from the Archduke when I passed through Pesth in 1812.

My mother was anxious for our safety. She feared lest we should be denounced and the object of our relations with Alexander be betrayed. This was the topic of all our conversations.

The Governor of Galicia, Count Erdödy, came at this time to pay my father a visit.* A Hungarian by birth, he was preoccupied with an idea which he was constantly talking about. He wished to prove to the Poles that the best thing that could happen to them would be to be united to Hungary; for, he said, the Emperor of Austria had only put forward his claims to Galicia as King of Hungary. This language on the part of a high Austrian functionary proved how much strength the Magyar element still possessed.

---

* Pulawy then formed part of Austria, together with Lublin, Sandomir, and Cracow.

The annexation of Galicia to Hungary, if it had been possible, would doubtless have brought great material advantages to Galicia, would have conferred upon her a free government, and would especially have protected her against the many evils which she suffered during the fifty years which preceded the year 1848. What would have been the immediate result of such an annexation at that period it is difficult to guess. In any case the Poles would have gladly fraternised with the Hungarians; yet public opinion and the Polish national spirit would probably have been opposed to such a measure, besides which I do not think the Austrian Government of that time would ever have agreed to it.

Pulawy was just then recovering from a two-fold pillage to which it had been subjected during the war of Kosciuszko. The first occurred under the command of Count Bibikoff, and its results were long felt by the inhabitants of the village; the second, which was chiefly directed against the Palace, was carried out by the advanced guard of a corps under the orders of Count Valerian Zuboff. The Palace was completely sacked. All the ornaments were broken and destroyed. Valuable pictures were cut in pieces; the books of the library were stolen and dispersed in various parts of the Empire, and the only room that was spared was one which, as it had gilt wainscots and pictures by Boucher over the doors, the Cossacks thought was a chapel. All the provisions in the house—oil, wine, sugar, coffee, spirits, preserved meats, &c.—were thrown pell-mell into a basin in the middle of the courtyard, which was then used by the Cossacks as a bath. When we arrived, people were still employed in cleaning the ruins, rebuilding damaged walls or partitions, and repairing the library. In the middle of the vast courtyard before the Palace there was a little hill, a sort of *Monte Testacio*, composed of débris covered with earth. When our parents returned to their home they had some difficulty in finding rooms fit to live in, and the works of restoration were not completed when we left.

About this time we lost our friend Gorski, who died of an apoplectic stroke. I found him one morning complaining of pains in the head and difficulty of speech; a surgeon was called to bleed him, and he was put to bed. Dr Goltz, who was absent at the time, came too late to save him. Gorski remained unconscious, talked incoherently, and only complained of the pain in his head. He recognised me and I remember his smile with gratitude. I did not leave him; he died on the same day late in the evening, without pain. I felt his loss deeply. He was a true man, with nothing but justice and sincerity in his heart. He had often expressed a desire for a good and short life: his wish was accomplished.

Our three months' leave had now expired, and we returned to St Petersburg. We were sorry to leave our parents and our home, but we were anxious to see Alexander again and resume our relations with him. The letters I had received from him during our stay at Pulawy proved to me, if I had had any doubt on the subject, that he had not changed. We found him the same as before, both as regards his feelings and his opinions.

Towards the end of the year 1797, the follies and eccentricities which had agitated the Court of the Emperor Paul were succeeded by a period of comparative calm, which looked as if it were likely to last. When he was Grand-Duke he had, during his stay at Pavlovsk and Gatchina, conceived a passion for Mdlle. Nelidoff, maid-of-honour to his wife. This sentiment, which was entirely platonic, had continued to exist since his accession. Mdlle. Nelidoff had remarkable qualities of heart and mind, and had captivated the affection and confidence of the Empress. The latter thought she had nothing to fear from her rivalry, as she was tall, fair and handsome, while Mdlle. Nelidoff's figure, complexion, and features were in no way attractive; her only charms were her sparkling smile and her animated conversation. The two women had a perfect understanding with each other, and the result was that the Emperor's conduct, his selection of high officials, and even his policy, became less changeable and confused, and more consequent, than they had been before. Unfortunately this salutary influence did not last long. On the return of the Court from the coronation, it went to Gatchina, where Paul liked to pass the autumn. His presence added to the naturally depressing effect produced by this season of the year in Russia, as it is foggy and rainy, and the cold, though less intense, is more disagreeable than in winter. The friendship and the extreme confidence shown to us by Alexander, and the familiarity which he and his brother allowed us to use in our relations with them, amply compensated, however, for the tediousness and melancholy of the Court, and we did not complain. I recollect having had some very warm disputes with the Grand-Duke Constantine, in which I did not give way to him either in words or in gestures, and one day I had a struggle with him in which we both fell to the ground. I think it was the recollection of these familiarities of our youth that impelled Constantine to treat me with consideration even at times when he was all-powerful in Poland, and deeply irritated at my opposition. He attempted to cultivate similar relations with my brother to those which existed between Alexander and myself; but his intolerable temper made his company much less agreeable than that of Alexander, though it had the advantage of keeping my brother and myself together. While we were at Gatchina we made the acquaintance of Baron Wintzingerode, a young officer of much nobility of character, a protégé of the princes of Saxe-Coburg, whom Constantine had made his aide-de-camp. Our friendship with him never varied, and lasted until his death.

At the end of the autumn, the Court returned to St Petersburg for the winter. (I may mention here that during the years I passed in Russia the only interesting events that I witnessed happened in Court circles, and I am therefore obliged to be always speaking of the Court). Our King Stanislas Augustus was, I believe, located with his suite at the house known as the Marble Palace, and lived magnificently at the expense of the Government. His niece, the Countess Mniszek, was attached to his suite with her

husband.   He also had a certain number of chamberlains, among whom was Trembecki the poet.   We
often went to present our respects to his Majesty, who
received us with pleasure at all times.   I have often
seen him in the morning in his dressing gown, writing
what I was afterwards told were his memoirs.   I
never could learn what had become of this work, which
must have been very voluminous.   All I could
recover was the first volume, which only contained an
account of his embassy to Russia at the time of
Augustus III; the other volumes, which must have
been much more interesting, were either destroyed or
so well concealed, that so far as I know no trace of
them has been found.*

This unfortunate prince seemed to me to accept
his position too patiently.   He strove to make himself
agreeable to his masters who had dispossessed him,
and to indulge the capricious fancies of the Emperor,
who pretty frequently came with the Imperial family
to dine with him.   His dinners were exquisite and
served to perfection, thanks to the skill of his famous
maître d' hôtel, Fremeau, who alone reminded him of
his past existence.   The King and his suite, in order
to vary the entertainments he was able to offer to the
Emperor and Empress, were preparing a soirée with
private theatricals, when he was struck down by an
attack of apoplexy on the 2nd of February, 1793.
The news at once spread through the town, and we
hastened to the palace.   Dr Bekler had bled the
patient and employed all the resources of his art, but

---

* They have since been published at Posen (in 1862) under the title 'Mémoires
de Stanislas Auguste Poniatowski et sa correspondance avec Catherine II.'

in vain. The King lay on his bed unconscious, the persons of his suite stood round him in tears, and Trembecki, who had come to have a last look at his sovereign, fled into his room with a gesture of despair. The Emperor also came with the Imperial family. Baciarelli has painted this sad scene in a picture in which he has represented with remarkable talent the likenesses of all those who were present. The King was buried with suitable pomp in the Roman Catholic Church of the Dominicans at St Petersburg.

Stanislas Augustus was only mourned by those whose existence depended on his own; and he had no cause to regret life so far as his happiness was concerned. His conduct as a King had been such that no one looked upon him as a representative of Poland, and his end made no change either in her destinies or her hopes.* There were some people who, in view of the great expense which he had caused to the Imperial Treasury, thought his death had been accelerated for reasons of State. This no doubt is possible, but none of the circumstances of his illness seem to confirm such a suspicion, which, unhappily for Russia, always arises at the death of any illustrious personage in that country.

* Stanislas Augustus Poniatowski, the son of the famous statesman and soldier who twice saved the life of Charles XII and with the two Czartoryskis governed Poland during the reign of Augustus III, went with the English Minister Sir Hanbury Williams to St Petersburg in 1755 and there became the favourite of the Empress Catherine, then Grand-Duchess of Russia. Through the influence of the Russian Government, which had concluded a secret alliance with Prussia (21st April 1764) pledging the two powers to prevent 'by force of arms, if necessary,' the establishment of hereditary monarchy in Poland, Stanislas Augustus was, on the death of Augustus III, elected King (7th September 1764). Although at first he endeavoured to act independently of Russia, he was easily outwitted by the superior abilities and greater force of character of the Muscovite diplomatists, and after Poland had been thrice partitioned, he was held in confinement by the Russians at Grodno, and afterwards at St Petersburg, where he died as above described (see Chapter I.)

Things now seemed to be settling down: the Emperor's manias had diminished under the combined influence of the Empress and her friend, and the public also had become accustomed to Paul's way of acting by fits and starts. The life we led at Gatchina or at St Petersburg would have been well adapted for study, if we had known how to profit by it. Our time was regulated, and there was only one indispensable occupation during the day—the military parade; after passing an hour or two in this duty every morning, we had the whole day at our disposal except Sundays and holidays, when certain Court functions had to be performed. These were regarded as so important, that they liberated us from all social conventions and duties, so that there was plenty of time for other occupations, but unfortunately I did not avail myself of the leisure thus afforded me. Being attached to Alexander's person as aide-de-camp, my service obliged me to attend him at military parades, and I used to go to his apartments every afternoon to take his orders; this was our time for intimate conversation. It is also from that period that dates my acquaintance with Prince Peter Volkonski, adjutant of the Semenofsky regiment of the Guards, of which Alexander was colonel. His position placed Prince Peter on a footing of familiarity with Alexander, and he afterwards became his aide-de-camp, then major-general, and finally grand chamberlain, which post he continued to occupy under the Emperor Nicholas. Without possessing brilliant or very superior faculties, Volkonski was very systematic and persistent in his duties, and fulfilled them to the Emperor's entire satisfaction ; he also acquired information indispensable to an officer of high military rank. He was goodtempered, his advice was always sensible, and he did not hesitate to give it even when it caused displeasure ; moreover, he was always ready and willing to do a service. We passed much time together, and I constantly received from him proofs of good-will to which I gladly bear testimony after an interval of more than half-a-century, when our relations have been interrupted by forty years of separation and by revolutions and other events.

His wife, the Princess Sophia, who belonged to another branch of the Volkonski family that had been more favoured by fortune, had a quicker temper and a more generous heart, and she often showed herself a true friend to me, even since my total withdrawal from the Russian service—for which I am sincerely grateful to her. She never pardoned the Emperor Nicholas for having kept her brother for thirty years in the mines of Siberia ; he became old there, and was not restored to his sister and his family until the coronation of Alexander II. Her sorrow had separated the Princess Sophia from the Russian Court during the whole of Nicholas's reign.

Among the young men of the Court there was only one who was received into Alexander's intimacy : this was Prince Alexander Galitzin, one of the Gentlemen of the Chamber. He was called 'Little Galitzin' on account of his short stature, and pleased Alexander by his amusing gossip and his wonderful powers of mimicry, which enabled him closely to

imitate the appearance and the voice of every member
of the Court.   When we were alone without
Alexander, he used to imitate the Emperor Paul
with such accuracy that we feared lest he should be
arrested and punished.   He had been a passionate
admirer of the Empress Catherine, and notwithstanding her advanced age he would have gladly become
one of her favourites.   When I knew him he was a
thorough epicurean, devoting much calculation and
reflection to all possible enjoyments of every kind ;
but after Alexander's accession he determined to
enter on a more serious mode of life, and, encouraged
by the Emperor, became Procurator to the Senate.
Afterwards, probably under the inspiration of Alexander's piety, he became very devout, saw visions
with M. de Kocheleff, and was finally appointed
Minister of Public Instruction, a post which I should
never have thought him qualified to fill.   His appointment did not take place, I think, until the year 1822,
when I was still Curator of the University of Wilna.
Remembering ' Little Galitzin ' as I had known him,
I could not picture him to myself as a Minister
directing the public instruction of the Empire, as he
did not seem to possess any talent but that of amusing
people and making them laugh.   He was totally
without personal animosity—which did not, however,
prevent crying abuses from occurring at Wilna while
he was Minister, the result of which was that I was
obliged to resign my post of Curator.

There were sometimes select balls at Court, at
which the etiquette was not so strict as usual.   The
Emperor appeared at one of these balls in a dresscoat,

which he never wore on other occasions ; it was of dark red velvet and of an old-fashioned shape. He danced that evening with Mdlle. Nelidoff. It was a curious sight, which stills dwells in my memory. The Emperor Paul, short, with very large shoes, placed himself in the third position, rounded his arms, and bent his body in the manner then taught by dancing masters, while opposite him was a lady of equally short stature, who thought it her duty to respond to the would-be graceful airs and harmonious movements of her partner.

In May, 1798, the Court proceeded to Pavlovsk, the property and creation of the Empress Maria, which, considering the general appearance of the environs of St Petersburg, was a pleasant and gay place. The buildings and gardens had been enlarged under the superintendence of the Empress. She attempted to entertain her guests by assembling them after dinner to listen to a reading of a French translation of Thomson's 'Seasons.' The Emperor did not assist at these readings, and the idea was not a success ; everyone tried to escape what was generally voted to be a dull and somniferous entertainment.

The Emperor Paul wished this year to make a progress through part of his Empire. The Grand-Dukes took part in the journey, and my brother and myself accompanied them. The Emperor visited the Canal which joins the Volga to the Neva, thereby establishing a communication between the Caspian Sea and the Baltic. This work of Peter the Great, which does great credit to his genius and activity, passes in a diagonal line through the whole of the interior of Russia. Paul went to see the fleet of boats on the canal, some of which started for St Petersburg and others for Astrakhan.   M. de Sivers, notorious for the odious manner in which he carried out the second partition of Poland, was charged with the Works Department.   Being on a so-called tour of inspection, he went to meet the Emperor.   He looked old, thin, pale, and depressed, without any energy or distinction.   The very cold reception accorded to him by the Emperor showed him that he would not long remain at his post.

We passed by Tver on our way out, and on our return by Yaroslav and Vladimir.   These provinces are rich and populous, with an air of abundance and prosperity which strikes all who travel through them. It is in the interior of Russia that her true strength lies; if it were well administered by a government concentrated within reasonable limits, this region should by its resources and prosperity disgust the Russians with the task of being the tormentors and gaolers of neighbouring countries.

At Moscow, which was the first place to which the Emperor went, there was a considerable assemblage of troops, which he reviewed and ordered to perform some manœuvres.   They were regiments of the line which had not been trained like the Guards, and had not had time to obtain instruction in the new system.   The infantry was divided into two lines which marched in two columns, at the head of each of which was placed one of the Grand-Dukes.   They were to deploy at a given signal, and I remember with pleasure the activity with which we executed this movement, which was successful beyond our hopes, without any crowding or spreading out of the lines, each of which was composed of from twelve to fifteen battalions. The Emperor was highly satisfied at the order in which the troops marched, and liberally distributed rewards among the officers.

From Moscow we went by way of Nijni Novgorod to Kazan. The country between these places is fine, and might be rich through the fertility of its soil and the navigable streams which cross it in all directions, but it is little inhabited. Some of the inhabitants are still half-savage tribes, apparently of the Finnish race—Tchouvasches and Tcheremisses who have preserved their odd national costumes. I made sketches of them, which I gave to my old friend M. Wiesiolowski. At Kazan there are still many Tartars who have also preserved their ancient dress and customs, but I do not think they have any strong national spirit, any more than our Tartars of Lithuania. It is only further east, among the Nogaïs and the populations adjoining the steppes of Great Turtary or the slopes of the Caucasus, that this spirit shows itself and is accompanied by a warlike disposition.

The journey was performed with a rapidity which deprived it of the practical advantage that might have been gained if the Emperor had seen with his own eyes what was going on in the country. We returned without passing through Moscow, and our last stage was Schlusselburg, the fortress which was rendered famous by the catastrophe of the unhappy Ivan.* Paul embarked on the Lake of Ladoga, and while we were on the boat he called my brother and myself

* Ivan VI, killed in 1764 in attempting to escape from the fortress of Schlusselburg, where he had been confined since 1741.

and decorated us with the Order of St Anne of the second class as a reward for our services during the journey. This was the only honourable distinction I ever received in Russia.

We passed the remainder of the summer at Pavlovsk, and then moved to Gatchina for the autumn. This palace, which had recently been enlarged, looked like a prison ; it is built on a perfectly level plain, without trees or fields. The park had a sombre and melancholy air; the sun seldom shines there, and it was so cold and rainy that we had no temptation to walk. Military parades or manœuvres in the morning, and the French or Italian theatre in the evening, did but little to relieve the prevailing dulness. This latter part of the year 1798, and the beginning of 1799, brought much trouble and unexpected change into the situation of the persons who composed the Russian Court.

At the time of the capture of Kutaysk and the massacre of its inhabitants, a Turkish child, afterwards named Kutayschoff, who had escaped with his life, was adopted by Paul, who had him educated, and then made him first his barber, and afterwards his principal valet. At the beginning of Paul's reign I saw Kutayschoff bring some broth to his master at the training school, where the infantry and cavalry drilled during the winter. He was in his barber's dress, of middle size, a little stout, but alert and quick in his movements, very dark, always smiling, with Eastern eyes and a countenance displaying a sensual joviality. In this costume he looked a sort of Figaro ; but he was already the object of obsequious

salutations and hand-shakings on the part of most of
the generals and other persons who took part in
the drill. Soon his influence with his master made
him a dignitary of the Empire and an all-powerful
favourite. This metamorphosis was accomplished by
the autocratic wand of Czarism. In less than a year
he rose from a barber and a valet to be Grand-Equerry,
and astonished the Russians, by appearing successively
with the Orders of St Anne, St Alexander, and St
Andrew, accompanied by extensive grants of land
and money. He was not, however, promoted to
these honours all at once, and he would not have
got them so rapidly if the Empress and Mdlle.
de Nelidoff had continued to retain their influence
over the Emperor's mind. It was difficult, sometimes
impossible, for aspiring officials to get what they
wanted so long as the influence of the Empress
and her friend was preponderant, and this was the
principal cause of their defeat. Ambitious people
now made overtures to the favourite valet in order
to advise him and take advantage of the almost
magnetic power which he was able to exercise over
his master. The instigator and prime mover of this
plot was Count Rostopchin. He had been removed
from the post of Minister for War, succeeded by M.
Nelidoff, the nephew of the *demoiselle à portrait*,*
and even banished to Moscow, for Paul always acted
in extremes both with regard to people whom he liked
and those who no longer enjoyed his favour. Rostopchin was not the man to forgive such a slight,
and, determined to have his revenge upon those who

* See page 132.

had caused his fall, allied himself with Kutayschoff. In order to divert Paul from his attachment to Mdlle. Nelidoff, and to make him quarrel with his wife, it was insinuated that he was in leading-strings, and that all Russia was convinced that the two women reigned in his name. The plotters brought him a younger and prettier woman than Mdlle. Nelidoff, without her decided character. She was the daughter of Lapoukin, who had been Director of Police at Moscow under Catherine; Paul made her his mistress, and rewarded her father for his complaisance by making him a Prince and giving him the blue ribbon. Rostopchin was then appointed Minister of Foreign Affairs, and all the high functionaries who belonged to the Empress's party—the Princes Kourakin and their relatives, the chief of whom was the old Prince Repnin—lost their places and were banished to Moscow. The break-up of the party was complete; it was enough for any one to be suspected by the Emperor of having been protected or liked by the Empress to ensure his dismissal and banishment from the Court.

Paul now became more suspicious than ever. He thought his sons were not sufficiently devoted to his interests, and that his wife wanted to reign in his place. All who approached the Court were in constant fear and uncertainty, being exposed at any moment to be addressed in the presence of the whole Court by the Court-Marshal with some insulting message from the Emperor, and then to be sent into exile. It was like the Reign of Terror. The balls and Court festivals were arenas where each man risked his position and his liberty. The Emperor constantly fancied that sufficient respect was not shown to some person who was the object of his favour, or to the relations of that person and that this neglect was inspired by the Empress, and in such cases he at once ordered the supposed culprit to be dismissed from the Court. His fancies and his decisions were equally sudden, and were at once carried out.

Other sovereigns, after a fit of anger or extreme rigour, sometimes become calm and strive to soften the effects of their first decisions. This was not the case with the Emperor Paul. Usually, after giving a severe order with regard to a man who had displeased him, the punishment did not, after reflection, seem to him sufficient, and he often augmented it. All who belonged to the Court or came before the Emperor were thus in a state of continual fear. No one was sure that he would remain in his place at the end of the day, and in going to bed it was quite uncertain whether during the night or in the early morning some policeman would not come with a *kibitka* to drive you off at once to Siberia. This state of affairs began with the disgrace of Mdlle. Nelidoff, and continued with increasing aggravation during the remainder of Paul's reign. Mdlle. Nelidoff behaved with much pride and dignity. She left the Court, showed no desire to remain there, and did not attempt to return. She said with marked disdain to all who would listen to her, that nothing was more tedious than a Court life, and that she was glad at last to have left it.

Paul had a new hobby which sometimes diverted him from his fanciful suspicions and the rigours which followed them. He wanted to become Grand Master of Malta.* Political considerations had probably contributed to this wish, as of all the Powers that might have protected or possessed Malta, England, who had taken it, was the one that Europe liked least. Paul was at that time in intimate relations with the British Cabinet, which attached great importance to the active co-operation of Russia against France, and he may have thought that under these circumstances England would perhaps not refuse to cede to him a territory which she had only provisionally occupied with the express promise to return it to the Order of St John, to whom it belonged, and to place it under the protection of a power which should be designated by Europe. Paul was full of the idea of himself becoming Grand Master of Malta, and of uniting in his person both a title so famous in history and the power necessary for the protection of the independence of so important a station in the Mediterranean. Political considerations were less concerned in this idea than the vanity of posing as a hero of chivalry before the Princess Lapoukin. Being the supreme chief and defender of the Russian Church, he saw no difficulty in placing himself at the head of the principal Order of the Roman Catholic Church. The combined Cabinets, with the exception of England, carefully abstained

---

* The Order of St John, which had obtained possession of Malta in 1530 from the Emperor Charles V, was divided into eight 'languages,' each of which had its prior. The first Russian Knight of Malta was Sheremetieff, who was sent to the island in 1698 by Peter the Great to learn naval warfare, and diplomatic relations were then opened by the Order with the Court of St Petersburg. In 1774, a new priory of the Order was established in Poland, with six commanderships, each of which was to be held by a Pole. The property of the Order in Poland was transferred to Russia at the second partition, and this led to the selection by the Grand Master, Rohan, of M. de Litta as plenipotentiary to arrange with the Russian Government as to the disposal of this property.

from contradicting him. Count Litta and his brother,
the Papal Nuncio at St Petersburg, who afterwards
became a Cardinal, readily fell in with the Emperor's
plan and encouraged him in it. In Poland there
were still some commanderships of the Order, notwithstanding the bad repute into which it had fallen among
us by Prince Poninski having trafficked in its property
and been condemned by the Diet after the first partition ; and Paul created other commanderships in
Russia without troubling himself about differences of
creed Count Litta framed, in accordance with the
ancient rite, the ceremonial of a Grand Chapter of the
Order, in which the new Grand Master was to enter
on his dignities. The Emperor appeared several
times on his throne in the costume of Grand Master,
with the cross of the Order, which had been sent him
from Rome. Paul was passionately fond of ceremonies, he wished that people taking part in them
should preserve an imperturbable gravity and should
attach great importance to them. My brother and
myself were appointed Commanders of the Order, and
had to put on the ancient costume, consisting of long
cloaks of black velvet, with belts and embroidered
crosses. There had been some rehearsals of the ceremony of offering the Grand Mastership to the Emperor,
and the whole business had an appearance of theatrical
masquerading which made the spectators and even the
performers smile, with the single exception of the
Emperor, who was thoroughly identified with his
part. The secretary to the Chapter was an old
acquaintance of ours, M. de Maisonneuve, a Frenchman who when young had sought his fortune in

Poland, had had some success with the ladies, and had obtained through them rank in the army and the Cross of Malta. He came to Russia in his old age to restore his fortune, which he had squandered twice over. Count Litta appointed him his secretary, and in this capacity M. de Maisonneuve gave entire satisfaction, as he wrote fluently and was well acquainted with legal and diplomatic phraseology.

This hobby of the Emperor's produced a quarrel with England, who, without giving any definitive reply, refused under various pretexts to give up Malta. The only result of his assuming the rank of Grand Master was the marriage of Count Litta, who was relieved from his vow of chastity by the Pope, and became the husband of the Countess Skovronsky, the favourite niece of Prince Potemkin, still a handsome woman, though not in her first youth, who when Alexander became Emperor procured for her husband a large fortune and the important position of Grand Chamberlain, which he held until his death. Her daughter-in-law was the Princess Bagration, whose estates Count Litta administered with much regularity and zeal.

During these continual changes shameful and petty intrigues were as usual mixed up with the events of the day. While the Emperor believed himself to have broken the chains which he fancied had bound him, Kutayschoff entered into relations with Madame Chevalier, a handsome woman and a charming actress engaged at the Court Theatre, who was the object of the assiduous attentions of M. Bignon, the French Minister at Cassel, but had abandoned him on receiving more sumptuous offers from Paul's valet. These amorous intrigues led to mutual confidences which added piquancy to the moments which the Emperor passed with his servant, and augmented the latter's influence.

Paul's nervous excitement was increased by political events. Austria obtained the alliance and help of Russia, and Count Rostopchin, since his recall to the Court, had infused a spirit of firmness into the Foreign Office, which he directed with much activity and an ability all his own. The whole credit of the new coalition * and of its first successes was attributed to him, and his friends used to say with complacency that the two great men of the age were Pitt and Rostopchin. Marshal Souvaroff also was recalled; he had been since Paul's accession in exile on his estates and under close surveillance as a partisan of Catherine. Very censorious remarks of his were quoted about the Government of the Emperor Paul, and he made some rather unseemly jokes on the new organisation and uniforms of the army. But as soon as the Emperor wanted him he loaded him with honours and compliments. Souvaroff took the command of the army, and had some astonishing successes over the French, who were no longer led by Buonaparte. During the year 1796 and the following years we had rejoiced at Buonaparte's extraordinary victories, hoping that they might lead to the reconstruction of Poland. We used to call him 'the friend' in order not to compromise ourselves by mentioning his name; and now every victory gained over the French seemed to us a stab in the body of our country.

* Russia, Turkey, England, Austria, and Naples were then allied against France.

When Souvaroff's first successes became known, the Court was at Pavlovsk. The old Cossack General Denisoff was also there; he had been beaten by Kosciuszko at Raclavice. He took a malicious pleasure in examining our faces each time that the news of a victory was brought from Italy. He used to say to us: 'I told you the French would be beaten; it could not be otherwise. Russia will beat her enemies always and everywhere. She is invincible.' *Te Deums* were continually sung in the churches, while the Emperor still mingled thoughts of his mistress with those of politics, war, and piety, and placed at her feet the trophies of the victories gained by his armies. One day she praised an undecided tint known as chamois, and he at once ordered everything to be coloured with this tint. He ordered chivalrous plays to be performed in which he imagined himself to be the hero; sometimes he was a Bayard, at others a Nemours. He also published in the papers a challenge to any sovereign who differed from him to settle the difference by single-handed combat. This was addressed especially to the King of Prussia, who had refused to join the coalition. Paul would have been in a great difficulty if the challenge had been accepted, as he had not much personal courage, and was very timid on horseback, so much so that when he was in front of cavalry he never would allow them to charge.

My brother and I suffered with the rest from the Emperor's abrupt changes of temper. The fact that we were Poles, and the antecedents of our family— perhaps also charges made against us or casual

remarks uttered with or without intention—had led
Paul to suppose that we were liberals, or even
Jacobins in disguise. Yet he had treated us with
some kindness on various occasions at Court assemblages where we were near him. He especially
seemed to like my brother, and he sometimes joked
with him. When he was in a good humour Paul was
continually saying and doing things which he thought
witty. Once he told my brother to make a coarse
and insulting remark to one of the persons present.
My brother objected, but the Emperor repeated his
order with such a menacing air that he had no alternative but to obey. On another occasion when
Paul met my brother he put out his tongue at him ;
and during our stay at Peterhoff, seeing my brother
in one of the alleys of the garden leading to the
rooms of the Countess Schouvaloff, who had a very
pretty chambermaid, Paul took him by the shoulders
and told him to go away, adding 'That bird is not
for you.' He also asked him to tell him his adventures, and promised not to betray his secrets to any
one. The Grand-Duke Constantine was Governor of
Peterhoff, and was responsible for the military
service of the palace. One day the Bavarian Minister
passed out of the gates, and the officer in command
of the guard having omitted to report the circumstance, Paul sent him through my brother the usual
message that he was a fool. The Grand-Duke was
much disturbed at this incident, but the officer simply
replied that the message did not produce the slightest
effect upon him, as it came from a madman. This
shows the impression which was already generally

produced by the Emperor's conduct; and although
he had been kind to us, he gradually became irritated
at seeing us on such intimate terms with his sons.
Prince Bezborodko, who afterwards died suddenly—
which perhaps saved him from a disgrace which he
would certainly have experienced sooner or later, as
Paul looked upon him as a censor and an inconvenient
obstacle to his caprices—had advised Paul to send us
to the Austrian army with letters, but nothing came
of this proposal. The Emperor still suspected us,
and expressed his suspicions to General Levaschoff.
This old general had in his youth been a gambler and
a creature of Potemkin's, but he was very jovial and
good-natured, and liked to render people a service.
He hardly knew us, but he spoke in our favour.
Suddenly the Emperor turned upon him and said :
'Will you answer for them ?'—'Yes, Sire,' was the
reply. 'With your head ?   Mind what you say.'
The General stopped for a moment ; but to hesitate
was to ruin us.   He then said deliberately : 'Yes, I
will answer for them with my head.' This reassured
the Emperor for some time.   I had the story from
Levaschoff himself.   Our turn for promotion by
seniority to the rank of Lieutenant-General having
arrived, and this rank being incompatible with the
appointment of aide-de-camp to the Grand-Dukes,
the Emperor decided to make me Court-Marshal to
the Grand-Duchess Helena, who shortly after married
the Grand-Duke of Mecklenburg, and my brother
Equerry to the Grand-Duchess Maria, who was
betrothed to the hereditary Prince of Weimar.   These
places gave us the effective rank of Lieutenant-

General, but I was sorry not to be officially attached any longer to the Grand-Duke Alexander nor to be able to accompany him in his military duties. The change, however, did not in any way alter our relations.

Soon after I had to separate from my brother. Our parents had settled in Galicia, and wanted one of us to go to them and become an Austrian subject. The family decided that this should be my brother. He addressed a very respectful letter to the Emperor, in which he explained that in order to satisfy the requirements of the Austrian Government and the demand of his parents, he found it necessary to ask permission to join them in Galicia. Paul was indignant at this very natural step, which was amply justified, and his irritation was perhaps the greater as he had shown some special kindness to my brother. He was so angry that his first impulse was to send him to Siberia. Fortunately Kutayschoff, who liked my brother, and who had been spoken to on the subject by the Grand-Duke Alexander, succeeded in calming the Emperor's anger. My brother not only got permission to go, but was decorated with the order of St Anne of the first class. After he had left I felt very solitary, and gave myself up to sad reflections. About this time a messenger came from the army who was asked how the French officers dressed. He said among other things that they wore large whiskers. When the Emperor heard this, he at once ordered every man at the Court to shave off his whiskers, and the order was executed an hour afterwards. At the ball in the evening there were a number of, so to say, new faces, with blank spaces on their cheeks, showing where they had shaved. People laughed as they met each other. The order was conveyed by the Court-Marshal, Naryshkin, who himself saw that it was at once carried out.

After dinner there were cavalcades at Pavlovsk in which the Grand-Duchesses managed their horses with much grace and dexterity. The Empress, who was ordered to ride by her physicians, sat astride on her horse like a man, and only went at a foot pace. The summer was finer than usual. I was quartered in a solitary house at the entrance to a wood at the end of the Park. Here I was more isolated, and could fill up my day with some useful occupation. One morning I suddenly received a letter from Count Rostopchin, informing me that I had been appointed Russian Minister to the Court of Sardinia, that I must at once go to St Petersburg to get my instructions, and that then I should have to leave in eight days for Italy. This was a disgrace in the guise of a favour. The order saddened and displeased me; it was painful to me to leave the Grand-Duke Alexander, to whom I was sincerely attached, and several other friends who by their affection had mitigated the disagreeables of my stay in Russia. I left Pavlovsk next day, and Alexander expressed to me his sorrow at my departure. On recalling his words to me on that occasion, it seems to me that he was no longer the same as when I left him after the coronation of his father at Moscow. He had already looked more closely into the realities of things, and they had produced their effect. Some of his dreams—those especially which related to himself personally, and of which we had not again spoken for a long time—had vanished. Moreover, Alexander had not been able to resist entirely the temptation to do as the people round him did, and he had sought to divert his thoughts by paying court to the most celebrated beauties of the capital. He heartily bade me farewell, and promised to write to me as soon as he could. I asked the Minister to allow me to stop a few days with my parents on my road to Italy. He refused; but as my road passed in the vicinity of Pulawy, I hoped to see them, if only for a few moments.

CHAPTER X

1798-9

I REGRETTED the more my forced departure as I had made arrangements for employing my leisure in literary work, for which purpose the solitary house I occupied at the entrance to the forest of Pavlovsk was eminently suited. This was a pleasant illusion. One fancies that one can create something, but it is only when one sets to work that one becomes convinced that hard labour and more information are necessary to give adequate expression to a favourite idea, and that talent and perseverance are often wanting. On arriving at St Petersburg I proceeded to the Foreign Office as directed, but the documents I found in its archives gave me only a general idea of the duties of my post, and no instructions whatever were furnished me as to the special mission with which I had been entrusted. I passed eight days in preparing for my journey, and then left St Petersburg. At Miendrzyrzec I found my eldest sister, who had come to tell me news of our parents. We passed part of the

night and the following morning in relating our joys
and sorrows. Prudence did not allow me to stop any
longer or to go to see my parents. We parted in
the hope of meeting again at Vienna, where my
young sister Zamoyska was already staying, and
where the eldest also soon arrived.

Four years had elapsed since my brother and I
left Vienna. I was then proceeding to Russia to ask
as a favour that which was only justice—the restitution of our property; while now I came to Vienna as
the representative of the Russian Government. This
change in my situation produced an immense impression on Viennese society, and especially on the
Government functionaries. The few months I passed
here with my sisters were among the happiest of my
life. My aunt, the Princess Lubomirska, also lived at
Vienna in the winter; she had a house on the Bastei
(the old fortifications) and received all the most distinguished people in Viennese society, which was composed of women celebrated for their beauty and wit,
and of foreign travellers, who came there in crowds,
as France and Paris, closed to Europe, were just now
detested by the wealthier classes in all countries.

Vienna was, so to say, the capital of the Continental States which were allied with England
against the horrors of the French revolution. In the
midst of this select society, which was less Austrian
than European, my two sisters had a most amiable
and flattering reception. My younger sister was
then at the climax of her beauty, and my elder sister,
who also was beautiful, was especially distinguished
by the qualities of her mind. An accidental circum-

stance doubled the prestige which they exercised at
Vienna. By the order of the Emperor Paul, the
Grand-Duke Constantine was to join the army of
Souvaroff, which was then pursuing its victories in
Italy, and was to stop at Vienna on his way. My
sister, the Princess of Würtemberg, who had just been
divorced from the Grand-Duke's uncle,* was under
these circumstances in a difficult position. She was
the intimate friend of the Countess Razumovska,
née Thun, wife of the Russian Ambassador, and the
eldest of three sisters who by their beauty, their
grace, their wit, and their noble sentiments, were the
ornaments of Viennese society. The youngest, afterwards Lady Guildford, was at one time engaged to
Prince Joseph Poniatowski, and always loved him as
a brother. The Countess Razumovska, though the
wife of the Russian Ambassador, detested the Russians
in general as much as her two sisters did. But the
Ambassador, not knowing how the Grand-Duke would
treat my sister, already began to avoid her company,
and though he had professed to be her friend, did not
dare to give her any advice. When Constantine
arrived, there was a meeting of Russians at the
embassy, and as my sister used to go there every day,
and she did not want to make any demonstration
which might be prejudicial to me, she also was
present; but being received with evident embarrassment by the rest of the company, she remained
alone in a corner of the room. When, however,
Razumovski began to present to Constantine the
ladies who had come to meet him, the Grand-Duke

* See page 40.

asked for my sister, went to her, addressed her as his aunt, and conversed with her for some time and with much amiability about her two brothers whom he used to see daily at St Petersburg. When he left, all those who had held aloof from my sister were as eager in their protestations of friendship as they had been distant before. Next day Constantine came to her house, having announced his visit beforehand. Prince Esterhazy and several Austrian generals had to wait in the ante-room, and my sister, who was much vexed at this, begged him to allow them to come in; but he took a pleasure in tormenting them for more than an hour, talking and laughing without intermission. It amused him to keep them waiting; this, indeed, was his usual custom both in Austria and elsewhere. He always treated in this way strangers who wished to do him honour.

It was during my stay at Vienna this year that I made the acquaintance of M. Pozzo di Borgo, and he owed to our meeting the high position and immense fortune which he afterwards obtained. Pozzo was at that time a young man who rightly or wrongly imagined himself a martyr to patriotism. General Paoli, who had become celebrated in the seventeenth century for having defended the independence of Corsica against the armies of Louis XV, had been compelled to take refuge in England, where I often met him in 1790 at the house of the beautiful Mrs Cosway, an artist who used to receive the most distinguished people in London. In that year the English seized Corsica, and made Paoli the head of the Government; the latter appointed Pozzo his secretary of state,

which shows that he was already known as a man of
ability; and although he was at first a zealous advocate of the French Revolution, in Corsica he belonged
to the opposite party. The influence of England in
Corsica did not, however, last long. After the
capture of Toulon, the French republican and revolutionary party gained the upper hand, turned out the
English and their Government, and took possession
of the island. Pozzo thus became a refugee; and,
passionate and vindictive like a true Corsican, he
vowed eternal hatred to France and Buonaparte. He
received a pension from England, though he had no
employment or mission, and strange to say he never
inspired the slightest confidence in the British
Government, which, after giving him a pension, took
no further notice of him. He now exerted himself to
the utmost in all directions to satisfy his ambition.
As the protégé of Lord Minto, the British Ambassador,
father of the ex-Minister, and known for his diplomatic travels in Italy in 1848, Pozzo was received in
the salons of my sisters and of Madame Lanckoronska,
a lady who was universally respected, and thus formed
part of the Polish coterie, which at that time enjoyed a
high reputation in Vienna. This gave him the *entrée*
to the best society and the protection of the ladies
who were its chiefs. Though still young and generally
liked, there was something so underhanded and
mysterious in his conduct that he had not a single
friend or person who could say he was intimate with
him. This at least was the impression he produced
upon me when I first made his acquaintance. He
had a cultivated mind, and sometimes he seemed

inclined to cast a tinge of poetry over his life and to work at history, moral philosophy, and politics; but his face belied his words, and his only thought was how to obtain wealth and a high position. Although circumstances sometimes forced him to enter the sphere of sentiment, he never swerved from this dominant idea. Yet he was regarded at Vienna as an interesting man, as sincere, and as worthy of true friendship. The praises which were generally lavished upon him almost persuaded me that I had formed a mistaken impression of his character.

When I was at Vienna in 1790 Kaunitz was still living. His place was occupied by Thugut, whom I had known at Brussels, and who was now all powerful. He professed to be a friend of my father's, and when he was Ambassador at Warsaw he held his own against adverse pretensions so firmly, that he even offended the King. He was of humble birth, and that he should have been placed at the head of the Government was astonishing in a country like Austria. Thugut was an unshaken partisan of war, and gave up his portfolio after the Battle of Hohenlinden, to the Emperor Francis's great regret, as he possessed his entire confidence. He had extraordinary firmness of character, perseverance, and power of work. While he was Minister he scarcely ever went out, ate no meat, and lived entirely on fish and vegetables. When I afterwards saw him in 1820, his sole occupation was to go every evening to the Kasperle theatre, and his faithful friend, Count Ossolinski, was the only one that did not abandon him.

On my journey to Sardinia I was particularly

struck by the miserable appearance of the villages of Northern Italy as far as Verona. I paid a hurried visit to the principal buildings of Verona, Venice, and Mantua, having but little time to give myself up to the meditations to which those celebrated cities have always given rise in my mind. It is impossible for one who knows something of the arts and literature of antiquity not to feel their influence. In passing by these cities and their fields festooned by vines, my thoughts were full of Virgil and Shakespeare, of Othello and Romeo and Juliet. The country was in a pitiable state; it had been the theatre of war, and had passed from one conqueror to another. Its inhabitants, who were formerly citizens of the Cisalpine Republic, were accustomed to French successes and reckoned upon them; now that the French had been defeated, they were despondent and helpless. It was a melancholy season of the year, and the roads were almost impracticable. At the first stage beyond Mantua my carriage stuck in the mud, and we had to get oxen to extricate us. On arriving at Benedetto, an inhabitant of the place offered me supper, saying that he had shot a bird which was unknown in that country. He at the same time complained of the hardness of the times, watching me, like the rest of his countrymen, as he spoke, to find out what party I belonged to, and what opinions it would be safe for him to express. He gave me some excellent soup, but the bird was thin, black, and with an enormous head and beak; I think it must have been a crow. I passed twenty-four hours under his roof, and this Lombard, who in his heart sympathised with the

French, but feared the Austrians, made a strong impression upon me. The King of Sardinia, who, expelled from the Italian Peninsula by the French, had been forced to take refuge in the Island of Sardinia, had taken advantage of Souvaroff's victories to return and establish himself at Florence; he was encouraged to do this by the Court of St Petersburg, which had taken him under its protection. He could not yet venture as far as Piedmont, where the armies were standing opposite each other. The Battle of Novi had been fought, but Buonaparte was already coming back from Egypt, and Massena had shut himself up in Genoa. The Court of Vienna, too, was doing its utmost to prevent the King of Sardinia from returning to his dominions. At first it feared that his presence might interfere with its military and political plans, and the two Courts had long been estranged. Austria did not care for anybody but herself. Selfishness is no doubt common both among States and individuals, but Austria was more passionately and evidently selfish than any other Power, and this exclusive sentiment prevented her from having any generous impulse, or a friendly and sincere, or even honest policy towards others.

I arrived at Florence in the winter of 1798-9. On the night of my arrival there was a terrible storm, accompanied by thunder and lightning, which reminded me of other similar natural phenomena that preceded some of the gravest events of my life. My diplomatic occupations as the Russian Minister at the Court of King Emmanuel, which consisted only of a few faithful partisans, were not very arduous. My task was to restore courage to this unfortunate prince by assuring him of the friendly sentiments and the protection of the Emperor Paul, and to send to my Cabinet at least once a month a report, which it was difficult to make very interesting, as other Ministers were posted nearer to the places where great events were occurring than I was. I was limited to a certain kind of news, and yet I was expected to invest it with interest. The task was especially difficult to me, as since my arrival in Russia, I had felt nothing but indifference with regard to all I was required to do. This indifference enabled me to bear numerous trials with firmness and equanimity, and it was especially necessary in my new appointment, as I had to regard as a success what I could only consider a calamity. I had to keep up a correspondence with Souvaroff and forget the massacre of Praga,* and I had to write at the end of each of my despatches to the Emperor: 'Your faithful subject and slave (rab),' according to the formula then laid down by him.

The King of Sardinia reminded one a good deal—theological erudition apart—of James I of England as he has been described in history, and especially by Scott. The branch of Savoy, descended from an English princess, the daughter, if I am not mistaken, of James I, was the oldest of the branches of the Hanoverian line. The King did not like business, and though very pious, was fond of telling good stories, for, like his predecessor James, he had a turn for buffoonery. His wife, Queen Clotilda, was one of the sisters of Louis XVI; she used to be

---

* See page 73.

called at Versailles *le gros Madame,* on account of her enormous size, but when I was presented to her, she was extremely thin. Her eyes were still very beautiful, and her face and the sound of her voice had an expression of sweetness and melancholy.

The diplomatic body of which I formed part was composed of myself and Mr Wyndham, brother to Lord Wyndham, a celebrated member of the House of Lords; he was a stout Englishman who looked more like a brewer or butcher than a diplomatist. We both used to go to the King's residence on every Sunday and holiday. He occupied one of the palaces of the Grand-Duke of Tuscany; it was outside the town, and afterwards became one of his most splendid residences. We were always introduced by Count Chalembert, who was the so-called Minister of Foreign Affairs. The Count presented us to the King and Queen, the conversation usually turned on insignificant subjects, and it did not last longer than twenty minutes. After some jocular remarks the King would dismiss us, sometimes imitating the person of whom he had been speaking, which he did in a very comic way. The Queen used to bow to us with a melancholy smile. There was also a hungry subordinate diplomatist who did not go to Court; his name was Winterhalter, and he was Chargé d'Affaires of Prussia. This poor wretch was so badly paid that he hardly had enough for his living; but though his clothes were threadbare, he was constantly moving about and insinuating himself everywhere. He chatted incessantly, and in order not to lose his wretched pay he doubtless filled his daily report with endless gossip.

Though almost destitute, he had a big stomach and a
face like a full moon, and he was not devoid of
political ability.

Only a few Piedmontese families had followed
their sovereign ; they lived in complete isolation and
did not see or receive anybody.   M. Bailly de Saint-
Germain, formerly tutor to the King, was supposed
to be the Court Chamberlain, but no one ever saw
him or did business with him.   He once gave a dinner,
and this was the only official function he performed.
M. Dunoyer, Count Chalembert's right hand ; M.
de Lamarmora (uncle, I believe, of the General of
that name) ; M. de la Tour, Governor of Piedmont
at the time of the Austrian occupation ; and a nobleman from Sardinia, completed the number of the representatives of Piedmont.   Among the Florentines
only the Marquis Corsi used to visit the Piedmontese,
and he also called upon me.   Another house which
was an exception to the general rule was that of
Madame d'Albany, who had been divorced from the
Pretender, and was now the wife of Alfieri.   She
often gave dinners to which strangers were invited.
The painter Fabre was frequently at her house ; I
knew him long after at Montpellier, his native
town, where he had established a museum of
pictures and curiosities collected by Alfieri and left
by the latter to the Countess of Albany, who gave
them to Fabre and, if I am not mistaken, married
him.

While I was staying at Florence Alfieri enjoyed
robust health, and occupied the greater part of his
time in long walks.   While he was walking he used

to declaim aloud verses from his tragedies without paying the slightest attention to passers-by or to the objects which surrounded him. In the evening he looked tired and exhausted, and directly he returned from his rambles he used to sit down to a game of chess. His youth had been, as he himself says in his memoirs, a very stormy one. It was Madame d'Albany, to whom he was warmly attached, who had advised him to write the tragedies and other works which even during his lifetime had gained him a great reputation. Some years before I had met him in Paris. At first he was an ardent admirer of the principles of the French Revolution, but afterwards, disgusted by its excesses, he looked upon France with horror, and devoted all his zeal to the cause of King Emmanuel, strongly blaming himself for not having been constantly faithful to it. When some years later a sudden illness had deprived him of the means of continuing his usual walks, he concluded that he would soon die, and he passed away in a few days. He was a man of great merit, and looked upon events from a truly elevated point of view; but he was the slave of an exalted imagination, and was subject to illusions.

The inertia into which the Sardinian Court and the society of Florence were plunged, was too monotonous to be interesting; the days followed each other without bringing anything new. Under these circumstances I decided to go to Pisa to see M. Francis Rzewuski, formerly Marshal of the Polish Court. He was a friend of my parents, and I and my mother had lived in his house during our stay in Paris. He received me with great cordiality, though he was in pain ; he had already been attacked by the malady which ended in his death. He was very impatient as regards suffering, and always relieved it by taking opium. He did this with the approval of a physician who was a professor in the university of Pisa ; but there is no doubt that by taking so much opium he hastened his end, and that it did not prevent him from suffering horribly. We had known and loved M. Rzewuski since we were children. He always had some sweets for us, and we used often to go from Powonski to his house at Marimont, which he had fitted up with much luxury and taste. He was a man full of good qualities—amiable, beneficent, scrupulously honest, but too fond of ease ; he was generous and a great nobleman in the true sense of the word, of a race which is now extinct. Sometimes he would not show himself to his guests, though he treated them with munificent hospitality. When he was in good health he liked to come down to his meals, and was very fond of conversation, which he made very interesting by relating a number of anecdotes. One of these referred to his stay at St Petersburg. He had been sent there by the King after his accession, and was on very friendly terms with Count Panin, Chancellor of the Empire, and tutor to the Grand-Duke Paul. Being one day at the Count's house he took the young prince on his knees, when the latter had a fit. 'I was never so frightened in my life,' he said, 'and I took good care not to play again with this sickly child, who might have died in my arms.' He knew all the scandalous gossip of Warsaw and St Petersburg by heart, and was much attached to the

King, though after being for a long time his Minister he at once abandoned the Court when he perceived that the King was not faithful to his engagements.

I profited by my leisure at Florence in visiting the masterpieces of art in the galleries, and in studying the Italian language. I read Dante with a priest who was remarkable for his extreme cowardice, and was constantly repeating the expression 'ho paura,' which at that time people were not ashamed to use. The Italians have greatly changed since then.

This tranquil and monotonous existence lasted all the winter; in the spring people's faces began to lengthen, they talked in whispers, and signs of great anxiety followed the placid security of the previous months. At length we all had the news of the crossing of the Alps by Buonaparte and of the battle of Marengo and its results. Sommariva disappeared with his troops, and the King of Sardinia with all his Court, myself included, hastily packed our things to go to Rome.

The impression produced by the sight of Rome, when one comes there for the first time, is indefinable. One gathers together all one's recollections, one strives to remember all one has learnt, read, and heard of this ancient capital of the world, and to combine all these echoes of the soul to make them more sonorous. It is difficult to realise the idea that you are really at the spot where such great events have occurred, that you tread the soil trodden by such great men. At the age especially when one has just completed the study of the classic writers who tell you what has passed and give you the names of those

who have lived at Rome, the very name of the Holy
City raises up a multitude of thoughts.   You do not
see things as they really are, but by a magical effect
of imagination you see them as they were formerly ;
the present puts on the pomp and the colours of the
past.   Directly I had alighted from my carriage I
hurried to the Capitol and the Palatine Hill.   I could
not subdue my impatience—I could not sufficiently
occupy my eyes and my imagination with the sight of
the places which had witnessed such great actions.
' Is it possible,' I said to myself, ' that it was here
that lived the Scipios, the Catos, the Gracchi, the
Cæsars, that it was here that Cicero thundered and
that Horace sang ? ' and I recalled to my memory all
that had since my infancy been the object of my
admiration and my sympathies, all that history and
the poets had taught me.   I regret much that at the
time of which I am speaking the Christian antiquities
of Rome did not interest me as greatly as they do now ;
all my dreams were only of heroic but pagan Rome.

Penetrated with these grandeurs of the past, I
thought of nothing else during my stay in the Holy
City.   I determined to visit every trace of its antiquity,
and by examining the ruins and studying all that had
been written on the streets and buildings of ancient
Rome, to construct the plan of the city as it appeared
at different epochs.   My idea was to make not only
general plans, but a series of drawings of portions of
Rome, such as the Tiber, the seven hills, and the
edifices built upon them, so far as imagination can
picture them—beginning with the first foundation of
Rome on the Palatine hill and the Capitol, then show-

ing her as she was under the Kings and in the various
phases of the Republic, when she was still built of
brick, and finally under Augustus, when she became a
city of marble. Each of these drawings was to represent something characteristic of the epoch. The above
plan, which to me was new, had been conceived by
others, but it has never been thoroughly executed.
The drawings representing the open spaces, the
temples, and the forts of the city divided into seventeen
districts (*regioni*) occupied me during the whole period
of my stay. I wished my work to be exact and conscientious, and to make it so required much time,
expense, and research. It was necessary to consult a
multitude of authors, to check their statements, to
employ antiquaries, architects and draughtsmen. I
did not finish the work; all I could do was to begin
it. I had a very good plan and two water-colour
drawings made of the city. One represented the
Forum as it was at the time of the Republic, with a
crowd of people opposite the Palatine hill, as was
usual in stormy times; an orator above the rostra;
and the *via sacra* with the edifice where the voting
was to take place. The other drawing, which was of
large size, also represented the Forum, but on the side
opposite the Capitol. The subject was the triumph
of Germanicus. All the temples on the slope of the
Capitoline hill were there, and Tiberius, his face distorted with hatred and rage, was represented as
coming out of one of them accompanied by the
members of the Senate. A third drawing, which I
ordered to be made during my absence, was to represent the grottoes on the Tiber near the Palatine hill

during the first period after the foundation of Rome;
but it did not in any way carry out my idea.

My enforced absence from my country, my family,
and my friends, and the fact that my position was un-
congenial and without aim, plunged me into a sort of
lethargy similar to that which had oppressed me on
my first arrival at St Petersburg, and the gravest and
most unexpected events could not rouse me. During
the whole of my life the sole motive of my actions
has always been one exclusive and dominating sentiment—the love of my country. That which did not
in some way promote the welfare of my fatherland or
of my fellow-countrymen had no value in my eyes,
while the most futile matters relating to Poland
interested me. Thus at Warsaw there was a good
French theatre and a very indifferent Polish one; yet
I went to the latter much oftener than to the former.

The period of my stay in Rome was, however, by
no means barren of events. Pius VI, who had been
elected Pope at Venice, entered the Holy City while
it was still suffering from the excesses committed by
the French troops. I recollect that at a reception of
Romans and foreigners at the house of Monsignor
Consalvi, who had just been promoted cardinal, the
Russian Consul, wishing to pay him a compliment,
awkwardly predicted that he would become Pope, and
that Consalvi very sincerely protested against the
idea. I may say in passing that in my official reports
I did not hesitate to censure the French for their
conduct. This seemed greatly to astonish M.
Karpoff, the first secretary of the legation, an old
Russian official who had probably been instructed to

watch my movements. Knowing the sympathy generally felt by the Poles for France, he almost reproached me for my severity ; but I replied that if the French behaved badly I could not speak well of them. All men, whether French or not, lose on a nearer view much of the prestige and enthusiasm which they inspire at a distance.

The friendly relations which had existed between the Emperor Paul and Austria began about this time to grow cool. There were various reasons for this ; I will give some which are not generally known. The Grand-Duchess Alexandra, the eldest of Paul's daughters, who, as I stated in a previous chapter, was intended by Catherine to marry the King of Sweden, became the wife of the Archduke Joseph, Prince Palatine of Hungary. This union was contracted at a period when the Courts of St Petersburg and Vienna were on the best terms with each other, and at the time when Souvaroff had gained his victories in Italy. The Archduchess was of uncommon beauty ; her features resembled those of her brother Alexander, she was most graceful, and she possessed all the moral qualities which are the highest ornaments of her sex. When she came to Vienna, she inspired universal admiration, respect, and enthusiasm, without in any way seeking it. Her popularity extended from the highest classes of the capital to the most populous districts of Vienna. This displeased the Neapolitan wife of the Emperor Francis II, a woman of jealous and eccentric character and of extraordinary habits. She loved monsters, and filled her gardens with burlesque statues. There was something underhand and cunning in her manner, and she never looked one straight in the face. The only persons with whom she was intimate were her servants, who never ventured to rival her in beauty or wit; she gave them *bizarre* banquets and private theatricals in which she played herself, and her husband, whose mind was also not very brilliant or suited to a more distinguished society, used to take part in these entertainments, of which singular stories were related at Vienna. The Archduke Joseph's beautiful and amiable wife was regarded by the Austrian Empress as a rival, and she rendered the Archduchess's life so intolerable that the latter had to withdraw with her husband to Ofen. She was Paul's favourite child, and when he learnt how she had been treated he flew into a rage, demanded that she should be sent back to St Petersburg, and even threatened war. Her death, which happened almost simultaneously with that of her father, rendered any further action useless, but it plunged the whole of St Petersburg in deep mourning, while Austria, having re-established herself in Italy, had begun to treat the Russian Cabinet with less deference. The Austrians had sent away Souvaroff with little ceremony, and thinking themselves already masters of the country, they were glad to rid themselves of an inconvenient and haughty ally. Then came the defeats of the Russians in Holland and Switzerland, which contributed still further to estrange Paul from Austria. Buonaparte, taking advantage of this change, hastened to send back to Paul all the Russian prisoners, clothed in new uniforms and well provided in every respect. This friendly step on the part of the First Consul gained the Emperor's heart, and he declared to his Ministers and the people with whom he was intimate that Russia had been too lavish of her blood and money for Austria, who only repaid her by ingratitude. He enlarged on Buonaparte's 'noble conduct,' and interpreted it as a sign that he sincerely wished for the alliance of Russia ; he had, Paul said, suppressed anarchy and the demagogues, and there was no good reason why Russia should not come to an understanding with him. Paul accordingly sent General Levaschoff to Naples to mediate between the French Government and that of the two Sicilies. In passing through Rome the General gave me a letter from Count Rostopchin, the Foreign Minister—the first I had received from him—introducing General Levaschoff to me and instructing me to give him my services. I did this readily, for the General was not only a good companion, but was very friendly. Soon after I received a second missive from Count Rostopchin informing me that the Emperor, not being satisfied with the conduct of the Sardinian Court, wished me to leave it under the pretext of visiting Naples.

I was delighted at this order, and left for Naples at once. The Court was not there ; its only representative was the Chevalier Acton, an all-powerful Minister, who had left Sicily to govern the kingdom. Though Naples, thanks to its brilliant sun and its unequalled position, cannot be otherwise than beautiful, it had at that time a very melancholy appearance.

M. Italinsky, afterwards envoy at Constantinople and then at Rome, a Ruthenian and formerly a surgeon, had for some years been at Naples on a diplomatic mission. He was, or at least he tried to be, a learned man. He studied archæology and physics, and knowing how to do his own business people concluded that he would also know how to do that of others. In ordinary matters he certainly acquitted himself very well, but he was never very successful, either from want of capacity or of good fortune, in dealing with affairs of greater importance. He owed his favour with Catherine to some letters on the eruptions of Mount Vesuvius, and he always stated at the end of his despatches that he had blotted them with some of the volcanic ash that had fallen upon Pompeii eighteen centuries before. He was also helped in his career by his ill-health. He suffered from a sort of aneurism which obliged him to lead a very regular life, but it lasted many years.

The Court of Naples sought to take advantage of the friendly relations which had been established between Paul and Buonaparte. It solicited the Emperor's intervention against the advance of the French, which people thought would, after Marengo, be continued to the most southerly point of the peninsula. Italinsky proceeded, at the instigation of the Chevalier Acton, to Florence, where Murat then was, to obtain some favourable conditions for Naples; but his efforts produced no result. He started before my departure from Rome, and M. Karpoff, my first secretary, being jealous of Italinsky, and wishing to revenge himself for his sarcasms, called this fruitless journey 'The Italinsky Pilgrim-age.'

On my arrival at Naples I requested Italinsky to present me to the Chevalier Acton. We found him at a table covered with papers. He was a thin, sickly-looking man, with a gaunt and sallow counten-ance and black eyes. His demeanour showed at every movement the ravages of time ; he walked with a stoop, and constantly groaned under the weight of his labours and misfortunes. Yet he was said to be the favourite lover of the Queen Caroline, who was the absolute mistress of her husband and the kingdom. Nothing was done except by her will, and even official letters bore her signature by the side of the King's, to show that they governed together. She had all the activity of her brother, the Emperor Joseph ; this was sufficiently proved by her sparkling glance, her quick movements, and her shrill voice. I saw her at Leghorn when she was disembarking with her daughters, one of whom, the Princess Amélie, after-wards married Louis-Philippe. Maria Theresa had fashioned her daughter's mind to domination long before she was married to King Ferdinand. This habit of governing afterwards became her passion. She also had a succession of favourites ; her fiery temperament was stimulated by the Neapolitan climate, and it would have been difficult to believe her boast that she had never had a child of whom Ferdinand was not the father, if there were not an unfortunate likeness between them and Ferdinand— not only as regards personal appearance, which, in his case, was anything but attractive, but also as to character and mind. Queen Amélie was the only exception to this; her rare moral qualities were in strong contrast to the characteristics of Caroline's other children.

The Russian army corps which then occupied Naples was under the command of General Borozdin, the eldest of three brothers. There was at one time some idea of pushing on the combined forces as far as Rome in order to check the French advance, and the General had himself gone to Rome with this object. But he could not come to an understanding with General Roger de Damas, the commander of the Neapolitan troops, as to who was to have the general command, and the plan was dropped, fortunately for the two generals, who would otherwise have inevitably been defeated. General Borozdin was a dandy of the time of Catherine; he was very amiable in society, but his military talents were doubtful. Being in the most voluptuous of climates and furnished with ample means by the Neapolitan Government, which reckoned on the Russian troops more than on its own, Borozdin had all a Russian can desire—display and enjoyment. To complete his pleasures, fortune had also placed in his hands a conquest which he valued more highly than any other. A British Consul who had married a young and charming lady had thought fit to escape from Naples directly he heard of the defeat of the Austrians at Marengo and the victorious march of the French towards .Florence and the south. In order not to expose his young wife to the dangers of a precipitous journey, he determined to place her in the charge of General Borozdin, with whom he was on intimate terms. The worthy Englishman doubtless thought he had deposited his treasure in safe hands, but the temptation was too strong. The lady was like a rosebud, and Borozdin had with the husband's permission located her in the house where he himself lived, on the plea that he would thereby be able to take better care of her. The result may be imagined. When the panic of a French invasion was over, the Consul returned, took back his wife, and could not sufficiently express his gratitude to his friend for the service he had rendered him. Shortly after, when I left Naples to go back to Rome, the General accompanied me. He was in very good spirits, and did not speak any more about the Consul's wife, whom he had doubtless soon forgotten.

CHAPTER XI

ASSASSINATION OF THE EMPEROR PAUL.

THE news of the death of the Emperor Paul suddenly fell upon us like a clap of thunder in a summer sky. The first result of the unexpected news was astonishment accompanied by a sort of fear, but these sentiments were soon followed by others of joy and relief. Paul had never been loved even by those whom he had benefited. He was too fantastic and capricious; no one could ever rely upon him. The messenger who brought the news to the legation looked as if he were deaf and dumb; he did not answer any questions, and merely uttered unintelligible sounds. He was terrified, and had been ordered to keep silence. All he did was to convey to me a few words from the Emperor Alexander, who asked me to come to St Petersburg at once.

[The following is a translation of Alexander's letter :—

March 17th 1801.

You have already heard, dear friend, that owing to the death of my father, I am at the head of affairs.

I do not mention any details, as I wish to give them to you by word of mouth. I write to ask you at once to hand over all the affairs of your mission to the next senior member of it, and to proceed to St Petersburg. I need not tell you with what impatience I am waiting for you. I hope heaven will watch over you during your journey and bring you here safe. Adieu, dear friend, I cannot say more. I enclose a passport for you to show at the frontier.

Alexander.]

This order gave me immense pleasure. Italy is undoubtedly a delicious country, full of interest, especially for those who have leisure to study it. The wars which had ravaged it had at this period deprived it of some of its charms, though the ravages were in themselves not without interest. But I was far from my country, my family, and all I loved; I was sad and solitary; I was never quick to make acquaintances; much time and peculiar circumstances were necessary to break the ice which separated me even from people whom I saw often. My old friendships, though not numerous, are dear to me, and I do not feel inclined to contract new ones. It was with inexpressible pleasure, therefore, that I made my preparations for departure; but I could not leave Naples without visiting Vesuvius, Herculaneum, Pompeii and Portici. As I was ascending Mount Vesuvius, I stumbled and began to slip down towards the crater, when the guide ran up, gave me his hand, plunged his iron-shod staff into the moving débris, and thus saved my life. The idea of death was at

that moment very painful to me; I was about to
return to my people, and to exchange a passive for an
active existence. I felt that I was more attached to
life than ever, as radiant visions of hope, not yet dis-
pelled by experience, were floating before my eyes.

On the day following that on which the news of
the death of the Emperor Paul was communicated to
us, the messenger sent from St Petersburg by the
Neapolitan Ambassador brought us a circumstantial
account of the catastrophe. It did not astonish me,
as I saw before my departure that the whole of the
Court was planning a conspiracy against the Emperor.
At Naples the general impression was one of joy
almost exceeding the bounds of decency. On the
second day after the messenger's arrival, General
Borozdin gave a ball to which he invited the best
society of the town. The dancing was kept up all
night, and the General encouraged by his example
public demonstrations of a gaiety which, to say the
least, was ill-timed. The wife of the British Consul
was conspicuous at this fête in a pink dress.

My companion on the journey from Rome to
Florence was General Levaschoff; he was very
amiable and full of anecdote. He had been sent to
Naples with the secret intention of negotiating an
armistice between the belligerents. The Emperor
Paul, who had withdrawn from the coalition, wished
by this means to avoid all reproach; and General
Levaschoff had been despatched immediately after the
defeats in Holland and Switzerland on the pretext of
visiting Italy for his pleasure. His instructions were
drawn up by Count Rostopchin, then Foreign

Minister, who was shortly after deprived of his portfolio and retired to Moscow, upon which Paul broke
off his relations with Austria, declared war against
England, and prepared to enter into a cordial alliance
with Buonaparte. All this happened during my
absence, and although I was on good terms with
Kutayschoff,* I never could learn the exact details
either of Levaschoff's mission or of Rostopchin's
dismissal. Levaschoff's negotiations, which he was
authorised by the Cabinet to continue after Paul's
death, were not successful. The French negotiators
at once suspected that Alexander would not be so
easy to manage as Paul had been. This was doubtless
also Murat's opinion, for, without waiting for instructions from Paris, he occupied the whole of Tuscany,
and continued his advance. The more he suspected,
however, the more loudly he proclaimed his belief in
the maintenance of a friendly understanding between
France and Russia. He occupied the palace of the
Duke of Tuscany, where he gave me and General
Levaschoff a splendid dinner to which all the generals
and the principal people of Florence, comprising some
sixty persons, were invited. We sat on each side
of Madame Murat, who was very slim and pretty.
Murat, who sat opposite, paid us constant attention,
and was more amiable than his wife. He proposed
the health of the Emperor of Russia, and afterwards
drank the health of both of us. When the General
went to see him in his box at the play he observed
that above his head were the Russian and French
flags crossing each other.

* The Emperor's barber. See page 184.

Before leaving Italy I went to Leghorn to bid
farewell to Marshal Rzewuski, whom I found very
ill. I met at his house several of my countrymen;
among them was Sokolnicki, a very active officer of
engineers whom I had known in Lithuania during our
campaign of 1792,* and Rozniecki, who was with me
in the camp of Golomb and in the skirmish at Granno.
Both heartily shook me by the hand, recalling with
emotion the events we had witnessed together.
Rozniecki told me that he had introduced into the
Polish legions the system of drill practised at Golomb,
which made the Polish cavalry of the republican army
superior in rapidity of movement to the French
cavalry. I left Rzewuski with a heavy heart, and
this illustrious man, proved friend, and worthy citizen
passed away soon afterwards. He is buried in the
Campo Santo at Pisa. His family intended to erect
a monument to his memory, but I believe they did
not carry out their intention.

After staying two days at Vienna, I went on to
Pulawy, where I found the whole of my family; but
much as they wished me to stay, they felt that it was
necessary I should go on at once. I travelled day
and night until I reached St Petersburg, where my
brother joined me soon after.

I approached the Russian capital with mixed
feelings of joyful impatience to see the persons to
whom I was attached, and of uncertainty as to the
changes which time and new circumstances might
have produced in them. A messenger met me at
Riga with a friendly note from the Emperor and a

* See page 53.

written order for post-horses to accelerate my journey.
The note was addressed to me in the Emperor's own
hand, and gave me the title of Privy Councillor,
which gives the rank of General. I was surprised at
this rapid promotion, which I decided not to accept.
When I arrived at St Petersburg I showed Alexander the envelope, and he admitted that he had
given me the title in a moment of forgetfulness, but I
could have taken advantage of the mistake had I
wished to do so. I never received any rank or
honorary distinction in Russia than that which had
been conferred upon me by the Emperor Paul.

The first impression produced upon me by the
Emperor Alexander confirmed my presentiments.
He had just come back from parade, and was pale
and tired. He received me cordially, but with a sad
and depressed air, as if he were under a feeling of
constraint. Now he was the master, I thought I
observed in him—perhaps wrongly—a tinge of reserve and embarrassment which pained me. He took
me into his room. 'You have done well to come,'
he said; 'our people expect you with impatience'—
alluding to some persons who he thought were more
enlightened and liberal than the rest, whom he regarded as his particular friends, and in whom he
placed entire confidence. 'If you had been here,'
he added, 'things would not have turned out as they
did; I should never have been led away if I had
had you by my side.' Then he spoke to me of his
father's death with inexpressible grief and remorse.
We often returned to this subject, and Alexander
gave me full details of it which I shall repeat below,

together with information communicated to me by other actors in the tragedy. As regards the matters which had formerly absorbed our attention, and as to which I wished to ascertain how far his feelings had been changed by his sudden elevation to the throne, I found him much as I expected; not quite aroused from his past dreams, to which he still always returned, but already in the iron hands of reality; yielding to force, and not yet knowing the extent of his power or how to use it.

Alexander told me that the first man who spoke to him about the plans of the conspirators was Count Panin, and he never forgave him. This personage seemed destined more than anyone else to play an important part in the affairs of the Empire, and he had all that was wanted for such an undertaking; a celebrated name, uncommon talents, and much ambition. While still young he had made a brilliant career. He was appointed Russian Minister at Berlin, from which post he was recalled by the Emperor Paul to be a member of the Council of Foreign Affairs under the orders of Prince Alexander Kourakin, his maternal uncle and Paul's faithful friend, the companion of his infancy and youth, who alone of the leading men at the Imperial Court had escaped the Emperor's caprices and remained steadily in favour. Besides his relationship to Prince Kourakin, Count Panin was the son of the eminent General of that name, and the nephew of the Minister who had been the Grand-Duke Paul's tutor. These antecedents gave Count Panin a certain assurance and air of importance. He was a tall, reserved-looking man, and wrote in excellent French; his despatches were perfect in every respect both as regards matter and style. He had the reputation of being a man of great talent, energy, and good sense, but of dry and imperious character. After remaining for some months in the Foreign Office, he displeased the Emperor, who deprived him of his appointment and sent him back to Moscow. As will be seen further on, Panin was one of the chief leaders of the conspiracy which brought about Paul's death, though he did not actually take part in it. During my previous stay in the Russian capital I had never met him, for having entered the diplomatic career at an early age, he scarcely ever came there. His wife, a Countess Orloff, did not follow him abroad; she was good and amiable, and had been very kind to me. When I returned to St Petersburg she insisted on bringing me and her husband together, and did everything in her power to make us friends, but without success. Apart from other reasons, the Count's exterior would, I think, almost have alone been sufficient to make this impossible. I have often been struck by his icy expression; his impassive countenance, on a body as straight as a spike, did not induce one to address him. I saw him but little, however, and my judgment of his character might have been erroneous and even unjust.

The two Counts Panin and Pahlen were at that time the strongest heads of the Empire. They saw further and more clearly than the other members of Paul's Council, to which both of them belonged; and they agreed to initiate Alexander into their plans.

It would not have been prudent to attempt anything without being assured of the consent of the heir to the crown. Devoted fanatics or enthusiasts might no doubt have acted otherwise. By not implicating the son in the dethronement of his father, by exposing themselves to a certain death, they would have better served both Russia and the prince who was to be called upon to govern her ; but such a course would have been almost impracticable, and it would have demanded an audacity and antique virtue which in these days very few men possess. Pahlen, as Governor of St Petersburg, had easy means of access to the Grand-Duke, and obtained from him a secret audience for Panin ; their first interview took place in a bath. Panin represented to Alexander the evils from which Russia was suffering and would continue to suffer if Paul continued to reign. He said that Alexander's most sacred duty was to his country, and that he must not sacrifice millions of people to the extravagant caprices and follies of a single man, even if that man was his father ; that the life, or at least the liberty, of his mother, of himself, and of the whole of the Imperial family was threatened by Paul's inconceivable aversion for his wife, from whom he was entirely separated ; that this aversion increased from day to day, and might prompt him to the most outrageous acts ; and that it was therefore necessary to save Russia, whose fate was in Alexander's hands, by deposing Paul, which would be the only means of preventing him from inflicting greater calamities on his country and his family, and securing to him a quieter and more happy life. This speech produced a great impression on Alexander, but it did not convince him. It required more than six months to enable his tempters to obtain his consent to their plans. Pahlen had at first left all the speaking to Panin, who was an adept at specious arguments; but when the latter was sent to Moscow, Pahlen completed the work of his colleague by hints and allusions, intelligible only to Alexander himself, which were so skilfully introduced, with a military frankness which he made almost as effective as eloquence, that Alexander became more and more persuaded that the aims of the conspiracy were just and good.*

It was a thousand pities that a prince so anxious and so well qualified to be a benefactor to his country did not hold entirely aloof from a conspiracy which resulted almost inevitably in his father's assassination. Russia certainly suffered much under the almost maniacal Government of Paul, and there are no means in that country of restraining or confining a mad sovereign; but Alexander felt and exaggerated in his own mind all his life the sombre reflection of the crime committed on his father, which had fallen on himself, and which he thought he could never wipe out. This ineffaceable stain, although it was brought about solely by his inexperience and his total and innocent ignorance of Russian affairs and the Russian people, settled like a vulture on his conscience, paralysed his best faculties at the commencement of

---

* Pahlen had the reputation of being one of the most astute men in Russia. There was no one like him to get out of a difficulty, and to advance his interests in spite of all obstacles. He fell, however, just at the moment when he seemed to have nothing to fear. He came from Livonia, where they used to say of him: 'Er hat die Fiffologie studiert' (he was a student of Fiffology—from the German word, *fiffig* cunning).

his reign, and plunged him into a mysticism sometimes degenerating into superstition at its close.

At the same time it must be admitted that the
Emperor Paul was precipitating his country into
incalculable disasters and into a complete disorganisation and deterioration of the Government machine.
Paul governed intermittently, without troubling himself about the consequences, like a man who acts
without reflection according to the impulse of the
moment. The higher classes, the principal officials,
the generals and other officers of rank—all, in a
word, who thought and acted in Russia—were more
or less convinced that the Emperor had fits of
mental alienation. His reign became a rule of terror.
He was hated even for his good qualities, for at
bottom he desired justice, and this impulse sometimes
led him to do a just thing in his outburst of rage ;
but his feeling of justice was blind, and struck
at all without discrimination of circumstances ; always
passionate, often capricious and cruel, his decrees
were constantly suspended over the heads of the
military and civil officers, and made them detest the
man who thus filled their lives with uncertainty and
terror. The conspiracy had the sympathy of all, for
it promised to put an end to a régime which had
become intolerable. A sovereign may commit grave
mistakes, bring evils on his country, cause its wealth
or its power to decline, without exposing himself to
death as a punishment for his misdeeds. But when
the sovereign authority weighs at every moment on
each individual in the State, and continually disturbs
like a fever the peace of families in the ordinary

relations of life, passions are excited which are much
more formidable than those produced by evils which,
though affecting the entire community, are little felt
by individuals. This was the real motive of Paul's
assassination. I utterly disbelieve the story that
English money contributed to this event. For even
supposing—and I am sincerely convinced there is no
foundation for such a belief—that the English
Government of that day was devoid of all feelings of
morality, such an expenditure would have been
totally unnecessary. The deposition, if not the
murder, of Paul had become inevitable in the natural
course of events. Even before my departure from St
Petersburg it was the fashion among the young men
of the Court to talk freely on this subject, to make
satirical epigrams on Paul's eccentricities, and to
suggest all kinds of absurd plans for getting rid of him.
The universal aversion to his rule was shown, often
without any attempt at concealment, on every possible
occasion ; it was a State secret which was confided to
all, and which no one betrayed, though the people
lived under the most redoubted and the most suspicious
of sovereigns, who encouraged espionage, and spared
no means of obtaining exact information not only
of the actions, but of the thoughts and intentions
of his subjects. The wish to get rid of the Emperor
Paul showed itself more strongly the nearer one
approached the Court and the capital, but it did not
really become active until almost at the moment of
its execution. Notwithstanding the extreme favour
with which the conspiracy was regarded in the most
distinguished society of the Empire, it could not have

attained its objects, and would probably have been discovered, if the appointment of Governor-General of St Petersburg, which placed at his disposal the garrison and the police, had not been in the hands of the chief promoter of the enterprise.

One day the Emperor said, with a scrutinizing glance at Pahlen: 'I hear a conspiracy is being formed against me.' 'Such a thing is impossible, Sire,' replied the General with his frank and good-natured smile; 'it cannot be formed unless I belong to it.' This reassured Paul, though it is said that his suspicions were aroused by anonymous letters, and that on the eve of his death he had sent for General Araktcheyeff to give him the place of Governor-General of St Petersburg, after dismissing Pahlen. If Araktcheyeff had come in time St Petersburg would have been the scene of many tragic events; he was a man imbued with a strong sentiment of order and with an energy which sometimes grew into ferocity. His return would probably have been followed by that of Count Rostopchin, and Paul might then have been saved. He had dismissed so many of his Ministers that he was surrounded by incapable men to whom he had given the highest offices of State. Prince Kourakin continued to direct Foreign Affairs with much kindness of heart and little wisdom, while an insignificant man named Obalianinoff held the important post of Procurator-General, involving the direction of the police and the whole administration of the Empire, solely because he had formerly been steward of the Gatchina estate. Kutayschoff was still the man in whom Paul most trusted. When he was arrested on the day after his master's death, letters were found in his pocket revealing the objects of the conspiracy, the time when it was to be executed, and the names of the conspirators. But he never opened his letters directly he received them. His favourite saying was 'business to-morrow,' and he put these important letters in his pocket in order not to interrupt his pleasures that evening.

Paul had just finished the construction at immense expense of the palace of St Michael.* This building was erected after his own designs, and was a sort of fortified castle where the Emperor thought his life would be safe. 'I never felt happier or more at ease,' he said when he took up his residence in this palace, and he became more self-indulgent and autocratic than ever.

Although everybody sympathised with the conspiracy, nothing was done until Alexander had given his consent to his father's deposition. The men who undertook to carry out the plan were Pahlen and the two Zuboffs, whom Paul had recalled from exile and loaded with favours, thinking he had nothing to fear from them now he was in his new castle. Their first step was to induce a number of Generals and other officers of rank who were their friends to come under various pretexts to St Petersburg; and this was rendered more easy by the fact that Paul himself had invited many high functionaries and Generals to be

---

* The swindling which took place at the erection of this building is almost incredible. The chief architect, B . . ., was an Italian foreman, whom Count Stanislas Potocki had brought from Italy, and who passed from Warsaw to the service of the Grand-Duke Paul at Gatchina. B . . . 's commissions on the work he performed were enormous, and he left a large fortune to his daughter's husband and their children, who became Russian diplomatists.

present at the fêtes he was about to give on the marriage of one of his daughters. Pahlen and the Zuboffs took steps to enlist the services of some of the more eminent of the Generals, without stating positively what they intended to do. But it was necessary to act at once, for the slightest imprudence or revelation might place the Emperor in possession of their secret, and he was already so suspicious that he might at any moment take some step which would be their ruin. It was not known whether he had already sent for Araktcheyeff and Rostopchin. The former lived at twenty-four hours' journey from St Petersburg and might come at any moment. Doubtless he and Rostopchin would endeavour to moderate the Emperor's excesses, but their influence would probably not be sufficient to put a stop to the severities he wished to exercise with regard to several members of the Imperial family. It was evident that any further delay or vacillation would be most dangerous, and might be the cause of incalculable calamities; and the conspirators accordingly decided to strike the blow on the 3rd of March, 1801.

On that evening Plato Zuboff gave a grand supper, to which were invited all the Generals and other officers of rank who were supposed to approve of the objects of the conspiracy. These were only now clearly explained to them, as the only way to secure the enterprise against accidents was for two or three leaders to prepare it, and not to announce it to the others who were to take part in it until the moment for its execution should arrive.

Zuboff represented to his guests the deplorable condition in which Russia was placed by the insanity of her sovereign, the dangers to which both the State and each individual citizen were exposed, and the probability that new and more outrageous excesses might at any moment be expected. He pointed out that the insane act of a rupture with England was contrary to the essential interests of the Russian nation, dried up the sources of its wealth, and exposed the Baltic ports, and the capital itself, to the gravest disasters; and that none of those whom he addressed could be sure of their fate on the morrow. He enlarged on the virtues of the Grand-Duke Alexander, and on the brilliant destinies of Russia under the sceptre of a young Prince of such promise, whom the Empress Catherine, of glorious memory, had regarded as her successor, and had intended, if she had not been prevented by her death, to place on the throne. He concluded by declaring that Alexander, rendered desperate by the misfortunes of his country, had decided to save it, and that all that was now necessary was to depose the Emperor Paul, to oblige him to sign a deed of abdication, and, by proclaiming Alexander Emperor, to prevent his father from ruining both himself and his Empire. Pahlen and both the Zuboffs repeated to the assembled guests the assurance that the Grand-Duke Alexander approved of their plan. They were careful not to say how much time it took them to persuade him, and with what extreme difficulty and with how many restrictions and modifications his consent was finally obtained. The last point was left vague, and everyone probably explained it after his own fashion.

When the company had been made to understand that Alexander's consent had been given, there was no further hesitation. Meanwhile champagne was drunk freely and there was general excitement. Pahlen, who had gone away for a short time on business connected with his functions as Governor-General, came back from the Court and announced that the Emperor did not seem to suspect anything, and had said good-night to the Empress and the Grand-Dukes as usual. Those who had been at supper in the palace afterwards said they recollected that Alexander, when he took leave of his father, did not change countenance or show that he was conscious of the scene which was preparing. Probably they did not look at him, for he has often told me how agitated he was, and certainly the risks he ran not only for himself, but for his mother, his family, and many others were enough to make him sad and anxious. The Grand-Dukes were always obliged to maintain an attitude of strict reserve before their father, and this constant habit of concealing their emotions and thoughts may explain why at this grave and supreme moment no one perceived in Alexander's countenance what was passing in his mind.

At the Zuboffs' house the guests had become so convivial that time went fast. At midnight the conspirators set out for the Emperor's palace. The leaders had drunk but moderately, wishing to keep their heads clear, but the majority of those who followed them were more or less intoxicated; some could even hardly keep their legs. They were divided into two bands, each composed of some sixty Generals and other officers. The two Zuboffs and General Bennigsen were at the head of the first band, which was to go to the palace direct; the second was to enter through the garden, and was under the command of Pahlen. The aide-de-camp in waiting, who knew all the doors and passages of the palace, as he was daily on duty there, guided the first band with a dark lantern to the entrance of the Emperor's dressing-room, which adjoined his bedroom. A young valet who was on duty stopped the conspirators and cried out that rebels were coming to murder the Emperor. He was wounded in the struggle which ensued, and rendered incapable of further resistance. His cries waked the Emperor, who got out of bed and ran to a door which communicated with the Empress's apartments and was hidden by a large curtain. Unfortunately, in one of his fits of dislike for his wife, he had ordered the door to be locked; and the key was not in the lock, either because Paul had ordered it to be taken away or because his favourites, who were opposed to the Empress, had done so, fearing lest he should some day have a fancy to return to her. Meanwhile the conspirators were confused and terrified at the cries of Paul's faithful defender, the only one he had at a moment of supreme danger when he believed in his omnipotence more than ever and was surrounded by a triple line of walls and guards. Zuboff, the chief of the band, lost heart and proposed to retire at once, but General Bennigsen (from whom I obtained some of these details) seized him by the arm and protested against such a dangerous step. 'What ?' he said, 'You have brought us so far, and now you want to withdraw ? We are too far advanced to follow your advice, which would ruin us all. The wine is drawn, it must be drunk. Let us march on.'

It was this Hanoverian that decided the Emperor's fate ; he was one of those who had only that evening been informed of the conspiracy. He placed himself at the head of the band, and those who had most courage, or most hatred for Paul, were the first to follow him. They entered the Emperor's bedroom, went straight to his bed, and were much alarmed at not finding him there. They searched the room with a light, and at last discovered the unfortunate Paul hiding behind the folds of the curtain. They dragged him out in his shirt more dead than alive ; the terror he had inspired was now repaid to him with usury. Fear had paralysed his senses and had deprived him of speech ; his whole body shivered. He was placed on a chair before a desk. The long, thin, pale, and angular form of General Bennigsen, with his hat on his head and a drawn sword in his hand, must have seemed to him a terrible spectre. 'Sire,' said the General, 'you are my prisoner, and have ceased to reign ; you will now at once write and sign a deed of abdication in favour of the Grand-Duke Alexander.' Paul was still unable to speak, and a pen was put in his hand. Trembling and almost unconscious, he was about to obey, when more cries were heard. General Bennigsen then left the room, as he has often assured me, to ascertain what these cries meant, and to take steps for securing the safety of the palace and of the Imperial family. He had only just gone out at the door when a terrible scene began. The unfortunate Paul remained alone with men who were maddened by a furious hatred of him, owing to the numerous acts of persecution and injustice they had suffered at his hands, and it appears that several of them had decided to assassinate him, perhaps without the knowledge of the leaders or at least without their formal consent. The catastrophe, which in such a case was, in a country like Russia, almost inevitable, was doubtless hastened by the cries above referred to, which alarmed the conspirators for their own safety. Count Nicholas Zuboff, a man of herculean proportions, was said to be the first that placed his hand on his sovereign, and thereby broke the spell of imperial authority which still surrounded him. The others now saw in Paul nothing but a monster, a tyrant, an implacable enemy—and his abject submission, instead of disarming them, rendered him despicable and ridiculous as well as odious in their eyes.

One of the conspirators took off his official scarf and tied it round the Emperor's throat. Paul struggled, the approach of death restoring him to strength and speech. He set free one of his hands and thrust it between the scarf and his throat, crying out for air. Just then he perceived a red uniform, which was at that time worn by the officers of the cavalry guard, and thinking that one of the assassins was his son Constantine, who was a colonel of that regiment, he exclaimed: ' Mercy, your Highness, mercy! Some air, for God's sake!' But the con-

spirators seized the hand with which he was striving
to prolong his life, and furiously tugged at both ends
of the scarf. The unhappy Emperor had already
breathed his last, and yet they tightened the knot
and dragged along the dead body, striking it with
their hands and feet. The cowards who until then
had held aloof, surpassed in atrocity those who had
done the deed. Just at that time General Bennigsen
returned. I do not know whether he was sincerely
grieved at what had happened in his absence; all
he did was to stop the further desecration of the
Emperor's body.

Meanwhile the cry ' Paul is dead !' was heard by
the other conspirators, and filled them with a joy
that deprived them of all sentiment of decency and
dignity. They wandered tumultuously about the
corridors and rooms of the palace, boasting to each
other of their prowess; many of them found means
of adding to the intoxication of the supper by breaking into the wine cellars and drinking to the Emperor's
death.

Pahlen, who seems to have lost his way in the
garden, came to the palace with his band immediately after the deed had been consummated. It is
said that he had delayed his arrival on purpose, so as
to be able to profess to have come to the Emperor's
assistance in case his colleagues should have failed.
Be this as it may, he was extremely active directly
he arrived, giving the necessary orders during the
rest of the night, and omitting nothing which could
give him a claim to reward as the prime mover and
commander of the enterprise.

It will be seen from the above narrative how easy it would have been for the undertaking to have been foiled by an accident, notwithstanding the precautions which had been taken to ensure its success. The conspiracy had the sympathies of the higher classes and most of the officers; but not of the lower ranks of the army. The persons who suffered from Paul's insane fits of rage and severity were usually the higher military and civil officials; his caprices very seldom affected men of the lower ranks, who, moreover, were continually receiving extra pay and rations of bread, wine, and brandy when they were on drill or on a parade. The punishments to which the officers were exposed did not therefore produce any unpleasant impression on the common soldier; on the contrary, they were a sort of satisfaction to him for the blows and ill-treatment he constantly had to endure. Moreover, his pride was flattered by the great importance attached to his calling, for to Paul nothing could be more important than a foot raised too soon on the march, or a coat badly buttoned on parade. It amused and pleased the soldiers to see their Emperor dispensing endless punishments and severities among the officers, while he took every opportunity to afford to the men ample compensation for the work and trouble that was required of them. The soldiers of the Guard, many of whom were married, lived with their families almost in opulence, and both they and those of the other regiments were satisfied with and attached to their Emperor. General Talyzin, one of the principal conspirators, who was very popular among the soldiers, had undertaken to bring to the palace one of the battalions of the first regiment of the Guard which was under his command. He assembled the men after leaving Zuboff's supper, and began to tell them that their fatigues were about to cease, and that they would now have an indulgent and kind sovereign who would not impose upon them the rigorous duties they had hitherto had to perform. He soon perceived, however, that his words were not listened to with favour; the soldiers preserved a gloomy silence, their faces had a sombre expression, and some murmurs were heard. The General cut short his speech, uttered in a sharp tone of command the words ' Right wheel—march,' and the battalion, which had now again become a machine, marched to the palace, all the outlets from which it occupied.

Count Valerian Zuboff, having lost a leg in the Polish War, could not belong to either of the bands of the conspirators. He entered the palace soon after the death of the Emperor became known, and then went to the guard-room to sound the opinions of the soldiers. He congratulated them on having a new and a young Emperor; but this compliment was ill received, and he was obliged to leave the room hastily to avoid disagreeable manifestations. All this shows how easy it would have been for Paul to crush the conspirators if he had been able to escape them for a moment and to show himself to the guards in the courtyard. It also shows how illusory and impracticable was Alexander's plan of keeping his father in confinement. If Paul's life had been saved, blood would have flowed on the scaffold, Siberia

would have been crowded with exiles, and his vengeance would probably have extended to his sons.

I will now describe what happened during this
terrible night in the part of the palace which was
inhabited by the Imperial family.   The Grand-Duke
Alexander knew that his father would in a few hours
be called upon to abdicate, and without undressing he
threw himself on his bed full of anxiety and doubt.
About one o'clock he heard a knock at his door, and
saw Count Nicholas Zuboff, his dress in disorder, and
his face flushed with wine and the excitement of the
murder which had just been committed.   He came up
to Alexander, who was sitting on his bed, and said
in a hoarse voice : ' All is over.'   ' What is over ? '
asked Alexander in consternation.   He was somewhat deaf, and perhaps he feared to misunderstand
what was being said to him, while Zuboff on his side
feared to state exactly what had been done.   This
somewhat prolonged the conversation; Alexander had
not the least idea that his father was dead, and did
not therefore admit the possibility of such a thing.
At length he perceived that Zuboff, without clearly
explaining himself, repeatedly addressed him as
' Sire ' and ' Your Majesty,' while Alexander thought
he was merely Regent.   This led to further questioning, and he then learnt the truth.   Alexander was
prostrated with grief and despair.   This was not
surprising, for even ambitious men cannot commit a
crime or believe themselves the cause of one without
repulsion, while Alexander was not at all ambitious.
The idea of having caused the death of his father
filled him with horror, and he felt that his reputation

had received a stain which could never be effaced. As for the Empress, directly the news reached her she dressed hastily and rushed out of her apartments with cries of despair and rage. Perceiving some grenadiers, she said to them repeatedly : ' As your Emperor has died a victim to treason, I am your Empress, I alone am your legitimate sovereign ; follow me and protect me.' General Bennigsen and Count Pahlen, who had just brought a detachment of men whom they could trust to the palace to restore order, strove to calm her and forced her with difficulty to return to her room. She had scarcely entered it, however, than she wished to go out again, although guards had been placed at her door. At first she seemed determined at all risks to seize the reins of government and avenge her husband's murder. But though she was generally respected, she was not capable of inspiring those feelings of enthusiastic devotion which cause men to act impulsively and without weighing the consequences. Her appeals to the soldiers (which were perhaps rendered somewhat ridiculous by her German accent) produced no effect, and she retired in confusion, vexed at having uselessly disclosed her ambitious views.

I never heard any details of the first interview between the Empress and her son after Paul's assassination. Subsequently they came to an understanding with each other ; but during the first terrible moments Alexander was so absorbed by his remorse that he seemed incapable of saying a word or thinking of anybody. His mother, on the other hand, was in a passion of grief and animosity ; the only member of the Imperial family that retained her presence of mind was the young Empress. She did her utmost to console Alexander and give him courage and self-reliance. She did not leave him during the whole of the night, except when she went for a few moments to calm her mother-in-law and persuade her to stop in her room and not expose herself to the fury of the conspirators. While in this night of trouble and horror some were intoxicated with triumph and others plunged in grief and despair, the Empress Elizabeth alone exercised a mediatory influence between her husband, her mother-in-law, and the conspirators.

During the first years of his reign, Alexander's position with regard to his father's murderers was an extremely difficult and painful one. For a few months he believed himself to be at their mercy, but it was chiefly his conscience and a feeling of natural equity which prevented him from giving up to justice the most guilty of the conspirators. He knew that there was a general sympathy for the objects of the conspiracy, and that those who had personally taken part in their realisation had only decided to do so when they were assured of his consent. It would have been difficult under these circumstances to distinguish between degrees of guilt; every member of the society of St Petersburg was more or less an accomplice in the fatal deed, for those who wished Paul to be deposed must have known that his deposition, if resisted, might have involved his death. If the assassins alone had been brought to trial, they would certainly have accused the other conspirators

and have referred to Alexander's consent in justification of their action, though the crime had been committed against his express wish.   Moreover, he did
not for many years know who they were, as all the
conspirators were interested in keeping the secret.
The assassins all perished miserably, including Count
Nicholas Zuboff, who, not daring to show himself at
Court, died in retirement, consumed by illness, by
remorse, and by disappointed ambition.

Although Alexander's mother continually urged
him to proceed against his father's murderers, it was
not possible for him to do so by the ordinary and
public legal means.   He looked with horror upon
those who had led him to give his consent to the
conspiracy, and he used every other means in his power
to discover and punish the assassins.   General
Bennigsen was removed from his post of Governor-
General of Lithuania, which was given to General
Kutuzoff, and it was not until the year 1806 that
Bennigsen's military reputation compelled Alexander to place him at the head of the army which
fought at Eylau and Friedland.   Prince Plato Zuboff,
the ostensible chief of the conspiracy, failed, notwithstanding all his efforts, to obtain any appointment,
and feeling that his presence was disagreeable to the
Emperor, he retired to his estates, married a handsome Polish woman, and then went abroad.   His
bad reputation, however, everywhere preceded him,
and he died obscure and unregretted.

As for General Pahlen, he at first thought himself
strong enough to maintain his position without
support.   It was he who took the external and

internal measures which had become urgently necessary by the probability of the British fleet entering the waters of Riga, Revel, and Cronstadt, after the battle of Copenhagen. Nelson had won this battle shortly after the Emperor Paul was assassinated.* The news did not become public for some days, and in the trouble and confusion which followed, Pahlen took into his own hands the reins of State, wishing to add to his important functions as Governor-General of St Petersburg the still more important ones of Secretary of State for Foreign Affairs. The proclamations issued at that time were all signed by him; nothing could be done except through him and with his consent; he affected to protect the young Emperor, and scolded him when he did not do what he wished, or rather ordered. Alexander, overcome with sadness and despair, seemed to be in the power of the conspirators; he thought it necessary to treat them with consideration and bend his will to theirs.

Just at this time the important post of Procurator-General, which combined the direction of all the administrative departments of the Empire, became vacant by the dismissal of one of Paul's favourites who had occupied it. Alexander had the happy idea of selecting for this place General Beklescheff, who had been summoned by Paul to St Petersburg perhaps with the same object. He was a Russian of the old school, with coarse and abrupt manners, ignorant of the French language or barely under-

---

* Paul was assassinated on the night of the 23rd of March 1801 ; the battle of Copenhagen was fought on the 2nd of April, 1801.

standing it, but firm, straightforward, and compassion-
ate for other people's misfortunes.   His reputation as
a man of high character was generally established,
and he had even preserved it while he was Governor-
General of the Polish provinces of the South, where
he showed himself just to the people he governed and
severe to his subordinates.   He had done his best to
prevent robbery and falsehood, and did not permit the
officials to sell justice by auction as other Russian
governors did.   When he left he was followed by the
gratitude of the people whom he had ruled.   No more
difficult task can be given to a high Russian official,
and not many have acquitted themselves so well.   He
knew nothing of what was going on beyond the
frontier, but he was thoroughly acquainted with the
ukases and the routine of Russian administration; he
executed them with rigour, but with all the justice of
which they were capable.   He had been a complete
stranger to the conspiracy, and Alexander complained
to him of Pahlen's dictatorial ways.   Beklescheff,
with his usual abruptness, expressed surprise at a
Russian autocrat complaining that he did not do as
he pleased.   'When flies annoy me,' he said, 'I
drive them away.'   The Emperor took the hint, and
signed an order directing Pahlen at once to leave St
Petersburg and proceed to his country house.
Beklescheff, who was an old friend of Pahlen's, undertook as Procurator-General to take this order to him
and make him leave within twenty-four hours.   He
came to Pahlen early on the following morning, and
the latter at once obeyed the Emperor's decree.   This
event made much noise at St Petersburg, and Alex-

ander was accused of duplicity because on the day before Pahlen was banished he had behaved to him as usual when he received his daily report. He could, however, hardly have done otherwise, and the fact is that this act of absolute sovereignty on the part of the young Emperor displeased and alarmed the leaders of the conspiracy.

The views of the Zuboffs as to the conspiracy were communicated to me by Count Valerian Zuboff a few days after my return to St Petersburg. He complained that the Emperor did not declare himself for his true friends, who had placed him on the throne and had not feared any danger they had incurred in his service. The Empress Catherine had acted otherwise; she had always supported those who had helped her, and had not hesitated to maintain them in power. By this wise and sagacious conduct, said Zuboff, she had been able always to reckon on their devotion. No one hesitated to make a sacrifice for her, as such sacrifices were always rewarded; but Alexander was exposing himself by his vacillating conduct to the most serious consequences, and was discouraging his best friends. Zuboff added that the Empress Catherine had expressly enjoined him and his brother to look upon Alexander as their only legitimate sovereign, and to serve him alone with unshaken zeal and fidelity. This they had done, and what was their reward? He said this to exculpate his brother and himself in the eyes of the young Emperor with regard to the assassination of his father, and to prove to him that their conduct was the necessary result of the engagements Catherine had demanded of them as to her grandson. But they did not know that Alexander, and even his brother Constantine, by no means regarded their grandmother's memory with veneration or attachment. During this conversation, which lasted more than an hour, I several times interrupted the Count to explain the young Emperor's conduct. It was evident that the Zuboffs wished me to communicate their views to the Emperor, and though I did not promise, I considered it my duty to do so. Their statements produced but little impression on Alexander, but they showed that the conspirators were still very proud of their achievement, and that they felt convinced they had done a great service to Russia, had a right to Alexander's gratitude and confidence, and were necessary to the security and prosperity of the new reign. They even hinted that their discontent might be dangerous to him. Alexander, however, was deaf both to their arguments and their threats. He could not look with favour on his father's murderers, or give himself up into their hands. Moreover, he had already dismissed Pahlen, who was perhaps the only one of the conspirators who by his ability, his connections, his boldness, and his ambition, could inspire serious fear or become really dangerous. Alexander also dismissed other leaders of the conspiracy who were not dangerous, but the sight of whom was odious and disagreeable to him. The only leader who remained at St Petersburg was Count Valerian Zuboff, who was a member of the Imperial Council. His amiability and frankness pleased Alexander and inspired him with confidence; and this feeling was

confirmed by the attachment which the Count professed (I think sincerely) to have for the Emperor
personally, and also by his indolence, his unwillingness
to take appointments to which onerous duties were
attached, and especially by his amours, which occupied
nearly the whole of his time.

The punishment of Pahlen and the other leaders
of the conspiracy was the most painful that could have
been inflicted on them, and Alexander punished himself with more severity than the others. His grief
and the remorse which he was continually reviving
in his heart were inexpressibly deep and touching.
In the midst of the pomp and the festivals of the
coronation, the young Emperor was reminded of the
similar ceremonies which had been passed through
by his father, and he saw in imagination Paul's
mutilated and blood-stained body on the steps
of the throne which he was now himself to ascend.
This brilliant display of supreme power, instead
of rousing his ambition or flattering his vanity,
increased his mental tortures, and he was never,
I think, more unhappy. He remained alone for
hours, sitting in silence with fixed and haggard
looks.

With me, as the confidant of his secret thoughts
and troubles, he was most at his ease, and I sometimes
entered his room when he had been too long under
the painful influence of these fits of despair and
remorse. I tried to recall him to his duties; he
acknowledged that a painful task was before him,
but the severity of his condemnation of his own
conduct deprived him of all energy. He replied to

all my exhortations and words of encouragement and hope: 'No, it is impossible, there is no remedy. I must suffer. How can I cease to suffer? This cannot change.'

Those who approached him often feared that his mind would be affected, and as I was then the only person who could speak to him freely I was constantly urged to do so. I think I was of some use in preventing Alexander from succumbing under the weight of the terrible thought that pursued him. Some years later, the great events in which he took a leading and glorious part gave him some consolation and for a time, perhaps, absorbed all his faculties; but I am certain that towards the end of his life it was the same terrible thought that so depressed him, filling him with a disgust of life and a piety which was perhaps exaggerated, but which is the sole possible and real support in the most poignant grief. When we returned to this sad topic, Alexander often repeated to me the details of the plan he had formed to establish his father in the Palace of St Michael and afterwards to enable him as much as possible to reside in the Imperial Palaces in the country. 'The Palace of St Michael,' he said, 'was his favourite residence, and he would have been happy there. He would have had the whole of the winter garden to walk and ride in.' Alexander intended to attach a riding-school and a theatre to the palace, so as to bring together within its precincts everything that could have amused the Emperor Paul and made his life happy. He judged of his father by himself. There was always in his noble character a feminine element, with its strength and weakness. He often used to make plans which could not be realised, and on this idealistic foundation he raised complete structures which he made as perfect as possible. Nothing was more impracticable—especially in Russia—than the romantic means which Alexander had devised of rendering his father happy, while depriving him of his crown and of the possibility of tormenting and ruining the country. Alexander was not only young and inexperienced; he had almost the blind and confiding inexperience of childhood, and this characteristic remained with him for some years until it was destroyed by the realities of life.

I have not concealed anything in regard to the catastrophe which inaugurated his reign, for this was the best way of doing him justice. The complete truth, without any restriction, exculpates him up to a certain point from an odious accusation, and explains how he was led into an action which he abhorred and why he seemed not to have punished the assassins with sufficient rigour. I have shown how inexperienced and unambitious he was, and what were the plausible and even honourable motives by which he was actuated. We may pity Alexander, but we must hesitate to condemn him.*

---

* M. de Langeron's account of the assassination of the Emperor Paul is true, but it does not give the whole truth, as it does not explain how Alexander was induced to give his consent to his father's deposition and why he did not bring the conspirators to trial. (*Note by Prince Adam Czartoryski.*)

CHAPTER XII

1801-2

THE opinions and sentiments which had seemed to
me so admirable in Alexander when he was Grand-
Duke did not change when he became Emperor;
they were somewhat modified by the possession of
absolute power, but they remained the foundation
of all his principles and thoughts. They were for
many years like a secret passion which one dares not
acknowledge before a world incapable of compre-
hending it, but which constantly dominates us and
colours our actions whenever its influence can make
itself felt. I shall often have occasion to return to
this important subject in explanation of Alexander's
character, for at other times the Emperor, being
thoroughly aware of his power and the obligations it
imposed upon him, might have been compared to a

man who still likes to amuse himself with the toys
of his childhood, and leaves his favourite recreation
with regret in order to return to the occupations and
duties of real life.

There was no longer any question of the old
reveries of extreme liberalism ; the Emperor ceased
to speak to me of his plan of giving up the
throne, or of the document he had made me write.
But he was constantly thinking of more practical
matters, such as the administration of justice, the
emancipation of the masses, equitable reforms,
and liberal institutions ; this was his diversion when
he was alone with me. He understood the often
insurmountable obstacles which the most elementary reforms would meet with in Russia ; but
he wished to prove to those with whom he was
intimate that the sentiments he had expressed to
them were still the same, notwithstanding the
change in his position. It was necessary, however,
not to disclose them, and still less to take a pride in
them, in the presence of a public which was at that
time so little prepared to appreciate them, and
would have regarded them with surprise and horror.
Meanwhile the government machine continued to
work according to the old routine, and the Emperor
was obliged to take part in its management. In
order to remedy the discrepancy between Alexander's
opinions and his acts, he established a Secret Council
composed of persons whom he regarded as his friends
and believed to be animated by sentiments and
opinions in conformity with his own. The first
nucleus of this Council was formed by the young

Count Paul Strogonoff, M. de Novosiltzoff, and myself. We had long been in near relations with each other, and these now became more serious. The necessity of rallying round the Emperor and not leaving him alone in his desire of reform drew us more closely together. We were regarded for some years as models of intimate and unshakeable friendship. To be superior to every personal interest, and not to accept either presents or distinctions, was the principle of our alliance. Such a principle could not take root in Russia, but it was in accordance with the ideas of Alexander's youth and inspired him with special esteem for his friends. I was the sole author of the principle, which indeed was specially suited to my peculiar position. It was not always liked by my companions, and the Emperor himself afterwards grew tired of servants who wished to distinguish themselves by refusing to accept rewards which were so eagerly sought by everyone else.

The understanding between us had, as I have shown, begun at the coronation of the Emperor Paul at Moscow, and we had for a long time been on intimate terms, as we met daily at Count Strogonoff's. The fourth member admitted by the Emperor to the Secret Council was Count Kotchoubey. Being the nephew of Count Bezborodko, a Minister who had been held in high esteem by the Empress Catherine, he was sent when still very young to the embassy at Constantinople, and was recalled under the Emperor Paul to give place to M. Tamara. While at Constantinople he conducted himself to the satisfaction of his Government, and was perhaps the only Russian who was well treated in the capital. This was at the time of our grand Diet,* and during the reign of Leopold, when Russians used to be received by ladies in drawing-rooms in a manner anything but flattering. I remember the Countess Caroline, afterwards Lady Guildford, being asked by Count Tchernitcheff to insult him in order to enable him to gain a wager, upon which she said : 'You are a Russian.' But to return to Count Kotchoubey. He had acquired a certain European varnish and grand manners which made him a favourite in society. Vanity, a general defect among men, and especially among Russians and Slavs of all kinds, exposed Kotchoubey to sarcasms from other vain people, but he was too good-natured to resent them. He was also accustomed to business, but he had not much knowledge ; his intelligence was clear, but not deep, and he had more good-nature and sincerity than are usually found in Russians. This did not save him from certain weaknesses characteristic of his nation—a great wish for place, for distinction, and especially for a fortune to cover his expenses and those of his family, which had become very numerous. He showed an extreme readiness to adopt any opinion that might be in fashion and to follow any lead imposed upon him by a superior will or by the conventions of society. When he was with us he professed liberalism, though with a certain reserve, as it was not to be reconciled with his real opinions. His vanity was such that it betrayed itself when he strove most to conceal it, which ex-

* The Diet which passed the Constitution of the 3rd of May, 1791. It sat for four years, from 1788 to 1792. (See page 52).

posed him to the satire of my two colleagues. I did not join in their jokes, as he had estimable qualities and showed me much friendly feeling, of which I had strong evidence some years later.

We were privileged to dine with the Emperor without a previous invitation, and we used to meet two or three times a week. After coffee and a little conversation, the Emperor used to retire, and while the other guests left the palace, the four members of the Secret Council entered through a corridor into a little dressing-room, which was in direct communication with the private rooms of their Majesties, and there met the Emperor. Various plans of reform were debated; each member brought his ideas, and sometimes his work, and information which he had obtained as to what was passing in the existing administration and the abuses which he had observed. The Emperor freely expressed his thoughts and sentiments, and although the discussions at these meetings for a long time had no practical result, no useful reform was tried or carried out during Alexander's reign which did not originate in them. Meanwhile the Official Council, namely, the Senate and the Ministers, governed the country in the old way. Directly the Emperor left his dressing-room he came under the influence of the old Ministers, and could do nothing of what had been decided upon in the Secret Council; it was like a masonic lodge from which one entered the practical world.

This mysterious Council, which was not long concealed from the suspicions, or ultimately from the knowledge, of the Court, and was designated 'the young men's party,' grew impatient at not obtaining any result whatever from its deliberations; it pressed the Emperor to carry out the views he had expressed to us and the proposals he considered desirable and necessary. Once or twice an attempt was made to induce him to adopt energetic resolutions, to give orders and make himself obeyed, to dismiss certain superannuated officials who were a constant obstacle to every reform and to put young men in their place. But the Emperor's character inclined him to attain his end by compromises and concessions, and moreover he did not yet feel sufficiently master of the position to risk measures which he thought too violent. In our Council Strogonoff was the most ardent, Novosiltzoff the most prudent, Kotchoubey the most time-serving, and I the most disinterested, always striving to curb undue impatience. Those who urged the Emperor to take immediate and severe measures did not know him. Such a proposal always made him draw back, and was of a nature to diminish his confidence. But as he complained of his Ministers and did not like any of them, an attempt was made in the Council, before inducing him to change them, to discuss the matter in a practical spirit, apart from the abstract considerations of reform which had previously occupied us. Strogonoff accepted the post of Procurator of the First Department of the Senate; and Novosiltzoff was appointed one of the Emperor's secretaries, a place which gave him many advantages, as every letter addressed to the Emperor passed through his hands, and he had a right to publish the

Emperor's ukases. His special department, however, was at first to deal with promoters of public undertakings, who are sometimes men of talent, but more often adventurers of very doubtful honesty who flock to Russia from abroad at the beginning of each new reign. This was a duty for which he was qualified by his varied knowledge in matters of finance and industry, and it was at the same time a school which did much to form his character. I must not here forget the fifth member of the Secret Council, M. de la Harpe, Alexander's tutor, who had come on a visit to his former pupil. He did not take part in the after dinner meetings, but he used to have private conversations with the Emperor, and frequently handed to him memoranda reviewing all the branches of the administration. These memoranda were first read at the secret sittings, and afterwards passed on from one member of the Council to the other to be considered at leisure, as they were interminably long. M. de la Harpe was at that time about forty-four years of age; he had been a member of the Swiss Directory, and always wore the uniform of that appointment, with a large sword fastened to an embroidered belt outside his coat. We were all of opinion that he did not merit his high reputation and the esteem in which Alexander held him. He belonged to the generation of men nourished with the illusions of the last part of the eighteenth century, who thought their doctrine a sort of philosopher's stone, or universal remedy which removed all difficulties to the regeneration of society. M. de la Harpe had his own particular panacea for Russia, and he explained it in such diffuse papers that Alexander himself had not the courage to read them. One of his favourite phrases was *organisation réglementaire;* an important idea no doubt, but he used to repeat it so often and with such emphasis that it was at last attached to him as a sort of nickname.

The Emperor, perhaps without admitting it to himself, began to think less of the capacity of his former tutor, though he was always seeking reasons for raising him in our esteem; his character he always continued to value highly. He did not like us to cast ridicule on the inanity of M. de la Harpe's papers, and he was always much pleased when we praised any of his former tutor's suggestions. But in truth M. de la Harpe had little or no influence on the reforms which Alexander afterwards introduced. He had the good sense to hold aloof from our meetings, and the Emperor himself preferred this, in order, I suppose, to avoid the scandal which might have been produced by an ex-director of the Swiss Republic and a recognised revolutionist preparing reforms for the Russian Empire. He was, however, recognised as one of our colleagues; there was always a chair ready for him at our meetings, and when he left St Petersburg he assured us that he would still in spirit take part in our deliberations.

Immediately after the Emperor's accession the Margravine of Baden, mother of the Empress Elizabeth, hastened to St Petersburg, being happy and impatient to see again a beloved daughter from whom she had been separated for seven years. She was accompanied by the Margrave of Baden, her husband, son of the reigning Grand-Duke, and the Princess Amelia, the eldest of their children.   These visitors represented an influence totally opposed to the principles which were at that moment being advocated by M. de la Harpe at St Petersburg.   The Margravine was the sister of the first wife of the Emperor Paul,* who died in Russia while still young and beautiful, and was more regretted by the Empress Catherine, her family, and the whole Court than by her husband, who discovered after her death from some letters which she had imprudently kept that he was not the sole possessor of her heart.†

The Margravine was tall, with a grand air and much dignity in her movements, and it was evident that in her youth she must have been beautiful.   She had justly obtained a high reputation for wisdom, prudence, and wit, which placed her far above the generality of German princesses of similar rank.   The Empress Dowager, instead of rejoicing at the prospect of the Margravine's influence counteracting that of M. de la Harpe, took umbrage at it; the two princesses were too unlike each other to agree. Moreover, the Margravine had brought about the marriage of her youngest daughter with the King of Sweden, who had refused the Grand-Duchess Alexandra.‡   This marriage, which at that time was

---

* A third sister was married to the Grand-Duke of Saxe-Weimar ; she had a daughter who was married to the Duke of Mecklenburg, and became the mother of the Duchess of Orleans. I recollect that when the Duchess of Orleans arrived in Paris I was struck by her likeness to the members of her family whom I had known in Russia. (*Note by Prince Adam Czartoryski.*)

† The gentleman who had attracted the Grand-Duchess's attention was Count Andrew Razumovski, then young and strikingly handsome. He made so many conquests among the ladies of St Petersburg that he was sent as ambassador to Stockholm, and afterwards to Naples, where he gained the favour of the Queen. (*Note by Prince Adam Czartoryski.*)   ‡ See page 135.

regarded as the most brilliant in Europe, was a triumph of which the Margravine was very proud, and did not contribute to reconcile her with the Empress Dowager, especially as the eldest of the daughters of the House of Baden, the twin sister of the Princess Amelia, had married the Elector, who afterwards became King of Bavaria, while none of the Russian Grand-Duchesses had attained so elevated a position. On the other hand, the Margravine was disappointed to see that the Empress Dowager retained all the advantages of a reigning sovereign and had not given up any of them to her daughter-in-law. When Alexander ascended the throne, being desirous above all to appease the continual regrets of his mother since the catastrophe which had made him Emperor, he left her the dower of a million roubles which Paul had assigned to her at the beginning of his reign, and added nothing to the moderate allowance of which his wife was in receipt as a Grand-Duchess. The latter readily and graciously accepted this arrangement, which afterwards placed her in a painful position, and deprived her of the means of responding to the numerous applications for assistance which were addressed to her. The Empress Dowager continued to have the sole direction of various charitable, educational, and even manufacturing, establishments with which she had been charged during the preceding reign, while the Margravine would have liked her daughter to take a more active part in affairs and to be in a position to distribute the largesses and benefits which one has a right to expect from the wife of the sovereign.

I was very amiably received by the Margravine, and afterwards she honoured me for many years with marks of her kindness. She often spoke to me about the Emperor with the most lively interest. She feared that the reforms he was contemplating would prove ill-timed, hurtful, and dangerous, and wished him to be dissuaded from introducing them ; she did not approve his tendency to diminish the ceremonial and the splendour of the Court, and she especially objected to his assumed simplicity of manner, which, she said, made those who approached him and whose duty was to obey him too familiar, thereby giving his Court an appearance ill-suited to the greatness of the Empire. She pointed to the example of Buonaparte, who, she said, was better acquainted with mankind and with what was neces- sary to obtain its respect, its obedience, and its admiration ; who surrounded himself by pomp and magnificence, and neglected nothing that could aug- ment the prestige without which supreme authority cannot be maintained. She wished to rouse Alex- ander's ambition, to make him profit by the lessons which so great a genius was then giving to the world, and to induce him to become Napoleon's rival without being his enemy, so that the acts of his Government, like those of the First Consul, should be continual proofs of greatness, of strength, and of decided will. The Russians, she said, want such a Government quite as much as the French.   I communicated these conver- sations to the Emperor ; I thought some of the things said by the Margravine were just and true, and that they might strike him and be of use to him.   But they made no impression whatever. He admired Napoleon, but did not think himself capable of imitating him. They were two opposite natures, and their lines of action were different. It was not till many years after that a supreme danger, the boundless ambition of the ruler of France, and his incredible blunders, gave Alexander an opportunity of showing great though always defensive qualities, which enabled him to conquer his rival. After some months' stay, the Baden family left St Petersburg to visit the Queen of Sweden, the youngest sister of the Empress Elizabeth, at Stockholm. During this journey a great misfortune happened: the Margrave died in consequence of a carriage accident. This made it impossible for the Margravine to reign over the Grand-Duchy, and had fatal consequences for her family.

During the summer of 1801 the Secret Council continued to meet. The only measure it decided upon before the coronation was the dismissal of Count Panin, whose participation in the conspiracy which brought about the death of Paul filled Alexander with dislike and suspicion. After much discussion it was resolved that Panin should be succeeded as Minister of Foreign Affairs by Count Kotchoubey, but should be allowed to remain at St Petersburg. The Emperor, wishing to avoid disagreeable scenes, treated Panin as a Minister up to the last moment, and this again was interpreted as a sign of duplicity. The Emperor's will was notified to Panin by letter, and Kotchoubey entered upon his duties to the great satisfaction of Alexander and of our council.

So long as Panin remained at St Petersburg he

was surrounded by spies, and the Emperor every day received reports from the secret police stating in detail all that Panin had done from the morning till the evening, where he had been, whom he had spoken to in the street, how many hours he had passed out of doors, who had visited him, and as far as possible what he had said. These reports were read in the Secret Council, and were drawn up in the mysterious style affected by police agents to give a certain interest to the most insignificant circumstances. They did not really contain anything remarkable, but the Emperor was extremely anxious, and was always suspecting Panin of new plots. He had no peace till Panin had left St Petersburg, which he did soon after, knowing that he was everywhere pursued by spies, and that his presence was disagreeable to the Emperor. He subsequently received orders never to show himself in any town where the Emperor might be staying, and passed the rest of his life in retirement at Moscow or in the country.

In this way three of ' ours,' as the members of the Secret Council were called by the Emperor, were placed in the sphere of practical affairs, and obtained experience of the difficulties and obstacles which are met with directly one becomes a wheel in the government machine. As for me, I had no ambition to serve Russia; I was there merely by accident, like an exotic plant in a foreign land, with sentiments which could not, as regards their full scope, be brought into entire accord even with the intimate opinions of the friends whom accidental and quite ordinary circumstances had given me; and I remained the only

member of the Secret Council that had held aloof
from practical life, and was glad not to enter it. I
was often tired of my position, and yearned after
my country and my parents ; I wished for nothing
so much as to go back to them, and the only thing
that retained me was my personal attachment to the
Emperor and the wish to be able to serve my country
through my influence with him. But this hope often
seemed entirely to disappear. The dreams of my
early youth had vanished like the morning mists
before the sun's rays, and whose was the blame?
Could I expect of men more than they can or know
how to give ? Those whose pretensions and hopes are
in advance of realities and possibilities in this short
life of ours are doomed to cruel disappointment; but
when one's illusions have gone, one hopes at least not
to be deprived of some prospect of happiness, and this
was in many respects denied me. I accordingly often
thought of leaving St Petersburg. The Emperor
spoke to me of Poland at more and more prolonged
intervals; when he found me anxious and discouraged,
he returned to the subject, but no longer in the same
way. He used to console me vaguely or keep silence
on a matter with which he found it more and more
difficult to deal, though it was the only real bond of
connection between us. At the same time, while
avoiding precise explanations, he wished me always
to believe that on this point as on many others he
had not changed his opinions or his intentions. But
in his position what could he do and what could I
reasonably ask for ?

On my return to St Petersburg, I had no longer

found there Buonaparte's aide-de-camp, Duroc, who had come with another officer to compliment Alexander on his accession. Paul's death was a severe blow to the First Consul; he had hoped much from a sovereign who would never admit that what he ordered was impossible. Fortune had favoured Buonaparte in his efforts to gain the good-will of the Emperor Paul. The news of the Russian prisoners who had been clothed and sent back to their country by France, and that of other advances skilfully made to Russia, had arrived at St Petersburg at the moment when Paul was in a violent rage with Austria and England, partly on account of the defeat of the Russian armies in Switzerland and Holland, which Paul attributed to the lukewarmness of the allies, and partly because of the capture of Malta, which Buonaparte had offered Paul, and which the English, now masters of the island, had refused to give up to him, although he had already been appointed Grand-Master of the Order. Under these circumstances, Paul, always passionate and impulsive, took a violent fancy to Napoleon and the French Government, whom he had detested, and an equally violent dislike for the allies, who had been the particular objects of his affection and zealous support. As usual with him, his likes and dislikes became stronger as time went on. After the chivalrous challenge which I have already mentioned,* he concluded a maritime alliance with Denmark and Sweden with the object of closing the Baltic to the English, and maintaining the inviolability of neutral flags. France, Spain, and Holland were to join their

* See page 192.

fleets to those of the Northern powers in order to destroy the maritime supremacy of England. Paul had ordered the whole of the Don Cossacks to march at once to India under the command of their attaman Platoff; and although this order had spread consternation among the Cossacks, and their chief did not know how to execute it, he was preparing to obey it.

What would have happened if Paul had continued to reign it is not easy to say. Nelson's expedition to Copenhagen had certainly foiled the plan of a naval combination against England, but its success had been almost entirely due to Nelson's boldness and good fortune. If the Danes had had the courage to persevere, this rash enterprise might have ended very differently. So great, however, was the terror inspired by Paul that the Danes adhered to his alliance in spite of their defeat. He had ordered his coasts and his harbours to be placed in a state of defence, and I doubt whether the British fleet could without considerable reinforcements have attempted an attack upon Cronstadt or Revel; if not, time would have been given for reforming and strengthening the alliance of the naval powers.

Paul's sudden death at once dissipated all the difficulties of the coalition, and created new ones for Napoleon, as it lost him a powerful friend. In his infatuation for the First Consul, Paul had persuaded himself that it did not matter whether the ruler of France were legitimate or not, so long as he could make himself obeyed. He had accordingly expelled Louis XVIII from his dominions,* and encouraged

* Louis returned to Russia after Paul's death.

Napoleon in his ambition to become Emperor of
France. His death changed everything. The naval
alliance lost its strength and value, there was no
further necessity for fortifying the coasts and
harbours, and trade, which had been suspended in
Russia to the great detriment of the proprietors of
mines and land, resumed its ordinary course, while
the Don Cossacks, who had already proceeded on a
day's march towards the Caucasus, turned their
horses' heads homewards and crossed themselves in
gratitude for the abandonment of Paul's insane enterprise.

The immediate result of Paul's death, so far as
European politics were concerned, was an arrangement between Russia and England. The state of
war which Paul had maintained against that power—
which had long been Russia's best customer for iron,
corn, wood for building, sulphur, and hemp—was one
of the principal grievances of the Russian people
against their Emperor, and immediately after his
death the Government hastened to effect an arrangement with England which showed how eager Russia
was to effect a reconciliation at any price. The
interests of her maritime allies were not sufficiently
considered, and essential points on the question of
the neutral flag were either passed over in silence or
left in doubt. The cessation of hostilities was the
great object aimed at. Alexander had in reality
no great sympathy for England. His education had
given him ideas and inclinations totally different
from those of the policy of Pitt ; and Napoleon's aide-
de-camp Duroc was accordingly received by him with

a sincere cordiality which was hardly to be expected in a moment of reaction against Paul's infatuation for the First Consul.   Duroc's reception was, indeed, the result of Alexander's secret and personal sympathy for the principles of 1789, which had been inspired in him by M. de la Harpe.   Alexander was glad to see at last Frenchmen of the famous Revolution, who he supposed were still Republicans ; he regarded them with curiosity and interest, having talked and thought so much about them.   Both he and the Grand-Duke Constantine took great pleasure in addressing them as ' citizens,' thinking that the title was one they were proud of.   This was a great mistake, and Napoleon's envoys had repeatedly to point out that the term had gone out of fashion in France before Alexander and his brother ceased to use it.   Napoleon's chief motive in sending his confidential aide-de-camp to St Petersburg was to sound the young Emperor as to his feelings with regard to a French alliance.   I was told that Duroc wrote to Napoleon that there was no cause for either hope or fear ; this statement was at the time perfectly accurate, and was founded on an exact knowledge of Alexander's character at the beginning of his reign ; but later on it was belied by events.

Count Panin, who was then Foreign Minister, had concluded a convention with Duroc which did not mention any of the difficulties that had long sown discord between the two countries, and had prevented them from being at peace with each other.   In this convention there was only one remarkable article, and it was directed against Poland and the Poles.

Russia and France engaged reciprocally not to protect political refugees, and not to help them in their efforts against the order of things established in their respective countries.   This article was aimed by France against the Legitimists, and by Russia against the Poles.   Thus Alexander's first public act was an abandonment of the sentiments which had united us. He did not tell me anything of it, and it was doubtless a very natural arrangement to make between two countries that wished to be on good terms with each other; it was the necessary consequence of an agreement between Russia and France, which must be always fatal to the Poles.   I made this remark with some sadness to the Emperor, who answered with embarrassment that the article had no real significance, that he could not avoid accepting it, as it had been proposed by France and agreed to by Count Panin, that it was a mere formality which ought not to cause me any anxiety, and that the destinies of Poland were as dear to him as ever.   The best and most powerful man can do nothing if circumstances do not permit him to act and to keep his promises; and it may safely be asserted that Alexander was the only sovereign of that time who, without publicly admitting it, still remembered and busied himself about the future of Poland.   She had for the moment been forgotten by all Europe, with France at its head. Since the treaty of Lunéville there had not been any Polish troops in France; the legions were either broken up or sent to St Domingo never to return.*

* The Polish legions were formed in Italy by Dombrovski in 1797, with the object of restoring Poland to her former independence.   They rendered great services to France in her Italian campaigns, but were afterwards abandoned by Napoleon, who did not wish to offend the partitioning powers.

Our patriots, having lost all hope for their country, had retired from the French service, and the glorious fall of Kosciuszko and the massacre of Praga had been effaced by the misfortunes we had suffered in other countries. No one thought of us, and it is not surprising that this general oblivion should have had some influence on Alexander's disposition in our behalf.

Not having any wish to take a prominent part in Russian affairs, and often losing the hope which had sustained me of being able to serve my country, I continually had fits of depression and did not conceal my wish to go back to my parents. The Emperor, to fulfil his old promises and prove to me that he had not changed, generously determined of his own initiative to give the inhabitants of the Polish provinces he governed proofs of his good-will. This sometimes raised my spirits and consoled me for the impossibility of realising brighter hopes whose disappointment became the regret and torment of my life. In the two first years of Alexander's reign I had the happiness of rendering services to many of my countrymen who had been sent to Siberia either by Catherine or by Paul, and had been forgotten in their banishment; these were restored by Alexander to their liberty and their families. Their sentences were cancelled, their confiscated estates were given back to them, either in land or in money, and the refugees who had served in France or in the legions were allowed to come back without any difficulty. The Emperor also interfered on behalf of the Poles confined in the fortress of Spielberg and other foreign prisons, and his wishes were zealously carried out by Kotchoubey, Panin's successor at the Russian Foreign Office. The abbé Kollontay, who was regarded as the most revolutionary of the Poles, was set free and came to live and die in the part of Poland which was under Alexander's rule. Count Oginski and several others were also invited to return ; they were received with distinction and were given back their fortunes, which were in several cases considerable. The days of persecution, of political trials and en-quiries, of suspicious precautions, had gone by, and for some time the Poles were trusted and left at peace by their Russian rulers.

The Emperor also wished to improve the admin-istration and regularise the course of justice in the Polish provinces. He looked for Poles capable of filling the principal posts, which had previously been occupied by Russians. Trials were expedited and made more equitable, both on the spot and in the third department of the Senate of St Petersburg, which was the final Court of Appeal charged with cases arising in the Polish provinces. These acts deserved our gratitude, but could not com-pensate us for the loss of our national existence, and they were far from realising the hopes expressed in the conversations of our youth. While consoled from time to time by the advantages which were granted to my countrymen, I could not see what more I could obtain for my country. My life was one continuous struggle between the consolation of having done some good and the regret—not to say the self-reproach—of never being able to reach the object of my wishes and

hopes. When I felt that the realisation of the noble
sentiments Alexander had expressed for my country
was indefinitely postponed, I was utterly discouraged,
and felt invincible disgust for the Court and all its
members. Although on intimate terms with my
colleagues of the Secret Council, I could not entirely
confide in them; their Russian thoughts and feelings,
which they often expressed, were too incompatible
with my hopes. It was to Alexander only that I
could freely disclose my sadness and its cause. Our
old intimacy, though it was more restricted, had not
ceased, and while my position with regard to current
affairs was insignificant, I still possessed the Emperor's
confidence more than any one else; when he was with
me he was more confiding and more at his ease than
with the others; I understood him better, and could
more freely tell him the truth about men and things,
and even about himself.

Our secret interviews were interrupted by the
coronation at Moscow. The recollection of this
ceremony, to which I have already alluded, left me a
painful impression. I know nothing more disagreeable than these occasions, when everything is thrust
out of its accustomed order. Festivals generally give
me a feeling of emptiness and melancholy; there is an
inflated and exaggerated spirit about them which
causes fatigue and is typical of the vanity of human
things. The gaiety which would be naturally elicited
by the occasion disappears directly it becomes obliga-
tory. One gets tired of the long periods of waiting,
during which one has ample time to think of the
nullity of such pleasures; and while surfeited with

inaction, one is incapable of action. In Russia these festivals are very sumptuous, and comprise innumerable masked balls, banquets, illuminations, fireworks, and popular amusements of all sorts. I have seen so many of them that I look upon them with aversion, and I am truly glad whenever I can avoid them.

The melancholy shed over the beginning of Alexander's reign was in strong contrast to the brilliancy with which it was endeavoured to invest his coronation. The father's tragical death and the son's remorse deprived these fêtes of the vivacity and freshness they should have had, and the joy which was at first felt by the people at their deliverance from the fantastic tyranny of the Emperor Paul was followed by the exhaustion produced by deceived expectations, as often happens at the beginning of a new reign, when all classes imagine their hopes will be realised, and are always disappointed. The young and handsome couple who were to be crowned did not look happy, and could not inspire a joy or satisfaction which they did not appear to feel themselves. Alexander had not the art of influencing and contenting those whom he wished to please ; this faculty, so necessary to a sovereign, was absent in him, especially at the beginning of his reign.

The ceremony of the coronation increased his sadness ; he had never more strongly felt remorse at having contributed, though against his will, to his father's death. I again strove to pacify him by reminding him of the great task he was called upon to perform ; these exhortations were only partially effectual, but they contributed to give him sufficient self-command not to betray his despair in public. The recollection of that time is one of the saddest of my life, and I cannot recall it without painful emotion.

The Court returned to St Petersburg for the winter, and our after-dinner meetings were resumed. They were soon interrupted, however, by the meeting of Alexander and the King of Prussia * at Memel in the spring of 1802.

The Emperor was at that time beginning to pay special attention to foreign affairs. Kotchoubey, the Foreign Minister, had adopted a system which he believed to be in entire conformity with the Emperor's opinions and views, and at the same time with his own. This was to hold Russia aloof from European affairs, and to keep on good terms with all foreign Powers, so as to devote all her time and attention to internal reforms. Such was indeed the Emperor's wish and that of his intimate advisers, but none of them had adopted it with more conviction, or maintained it with more persistence, than Kotchoubey. Russia, he used to say, is great and powerful enough both as regards population and extent of territory, and geographical position ; she has nothing to fear from any one so long as she leaves other Powers in peace ; and she has too often mixed herself up with matters which did not directly affect her. Nothing had happened in Europe but she claimed to have a part in it ; she had made costly and useless wars. The Emperor Alexander was now in such a fortunate position that he could remain at peace with

* Frederick William III.

all the world and devote himself to internal reforms. It was at home, not abroad, that Russia could make immense conquests, by establishing order, economy, and justice in all parts of her vast empire, and by making agriculture, commerce, and industry flourish. European affairs and European wars were of no advantage whatever to the numerous inhabitants of the Russian Empire; they only lost their lives through them or had to furnish new recruits and taxes. What was necessary to their prosperity was a long peace and the incessant care of a wise and pacific administration—a task eminently suited to the Emperor, with his ideas of reform and liberal government.

This system was somewhat similar to that advocated by the English radicals. The idea is plausible and not without a basis of truth, but it has the disadvantage of reducing to insignificance and humiliation the State which follows it too literally, as by so doing it incurs the risk of becoming the vassal and tool of more enterprising and active States. Moreover, a consistent adherence to such a system would require much tact and firmness to avoid damaging compromises, which, in the then existing state of European relations, would have become almost inevitable. This is what happened to the Emperor Alexander in the case of the Memel interview.

The Prussian and Russian sovereigns had both expressed a wish to meet each other. The former thought this would be a means of facilitating to his advantage the question of indemnities in Germany, which at that time was being dealt with under the influence of France, while Alexander's sole object was to become personally acquainted with his neighbour and relative. He had a liking for the Prussians and their King which arose from his military education at Gatchina, and he looked forward to seeing the Prussian troops, of whom he had a great idea; he would, moreover, get an opportunity of augmenting his knowledge of drill, uniform, and parades, to which he attached great importance. He also wished to make the acquaintance of the beautiful Queen of Prussia, and to appear before her and her Court as the Emperor of Russia. For all these reasons he started on his journey with much anticipation of pleasure, and he was accompanied by Kotchoubey as Foreign Minister, Novosiltzoff as Secretary, and Count Tolstoï, who had administered the affairs of his house when he was Grand-Duke, as Marshal. Tolstoï was sincerely attached to the Emperor, and was very zealous in his service; but he possessed little intelligence or instruction, and was often laughed at by Alexander, though he placed implicit trust in his fidelity.

At Memel, where the same sovereigns had afterwards to meet in very different circumstances, there were many parades, reviews, and balls. The Emperor contracted a personal friendship for the King of Prussia to which the latter afterwards owed the preservation of his monarchy, and the King hastened to take advantage of the good impression he had made on Alexander to secure his consent and support for the arrangements which were then preparing between Prussia and France with the object of withdrawing Germany from the influence of the Church. Kotchoubey had been opposed to the interview, whose consequences he foresaw ; he endeavoured to dissuade the Emperor from going to Memel, and went there himself very unwillingly. To interfere in the affair of the indemnities would be contrary to the principle of non-intervention adopted in the Secret Council, and would be playing into Prussia's hands. What especially displeased Kotchoubey in the proposed arrangements, and made him wish not to take part in them, was that the disposal of the indemnities was left entirely to Napoleon's good pleasure, and that the latter might consequently be regarded as the prime mover in the whole business. But the two sovereigns settled the matter personally, without consulting their Ministers—a bad way of dealing with political affairs, as it necessarily makes dupes of those who are straightforward, disinterested, and generous.

It was also at this first interview at Memel that began the Platonic coquetry between the Emperor of Russia and the Queen of Prussia—a sort of connection which was especially pleasing to Alexander and to which he was always ready to sacrifice much time. It very seldom happened that the virtue of the ladies to whom Alexander paid his attentions was really in danger. The Queen was always accompanied by her favourite sister, the Princess of Salm, now Duchess of Cumberland,* about whom there was much scandalous gossip. She relaxed the Court etiquette, made conversation more merry, and introduced more familiarity into intimate society. She was thoroughly informed of her sister's secret thoughts, and would have been of her secret actions if there had been any.

* Afterwards Queen of Hanover.

After one of his interviews the Emperor, who then had transferred his affections to some one else, told me he was seriously alarmed at the distribution of the rooms which communicated with his, and that at night he used carefully to lock his bedroom door to prevent his being surprised and led into dangerous temptations which he wished to avoid. He even said this plainly, with more frankness than gallantry, to the Queen of Prussia and her sister.

On returning from Memel, the Emperor made a tour in Lithuania, and showed that he took an interest in the Poles by distributing some favours and repairing some acts of injustice, and at the same time holding out the prospect of further benefits. All this was very hurriedly done, as is usually the case during the tour of a sovereign in his dominions. When he arrived at St Petersburg, the treaty relative to the indemnities was made public, and it turned out to be a general distribution of ecclesiastical property in which Prussia had the largest share. In Paris the property was sold by auction: the First Consul took the leading part in the arrangements, but Talleyrand was entrusted with the details of the distribution, and as a rule the highest bidder got the property. Right had little chance unless it had money to back it. Germany was parcelled out for the advantage of Prussia—whose favour the First Consul wished to gain—and of the distributors in Paris. The importance of France was sensibly increased, while that of Russia was greatly diminished; she played a secondary part and was led into giving her assent to an arrangement which was far from honourable in its origin and the results of which she could hardly approve. Kotchoubey was much distressed, and in the salons people talked of the insignificant part Russia had been made to play. France, on the other hand, boasted of her triumph, and the Prussian Ministers were delighted. In order to gild the pill for Russia, Napoleon offered some advantages to the houses of Würtemberg and Baden, which were allied with her; but these States felt that their fate must ultimately depend on the good-will of France, and not on the power of Russia. As for the Duke of Oldenburg, the Empress Dowager's son-in-law, he complained of the prejudicial effect of the treaty upon his estates, but he could not obtain any redress: Napoleon had been offended by his strong German feeling and his stiff manners.

The meetings of the Secret Council were now resumed, and they had become the more important as three of its members—Kotchoubey, Novosiltzoff, and Strogonoff—were now in the service of the State. Novosiltzoff's ante-chamber began to fill; men with new ideas sought and obtained employment. Many matters passed through his hands and were influenced by his liberal leanings. The Emperor found him useful for giving Russian forms to his European aspirations. We were also supported by some of the older and more distinguished functionaries of the Empire. One of these was the father of Count Paul Strogonoff, who had passed the greater part of his life in Paris at the time of Louis XV. He had been in the society of Grimm, d'Holbach, and d'Alembert; he had been a frequent visitor in the salons of celebrated women, where the greatest noblemen used to meet men of letters; his conversation was full of the anecdotes and good sayings of that day, and he had in many things adopted its opinions. He was very impulsive and enthusiastic, but the slightest obstacle sufficed to cool his enthusiasm. He was a singular mixture of the encyclopædist and the old Russian boyard. His mind and his language were French, his manners and customs Russian; he had a great fortune and many debts, a large elegantly furnished house, a good picture gallery, of which he had himself drawn up a catalogue, and an immense number of servants (including some French valets) whom he treated as slaves, though with great kindness. He was surrounded by disorder, and his servants robbed him; but he did not care. He kept open house, and anybody could come to meals on certain days in the week. The society was less mixed, and included more learned men and artists, than at the house of the Grand Equerry Narishkin, and the complete absence of etiquette, together with the Count's extreme amiability, made his house very pleasant. He had taken a great liking to me, and was angry when I did not come to his dinners; he treated me as one of the family.

By natural inclination and by his French training the Count was liberal so far as his words and desires were concerned. He wished to give happiness and liberty to everybody; but at the same time he was a thorough courtier, and the favour and consideration of his sovereign was to him a necessity. He was not ambitious or desirous of place; but a cold reception or a frown from the Emperor made him unhappy and deprived him of all energy and rest. He had been liked by Catherine, by Paul, and by the Empress Maria, and he was especially so by Alexander. The latter was his son's friend, and was very fond of the young Countess, who by her amiable character had obtained a great influence over him. At the old Count's he felt in his element, for he used to meet people who understood and appreciated those modern and liberal ideas which were at that time Alexander's secret passion.

The special favour enjoyed by the Strogonoff family at the beginning of Alexander's reign gave the old Count more weight than he had ever had before, and as he was a senator, and his Russian manners had gained him much popularity among the nobility of the district of which he was Marshal, his enthusiastic approval of the new ideas which were supposed to be entertained by Alexander and the members of the Secret Council was very valuable to the latter. An even more important supporter was Count Alexander Vorontzoff, who was regarded in Russia as one of her ablest statesmen. He and Count Zavadovsky had been Count Bezborodko's friends; they used to come to see him to talk about public affairs, and it is said that when they left Bezborodko used to have the doors and windows opened, and to wander about the rooms panting, fanning himself, and saying, 'Thank God, the pedagogues have gone,' as they were constantly reproaching him for his indolence and his yielding temper. They were, however, true friends. I do not know what induced Count Vorontzoff to

withdraw from public affairs during the reign of
Catherine. He used to have fits of bad temper, and
his ambition was not easily satisfied. While Paul
was on the throne the Count had the good sense
to remain in retirement, although Paul was very well
disposed towards the Vorontzoff family on account of
the *liaison* of Peter III with one of their sisters. It
was only at the time of the new Emperor's accession
that Vorontzoff reappeared at St Petersburg, with
the reputation he had enjoyed during the reign of
Catherine still further increased by his having so
long and so wisely remained in retirement. He did
not join the old Ministers, most of whom were inferior to him in knowledge and judgment, and whom
it would have been necessary to dismiss in order to find
a place for him. The position he assumed was a more
elevated one; he undertook the task of reconciling
the Emperor's ideas with those of the old Russian
routine, of moderating the changes which he foresaw
might arise from Alexander's inclinations. It was
easy to adopt and at the same time to guide them,
and thereby to gain favour and power. Vorontzoff
accordingly entered the 'young men's party,' feeling that in order to rise it was necessary to free one's
self from the old traditions, and that in any new
arrangement the first place would be secured to
him.

Vorontzoff's brother Simon had also arrived at St
Petersburg after a long absence. He had very fixed
opinions and sentiments, and was always a blind and
passionate partisan of any idea he adopted, or any
man he chose as his idol. During the revolution

which placed Catherine II on the throne he was a
subaltern officer in the grenadiers, and loudly declared
himself in favour of the unfortunate Peter III, which
did not prevent him from being afterwards employed
by Catherine and appointed Ambassador in London.
It is known that one of Vorontzoff's sisters was Peter
III's mistress, while another was a *confidante* of the
Empress Catherine.   The zeal he had shown in his
youth for Peter III, induced the Emperor Paul to
recall him from London to St Petersburg, and offer
him the first posts in the Empire, but he refused
them all and asked to be left in London.   He had
acquired friends in England by his noble, frank, and
determined character, and had, so to say, taken root
in the country.   England had quite fascinated him ;
he loved her more than the most bigoted of Tories,
and he adored Pitt to such an extent that he looked
upon the slightest criticism or even doubt as to his
policy and doctrines as simple nonsense, and as showing an inexcusable perversion of mind or heart.   Besides his worship of England and Pitt, he cultivated
another which was more natural and of older date—
that of his elder brother.   He considered him the
ablest and most virtuous man in Russia, and his
decisions were to him oracles.   His devotion to his
brother was indeed touching, for it was quite spon-
taneous and sincere.   The two brothers were so
united that they did not even divide the property left
them by their father.   Alexander, who managed the
property, gave his brother his share, and there was
never the slightest altercation between them on the
subject.

Novosiltzoff, during the years he had passed in England while Paul was on the throne, had been a frequent visitor to Simon Vorontzoff's house, to which he had been introduced by Count Strogonoff; he had gained his intimacy and confidence, and thus became a sort of bond between Alexander Vorontzoff and the 'young men's party.' Simon's arrival at St Petersburg made these relations more intimate and effective. His Tory opinions were regarded in Russia as extremely Liberal, and they had considerable influence on his brother, through whom they were transmitted to the Emperor, who was already elaborating a plan of reform. Alexander Vorontzoff was in no way opposed to certain Liberal ideas; on the contrary, he was inclined to adopt and support them, and this inclination was fostered by the traditions of the old Russian aristocracy which had wished to limit the power of the Empress Anne when she was called to the throne. He once told me that in passing through Warsaw in his youth, during the reign of Augustus III, to make a tour in Europe, he had thought that nothing could have been better or more fortunate for himself and his country than that he should be a great nobleman like those of Poland, with the same rights and privileges. The Russian aristocratic spirit of one of the brothers and the pure Toryism of the other both looked to the Senate for a solution of the problem. The basis and the source of all reforms should, they thought, be found in the Senate; by that body alone could they be carried out without danger. Yet, though various plans were discussed in the Secret Council, nothing was done. This discontented the Vorontzoffs,

and they agreed with the ' young men's party ' to take
a decided step to draw the Emperor out of the timid
inertia in which he had entrenched himself.

The country house of Kamienny Ostrog, where
the Emperor then lived, was separated from that
of Count Strogonoff by the river Neva, over which
there was a bridge.　The Emperor and Empress went
to dine at Count Strogonoff's, and the Vorontzoffs
were also there.　After we had got up from table,
the Emperor walked in the garden and went into
one of the pavilions, where he found Novosiltzoff;
we all followed him, and entered into conversation.
Simon Vorontzoff had been chosen as the speaker on
this occasion, as, having only just come from England,
and being a stranger to what had passed at St
Petersburg, he had a right to be regarded as impartial
and to state his views freely.　His speech was not as
eloquent as we had expected ; the Emperor, who was
very clever in raising objections and difficulties, repeatedly disconcerted both Simon and his brother.
They tried to prove to him that it was necessary to
do something, that improvements were expected of a
new reign, and that both Russia and Europe generally
expected them, especially of him.　These were only
vague phrases ; and when the Emperor asked what
line the improvements should take and how he was to
proceed, the Vorontzoffs could only answer that if the
authority of the Senate were re-established all difficulties would be removed.　They held that this body,
if restored to its power and dignity, would possess all
the safeguards and the means necessary for bringing
about the projected improvements.　Each sentence in

Simon Vorontzoff's speech began and ended with the Senate, and when he did not know what to say or answer he simply repeated the word. This affectation was somewhat awkward and ridiculous, and was more likely to chill the Emperor than to rouse him. The Senate had certainly much changed since its establishment by Peter I, and it could no longer be said even to have the power it enjoyed in the reigns which immediately succeeded that of the founder of modern Russia. In all difficult questions the Senate was always referred to, but it was nothing but a name; it was composed of men who were for the most part incapable and without energy, selected for their insignificance, and it could not therefore act as a mediator between parties or be of any weight either on one side or the other.

At length the Emperor's vague and floating ideas were consolidated into a practical shape. All the eccentric views which were mere fireworks were abandoned, and Alexander had to restrict his wishes to the realities and possibilities of the moment. He consoled himself by indulging in his hours of leisure, which were daily becoming more rare, in hopes of progress which enabled him not to give up entirely the dreams of his youth. These dreams seemed to me like a tree transplanted into a dry and arid soil and deprived of its exuberant vegetation, whose despoiled trunk puts forth a few weak branches and then perishes. The Emperor's first step was to issue an ukase or manifesto to restore the authority and dignity of the Senate; this was a prudent course, calculated to predispose the public for the changes which were to follow. In speaking of the Senate he spoke a language which the Russians understood and which flattered the nobility ; it was already the Supreme Court of Justice and Administration, for although every order of the Emperor, whether written or spoken, had the force of law, they had (especially those relating to general administration and the civil and criminal law) all to be addressed to the Senate, which was entrusted with the task of publishing them and seeing to their due execution. The various departments of the Senate were charged not only with trying on final appeal the civil and criminal cases of the empire, but also with punishing contraventions of the administrative regulations. It had the right of issuing ukases of its own founded on those of the Emperor, and, when necessary, explaining and developing them ; and it presented him with reports for his approval. The governors and financial authorities of the provinces were under its direct supervision, and it was their duty to send to the Senate regular and formal reports upon which the sovereign gave such orders as he pleased. It was accordingly called ' The Senate administering the Empire.' Its vague functions, partly judicial and partly executive, were not in accordance with modern ideas, being so cumbrous in form that they retarded and might even embarrass the course of government ; but there was no way of touching this ancient organisation without exposing internal affairs to even greater confusion, as the institution of the Senate had become part of the routine and the habits of the government machine. The Senate was consequently allowed to retain its

administrative functions, though it was intended to
let them fall by degrees into desuetude. All its
powers were confirmed in pompous terms of which the
author was Vorontzoff, and to them was added the
right of making representations on the Emperor's
ukases. It was at the same time laid down that all
the Ministers should make detailed reports of their
functions, which the Emperor would send to the
Senate for its opinion.

This, it was hoped, would be a first step in the
direction of national and representative government.
The idea was to deprive the Senate of its executive
powers, to leave it those of a Supreme Court of
Justice, and gradually to convert it into a sort of
upper chamber to which would afterwards be attached
deputies of the nobility who, either as part of the
chamber or as a separate body, would, for the
Emperor's information, state their views on the
management of affairs by the Ministers and on the
laws which were in existence or in preparation. This
plan was never carried out, and what really happened
was very different.

Those who think that the Senate of St Petersburg
can ever be of any importance for the destinies of
Russia are entirely mistaken, and only show that they
do not know Russia. The Russian Senate in its
present form is less able than any political body in
the world to make itself respected or to act on its own
initiative. It can neither give an impulse nor even
receive one; it is a marionette which one can move
about as one pleases, but which has no motive power
of its own.

Those who are tired of official life and wish to retire and live quietly in idleness are the sort of people who seek the appointment of Senator. The Senate thus becomes a receptacle for the indolent and the superannuated; all its work is done by the pro-curators and the secretaries, who decide questions at their pleasure and then take the decisions to the Senators, who as a rule sign them without reading them. These decrees are drawn up in a more diffuse and tedious style even than the official documents of other countries; the minutes in each case fill an immense volume, and it would require some courage to read them. One or two Senators who do read the decrees that are submitted to them for signature are spoken of with admiration as heroes. It is evident that such a political body is incapable of undertaking or following up any reform.

After laying the first stone of the edifice of a regulated legislative power, and devising a limit to the autocratic power, the Emperor turned his attention to the organisation of his government, so as to make its action more enlightened, more just, and more methodical. The government machine was irregular and intermittent in its action, and the administration was a chaos in which nothing was regulated or clearly defined. The only administrative authorities that were recognised were the Senate and the Committees of War, of the Navy, and of Foreign Affairs. These were not deliberative or consultative bodies; one of the members of each committee, usually the president, brought the reports of the committee to the sovereign and then informed it of his decisions. The Procu-

rator-General united in his person the offices of
Minister of the Interior, of Police, of Finance, and of
Justice ; but sometimes the sovereign created separate
departments, and the Empress Catherine placed the
conquered provinces under the direction of one of her
favourites, such as Potemkin or Zuboff, who were
independent of the Senate and reported direct to the
sovereign. Moreover, when the reports of the Senate
and the various committees were handed to the
sovereign by the Ministers or other high functionaries of State, they were often put away in a drawer,
and after some time had elapsed a decision totally
opposed to the one suggested was issued. Thus there
was practically no bar to the caprices of the sovereign.
Paul, who thought he was a great general, and was
especially jealous of any control over the army apart
from his own, appointed one of his aides-de-camp in
whom he had confidence to examine and submit to
him all the proposals of the War Committee, and all
promotions and appointments. The direction of
Foreign Affairs was nominally entrusted to a committee of three members, each of whom worked with
the sovereign separately, and had the management of
some particular question which was kept a secret from
his colleagues. This post was much sought after,
and Catherine's favourites obtained some magnificent
presents from foreign powers in employing for a
negotiation with which they had been charged by the
Empress one of the members of the Foreign Affairs
Committee on whose complaisance they could rely.
This was the case with Prince Zuboff and Count

Markoff, who were handsomely rewarded for advoca-
ting the two last partitions of Poland.

In the time of the Emperor Paul foreign affairs
were often directed by his favourite aides-de-camp.
The Vice-Chancellor or the eldest of the members of
the committee only had the direction of the administrative and financial branch, and of the current
correspondence. This system suited an able sovereign
like the Empress Catherine, who, notwithstanding its
disadvantages and a complete absence of unity, still
ultimately carried out a consistent policy. Paul, with
his incessant caprices and changes of mind, yet had a
most decided, almost furious, will which all the
wheels of the government machine had at once to
obey. But with a sovereign of vacillating character
it is evident that the system of administration above
described must lead to serious evils. The Emperor
was continually exposed to making mistakes, to
seeing only one side of a question; he was liable to
be confused by a mass of opinions from persons many
of whom had an interest in not letting him know the
whole truth; and he could never advance towards a
definite object. Russia therefore had reason to be
grateful to the Emperor Alexander and those whose
advice he then followed for having sought to introduce
more order and method in the Imperial administration.

The object of the reform was to establish a system
somewhat similar to those adopted in most other
European States by separating the departments, defin-
ing their limits, assembling in each department matters
of the same kind, centralising their management, and
thereby augmenting the responsibility of the principal

functionaries of State. It was hoped among other
things that this would be an efficacious means of
checking the numberless abuses and frauds which are
the curse of Russia. The Emperor accordingly
created for the first time Ministries of the Interior
and of Police, of Finance, of Justice, of Public Instruction, of Commerce, of Foreign Affairs, of War,
and of the Navy. As to the War Department,
Alexander continued the system adopted by his father,
insisting that everything relating to the army, down
to the smallest appointment, should emanate direct
from the sovereign, and that the army should know
it. The post of aide-de-camp charged with the management of the *personnel* of the army became gradually
converted, in imitation of Napoleon, into that of
Major-General, so as to show that Russia always
considers herself in a state of war, and wishes to be
in a position to make war at any moment. In the
manifesto establishing the changes above referred to,
it was stated that all the Emperor's ukases were in
future to be countersigned by one of the Ministers—
an attempt to introduce the principle of responsibility
—and the Ministers were directed to meet in a
council, in which they were to discuss the most
important questions of State. This was a new
administrative machine superior to the Senate, which
retained all its functions and was invested with new
ones; but those which related to administration
properly so called, became in its case almost purely
formal. By the creation of the new Ministers the
administrative authority of the Government was
concentrated, while hitherto it had not had any legal

or definite status except in the person of the sovereign. The Council of State also was not changed, although some of its most eminent members became Ministers. The Emperor continued occasionally to refer to this Council various disagreeable or complicated questions, in order to give it something to do, and not let it die too soon ; but it speedily perished through its insignificance, and Alexander afterwards created another Imperial Council on quite a different and much more extensive plan.

These changes, which elsewhere would seem the very A B C of politics, seemed at that time to the Russians novel and immense. The manifesto made much noise in the whole Empire and especially in the salons of St Petersburg and Moscow ; each man had his own opinion of it, and the majority judged it not by its intrinsic merits or the benefits it might confer on the State, but by the effect it would be likely to have on their own advancement. Those who obtained places approved it, while those who remained in the cold criticised the juvenile infatuation that wished to change the old and venerable institutions under which Russia had become great. The personages high in office who had not been consulted, and did not expect so considerable a change, were taken by surprise, finding themselves eclipsed by those who during the reign of Paul and the beginning of that of Alexander had held aloof. They strove to vent their disappointment by smiling with pity at the young men who were trying to reform the Empire, and at the foolishness of some older men who consented to be the instruments of a servile and awkward imitation of

foreign institutions. The easy good-nature of the
Emperor encouraged these criticisms, so far as they
were possible in Russia, and they found a certain
amount of support in the Empress Dowager, who was
annoyed, without admitting it, at not having been
more consulted by her son and at not being able to
influence his decisions. She perceived in all these
novelties a germ of liberalism whose development
she feared, and her salon became a centre of opposition where people came to express their discontent.

The head of the new administration was Count
Alexander Vorontzoff, who was made Foreign Minister, and also Chancellor—a title of which he had
long been ambitious, and which had not been given
to any one for many years. Kotchoubey left the
Foreign Office without regret, even with pleasure, as
he thought nothing could be done in it under that
system of impassiveness which he considered most
suitable to Russia and most in conformity with the
Emperor's character and his views and wishes ; he
threw himself with extreme ardour into the new
sphere of action opened to him by his appointment
as Minister of the Interior. The important branches
of police and general administration of which this
department was composed had until then been buried
in the mass of the functions attributed to the Senate,
to the Procurator-General, and occasionally to some
of the sovereign's secretaries. Kotchoubey had
entirely to reorganise an administration which had
been long neglected, and which in the more distant
provinces was without any direction or supervision,

and given up to all the abuses arising from the ignorance and cupidity of subordinate officials. It was
a noble and arduous task, and if he did not succeed
as well as he had wished, it was not for want of
zeal or good-will. He began by organising his office,
dividing it into several sections, each of which
had to deal with a distinct branch of the vast department. He invited the assistance of all the able
and experienced officials he could find, and endeavoured to raise in general estimation the post of
Governor of a province by appointing in that capacity
men whose character and position afforded guarantees
of integrity, and who, though inexperienced in official
work, were likely soon to obtain the necessary
knowledge. It seemed as if order was going to break
through the chaos, and the immediate effects of the
change were soon felt by the people. One of the
reforms he introduced was in the supply of salt, which
in Russia is a matter of great importance. This was
not nominally a Government monopoly, but the
Government alone was able to supply salt to all parts
of the Empire by obtaining it from the salt marshes
or distilling it from sea-water. Kotchoubey took
steps to reduce the cost of production and of convey-
ance to the lowest possible point, so as to enable the
people to buy salt more cheaply, and the Government
to be repaid its expenses.

The new Finance Minister was Count Vasilieff, a
capable and honest official who had in financial
matters been the right hand of Prince Viaziemskoy,
the only Procurator-General who had been mentioned
with praise at the time of the Empress Catherine.

In the various changes which had taken place since the Prince's death in 1794, M. Vasilieff, as treasurer of the Empire, had been indispensable; he was a steady worker, appreciated new ideas, and adopted them when he thought they were opportune. All the branches of the public revenue, the brandy traffic, the Imperial Bank, etc., were comprised in this department, to which was added the mines department, which had been reorganised on a larger scale.

The functions of Minister of Justice were united to those of Procurator-General of the Senate. General Beklescheff did not wish to stop in this department, as it had been deprived of the greater part of its functions by the creation of the Ministers of the Interior and of Finance; and he was succeeded by the Senator Dzierzanin. He was the personal choice of the Emperor, without communication with the Secret Council. A worthy man, and the writer of some much admired lyrics which were full of owing and passion, he was imperfectly educated and knew no language but Russian. The Emperor had been attracted to him by his ardent sentiments and poetic dreams, not being able to resist fine phrases; the vaguer they were the better they pleased him, as he could then easily assimilate them to his hopes, which also were not very clear. He liked expressions of energetic liberalism, and was especially attracted by admiration of himself when it was couched in the language of devotion to the cause of humanity.

The Emperor had direct and special relations with certain persons whom he himself introduced at our meetings; he liked to patronise them and defend

them against objections raised sometimes by people
who knew them more intimately.   It gave him
pleasure to have these relations without the knowledge of his friends, who already at that time had
begun to displease him because they were so united
among themselves.   Yet it was absolutely necessary
to introduce members of 'the young men's party'
into the administration, for all Alexander's hopes
rested upon them for the zealous continuation and
accomplishment of the reforms he had at heart.
Kotchoubey was provided for, but what was to be
done with the others?   It would be too much to
make them Ministers, and it was accordingly decided
that assistants to the Ministers should be appointed;
in this way the Emperor's friends would be able
to direct their chiefs in accordance with the Emperor's
views, and to keep him fully acquainted with what
was going on.

Count Paul Strogonoff was at his request appointed assistant to the Minister of the Interior, and
Novosiltzoff obtained the post of assistant to the
Minister of Justice, retaining his former appointment
of Secretary to the Emperor.   This gave Novosiltzoff
the most important place in the administration, as it
was through him that the Emperor was to begin the
work of reforming jurisprudence and the existing
laws.   He was well qualified for the task, as he had
studied jurisprudence and political economy in England, and had made good use of the opportunities
thereby afforded him of becoming conversant with
those subjects.   No one in Russia was at that time
his superior in that administrative knowledge which

was then only to be obtained by reading French and English works. His practical mind rejected all vain theories; he possessed skill and tact in dealing not only with individuals, but with the Russian public, which he knew thoroughly. He had bad qualities also; but these had not yet developed themselves. One of his greatest merits was that he seconded Alexander's wishes as to the improvement of the condition of the peasants, and he drew up the first ukase on this subject. He also reconstituted the commission for the revision of the law. This commission had been formed by the Empress Catherine, who thereby gained the flattering appreciation of Voltaire and the Diderots; but the only result was the publication of the philanthropic and philosophical instructions addressed by Catherine to the commission. It was dissolved soon after, and its proceedings were never made public. The new commission was organised by Novosiltzoff with the assistance of a German jurist, Baron Rosenkampf, on a vast and well-conceived plan. It was directed to codify all the existing Russian laws, which were very numerous and often contradicted each other, classifying them according to subjects, omitting such as were obsolete, and adding new ones when necessary, but taking care to retain in the new codes all that had entered for many years into the life of the Russian people, even if not quite reconcilable with the ideas of modern jurisprudence. The system adopted was somewhat similar to that of Justinian; but the task of the Russian codifiers was far more difficult than that of the Roman ones. The latter merely had to select and classify out of a somewhat confused mass of laws, most of which were admirable examples of wisdom and legislative science, while in Russia the laws were not only confused, but in many respects defective and insufficient. For such a work not only jurists, but real legislators were wanted. A similar code was to be prepared for the outlying provinces of the Empire, such as Livonia, Esthonia, Courland, and the Polish provinces of Little Russia, each of which had its own particular language, laws, and customs.

This great undertaking was begun methodically and pursued for some time with activity; Novosiltzoff was allowed by the Minister of Justice to make it his exclusive occupation. The classifications were prepared by Baron Rosenkampf, and so long as they were adhered to the work progressed; but it did not produce the results which were expected of it. This is usually the case in Russia; if there is no immediate result, the persons entrusted with the execution of the work are changed, and it has to be begun over again.

I was the only member of the Secret Council who remained without employment. Alexander offered me, with Count Vorontzoff's concurrence, the post of assistant to the Minister of Foreign Affairs, and all my friends, the Emperor especially, pressed me to accept the offer. I hesitated for a long time, feeling how much surprise and dissatisfaction such an appointment would cause in Russia. The Emperor observed that during my mission to the King of Sardinia I had made myself favourably known by my despatches, and that my nomination to the Foreign Office ought

not therefore to be a matter of astonishment,
besides which Count Vorontzoff, who alone had
a right to be consulted on the subject, had consented
to my becoming his assistant. I replied that he
(the Emperor) knew more than anyone my feelings
with regard to my country; that they could never
change, and that I had some reason to fear that they
might be incompatible with the duties of the appointment he wished to give me; the safest and most
proper course, therefore, would be for me not to accept
it. To this Alexander rejoined that he did not at
present anticipate any such contradiction as that
which I feared; that I should always be at liberty to
give up my post if such a contradiction were to arise;
and that, on the contrary, he thought that events
would occur which would be favourable to my views.
He added some very flattering expressions with regard
to my qualifications for the post. It is every man's
duty, he said, to pay his debt to humanity; when one
has talents one must not refuse to employ them in the
most useful way. I still declined, but Alexander was
bent on my taking the appointment; this was one of
his irresistible fancies which nothing could induce him
to abandon until they were satisfied. His persistence
and kindness to me were such that at length I
yielded, on the express condition that I should
be allowed to resign the appointment directly
its functions should become incompatible with my
feelings as a Pole. My chief object in this was, by
spending some years in the Emperor's service, to
prove to him my sincere attachment and my gratitude for his friendship and confidence. I accepted

with some sadness, as by so doing I was entering on
a new career full of pitfalls which would retain me at
St Petersburg, where I was always like an exotic
plant which could not take root; I felt I could not
enjoy life unless I were with my own people.

I will not pretend that I had more foresight and
prudence than was really the case. In accepting the
post which was offered me, I was determined not to
do anything which might exercise an injurious influence on the destinies of my country; but I had
no clear or decided idea as to the nature of the services I might be called upon to render to Poland in
my new position. In this respect, a substantial bait
was offered me as a reward for having at length yielded
to the Emperor's wishes. He entrusted to me the
direction of the schools in the eight Polish provinces, which at that time constituted the whole
of that portion of Poland which belonged to his
dominions.

The creation of a Ministry of Public Instruction
was　remarkable innovation in Russia which was
fruitful of great and salutary results, and posterity
will owe gratitude both to Alexander and to the
young men, then so much criticised, who supported
him in his plans and gave them practical shape by
dividing into special branches the confused organisation which was then in existence. Nothing could be
more wretched or insufficient than public instruction
in Russia up to the reign of Alexander. There was
an Academy of Sciences at St Petersburg which
owed its only celebrity to the presence of some
learned men whom the Government had brought to

the Russian capital from abroad. Euler came when he was already an old man, and died there soon after The transactions of this Academy were for the most part written in the French and German languages, it had no relations whatever with the country, and exercised no influence on its progress. At Moscow there was a university which was equally isolated, and was attended by not more than a hundred students maintained at the expense of the Government. The only other educational establishments in Russia proper were the so-called 'National Schools.' The teaching in these schools was bad and extremely meagre; the teachers were poor wretches whom idleness and *ennui* had rendered drunkards, and no respectable person sent his children to them. The establishment of the Ministry of Public Instruction completely changed all this. The existing universities of Moscow, Wilna, and Dorpat were better endowed, and three new ones were created those of St Petersburg, Kharkoff, and Kazan,—each forming an educational centre for a prescribed district, in which it directed all the educational arrangements. The University of Wilna was exclusively Polish, and during the next few years the whole of Russian Poland was covered with schools in which Polish feeling freely developed itself. This University, to which I appointed the most distinguished literary and scientific men of the country, and some eminent professors from abroad, directed the movement with admirable zeal and intelligence, and its consequences, which the Russians afterwards deeply regretted, seemed at that time to flow naturally from the Emperor's generous intentions with

regard to the Poles. The University of Kazan was
to look after the instruction of the Tartars and of
Siberia generally. Each university had its curator,
and the curators formed a council of public instruction,
the President of which was the Minister. The
persons appointed to these posts by the Emperor were
such as to give a hope that the work of public instruction would be pushed forward with zeal and success.
General Klinger, commandant of one of the cadet
corps, was appointed curator of Dorpat. He was a
distinguished German author, with liberal opinions
which might almost be called utopian, although he
had been in the service of the greatest despots ; his
intentions, however, were good, and he was full of
zeal for the advancement of science and instruction.
His eccentric and dreamy views were expressed with
a German bluntness which gave him an appearance of
frankness and energy, and all this had gained him
Alexander's favour. Count Severin Potocki was
appointed Curator of the University of Kharkoff,
which was the centre of a district the inhabitants of
which were strongly desirous of obtaining the means
of instruction. Count Severin, as a Pole, had been
treated with great consideration by Alexander when
he was Grand-Duke ; he had been admitted, like my
brother and myself, into his familiar circle, and was
one of his most enthusiastic admirers. The Emperor
appointed him not only curator of Kharkoff, but also
senator of the third department of the Senate, which
issued decisions on appeals against measures taken by
the administrations of the Polish provinces. Count
Severin obtained some celebrity in Russia as a senator,

and in his capacity of curator he showed zeal and perseverance.

The universities which were most progressive were Wilna, Dorpat, and Kharkoff. The nobility of Livonia, Esthonia, and Courland did not look with favour upon the University of Dorpat, which had declared itself the protector of the peasants and the bourgeoisie. One of the professors of this university was named Parot; he was a worthy man who expressed boundless attachment to the Emperor Alexander, and was very anxious about his health. Once Madame Parot sent a waistcoat, woven by herself, which she said would preserve the Emperor's life. Parot begged him to wear it, and by such manifestations of affection he gained Alexander's favour, and had private conferences with him during his frequent journeys to St Petersburg. The Curator of Moscow was M. de Mouravieff, one of the gentlemen formerly attached to Alexander's service when he was Grand-Duke, and also his former secretary. He was a worthy man, but excessively timid and quite devoid of energy. The Emperor appointed him assistant to the Minister of Instruction in order that it should not be said that young men only performed the duties of assistant, and that these posts were created only for the members of the Secret Council. Novosiltzoff was appointed Curator of St Petersburg. As there was already in that capital a faculty of medicine dependent on the Ministry of the Interior, and a faculty of law could not be established before the commission for the revision of the laws had terminated its labours, Novosiltzoff for the present confined himself to establishing a faculty of philosophy, with the special object of training professors of the exact sciences, of administration, and of literature, This faculty began brilliantly by turning out some distinguished pupils, but they did not afterwards realise the hopes that had been formed of them, and the institution perished without leaving any durable results. A university with privileges and endowments would have better maintained itself, as was shown by the universities of Moscow and Kharkoff, which, though they declined, were still active in the midst of the indifference and oblivion by which they were long surrounded.

Count Zavadovsky was appointed Minister of Public Instruction. He had been secretary to Count Romantzoff at the same time as Prince Bezborodko, and they had remained friends ever since. Count Romantzoff had presented them both as secretaries to the Empress Catherine, and this was the origin of their brilliant fortunes. Bezborodko, to whom I have already referred, soon rose by his great capacity for work ; he enjoyed the confidence of his sovereign and attained to the highest dignities. Zavadovsky's success was obtained by other means. The Empress made him her favourite ; he became attached to her and was very unhappy when after six months had elapsed he was dismissed. His friends Bezborodko and Vorontzoff endeavoured to console him, and the presents which Catherine always lavished on a dismissed favourite were in his case richer than usual, as she recognised in him other merits than those which had merely attracted her fancy. He afterwards married, and continued to be well received at Court. His friendship with Vorontzoff, and the reputation for writing pure Russian which he had gained by certain manifestoes that he had written for the Empress Catherine, obtained him the post of Minister of Instruction. He was a man of just and benevolent character, but of somewhat stolid mind. He was not quick of intelligence, and did not perceive shades of meaning, while at the same time he wished to understand new ideas, and not to be reckoned among those who could neither learn nor forget anything. Yet he possessed in a high degree one of the most marked traits of a Russian administrator— profound submission to everything that comes from superior authority. He was enthusiastic in his admiration of classic writers and was fond of quoting the passages he remembered. The literature of his own country also greatly interested him. By a singular accident he had learnt Latin in one of the Polish schools managed by the Jesuits; he had not forgotten his Polish, and he prided himself on his knowledge of that language, speaking with much admiration of our ancient poet John Kochanowski,* some fragments of whose poems he knew by heart. All this gave him a certain predilection for Poland and the Poles; as was shown even at his dinners, which always consisted of Polish dishes.

While the other curators were often overruled in their projects by the Minister, who was not always disposed to yield to ideas of reform and progress, I never had to complain on this score. Vorontzoff

* Born 1530. Died 1584.

always trusted me implicitly, and he was always most kind in supporting every proposal I made. I owe him much gratitude for the condescension, the frankness, and the friendly feeling with which he always treated me.

CHAPTER XIII

1803-4

DIFFERENCES WITH SWEDEN.—THE CHANCELLOR VORONTZOFF'S POLICY.
—THE FOREIGN AMBASSADORS—AUSTRIA, PRUSSIA, ENGLAND,
FRANCE, AND SWEDEN.—ALEXANDER'S PROFESSED LIBERALISM
PUT TO THE TEST.—HIS FOREIGN POLICY AND THAT OF NAPO-
LEON.—PRINCE CZARTORYSKI BECOMES UNPOPULAR AT COURT.—
A DUEL.—THE CHANCELLOR'S ILLNESS.—NAPOLEON AND THE
RUSSIAN AMBASSADOR.

DIRECTLY after my appointment I was admitted to all
the Chancellor's Conferences with the Foreign Ministers, and I drew up the protocols which he took to
the Emperor. I did this work with much care, and
to his satisfaction. A well-written protocol often
gives precision and clearness to a desultory conversation. Vorontzoff was satisfied with what I made him
say, as it expressed what he thought, though in a more
complete manner than he had himself done; I had
guessed his intentions, and this greatly pleased him.
The practice I thus gained was very useful to me, and
the conferences at which I was present enabled me to
be fully informed of the relations of Russia with
Foreign Governments. It was also my duty to draw
up the despatches which resulted from these conferences, and the Emperor's rescripts to his Ministers

abroad. Having accepted these functions, I threw myself heartily into the work. I sometimes wrote incessantly for eight or nine hours at a time. This produced a sort of nervous disorder which Dr Rogerson said might have serious consequences; but I was young, and did not pay any attention to his counsels. Later on I had reason to regret that I did not do so.

The policy of Russia was in essence the same under Vorontzoff as it had been under Kotchoubey; but it became stronger and more dignified in form. Its leading principle, which was well adapted to Alexander's character and projects, was to be on good terms with all the world, and not to interfere in European affairs, in order to avoid being carried too far; in a word, carefully to avoid difficulties without appearing to fear them. The principle was not changed; it was only the way of carrying it out that was different. The Russian Cabinet assumed a tone of hauteur which deceived people as to its true policy, and somewhat reminded one of the spirit of Catherine's diplomacy. The Chancellor was very careful to avoid any quarrel, or even slight estrangement, with any of the great Powers; but he was not sorry when an opportunity presented itself to frighten the weak ones and crush them under the weight of Russian power. This is what happened with Sweden. The two Governments had a difference as to the possession of a wretched little island in a river which at that time separated Finland proper from the Russian province of that name. The point at issue was on which branch of the river was to be the bridge constituting the frontier. This question had been pending for some time, and the Chancellor resolved to cut the knot. He addressed Sweden in a dry and imperious tone, and I was very glad that I was not asked to write the despatches on this matter, which were in Russian; my abstinence afterwards obtained for me proofs of confidence on the part of the King of Sweden and his Government. At the same time Russia seemed to prepare for a rupture, and Russian generals were sent to inspect the Swedish frontier. The Emperor himself went there, and I accompanied him with Strogonoff and Novosiltzoff.

We passed along the greater part of the frontier on horseback. The soil mostly consists of a slight layer of earth on a substratum of granite, and there is some extraordinary scenery, with magnificent water-falls, but the country was not populous, and we often had to sleep in thinly scattered villages, at the houses of the clergy, some of whom knew no other language than the Finnish. The villages and parsonages were surrounded by meadows, but the general appearance of the country was melancholy and arid. I refer here only to the portion of Finland which at that time belonged to Russia, as other portions are rich and abound in corn. Beyond the town of Abo the country looked more cultivated, and the people seemed more prosperous. We visited the disputed island, and the fortress and harbour in its vicinity, which in case of war were to form the basis of our operations. General Suchtelen, then commander of the engineers, and afterwards Russian Minister in Sweden, was having some works constructed in this fortress according to a new system of his own invention; it was more simple, he said, than those of Vauban and Coëhorn, which it combined and made more effective.

The King of Sweden was very obstinate in his resistance to the demands we had made in so imperious a tone. Count Stedingk, the Swedish Ambassador at St Petersburg, often expressed to me his astonishment on this subject, and shrugged his shoulders in speaking of the offensive way in which Russia dealt with a matter which in reality was quite unimportant. Sweden resisted for a long time, and we continued preparations for war. She had to give way at last, but the conditions imposed upon her were insignificant, and Sweden could not be mad enough to make war on account of them. The Chancellor was very proud of his victory, but it might easily have been obtained without humiliating Sweden—which I think would have been preferable. The conduct of Russia left a bitter feeling in the mind of a neighbour which had already been often ill-treated, and which, notwithstanding its relative weakness, might on occasion do much harm. But Vorontzoff knew Russia, or at least those who spoke in her name. He knew that every demonstration of power, even if unjust, pleases the Russians; that to domineer, to command, to crush is a necessity of their national pride. Not being able to overcome the strong, the Chancellor attacked the weak, hoping thereby to bring into prominence the young Emperor's government. I am convinced that this was one of the motives which induced him loudly to proclaim his pretended victory over Sweden; but the Russian public was not deceived. There was at that time in the two capitals among the civil officials and in the army—the class which afterwards formed the elements of public opinion—a vague desire of improvement, or rather of events which should be more interesting, more profitable, and especially more flattering to their vanity. It must be admitted that the Emperor Alexander did not at that time have public opinion on his side, and this was indeed but seldom the case during the whole of his reign. At that period especially his conduct was too natural, his views too pure and too much in conformity with the welfare of the great majority of his subjects, to be appreciated by a country whose upper classes had tasted of a corrupt civilisation and had been excessively indulged in their avidity and vanity. The goodness, the kindness, and the pure intentions of Alexander as he then was did not suffice to make him popular. Notwithstanding all the Chancellor's efforts, no great satisfaction was expressed at the advantage gained by him over an adversary of such little importance as Sweden ; on the contrary, the old Minister was reproached for attempting to throw dust in the eyes of the public and take advantage of its vanity.

Count Sauvan was then the Austrian Ambassador ; he used always to come to the Chancellor in full dress, and conferred with him in a very solemn manner. The policy of Austria was at that time lachrymose and sentimental. The peace of Lunéville had only lately been signed,* and the Vienna Cabinet sought for consolation. Russia did not reject its mournful

* On the 29th of February, 1801.

representations, but only replied by assurances of interest and good-will which meant nothing. Prussia was represented by Count Goltz; the only qualities which had obtained him advancement were a good memory, a knowledge of routine, and a kind heart, and he was completely under the domination of his wife, remarkable for a somewhat noisy and brusque vivacity. When Prussia, perfidiously violating the treaties of the past ten years, took her share of the plunder of Poland, he succeeded M. Lucchesini as Ambassador at Vienna. He treated me with a deference which betrayed a feeling of regret, almost of shame, at the conduct of his Government towards my country. His predecessor at St Petersburg was M. Tauentzien, afterwards known as one of the ablest of the Prussian generals. While my mother was at Berlin on the occasion of my sister's marriage with the Prince of Würtemberg, he was an officer of the Guards, and often came to her house, where he was deeply smitten by Mdlle. Constance Narbutt (afterwards Madame Denbowska). She refused his offer of marriage, but the only result was that during his stay at St Petersburg he often asked me and my brother to dinner. The relations of Russia with Prussia were purely personal between the two sovereigns, as there was no sympathy between the Cabinets, the armies, or the people of the two States. Prussia's equivocal conduct, her base submission to France, and the acquisitions which she obtained by it, were much disapproved by the Russians, who did not spare their sarcasms on the subject. The Emperor, however, remained faithful to his friendship with the King, and to the high opinion he had formed of the Prussian army. This perseverance, which was often blamed at St Petersburg, was nevertheless of great advantage to Russia, as she managed thereby to attract Prussia to her side and make her a sort of satellite.

England had just concluded the peace of Amiens. Her ambassador at St Petersburg was Sir John Warren, an excellent admiral, but an indifferent diplomatist. He was a perfect representative of the nullity and incapacity of the Addington Ministry which had appointed him. In those days the English Government was seldom happy in its choice of ambassadors. The diplomatic service, though much sought after, contained few able men; the most important posts were given by favour or through party arrangements, either to satisfy some supporter of the Ministry or to obtain a few more votes in the House of Commons. Other promotions were entirely by seniority; want of knowledge or of intelligence was no disqualification. It was generally remarked at that time that there was neither ability nor zeal among the great majority of English diplomatists. All this is entirely changed; the English diplomatists are now among the ablest in Europe.

General Hédouville represented France. He had obtained a reputation as a General by his pacification of La Vendée, but he did not seem very likely to sustain the reputation of French diplomacy, whose cleverness and general ability seemed even to increase under the Consulate and the Ministry of Talleyrand. In selecting a Minister so benevolent and quiet, not to say tedious, in manner and conversation, the French

Government probably intended to reassure and tranquillise those whose friendship it wished to gain. He represented one of those dead calms which in diplomacy follow or precede a storm.

There was nothing important or even interesting in the relations of Russia with the other great Powers; they reduced themselves, so far as I remember, to an exchange of rounded phrases the drift of which was: 'Let us be quiet and avoid all embarrassments and conflicts.' This feeling was shared even by the Governments which had suffered from the peace; they would have been glad to strike another blow in the hope of regaining what they had lost, but they did not dare to confess it. Even England did not expect a speedy rupture. Austria groaned only in secret, and when she thought she could complain without compromising herself; while Prussia congratulated herself on her constant neutrality and looked upon it as a source of prosperity and progress. France, too, seemed to have turned all her attention to internal affairs. The First Consul was organising the administration and the laws of the country; but all eyes were still turned to this vigorous sap which could not long be satisfied with the immense territories it had already fertilised. All continental Europe feared France, while Russia, although she was both pacific and inoffensive, assumed a tone which denoted a consciousness of equal power and a feeling of independence. The relations of the Chancellor with General Hédouville showed a friendliness based on mutual consideration. A convention of no great significance was concluded, and the Chancellor took the opportunity of offering to the French Minister the usual present of 4000 ducats and a gold snuff box adorned with diamonds and the Emperor's portrait. The Chancellor was ill, and received the Ambassador in bed while the ratifications were being exchanged. The presents were laid out on the bed, and I never saw a face so beam with pleasure as did the General's when he saw the bags of ducats. Forgetting all decorum and the little speech he should have delivered on the Emperor's portrait, his eyes were fixed on the money-bags, and he carried them away with an expression of delight which was quite comic. He was a very worthy man, however, and everyone would have been glad to see him so happy if he had been a little more dignified in showing his joy.

Among the members of the diplomatic body the most remarkable was Baron Stedingk, the Swedish Ambassador. He was distinguished both by his wisdom and by his noble sentiments; with a simple exterior, his conduct also was marked by simplicity, by tact, and by perfect loyalty, and was strictly honourable in the highest sense of the word. He had that rare perspicacity which always appreciates both men and events at their true value. In his youth he had served with distinction against the English in the American war, and had been decorated with the cross of St Louis, which, being a Protestant, he wore with a blue ribbon. Afterwards, being honoured with the confidence of Gustavus III, he distinguished himself at the head of the army corps which fought the Russians in 1789 and 1790. When peace was signed he was appointed Ambassador at the Court of St Petersburg, where he was already known by his military successes. He remained at this post during three consecutive reigns, serving his country in the most difficult emergencies, without ever losing any of the high consideration he had acquired. Of all the men I ever met he seemed to me one of the best and the most worthy of confidence; he was a man whom one could not help liking, and whom one would wish always to have for a friend. I think he was mine, so far as he could be in view of our different positions, which afterwards entirely separated us. As second in the Ministry, I was not obliged to take an active part in the difficulty which had arisen between Russia and Sweden, and the Chancellor wished to conduct the matter himself in order to gain the merit of having brought it to a triumphant conclusion. His insulting affectation of superiority, and the way in which he deprived a weaker power of a worthless island which was only taken to humiliate her, inspired me with profound repugnance, and, as I have already remarked, this gained for me marks of gratitude and confidence from the Swedes.

The progress of internal reform in Russia was abruptly stopped by an unexpected incident. Count Severin Potocki, who, as I said above, was a great admirer of the Emperor, often addressed memoranda to him on various subjects. The Senate had received from the Emperor, among other important prerogatives, the right of making representations to him, but it had hitherto not made any use of this right. Count Severin naturally thought the Emperor was sincere

in his liberal opinions; the Emperor himself thought
so; and the Count therefore imagined it would be a
good thing, and would please his Imperial master, if
the Senate were prompted to exercise its prerogatives. For this an opportunity soon presented itself.
Although almost every noble in Russia entered the
army, he was not obliged to do so, and could leave
it when he thought proper. This double privilege
was granted by Peter III in an ukase for which
many blessed his memory. Alexander, however,
restricted the privilege to nobles who held the rank of
officer; those below that rank were obliged to serve
for twelve years. This was looked upon as an attack
on the guaranteed rights of the nobility, and produced a deep and painful sensation. The Minister of
War, an old military bureaucrat of low origin, was said
to be the author of the new ukase, and Count Severin
Potocki proposed to the Senate that it should address
representations to the Emperor on this violation of
the nobles' charter. His proposal was read to the
general assembly of all the departments, and the
senators, seeing that one of the confidential advisers
of the Court was taking the initiative in the matter,
and that his opinion was warmly supported by Count
Strogonoff, thought they could safely vote in its favour.
They gladly did this, under the impression that by so
doing they could without danger assume an air of
independence in a matter to which it was believed the
Emperor did not attach any serious importance.
Count Severin's proposal was adopted, notwithstanding the opposition of the Procurator-General (Minister
of Justice), which was supposed to be feigned in order

to give more appearance of reality to the little scene which it was believed had been got up for the occasion. Count Strogonoff, who was deputed with two other senators to take the representations of the Senate to the Emperor, readily set out on his mission; but the deputation was received by Alexander very coldly, and Strogonoff, disconcerted and not knowing what to say, withdrew. The Emperor sharply reprimanded the Senate, ordered it not to meddle with things which did not concern it, and directed it by a new decree to carry out the very ukase against which it had appealed. To my great astonishment it was Novosiltzoff who was the agent of the Emperor's unjust anger in this matter. This failure of the first move of the Senate in the direction of liberalism sufficed to discourage people whose generous aspirations were not, it must be admitted, very strong. The Senate did not again attempt any independent action, and its rights became a dead letter. At my first interview with the Emperor after this incident, I could not help smiling at his extreme alarm in presence of the new attitude of the Senate. My jocular remarks on this point were ill received by Alexander, and I believe they left in his mind a certain anxiety as to my liberal tendencies which afterwards came back to him. This was an indication of Alexander's true character, which then appeared to me in a novel and unfortunately too real light. Grand ideas of the general good, generous sentiments, and the desire to sacrifice to them part of the Imperial authority, and resign an immense and arbitrary power in order the better to secure the future happiness of

the people, had really occupied the Emperor's mind
and did so still, but they were rather a young man's
fancies than a grown man's decided will. The
Emperor liked forms of liberty as he liked the
theatre ; it gave him pleasure and flattered his vanity
to see the appearances of free government in his
Empire ; but all he wanted in this respect was forms
and appearances ; he did not expect them to become
realities. In a word, he would willingly have agreed
that every man should be free, on the condition that
he should voluntarily do only what the Emperor
wished.

Alexander never forgot Count Severin's indiscretion ; he was still received at Court on the same
footing as heretofore, but he no longer shared the
confidence and favour of his sovereign. The incident
gained him great credit at Moscow and in the ancient
provinces of the Empire, where he was regarded as a
true Russian patriot and a generous defendor of the
immunities of the nobility. This wave of popularity
had so much charm for the Count that it made him
forget his old Polish sentiments. In his youth, at
the diet of the 3rd of May, he had been an ardent
Polish patriot ; in his old age he forgot his country,
thought only of augmenting his fortune and living
pleasantly, and amused himself by opposing the
Russian Government. He got into the habit of travelling continually between his estates and the Senate,
reading much on the journey, and preparing the
speeches which he made every year either at Moscow
or at St Petersburg. His mind tended rather towards
doubt than action ; he seldom expressed any positive

opinion, and sentiment did not in any way affect his decisions, which were invariably prompted by considerations of personal interest. His self-love was greater than his fear, which could not indeed be very great, as Alexander, at that time especially, never persecuted anybody, and his displeasure could be incurred without danger. Count Severin retained as long as he liked his appointments of senator and curator, which gave him a circle of activity that pleased him. He was able and well informed, but made light of everything except what touched his material interests, and had no religious sentiments whatever. Such a man was destined to end his days without friends or sympathy. I did not see him again. Alexander had given him the use of a considerable estate for fifty years; I had done my best to arrange the matter, and later on I did some service to his son Leo. All this established a reciprocity of good feeling between us which lasted as long as I was in Russia, and afterwards gradually died out.

If it had been in the nature of man to be satisfied with what is practicable, Alexander ought to have satisfied the Russians, for he gave them a tranquillity, a prosperity, and even a degree of liberty which were unknown before his reign. But the Russians wanted something else. Like the gambler who seeks violent emotions, they were tired of the monotony of their prosperity. They did not like their young Emperor: he was too simple in his manners, too averse to pomp, too disdainful of etiquette. The Russians regretted the brilliant Court of Catherine and its abuses, the opening which it gave to so many passions, struggles,

intrigues and successes. They regretted the days of
the Imperial favourites, and the possibility of gaining
colossal positions and fortunes like those of Orloff and
Potemkin. The courtiers had no ante-chambers to go
to, and sought in vain for an idol before which they could
burn their incense; their platitude was condemned
to inaction, and there was no one to whom they could
cringe and bow. The grumblers at Moscow, too, did
not like the Court because it no longer afforded food
for their censure, while it did not offer them any of
the advantages which they valued. Their liberalism,
moreover, was very different from that of the Emperor
Alexander; he inclined rather to the democratic and
levelling ideas of the Emperor Joseph of Austria,
though in a milder form.

Only the Empress Dowager attempted to maintain the customs and the brilliancy of the old Court.
Alexander's Court was of an exaggerated simplicity,
totally devoid of etiquette, and he met his courtiers only
on intimate and familiar terms. The Emperor and his
family only appeared in full dress on Sundays and
holidays, when they went to church. Dinners and
soirées were mostly given in the private apartments,
and were quite different from what they had been in the
preceding reigns. Later on, Alexander became more
sumptuous in his receptions, but at the beginning of
his reign he was not sufficiently so. While Napoleon
surrounded himself with a pomp and ceremonial revived from the times of the monarchy, Alexander
liked to eclipse himself and to behave like an ordinary
citizen. His friends found fault with him for this—
especially the Margravine of Baden, his mother-in-

law, who wanted to give the young Emperor every possible quality and success. She endeavoured to stimulate him by the example of Napoleon, but in vain. The two Emperors went in opposite directions in everything; one demolished, while the other restored, old ideas; and the comparison made between them was not to Alexander's advantage in the eyes of the very Russians for whom he was working. He was, in fact, not at all popular during the first few years of his reign, although he was never more devoted than he was then to the good of his country. But men want to be dominated and fooled, and this necessity is nowhere so much felt as in Russia. At the beginning of his reign, Alexander did not know how to do this; he learnt it later, but even then, and notwithstanding his great success, he never attained the popularity and the moral power of his grandmother, who could have said of the Russians, as Buonaparte said of the French, that they were in her pocket.

The Emperor had made it a maxim to respect other people's opinions, and not to punish anybody for expressing them, so that no great courage was required to criticise the sovereign and tell him unpleasant truths. Full advantage was taken of this privilege, especially in the salons of the two capitals. Everything that the Government did was found fault with, and these criticisms, growing like the waves of a heavy sea, used in the same way to subside and grow again at the least breath of wind. Such was the constant state of opinion in Russia during the first year of Alexander's reign. The old courtiers used to say, in order to calm the anxiety of the young ones, that all new reigns began in the same way, and that the first years of the reign of Catherine were marked by the same pre-occupations. What people most objected to, however, in the case of Alexander, was my presence at his Court, and my appointment as assistant to the Minister of Foreign Affairs. A merely honorary title would not have shocked the Russians, but they could not accustom themselves to see me at the head of the department : a Pole enjoying the confidence of the Emperor, and initiated into all the secrets of State, was to them an intolerable innovation.*

This was a fertile subject of suspicion and calumny in the Russian salons. My parents had always been averse to Russian influence, and their fortune had been confiscated on account of their participation in Polish revolutions. That their son, who had never concealed his enthusiastic devotion to his country's cause, who had often loudly proclaimed it, and proved it by the national spirit in which he promoted public instruction in the Polish provinces, should be the intimate and confidential adviser of the sovereign, was naturally the subject of much comment. It was easy to imagine that I betrayed the interests of Russia, and that I would at any moment prove false to my duties as a Minister and a friend in order to advance the cause of Poland. All the ambitious men who thought themselves more worthy of the Emperor's confidence than a stranger—all the young men of

* 'Prince Czartoryski,' says Lord Whitworth in a despatch to Lord Hawkesbury (in the Record Office), dated January 4, 1803, 'for some years past the intimate and most confidential friend of the present Emperor of Russia, . . . is now second in point of precedency, but perhaps first in point of influence, in the Foreign Department.'

Alexander's Court—-were agreed on this point. But
their suspicions were unfounded. I do not think I
have ever been more zealous and devoted than I was
in the Emperor's service. He knew better than anyone my attachment to my country, and it was this
knowledge which was the first basis of our intimate
relations and the source of the esteem and friendship
with which he honoured me. He did not at that
time think that the welfare of Russia was really
incompatible with that of Poland. Perhaps he did
not have a very clear idea of that grave question, and
as its solution appeared distant, he did not think it
necessary to go very deeply into it. Meanwhile he
accepted the services which I cordially rendered him,
and he thought it just and proper to reward them by
giving me a certain liberty of action in regard to the
Polish provinces under his rule. I of course availed
myself of this concession; I reorganised public instruction in Poland on a larger and more national
basis, and made it more conformable with modern
ideas. The Russians could not understand my relations with Alexander, and indeed they were only to
be explained by the fact that we were both very young
and had become friends at an age when generous
impulses are stronger than reflection. The Russians,
however, attributed our connection to personal ambition and dissimulation on my part and silly good-
nature on that of Alexander. They imagined that I
secretly favoured France, and that I wished to bring
Alexander under the fascination of Buonaparte's genius.
It was to my influence that they ascribed the somewhat colourless policy adopted by the Emperor in

European politics, which they thought arose from my connivance with France. This was also the Empress Dowager's opinion, and she propagated it among the young officers of the army.

My position was not an easy one. The part played by Russia was certainly not so brilliant or preponderant as might have been desirable, and was not at all in accordance with Russian vanity or Russian pretensions. Alexander was eclipsed by Napoleon, who, at the pinnacle of military glory, introduced into diplomacy, hitherto so discreet, that bluntness and rapidity of decision which were the secrets of his success on the battlefield. He took the initiative in every European question, and daily gained ground, increased his preponderance, and showed that he intended to become the arbiter of Europe. I constantly heard Russians complain of the weakness and want of dignity of their Cabinet ; and if I had ascribed these faults to Alexander's character and opinions, I would have cast the whole blame upon him. Among the most active and ambitious of the malcontents was the young Prince Dolgorouky. He was the prime mover of the Russian party, and his passionate vexation at seeing a stranger occupy a post which he considered should have been given to him made him witty, much to the surprise of his friends. Being one of the Emperor's aides-de-camp, he was continually at Court, and I often met him, on which occasions he used to pursue me with reproaches and sarcasms on the indolence of the Russian Foreign Office. He provoked me so far that I once told him he should address his remarks to the Chancellor, who was the head of the department. He replied that he knew well there was an understanding between the Chancellor and myself to refer matters from one to the other in order to avoid the difficulty of a precise answer. The discussion almost became a quarrel, and the Emperor had to interfere to put a stop to Dolgorouky's remarks. We no longer spoke to each other, but he continued his intrigues with more animosity than ever. Under the reign of Paul we had been on very good terms, and he had shown me much confidence in an affair of honour which he had with M. de Wintzingerode, a worthy German, very stiff and punctilious. Having quarrelled with Dolgorouky, he challenged him, and both agreed to take me as the only witness of the duel. The scene of the encounter was a garden, and I loaded the pistols and placed the adversaries in such a way as to make it exceedingly difficult for them to hit each other. The result was that both missed, and the incident was closed by a complete reconciliation.

The Chancellor's health now began to break down. He was several times seriously ill, and he often thought of temporarily retiring to his estates near Moscow, though he had no wish to withdraw from political life altogether. One day when he was ill I was seated by his bed; he was in a high fever, and speaking with much animation, though somewhat delirious, he said several times: 'These young men wish to govern everything, but I will not allow it; I alone will remain at the head of affairs.' I thought it probable that some one had led him to suspect those

who were called the Emperor's friends; perhaps these
suspicions had spontaneously arisen in his mind. I
am convinced, however, that he never distrusted me,
or listened to the insinuations which people made
against me. The extreme and entire confidence which
he showed me lasted to the end of his life, which is
surprising, as so many people had an interest in
making us quarrel. He gave his confidence and
friendship to very few people; his sentiments were
delicate and noble, and although they were not based
on strict principle, they showed that he was kind-
hearted and sensitive. Always inclined to render a
service, he judged others with great indulgence, and
even at times when he spoke his mind most freely, I
have never detected in him any feeling of hatred or
desire for revenge. The Emperor, however, had an
invincible dislike for him, which increased every day.
His somewhat old-fashioned manners, his voice, his
deliberate way of speaking, even his gestures, were
antipathetic to him. During his frequent attacks of
illness, the Chancellor used to send me with his papers
to the Emperor, and the latter expressed his joy at
not being obliged to see him. In spite of all I said in
his behalf, he used to ridicule the old Minister, and
often told me he would like to be rid of him. I was
at this time in high favour with the Emperor, and he
spoke with marked approval of my drafts of despatches
and rescripts. He in no way opposed the Chancellor's
wish for rest; on the contrary, he encouraged it in
every way.

The friendly relations which had hitherto existed
between Russia and France began about this time to

be disturbed. Count Markoff, supposed to be the ablest man in Russia, and the prototype and almost the last living representative of the diplomacy of Catherine, had been sent as Ambassador to Paris. When Paul became Emperor Markoff fell into disgrace, and was banished to Podolia, on one of my father's confiscated estates. After Alexander's accession he hastened back to the capital, and Count Panin, who was then Foreign Minister, fearing in him a dangerous rival, decided to send him on a mission abroad. The most important task in foreign affairs was at that time the renewal of friendly relations with France, and for this it was necessary to send Napoleon an Ambassador capable of controlling and restraining his policy, and sustaining the dignity of Russia. Markoff, who was selected for this post, accepted it with eagerness, for he knew Alexander did not like him, and he was pleased at the idea of playing an important part in a capital where Napoleon and other personages already celebrated were influencing the destinies of the world. He did not, however, justify his reputation,* which had already been impaired by his extraordinary want of tact in the affair of the proposed marriage of the King of Sweden with the Grand Duchess Alexandra, which was the cause of Catherine's death. Notwithstanding his aversion for Napoleon and his Ministers, Markoff did not succeed in preventing the dismemberment of Germany to compensate the princes who had lost part of their

---

* Lord Whitworth, then English Ambassador in Paris, says of him : 'He has not the talent of inspiring confidence, and indeed his conduct here is such as to render any confidential intercourse with him extremely dangerous.' (Despatch to Lord Hawkesbury of November 16, 1802, in the Record office).

dominions, and to indulge the avidity of Prussia. The
Convention was sent to the Emperor for his approval
after it had been concluded, and when it was too late
to make any change in it. A more favourable result
would no doubt have been difficult to obtain, but
Markoff did not even attempt to do so; he did not
give the Cabinet of St Petersburg the necessary
time to state and defend its opinions, and compelled
it to accept the Convention like a child forced to obey
orders. He was a creature of the Zuboffs, and he
had voted with them for the partition of Poland; he
was the incarnation of an unscrupulous State policy
and a diplomacy without justice or pity; very extravagant, he was inflexible in money affairs, and though
fond of presents, he would not take them if by so
doing his pride would suffer. His face, seamed with
the smallpox, constantly expressed irony and scorn;
his round eyes and his mouth, depressed at the corners,
resembled those of a tiger. Though he had adopted
the language and the grand airs of the Court of
Versailles, his manners were haughty and rude. He
spoke excellent French, but what he said was generally harsh, trenchant, disagreeable, and totally devoid
of feeling.

Such was the pearl of Russian diplomatists sent
to Napoleon by Russia in evidence of her desire
to be on good terms with him. He was at first
received with much distinction, and he satisfied the
First Consul by his complaisance in the matter of the
indemnities; but after a time his scornful manner and
his sarcasms irritated Napoleon and gave rise to
violent scenes. One evening the latter looked about

for a Pole to give him an opportunity of venting his bile on the Russian Ambassador, thinking this would be the best way of mortally offending him. Seeing M. Z. . ., a stupid and insignificant personage who happened to be present, he took him by the button of his coat, moved him forward into the middle of the room, and after asking him whether he was a Pole, violently condemned the partition of Poland and the Powers which had committed and allowed it, after which he left without taking any notice of Markoff. Shortly after, the French Government sent a despatch to St Petersburg complaining of Markoff's conduct; but the Chancellor, feeling the necessity of demonstratively asserting the dignity of Russia, proposed to the Emperor that Markoff should be invested with the ribbon of St Andrew, which he had long desired. The Emperor entirely approved of this proposal, and Markoff appeared at his next audience of Napoleon decorated with the order, and looking more proud and satisfied than ever. This time the First Consul had not the laugh on his side; but Markoff did not think it right to remain in Paris after his triumph, and he was recalled at his own request.

MEMOIRS OF PRINCE ADAM CZARTORYSKI

VOLUME II

PRINCESS ELIZABETH CZARTORYSKA.
(Mother of Prince Adam.)

Copied from an old Miniature.

MEMOIRS

OF

PRINCE ADAM

CZARTORYSKI

AND HIS

Correspondence with Alexander I.

WITH

DOCUMENTS RELATIVE TO THE PRINCE'S NEGOTIATIONS WITH PITT,
FOX, AND BROUGHAM, AND AN ACCOUNT OF HIS CONVERSA-
TIONS WITH LORD PALMERSTON AND OTHER ENGLISH
STATESMEN IN LONDON IN 1832

EDITED BY

ADAM GIELGUD

TWO VOLUMES
WITH PORTRAITS

VOL. II

[An Alphabetical Index to this work will be found at end of this Volume.]

Contents

CHAPTER IV

1804

CHAPTER V

1804

CHAPTER VI

1804-5

CHAPTER VII

1805

CHAPTER VIII

1805

CONTENTS

CHAPTER IX

1805

CHAPTER X

1805

CHAPTER XI

1806

CHAPTER XII

1806

CHAPTER XIII

1806

CHAPTER XIV

1806

CHAPTER V

1806

CHAPTER XVI

1806

CHAPTER XVII

1809-10

CHAPTER XVIII

1810

CHAPTER XIX

1810-12

CHAPTER XX

1813

CHAPTER XXI

1813-14

CHAPTER XXII

1814-15

CHAPTER XXIII

1815

CHAPTER XXIV

1815-22

CHAPTER XXV

1831-2

CHAPTER XXVI

1834

CHAPTER XXVII

1839

CHAPTER XXVIII

CHAPTER XXIX

1853-5

CHAPTER XXX

1855-61

Memoirs of Prince Adam Czartoryski

✦—oo—✦

CHAPTER I

1804-5

PRINCE CZARTORYSKI APPOINTED FOREIGN MINISTER.—THE RUSSIAN
AMBASSADORS.—PETER THE GREAT'S FOREIGN POLICY.—PROPOSALS
AS TO THE EMANCIPATION OF SUBJECT NATIONALITIES.—SYSTEM OF
GENERAL EUROPEAN POLICY.

I now come to one of the most important epochs of
my life. Taking advantage of the Chancellor's wish
for temporary retirement, the Emperor took steps to
make it virtually permanent, being desirous of giving
over to me the complete direction of the department
of Foreign Affairs. This was one of his hobbies, and
he did not rest until he had satisfied it. The Chancellor had announced that his health obliged him to
take some rest. It was necessary to replace him, and
I asked him whom he would like to be his successor.
'You, of course,' he said; 'that would be in the regular
order of things, and could not be otherwise.' I have
already said that this was also the positive and pressing
wish of the Emperor. What could I do? Was I to
accept so difficult and dangerous a post? Should I

not rather give up everything and retire? But to retire at such a moment would have been to prove that I did not feel equal to the difficulties of the task offered to me. By remaining assistant to the Minister I had not gained anything, and if I became Minister I should not be more exposed to suspicion and calumny than before. But what most contributed to tranquillise my conscience was the thought that I might inaugurate a system of policy which, being based on equitable principles, might ultimately have a good influence on the destinies of Poland. I foresaw a rupture with France; the establishment of intimate relations between that power and Russia, which the Russians accused me of projecting, was far from my thoughts, for it was evident to me that any understanding between the two empires could only be fatal to Polish interests. Moreover, I was pressed on all sides to accept the Ministerial portfolio. The Emperor would not listen to any objection, and the young men who were my colleagues did not want our relations to be broken off by my retreat. Even the old Chancellor urged me to accept the post. He left it firmly persuaded that he would come back, but before the end of the year the state of his health, and perhaps the charms of a quiet life, made him change his views; he wrote to me that he had decided to quit the active service, but that he would not yet ask to be pensioned, as he feared to abandon me to the intrigues to which his absence would expose me. On leaving the capital he told me that when he came back he would keep open house, as was fitting for a Chancellor, although hitherto he had never invited any of the members of the diplomatic body. In leaving me in his place he was sure that he would be heartily received on his return, and he supported me with all the influence he possessed in the Government offices and in the Senate; he had none over the general public. He promised me to write often and give me his advice. We entered into a very voluminous correspondence, which touched me much on account of the friendship it showed, but which I soon could not follow or even read with attention, as my whole time was absorbed in public business.

I accepted the post of Foreign Minister, and the Emperor was as glad as a child; but the young Russian party did not conceal its anger and excitement. Even the Empress thought that I had some malevolent intention, or at least that I was wanting in delicacy towards the Emperor in accepting so confidential an appointment in the teeth of the general opinion (so at least she thought) and in spite of the conviction that I would thereby deprive the Emperor of the affection of his people. She now absolutely ignored me; this lasted more than a year, and did not cease until after Austerlitz. It will be seen that I had powerful adversaries; but having made my decision, I did not flinch, and only thought how to acquit myself of my task in the best possible way.

It so happened that just at the time when I was appointed Foreign Minister several important Russian diplomatists were at St Petersburg. I have already alluded to Count Markoff, who, when the Chancellor

retired, was more determined than ever to quit the
diplomatic career. He went to the estate Catherine
had given him, and worried his neighbours with in-
terminable actions at law. I made it my duty, so
long as he remained at St Petersburg, to consult him
on current affairs and on the difficulties which were
occurring between Russia and France; he gave his
advice with an air of cold and disdainful superiority,
and I think left with a conviction that the policy of
the Empire would be thrown into confusion. He had
a very small opinion of Alexander, but was always
ready to obey his slightest wish.

Count Razumovsky, who had come on short leave
from Vienna, said to me in a half-contemptuous tone:
'So it is you who are going to direct us?' 'So it
seems,' I replied. When he returned to his post he
only addressed despatches to me on current affairs,
and reserved more secret and important subjects for
the reports addressed by him direct to the Emperor.
This manœuvre was not successful. Alexander was
offended at the Minister whom he had selected being
so treated; he held that no one should have less
confidence in any public functionary than he had
himself, and ordered that all communications should
pass through me   Count Razumovsky then entered
into a private correspondence with me in which he
concealed nothing, and similar relations were established between me and Count Simon Vorontzoff, the
Ambassador in London. Vorontzoff was frank and
loyal, but his opinions on men and things were too
absolute, not admitting those shades between good

and evil which it is only just to recognise. He had unlimited confidence in the judgment of his brother the Chancellor, and adopted the favourable opinions he had formed of me. His correspondence shows the interest he took in defending me against slanderous accusations, and in maintaining me in the functions which I performed at the Emperor's wish and that of the Chancellor. I am paying a debt of gratitude in here recognising the numerous and persistent marks of affection he showed me, though I cannot approve his political views or conduct. His faults were a consequence of his simplicity of character, which prompted him to an unreserved admiration of England, the only country which at that time possessed liberal institutions. Count Simon was deeply attached to Mr Pitt and some of his colleagues, and had an almost unlimited admiration for them. This prevented him from impartially watching the march of events and perceiving the true interests either of Russia or even of Europe in the general scope of his policy. The same fault was to be found with the Russian Ambassadors at Vienna and Berlin, except that neither Count Razumovsky nor M. Alopeus redeemed their defects by the good qualities of Count Simon Vorontzoff. The intimate relations of Count Razumovsky with various prominent personages at Vienna, and the servility shown by Alopeus to the leading statesmen at Berlin, were the cause of many inaccuracies in the reports they used to send me. Their only desire was to be on good terms with the Governments to which they were accredited, and they

often nullified the effect of our communications by
attenuating them at their pleasure. To prevent such
abuses in future, the Emperor sent M. de Wintzingerode to Berlin. He was not disposed to be very
friendly to Prussia, and was determined not to conceal anything as to the military resources of that
Power or the uncertain policy of its statesmen. His
reports gave little hope of there being anything to be
expected from the co-operation of Prussia in the
event of a rupture with France.

Another special envoy, M. de Novosiltzoff, was
sent to London, as it was impossible to rely entirely
on the reports of Count Simon Vorontzoff. This
appointment was approved by the Chancellor and was
consequently satisfactory to his brother. When he
was last in Russia, the Ambassador had entered into
a closer acquaintance with Novosiltzoff, and highly
appreciated his intelligence and his political principles.
Novosiltzoff had, moreover, been ordered to pass
through Berlin, in order to sound the feeling of that
Court before proceeding with the same object to
London ; he was also, if circumstances should render
it desirable, to go to Paris to propose the most favourable conditions for the maintenance of peace.

After Count Markoff's retirement, the principal
personages of Russian diplomacy were Count Razumovsky and Count Simon Vorontzoff; and the
Chancellor's favourable opinion of me contributed
greatly to smooth down difficulties which might have
been raised by Ambassadors who were more experienced than myself. My Ministry was in some degree

a continuation of the preceding one, though it was difficult to maintain the passive system of peace and tranquillity that had been adopted by Kotchoubey and pursued with more self-assurance and dignity by the Chancellor. A country accustomed to the continual successes of Catherine or the escapades of Paul could not be satisfied with a subordinate and insignificant part, even if it was thereby assured uninterrupted internal prosperity. Moreover, the foreign policy of a great State should in my opinion not be passive or lethargic, without any interest for the general good; this narrow way of looking at politics, this imperturbable gaze which soon becomes spiritless because it is always fixed upon one's self, cannot be consistent with the feeling of power and the desire of achieving distinction by noble deeds. Such a system defeats its own object, for, by producing an incapacity to rise to larger and more generous considerations, it creates improvidence and timidity, and leaves free scope to the ambitions of others. This had certainly not been the spirit of Russian policy in former days. No State, except ancient Rome, ever had a vaster, a more active, or a more persevering policy, though we must admit that it always disregarded the principles of justice and right.

The Czars of Moscow had had the instinct of conquest since the reign of Ivan the Cruel; they employed artifice and violence by turns, and succeeded with rare ability in augmenting their territories at the expense of their neighbours. It was under Peter the Great, however, that Russian policy first assumed that decided and stable character which it has maintained to this day.   All the objects which Russia unceasingly pursues with indefatigable perseverance— amounting to nothing less than the subjugation of the greater part of Europe and Asia—were clearly conceived and designated to his successors by Peter the Great.   He gave the first fatal blows to Sweden and Poland ; he began the struggle with Persia and Turkey ; he placed himself at the head of the Greeks and Slavs, and created a European army and navy. The impulse which his iron will gave to the nation still continues, and by an extraordinary concourse of circumstances, Russia has come alarmingly near to the attainment of his objects without Europe having succeeded in stopping her.   Internal difficulties may from time to time have retarded her advance, but the spirit of Peter still hovers over his empire, and his pitiless ambition lies at the bottom of every Russian heart.

There was, however, a time when Peter's policy was forgotten and suspended ; this was at the beginning of Alexander's reign.   Young, candid, inoffensive, thinking only of philanthropy and liberalism, passionately desirous of doing good, but often incapable of distinguishing it from evil, he had seen with equal aversion the wars of Catherine and the despotic follies of Paul, and when he ascended the throne he cast aside all the ideas of avidity, astuteness, and grasping ambition which were the soul of the old Russian policy.   Peter's vast projects were ignored for a time, and Alexander devoted himself entirely to internal reforms, with the serious intention of making his Russian and other subjects as happy as they could be in their present condition. Later on he was carried away, almost against his will, into the natural current of Russian policy ; but at first he held entirely aloof from it, and this is the reason why he was not really popular in Russia. His character differed both in its good and its bad qualities from that of his people, and he was far from happy when he was in the midst of them.

After being placed at the head of affairs, I felt like a soldier who, being thrown by chance and friendship into the ranks of a foreign army, fights zealously from a feeling of honour and in order not to abandon his master and friend. Alexander's unbounded confidence made me feel it my duty to do my best to serve him, and to add lustre to his policy so long as I had the direction of it. Moreover, I firmly believed that it might be possible for me to reconcile the tendencies of the Russian nation with the generous ideas of its ruler, and to make use of the Russian craving for glory and supremacy for the general benefit of mankind. The object was a great but a remote one, to be pursued consistently and with perseverance, and to be executed with patience and skill. I thought it was worthy of the national pride of the Russian people. I would have wished Alexander to become a sort of arbiter of peace for the civilised world, to be the protector of the weak and the oppressed, and that his reign should inaugurate a new era of justice and right in European politics.

This idea quite absorbed me, and I endeavoured to reduce it to a practical form. I drew up a scheme of policy which I sent in the form of a circular to all the Russian representatives at Foreign Courts. This circular, which was intended to inaugurate the new system, and was based on the principles which I afterwards developed in my 'Essay on Diplomacy,'* prescribed a line of conduct characterised by moderation, justice, loyalty, and impartial dignity. My efforts in this direction, however, were fruitless, owing to the innumerable difficulties I encountered and the rapid march of events which brought about my fall. But, so long as I remained in office, I did my utmost to direct the course of Russian policy in accordance with the above principles, although not so completely as I should have wished. One is often compelled by circumstances to modify one's ideas, and to make painful concessions which sometimes frustrate plans long elaborated and cherished.

My system was just the one to delight Alexander in the mood in which he then was. It gave free scope to the imagination and to all kinds of combinations without requiring immediate decision or action. He was the only man in his Empire capable of understanding my aims and adopting my principles through conviction, and even as a matter of conscience. At the same time, he only entered into my ideas superficially; being satisfied with the general principles and the phrases in which they were expressed, he did

* 'Essai sur la Diplomatie, Manuscrit d'un Philhellène, publié par M. Toulouzan.' Paris and Marseilles, 1830.

not think of going more deeply into them or appreciating either the duties which the system imposed upon him or the difficulties which would necessarily impede its realisation. My colleagues, who seemed to share my opinions on many points, listened with approval to the details of my system of policy, which comprised the emancipation of the Greeks and the Slavs. So long as the only matter in question was the supremacy of Russia in Europe and the increase of her power, those who listened to me were on my side ; but when I passed to the objects and obligations which should be the consequence of such supremacy, to the rights of others, and the principles of justice which should check ambition, I observed that my audience grew cold and constrained.

My system, through its fundamental principle of repairing all acts of injustice, naturally led to the gradual restoration of Poland. But I did not pronounce the name of my country, not wishing to raise all at once the difficulties which a course so opposed to all preconceived ideas was sure to encounter. I spoke only of the progressive emancipation of the nations which had been unjustly deprived of their political existence, and I named the Greeks and Slavs as those whose restoration to independence would be most in conformity with the wishes and the opinions of the Russians. It was tacitly understood between the Emperor and myself that the principle was to be held equally applicable to Poland, but that for the present no mention should be made of that country. I felt the propriety and necessity of this. No Russian was ever on his own initiative or of his own will favourable to Poland; and I afterwards became convinced that there is no exception to this rule.

One day, when in an intimate conversation with my colleagues we spoke of the vicissitudes through which Poland had passed, Novosiltzoff told us that when he was travelling in that country at the time of the Kosciuszko Revolution, he was stopped by some peasants who asked for his passport. It was in German, and none of them could read it, so they sent to a German who lived in the neighbourhood. When the latter arrived, Novosiltzoff, who spoke German, begged him to interfere in his behalf, upon which the German assured the peasants that there would be no harm in letting Novosiltzoff pass, and he was then allowed to proceed to the army of the Prince of Nassau, who was besieging Warsaw. I strongly expressed my disapprobation of the German's conduct, which greatly astonished my colleagues, as they thought any step would have been justifiable to save Novosiltzoff. This showed how different were our respective points of view; and similar incidents often happened in the course of our relations. I had no reason to conceal my thoughts, and no one was better informed of them than the Emperor himself.

Although the new system of policy was often criticised on account of its vagueness and utopianism, it soon had serious and practical results. It was impossible to take a prominent part in European affairs, to come forward as a judicial and moderating influence, to prevent violence, injustice and aggression, without coming into contact with France at every step. She would have been a dangerous rival if she had wished to play the same beneficent part; but being led by the unlimited ambition of Napoleon, she sought to do the very contrary of what we wished. A collision sooner or later was inevitable.

Napoleon could not suffer any rivals in the career upon which he had entered. All the attempts which were made to act on an equal footing with him failed. His ally had either to carry out his plans or become his enemy. Scarcely had my system of policy been decided upon than by a sort of instinct our relations with the First Consul became colder, and the communications on both sides clearly showed by their tone that neither was disposed to make concessions to the other.

CHAPTER II

MATTERS had now arrived at such a point between Russia and France that any incident might have brought about a rupture between the two Governments; and this could not long be deferred under the system pursued by Napoleon. The origin of the rupture was in this case of a special kind, as no material interest was involved : it was simply a question of justice and right.

The seizure of the Duc d'Enghien,* by a French detachment in an independent country with which France was at peace, and his trial and execution which immediately followed, produced a general feeling of stupor and indignation which those who did not witness it could not easily realise. The Emperor Alexander and his family were most strongly impressed by it, and did not hesitate loudly to proclaim their horror and detestation of the deed. The news came on a Saturday; on the following day the whole

---

* The Duke was seized by the orders of Napoleon on the 15th March 1804, a Ettenheim, in Baden. He was taken to Vincennes, where he arrived on the 20th, tried by a military commission, and executed the same night.

of the Court went into mourning, and the Emperor and Empresses, as they passed after mass through the room in which the diplomatic body were in attendance, took no notice whatever of the French Ambassador, though they spoke to various persons who were next to him. It was indeed impossible for a Power which proposed to carry out the policy adopted by the Russian sovereign to be indifferent to such a violation of justice and international law. I drew up a note on the subject which made some noise at the time; it was sent to the French Ministry by M. d'Oubril, the Russian Chargé d'Affaires in Paris. In this note Russia loudly protested against a deed which seemed to show entire forgetfulness of the most sacred laws. She demanded a satisfactory explanation—which it was evidently impossible to give. The reply soon came: it was harsh and insulting. Talleyrand, at that time Minister of Foreign Affairs, reminded Russia that when Paul was assassinated, France did not consider herself justified in demanding an explanation. In handing me this despatch General Hédouville gave me a letter which was intended to soften the bitterness of its language. Talleyrand instructed the Ambassador to address himself to me especially. He said that Napoleon had confidence in my character and intelligence, and felt certain that I would use my influence to prevent the two countries from being exposed to break a harmony which was not only useful to themselves but necessary for the welfare of Europe. These coquetries did not of course produce any effect upon me; I regarded them as almost offen-

sive ; and I drily replied that all the papers would be
laid before the Emperor, that I had nothing to say
until I knew his wishes, but that it seemed to me
evident that a very different reply would have had
to be given if France had really wished to maintain
the friendly relations between the two countries.

There could no longer be any doubt as to the
course the Emperor should take ; indeed all was
foreseen at the time the first note was sent to Paris.
I was instructed to draw up a memorandum, stating
the question and proposing the means of dealing with
it. The matter was so urgent, in view of the conduct
of the French Government, that I had to work all
night at this document.

[The following is a translation of the memorandum
here referred to :—

April 5, 1804.

The incursion which the French have ventured to
make upon German territory in order to seize the Duc
d'Enghien and take him into France for immediate
execution, is an event which shows what is to be
expected from a Government which does not recognise
any check upon its acts of violence, and which treads
under foot the most sacred principles. His Majesty,
indignant at so flagrant a violation of the most binding
principles of equity and international law, is reluctant
to maintain any further relations with a Government
which is not restrained by any sense of duty, and
which, being stained by an atrocious crime, can only
now be regarded as a band of brigands. This act on

the part of Buonaparte should bring down upon France a cry of revenge and condemnation from all the European States and be the signal for a general opposition to him ; but if the other Powers, struck with terror and deprived of energy, keep a humiliating silence at such a moment, would it be right for Russia to follow their example ? Is it not for her, on the contrary, to lead the way in taking steps to save Europe from the ruin with which she is threatened ? His Imperial Majesty, being moved by these considerations and by a feeling of what is due to his dignity, thinks it necessary to order the Court to go into mourning for the death of the Duc d'Enghien, and proposes loudly to proclaim his indignation at Buonaparte's iniquitous proceedings. His Majesty is the less disposed to pursue any other line of conduct seeing that the outrage which has been committed upon the whole family of European States, and upon humanity itself, has taken place on the territory of a Prince nearly related to the Emperor, and thus affects him doubly. Our august master, considering that in future it will be not only useless, but dishonouring, to continue in relation with a Government which has so little respect either for justice or for common propriety, is inclined to send back the French embassy and at the same time to recall the Russian embassy from Paris.

The Emperor is firmly convinced that it would not be in accordance either with his personal dignity or with the honour of his Empire to remain passive after the event which has occurred ; but he does not

conceal from himself the partial and temporary inconveniences which might result from the decision which
he thinks it necessary to take. His Majesty wishes
to have the benefit of the wisdom of others in so
important a matter, and he has accordingly assembled
the members of his Council and diplomatists of known
experience and ability for this purpose.   He has
ordered me succinctly to lay before them the state of
the question and the decision he is disposed to take,
with the reasons which have led him to it, in order to
show the advantages and disadvantages which might
result to the welfare of the world in general and of
Russia in particular.

Since the re-establishment of the relations between
Russia and France it would be difficult to point to
any real advantage which has resulted from it to
Russia. The French Government has not kept the
solemn engagements into which it had entered with
us, and our representations on the subject in favour
of princes in whom the Emperor is interested have
had no effect. On the contrary, the First Consul
seems lately to have made it his task to cause Russia
incessant annoyance by unreasonable demands and
proceedings, notwithstanding the firmness with which
his Majesty has opposed them. This brief sketch of
the conduct of France towards Russia shows that we
would not lose much by suspending all relations with
her for the present. Such a course, besides being in
accordance with the Emperor's sense of dignity and
his outraged feelings of justice, also presents some
purely political advantages. It is to be expected that

an energetic step of this kind on the part of Russia at
the present moment would be likely more than anything else to stimulate a general combination among the
European States, to limit Buonaparte's ambition and
violence. One may hope that the Courts of Vienna
and Berlin would then also be led to take decisive
action. These two Governments, the latter especially,
acting from different motives, but both chiefly influenced by the terror with which France inspires
them, could not hitherto be persuaded to abandon
their attitude of passive submission, notwithstanding
the offers and the very strong representations his
Imperial Majesty has addressed to them. The
Emperor, in taking the initiative of declaring himself
in a manner which would leave no doubt as to his
views and system of policy, would be in a position to
address these two Courts in even more pressing
language than before—to which the presence of his
armies on the frontier would add weight—and would
be able to ask for categorical replies as to the conduct
they would pursue. Judging by appearances and the
information in our possession, the Cabinets in question, if they were thus obliged to come to a decision,
would elect to join Russia ; and it would perhaps be
impossible to induce them to do so in any other case.
The same might almost be said of Turkey, which
seems full of confidence and good-will towards us, and
quite alive to the dangers she has to fear from France.

Assuming, however, that Russia, after having
come to a rupture with the French Government,
should remain alone without an ally on the Continent,

what would she risk by such a course? To suspend diplomatic relations is not to make war, and France cannot directly attack us. To reach us she would have to invade other States which would then be forced to defend themselves and give us an opportunity of coming to their assistance. This could only increase the influence of Russia; an illustration of which is furnished by the part she played during the French Revolution, when, without being precisely at war, the relations between the two Powers were suspended. We should thus be freed from the embarrassments caused by our connection with France, and also from the presence of the numerous French agents spread all over the country.

Further, his Imperial Majesty may be sure to find in England, if necessary, a safe ally, always ready to join him.

Thus the advantages of the course proposed by his Majesty appear evident. Its disadvantages have also not escaped his attention, and they will now be here indicated.

There can be no doubt that as soon as the French Government is informed that Russia has decided to break off her relations with France, its first step will be to avenge itself on all the States that are protected and maintained by his Majesty. The kingdom of Naples will be its first victim in the south. Once the French are masters of that country, our troops at Corfu would be in danger so long as the reinforcements ordered by his Majesty (which cannot arrive for some months to come) do not reach them. In the

north it is possible that the French would attack
Denmark, which, though inclined to make a vigorous
resistance and certain to be promptly relieved by his
Imperial Majesty, is not prepared for so sudden an
aggression.

If the seizure of the Duc d'Enghien had taken place
three months later, Russia would have been in a much
better position to act. The views of Austria and
Prussia would then have been clearer and more decisive,
Denmark would have been ready, and our troops in
the Ionian islands, having been reinforced, would have
been in a position to secure Greece and relieve Naples
by means of an understanding with England. Buonaparte's difficulties would also have been increased;
and we should perhaps have done him a service by
furnishing him with a pretext for giving up his plans
of a Continental war which his Imperial Majesty,
desirous of sparing the blood of his subjects, would
not have wished to break out except under the most
favourable circumstances and after having exhausted
the means which might have been furnished by a
negotiation at Paris of all the European Powers.

However well-founded the above considerations
may be, the event which has just occurred obliges us
to disregard them, or at least only to treat them as
accessory. His Majesty cannot pass unnoticed the
atrocious proceeding of the First Consul without a loss
of dignity, and without showing Europe, France, and
Buonaparte himself, that the latter may do anything
with the certainty that no one will oppose him.

It would seem at first sight that a means might

be devised of attaining the object in a different way.
Without concealing its just indignation, the Russian
Court might, instead of coming to an immediate
rupture with Buonaparte, confine itself to going into
mourning for the Duc d'Enghien, declaring in Paris
that the Emperor could not see with indifference the
violation of German territory—especially of the dominions of the Elector of Baden, from which the Duc
d'Enghien had been dragged to his death—and asking
to be informed whether the French Government did
not disavow a deed so iniquitous and so much opposed
to international law.   This would lead to explanations
which might take some two months longer, and give
Russia time to complete her preparations in the North
and South of Europe.   The French Government would
doubtless not submit to the humiliation of acknowledging its misdeed, which would be almost as
damaging to it as the misdeed itself, and a rupture
would be the necessary consequence ; but we should
have gained time.   Against this plan it is to be remarked that directly it became known in Paris that
mourning for the Duc d'Enghien had been ordered at
St Petersburg, and especially that M. d'Oubril was
making a communication on the subject, the tenour of
which could not be otherwise than very disagreeable,
the First Consul would be the first to act by sending
back our embassy from Paris and recalling his from
St Petersburg.   He would thus show that he dares
to affront Russia and does not fear her power ; in a
word, a considerable part of the advantages which
would result from the action of Russia on this occa-

sion would be lost if Buonaparte were given the opportunity of forestalling us by a decision similar to that proposed by his Majesty, and thereby setting us at defiance in the eyes of Russia and of Europe.

The original idea, therefore, seems preferable. The first step is to put the Court into mourning; then we should recall our embassy from Paris, retaining the French one here until the Russian Chargé d'Affaires leaves France. Above all, two couriers should be sent to Naples and Copenhagen to warn the Governments in those towns of the decision of his Majesty and its probable consequences so far as France was concerned. As to Corfu, orders should be sent to the troops to hold themselves in readiness against any sudden attack, and pending the arrival of the reinforcements, to raise a corps of Albanians so as to strengthen our forces as much as possible. The details of the measures to be ultimately taken cannot be entered into here, and must form the subject of a separate memorandum.

In the official despatch which our Chargé d Affaires would present to the French Government on leaving Paris, its conduct relative to the German Empire and the Kings of Naples and Sardinia, in violation of the most formal engagements, should be forcibly commented upon. It might be thought that a last effort should on this occasion be made in favour of the princes who will immediately after be abandoned by Buonaparte, and as a proof of the interest his Majesty takes in them, that it should be proposed to him as the only acceptable satisfaction, and as an indispensable con-

dition for the maintenance of the relations between
Russia and France, that the compensation promised
to the King of Sardinia should be at once paid him,
and that the kingdom of Naples and all the countries
forming part of the Empire of Germany should be
immediately evacuated, with a solemn engagement
not to send French troops to them again. Such a
proposal, however, would be useless, and would perhaps only embitter the hostility of the First Consul
towards the princes in question. A refusal would be
certain, and should be avoided. Moreover, such a
proposal would not be in accordance with the idea of
his Majesty to break off relations with a Government
which no longer deserves to be called one, and with
whom any further connection would be dishonouring.
The more the Emperor's moderation and his generous
and disinterested principles are known, the greater
will be the impression made by his decision on the
French nation and the whole of Europe. If, however,
the French Government should really so much wish
to maintain its relations with Russia as to be disposed
to accept the above conditions, it would propose them
itself, and his Majesty could then, if he thought
proper, consider the proposal.

Having thus endeavoured briefly to state both
the beneficial and the injurious consequences which
might flow from the decision his Majesty believes
it to be his duty to take, and to show the difficulties
which would arise in executing it, I have to add that
the Emperor wishes those whom he has to-day assembled to state their opinion, according to the data

I have set forth (which I am prepared to complete if they do not appear sufficient), on the best means of action under present circumstances, and especially as to whether reasons of State or of prudence would render it necessary to suspend a decision rendered imperative by the Emperor's sentiments and his feeling of dignity. Their opinion is also desired on the following points :—

(1) Whether it will be right, after the announcement of the Court mourning, at once to take final steps for a rupture, or to endeavour to gain time by negotiation.

(2) If the latter, in what sense the negotiations should be opened.

(3) How far consideration is due to the princes whose only hope is in the Emperor's protection.

(4) What steps should in any case be taken to provide as much as possible for the safety of these princes, and especially of the King of Naples, who is in the greatest danger.

(5) What steps should be taken generally in order not to lose any of the advantages which should be obtained from the Emperor's decision in a manner both honourable and glorious to himself, and to remedy the inconveniences which might be connected with it.

Having thus carried out his Majesty's orders, it only remains to me to point out the importance of keeping absolute secrecy as to the object of the discussion which is about to take place, as both the Russian Embassy and the princes, whom we wish to expose to the least possible risk, would be in great

danger if the matter should transpire. His Imperial
Majesty feels perfectly safe on this point, knowing
thoroughly the high character and the zeal for the
service of those whom he has assembled.]

The somewhat crude language of this memorandum
was owing to the haste with which it was drawn
up, there being no time to moderate the violence of
some of the expressions in it.   After reading it, the
Emperor called a Council and invited each of its
members freely to state his opinion, as he wished the
question to be thoroughly considered.   The discussion,
however, was not a very animated one.   The majority
of the Ministers took no interest in foreign politics,
and thinking they knew what was the Emperor's
wish, they had neither the capacity nor the inclination
to oppose it.   Kotchoubey was the only member of
the Council who gave a reason for his vote.   He said,
and every one felt the truth of his statement, that to
break off relations with France was not in any way
dangerous to Russia, as France could not reach her,
while such a step would spare Russia many embarrassments which are inevitable when one deals with a
government which claims to be the sole dominating
power in Europe.   Count Romantzoff, then Minister
of Commerce, and afterwards Foreign Minister and
Chancellor, raised some objections, as he had a leaning for Napoleon and an aversion to England.   He
was a diplomatist of the school of Catherine, and his
absolutist theories converted Alexander some years
later to the doctrines and tendencies of the old

Russian policy. He admitted that after what had occurred it would be difficult to abstain from taking some steps to prove to the world that Russia would not submit to an affront on the part of France, or allow her to have the last word; but he thought it would have been better not to place one's self in such a position. While recognising that considerations of honour and respect for international law should have due weight, he thought that material interests should also be considered, and that in announcing an irrevocable decision it was necessary to be certain of the advantages and support on which one could rely. Russia was free at any moment to cast her power on either side; her decision should, however, be based not on abstract principles, but on considerations of advantage and security. He asked whether the consequences of the step Russia was about to take had been duly weighed, whether we were clear as to the results we wished to achieve, and whether we had any security for the advantages which were expected to accrue or against the dangers which might arise.

I answered that the proposed course did not involve any danger to the Empire; that its object was to satisfy a sentiment of honour and equity, without any idea of obtaining advantages which we did not want; that the Emperor was satisfied to fulfil with dignity and honour a duty to the rest of Europe, and that his position left him ample time to consider what more should be done if the interests and the security of his Empire should require it. This ended the discussion; the Emperor approved the memorandum, and ordered its proposals to be carried into effect.

I then sent for M. de Rayneval, the French Chargé d'Affaires (the Ambassador having gone on leave), and handed him a note explaining the motives of the Emperor's decision, together with passports for his immediate departure. He received my communications very calmly, without making any remark, which indeed would in the circumstances have been superfluous. It was only right, at a moment when he was about to leave St Petersburg with the whole embassy, to remove as much as possible any difficulties or disagreeables attending so sudden a departure, and I accordingly helped him as much as I could in this respect. Both General Hédouville and M. de Rayneval afterwards thanked me for the services I had rendered them. The facts of the case were not correctly described by contemporary historians. The nature of the relations then established between France and Russia was unprecedented. The motive of the rupture was quite a novel one in the annals of diplomacy, for it was not a Russian prince that had been executed, and the Cabinet of St Petersburg had no direct grievance of its own. The sole cause of the rupture was the violation of international law. The result produced a state of things which was not war, and the subjects of the two States were not threatened by the dangers produced by war; it was simply an announcement that we could not remain in relation with a Power which had no respect for the most elementary principles of justice. The case was like

that of a man whose society we drop because his conduct is opposed to our principles, though not such as
to justify our sending him a challenge.

None of the other Powers followed the example of
Russia ; but it must be admitted that she was at that
time in an exceptionally favourable position.   She
alone of the Continental Powers had managed to preserve her dignity and her independence.   Unassailable
by Napoleon now he had no navy, she threatened him
by her disdainful calm, like the stationary cloud which
is believed to be loaded with storm and thunder.
Russia should have maintained this imposing attitude
as long as possible ; applications for support and
expressions of esteem and deference came to her from
all sides.   She should not have abandoned this unique
position unless it were proved that her interest and
those of the other powers required her to enter into
action ; but things turned out otherwise.

[The following communications on this subject
were addressed by Prince Adam Czartoryski to the
Chancellor :—

To Count Vorontzoff.

ST PETERSBURG, *May* 7, 1804.

I see with real pain from your last letters, Monsieur le Comte, that you were not quite satisfied with
what has been done in the matter of the Duc
d'Enghien, but I am none the less grateful to you for
the frankness with which you have expressed your
views.   You do not say anything as to the two notes

presented at Paris and at Ratisbon ;* yet in them we only lay stress on the violation of neutral territory, which is in accordance with your views. If your Excellency had seen the way in which the matter is considered here, and the sensation it has produced, you would have been convinced that even if I had thought the sort of pressure which had been put upon the Cabinet should have been resisted, I should not have been strong enough to do so, and that only a man of your weight and consideration could have had any chance of succeeding. No one could have wished for your opinion more than myself, but I assure you that the matter did not brook delay ; if anything was to be done, it had to be done at once.

I now come to the negotiations with Austria. The Emperor received your letter with gratitude, together with your observations which I communicated to him. The decisions which have been arrived at are, in principle, in conformity with your Excellency's opinion, and I flatter myself that the modifications I have introduced will meet with your approval. To make things safer I had a conference here with Count Stadion to discuss with him the draft of the autograph letter which was to be sent to Vienna. He raised difficulties on every word that was at all precise in its meaning, and I accordingly had to limit myself to vague and general expressions in which he concurred. Judging by the Ambassador's talk and the policy of his Court, the Emperor thought, as it

* This was the note addressed by Russia on the 7th May 1804 to the German Diet at Ratisbon, protesting against Napoleon's conduct.

seems to me with reason, that it would be better not
to settle anything for the present as to the renewal of
the Russo-Austrian Alliance, but to make it depend
on Austria's conduct, and the way in which she may
enter into the execution of more precise stipulations
should such be found necessary. . . .

The Emperor will leave shortly for Revel; he
will only be away ten days, as he does not wish to be
absent from St Petersburg until he knows what turn
things are taking. I am going with him, and M. de
Tatischeff has kindly undertaken to look after the
letters and receive the Ministers as he did when I was
away last year. Hédouville complains bitterly of the
way in which he is being treated in Russian society.
This is very wrong, and I wish I could prevent it.
He has just asked in the name of his Government for
a private audience of the Emperor, but it will be
refused.*

To Count Vorontzoff.
St Petersburg, *May* 29, 1804.

I write to-day, Monsieur le Comte, not to answer
your letters, for which I am infinitely grateful, nor to
render you an account of my correspondence since my
last letter and his Majesty's return, but only to send
you the replies we have received from Paris and
d'Oubril's reports as to what passed there. These
despatches are being copied, and in order not to delay
the departure of the messenger I have only time to

---

* He left St Petersburg and ceased to be French Ambassador there on the 7th
of June 1804.

tell your Excellency that the Emperor's personal
opinion is that at this moment he cannot with propriety continue his relations with France, unless she
consents to fulfil her engagements with us relative to
Naples, the King of Sardinia, and Germany ; and
that after the insulting note* which had been received
from Paris, he can only sacrifice his just resentment in
so far as not to cause injury to his allies.   If we
succeeded in bringing about the evacuation of the
kingdom of Naples, in obtaining an indemnity for the
King of Sardinia, and in liberating Hanover, the
Emperor's dignity will be intact, and he will have
done much good to his friends and to Europe ; if
France does not yield on these points, d'Oubril should
I think leave Paris, and Russia should decline to
recognise the newly proclaimed Emperor on any
other terms.   Meanwhile we will do our utmost also
to persuade Vienna, Berlin, and even Constantinople
to refuse the recognition without obtaining some
return.

Such, in brief, are our ideas here.   But his Majesty
desires above all to have your Excellency's opinion
on the subject.   There are some difficulties which
might impede the execution of the plan.   Supposing,
which is most probable, that all our demands are not
refused, and that France consents to evacuate Naples,
it will be necessary to negotiate as to the indemnity
to the King of Sardinia and even the evacuation of
Hanover, besides guaranteeing the neutrality of those
countries.   For this a Chargé d'Affaires would not be

* See page 15.

sufficient ; and M. de Tatischeff has had the good idea of sending in that case M. Stackelberg to Paris with full powers to treat, but without any diplomatic office.

Another question is the way in which we are to deal with various points of the French reply. A very delicate one is the allusion to the death of Paul, while in our despatches we spoke, not of the Duc d'Enghien's execution, but only of his seizure on neutral territory. This is characteristic of Buonaparte's maliciousness. Are we to take up this point ? And if·so, how ? Can we pass it over in silence, seeing that our Court has never admitted that Paul died a violent death, as is shown by the manifesto of the present Emperor? Moreover, Talleyrand's argument is as false as it is insulting, and they wish to reproduce it in the note which they will send to the Diet. On all these points the Emperor wishes for your ideas and advice. Tchourakoff will be with you again in three days, and I beg your Excellency to send him to me as soon after as possible, with your remarks on the principal points and in general as to the line of conduct you think should be adopted ; we will do our best as to the details. The interruption of all relations seems to me inevitable, and cannot do us any harm ; war will perhaps follow, but that depends upon the turn things will take. Meanwhile I can announce to you that the King of Prussia has signed a declaration* almost similar to ours ; it is in our hands, and it secures the rest of Northern Europe. He has at the same time, however, promised the French not to allow Russian

* Dated May 24, 1804.

troops to pass through his territory to attack them. All that relates to this matter will at once be sent you.

Hédouville has asked for leave on account of his health, and will leave Rayneval as Chargé d' Affaires. D'Oubril's messenger had not arrived, but after waiting a few days we could not keep Hédouville any longer, as he himself came several times to get his passport. He had no message to deliver when he went, and maintained an absolute silence as to the affairs of the day. I send you the note I gave him with his passports.

Vernègues has been given up and Cassini has left Rome. The Pope's Ambassador will be sent back; this decision seems to me indispensable, but I do not quite know what is the form in which it should be notified to him.

I should like to do everything for the best, but often I confess that I fear I do not acquit myself of my task as well as I should. The details you have kindly given me of your return here have given me great pleasure, and I feel very strongly this proof of your confidence. It is with real joy I shall see you here again; and I am always grateful for the advice your frankness and your friendship dictate to me. Pray excuse my bad writing and believe in my respect and sincere attachment.

P.S.—The news from Georgia are good. The Czar of Imeritia has submitted, and has taken the oath of allegiance.]

CHAPTER III

1804-5

AFTER the diplomatic rupture consequent upon the execution of the Duc d'Enghien, it became indispensable to come to an understanding with the only Power except Russia which thought herself strong enough to contend with France—to ascertain as thoroughly as possible what were her inclinations and designs, the principles of her policy, and those which she could be led to adopt in certain contingencies. It would have been a great advantage to obtain the concurrence in our views of so powerful and influential a State as England and to strive with her for the same objects ; but for this it was necessary not only to make sure of her present inclinations, but to weigh well the possibilities of the future after the death of George III and the fall of the Pitt Ministry. We had to make England understand that the wish to fight Napoleon was not in itself sufficient to establish an indissoluble bond between her Government and that of St Petersburg, and that such a bond, to be per-

manent, must be based not on a common feeling of
revenge, but on the most elevated principles of justice
and philanthropy.*

This was a delicate and difficult mission. It was
confided to Novosiltzoff, who, as a member of the
Ministry and of the Secret Council, was fully
acquainted with all our opinions and plans. As has
been already stated, he made numerous acquaintances
during his stay in England, and he had not only
obtained a perfect knowledge of the language, but had
studied the social organisation and the resources of
the country. He was also on intimate terms with the
Ambassador, whose personal feelings had to be considered ; and he thus seemed in every respect fitted for
the task entrusted to him. On leaving he was furnished with two sets of instructions, one official and
the other secret ; in the latter I endeavoured to
explain to him all the points we wished to gain, or as
to which it would be proper to sound the views of the
British Government. I also gave him a letter to Mr
Fox, who at that time had the entire confidence of the
Prince of Wales and the men of his party. Novosiltzoff found Mr Pitt not disposed to accept all our proposals, and the Ambassador, Count Simon Vorontzoff,
in his admiration of the narrow policy of the British
Cabinet, constantly opposed the modifications we
wished to introduce. Owing to the difficulties thus
raised, or to other reasons, Novosiltzoff did not exe-

---

* This was the first time that any Power proposed a settlement of European
differences by international arbitration. The idea was originated by Prince Adam
Czartoryski, and worked out by him with the assistance of the Abbé Piattoli (see
pages 92 to 94.).

cute the mission to our satisfaction. It required much prudence and reserve, but also great firmness in following instructions; while he only hinted at the conditions to which we attached the greatest importance, did not mention the name of Poland, and did not allude to the precarious state of Europe as a result of iniquities which demanded redress. There were also some points as to which he was instructed not to make any compromise without first referring to his Government. One of these was the demand that England should evacuate Malta, as she had bound herself to do. This question had been the subject of a debate in Parliament, during which Lord Nelson held that by evacuating Malta England would not expose herself to any serious inconvenience. Be this as it may, the haughty refusal of England gave us the right to withdraw from the negotiation at the beginning; our dignified attitude would have been a proof of our sincere desire for justice and the prosperity of Europe, and must have made a great impression on England herself, by showing her that our just reclamations should not be disregarded. Moreover, it would have given Novosiltzoff facilities for negotiating in Paris. Instead of doing this he hurried back to St Petersburg, leaving matters to be directed by England at her pleasure.

[A preliminary Treaty between Russia and England was, however, concluded on the 11th of April 1805. It stipulated that the contracting parties should endeavour to form a general league of the European Powers against Napoleon, and to collect a

force of 500,000 men for the liberation of Europe
from his yoke. The objects of the league were to be
the evacuation by the French troops of Hanover
and other parts of Northern Germany and of Italy;
the independence of Holland and Switzerland; the
restoration of the King of Sardinia in Piedmont;
and in general the establishment of a state of things
in Europe calculated to prevent future aggressions.
The secret instructions to M. de Novosiltzoff, and
other diplomatic papers relative to the Anglo-Russian
negotiations of this period, will be found in the
following chapters. As to the question of the possession of Malta by England, it is not referred to in
the Treaty, and was not raised by Russia until
after it was signed. Some curious information on
this subject will be found in the letters from Count
Vorontzoff in Chapter VIII (pp. 69 to 77), in Lord
Stanhope's Life of Pitt, Vol. III, p. 333, and in
an interesting collection of despatches edited by Mr
Oscar Browning under the title of 'England and
Napoleon in 1803,' which has been published by the
Royal Historical Society.

Lord Nelson's remarks on the article of the Treaty
of Amiens, which bound England to evacuate Malta,
were made during a debate in the House of Lords on
the Preliminaries of Peace with France on the 3rd
of November 1801. They were as follows (Parliam.
Hist. 1801):—'To speak next of Malta: when the
noble earl (Earl St Vincent, First Lord of the
Admiralty) sent him down, the Mediterranean was in
the hands of the French, and on his return from the

battle of Aboukir, he thought it his first object to
blockade it ; because he deemed it an invaluable piece
of service to rescue it from the hands of the French.
In any other point of view, Malta was of no sort of
consequence to this country. It was true it contained
a most extensive and commodious harbour, with a
strong fortification, which would at least require 7000
soldiers to man the works. By the preliminaries,
Malta was to be put into the possession of a third
Power, and he repeated that in any hands but those
of the French it became immaterial to us.'

The Russian emissary in the Anglo-Russian negotiations of 1804-5, M. de Novosiltzoff, afterwards
became notorious in Poland as the persecutor of
the Polish children in the University and the
Schools of Lithuania. Prince Adam Czartoryski,
in a letter addressed to his friend, Mr Fox Strang-
ways, Under Secretary of State for Foreign Affairs,
on the 18th of July 1836, thus speaks of him :
' The papers here announce the approaching arrival
at Brussels of M. de Novosiltzoff, President of the
Council of the Empire. Do you know him personally ?
You are aware that he played an odious part in the
history of the misfortunes of Poland, and that he is
regarded by my countrymen as the most implacable
and despicable enemy our country has ever had. I
should not be surprised if some Poles gave him a bad
reception should they meet him ; the sight of him would
make them furious by recalling all the evil he has done.
It is said that he is going to the Hague, and thence to
London. This unexpected journey of a personage

who has become eminent in Russia is probably not without a political object. Perhaps he is instructed to study the policy of England on the spot, and find out what you have decided to do in the East—to endeavour to calm you and delude you. He will speak to you of the old friendship between the two countries. Perhaps he will hold out to you a proposal of arrangement and an amnesty for the Poles. His language will be most conciliatory ; he will profess the most liberal opinions, and his mission, if he has a formal one, will be a mission of peace, of concord, of forgetfulness of all offence, and of the harmony and reciprocal confidence of past times. Be on your guard. There will not be a word of truth in all this. He is a man without faith or principles, but very clever and astute, and with much knowledge. He has been several times in England, both as a traveller and on a mission to Mr Pitt.']

[*The secret instructions given by the Emperor Alexander to M. de Novosiltzoff, and other documents relating to the negotiations with England in* 1804-5, *are in Chapters IV to IX. The concluding portion of the Memoirs forms Chapter X.*]

CHAPTER IV

1804

SECRET INSTRUCTIONS FROM THE EMPEROR OF RUSSIA TO M. DE
NOVOSILTZOFF.

COMPLETE as is the confidence which I place in the
zeal and experience of my Ambassador at the Court
of London, the nature and importance of the circumstances of the moment, which may become decisive
for the tranquillity of Russia and the fate of Europe,
require the presence in England at this juncture of a
man who, while having long enjoyed my unlimited
confidence, has been in a position to become thoroughly
acquainted with my opinions and views, and would be
thereby enabled both to inform me clearly and precisely how far the Court of London is inclined to
share them, and to direct in accordance with my
wishes any negotiations which might have to be
undertaken.

I could not make a better selection for so grave
and delicate a mission than by entrusting it to you,
as you fulfil all the conditions necessary for carrying
it out. I accordingly furnish you with these secret

instructions, which are to serve as a complement and a commentary to those received by my Ambassador, and will guide you in preventing any arrangement between Russia and England not based on principles, or likely to lead to results, contrary to my just wishes.

A combination of the resources and forces of Russia and Great Britain would no doubt constitute a vast mass of power, and might promise the most satisfactory results. But I would not wish to contribute to it unless I have the assurance that it will be employed for a really useful and beneficent object. I have already explained myself on the subject in my rescript to Count Vorontzoff of which you are the bearer. But several essential points could only be alluded to in general terms in that document; and it will be for you to take to England further explanations and developments in regard to them.

The most powerful weapon hitherto used by the French, and still threatening the other European States, is the general opinion which France has managed to promulgate, that her cause is the cause of national liberty and prosperity. It would be shameful to humanity that so noble a cause should be regarded as the monopoly of a Government which does not in any respect deserve to be the defender of it; it would be dangerous for all the Powers any longer to leave to France the great advantage of seeming to occupy such a position. The good of humanity, the true interest of the lawful authorities, and the success of the enterprise contemplated by the

two Powers, demand that they should deprive France
of this formidable weapon.

Such is the first object as to which I desire to
come to an understanding, if possible, with the
British Government, and you will point out that it
must be an absolute condition of an intimate and
cordial union between Russia and England. Being
repugnant to any reaction, I would wish the two
Governments to agree that far from attempting to
re-establish old abuses in the countries which will
have to be emancipated from the yoke of Buonaparte,
they should, on the contrary, be assured of liberties
founded on a solid basis. This is the principle which,
in my idea, should guide the conduct of the two
Powers, and their proclamations should always be in
accordance with it.

As, before thinking of the liberation of France,
we should have to deliver the countries which she
oppresses, the first thing to be considered would be
how to regulate their future position. The King of
Sardinia, with regard to whom Russia and England
have contracted engagements, could not be omitted in
the arrangement of the affairs of Italy, and he would
be perhaps the first to give us a useful example. The
safety of Europe requires not only that he should be
restored to the throne, but that his share of the
territories to be recovered from France should be as
large as possible. At the same time the two Powers,
while restoring him to the throne and increasing his
dominions, would be fully justified in jointly urging
him to give his people a free and wise constitution.

He will no doubt himself perceive that his own interest will require him to proclaim a promise to this effect and keep it. It is only by so doing that this prince would be able personally to be useful to the common cause.

The political existence of Switzerland is also of essential interest to the safety of Europe. It is necessary as much as possible to give that country a defensible frontier and strengthen it in its position with regard to other Powers. I think it should be given a Government, based on local requirements and the wishes of the people, which, without falling into the errors of the old system, should be strong enough to take advantage of the resources of the country and make its neutrality respected.

The same principle should guide our policy with regard to Holland, where the national character and wishes should be impartially considered in deciding upon the form of government which should be supported. If the restoration of a hereditary Stadtholder, with a suitably limited amount of power, should be found necessary, Russia and England might come to an understanding as to the selection of the family on which this dignity is to be conferred—either some German Prince who would have a right to our advocacy and on whom we could rely, or some member of the reigning family of Prussia or Denmark, so as to gain a claim to the alliance of one of these Powers ; or it might be made a compensation for concessions made by other States. . . . As regards Germany, its present position is certainly not compatible

either with the welfare of the German nation or of
Europe generally. Should we allow part of Germany
to be absorbed by the two Powers which have long
coveted it, and at most form a third great State in the
midst of Germany? Such a measure would involve
so much injustice towards the princes of the Empire
who would have to be dispossessed that it can hardly
be thought of. Could one succeed in establishing a
more intimate union, a sort of more concentrated
Federal Government among the various States which
compose the German Empire, and if so would it not
be desirable to exclude from it the Prussian and
Austrian monarchies, whose too unequal forces destroy
all balance and patriotism? This will have to be
maturely considered if the future organisation of
Germany should have to be dealt with.*

I now come to the line of conduct which I am
convinced it would be indispensable to pursue with
regard to France. After having by our successes
abroad, and by the just and liberal principles professed by us, inspired general respect and confidence,
we should declare to the French nation that our efforts
are directed not against her, but only against her
Government, which is as tyrannical for France as for
the rest of Europe; that our only object is to
deliver from its yoke the countries which it oppresses,
and that we now address ourselves to the French
nation not to preach revolt and disobedience to law,
but to urge all parties in France to trust the allied

* The same views as to Germany are expressed, almost in the same language,
in some notes made by Mr Pitt in 1803 (see Lord Stanhope's Life of Pitt, Vol. III,
p. 269).

Powers, whose only desire is to emancipate France from the despotism under which she is suffering and to make her free to chose any government she may herself prefer.

Assuming that, for the good of Europe and of France, it is necessary that the constitution there should be monarchical, any proposal to that effect would have to be made by the nation itself: one might' endeavour to suggest it, but any intention to that effect should not be declared too soon.

The Cabinets of St Petersburg and St James's will have to come to an understanding on all these points, and also as to the individual and family who might be called upon to reign in France—if the Bourbons, which of them, and what conditions he should be called upon to subscribe to, the most essential of which would be that he should submit to the constitution which would be adopted by the nation. I look upon the choice of a king as a secondary matter, and I will not for my part attach any importance to it except in so far as it might impede or facilitate our operations.

This is not the place or the moment to trace the different forms of government which should be established in these various countries. I leave you entire freedom to treat with the English Minister on this important subject. The principles should undoubtedly everywhere be the same, and it will be above all things necessary to agree as to that point. Everywhere public institutions should be founded on the sacred rights of humanity, and so as to produce the order which is their necessary consequence; everywhere they should be based on the same spirit of wisdom and benevolence. But the application of the same principles may vary according to locality, and the two Powers, in order to come to an understanding on this subject, will take steps to obtain on the spot just, impartial, and detailed information on which they can rely. It is in strictly following such a line of conduct, in tearing off the masks worn by governments which for their private objects alternately have recourse to despotism and to anarchy, carefully separating their interests from those of the people over whom they tyrannise, that we may hope for the sincere assistance of the latter, and produce a general enthusiasm for the good cause whose results would be incalculable.

The adoption of the course above indicated in intimate concert with England would not only be the true and perhaps the only means of restricting French power within its just limits, but would also contribute to fix the future peace of Europe on a solid and permanent basis. The object would be, first, to attach nations to their Governments, by making it only possible for the latter to act for the benefit of their subjects; and secondly, to fix the relations of the various States towards each other on more precise rules, which would be so drawn up as to make it the interest of each State to respect them. . . . When peace is made, a new treaty should be drawn up as a basis for the reciprocal relations of the European States. Such a treaty might secure the privileges of neutrality, bind the Powers who take part in it never to begin a war until after exhausting every means of mediation by a third Power, and lay down a sort of new code of international law which, being sanctioned by the greater part of the European States, would, if violated by any one of them, bind the others to turn against the offender and make good the evil he has committed. . . Should the two Governments agree in the line of policy thus sketched out, they will easily come to an understanding as to the conduct they should pursue with regard to the other Powers who would be made to join in the struggle. The fear of losing the support of Russia and the subsidies of England will decide Austria to follow our impulse in the war which she is already inclined to begin as our ally. As to Prussia, it will be difficult to induce her willingly to enter a combination against France. Her engagements towards Russia are known to you, and it will be for consideration whether it would not be better to force her to take a side either with or against us than that she should remain neutral. Russia especially can put great pressure upon her, and the Berlin Cabinet, by the double engagement it has taken not to allow either Russian or French troops to pass through its territory, might find itself in the difficult position it wished to avoid. But whoever may be our allies, the English Ministry, if it adopts our ideas, will feel the necessity of not allowing any other power completely to penetrate our views, and of only directing our allies towards the proposed object by such means as we may possess of acting upon them.

The Ottoman Empire is another country whose fate will have an influence on that of the rest of Europe. The most intimate concert is necessary between Russia and England with regard to the line of conduct which should be adopted towards Turkey. It cannot be disputed that her weakness, the anarchy of her administration, and the growing discontent of her Christian subjects, are all elements which stimulate speculative ambitions and are diametrically opposed to the principles which we hold are the only ones that can bring about a stable condition of tranquillity in Europe. It will doubtless be desirable to arrive at some arrangement with regard to Turkey which shall be in conformity with the good of humanity and the precepts of sound policy ; but it cannot at present be foreseen how far this could be done. The two Powers will not be wanting in loyalty even to an essentially tyrannical government ; and this would be the chief obstacle. But if the Porte joined France (for one can never be quite sure of the sincerity of its professions)—if a war and its results rendered the further existence of the Turkish Empire in Europe impossible—the two Powers would regulate among themselves the future fate of the parties concerned. So long as the Turkish Government can be preserved in Europe, it will be necessary not to lose its confidence ; but in any case the considerations hereinafter stated should not be lost sight of in our relations with it, and should be maturely weighed, especially before deciding as to the renewal of the treaty of alliance which the Porte proposes to Russia

and England. In consenting to the proposal, it will
be necessary at least to secure, if possible, a more
happy existence to the Christian populations which
are suffering under the domination of the Porte, and
by that very means to render such domination less
precarious; and since we should do so much to preserve the Turkish Empire, it would be desirable also
to foresee the advantage we could derive from its
government, weak as it is, to paralyse the opposition
of France, to which Power a rupture with the Porte
might be injurious in several respects. My ambassador in London, following the instructions in this
sense which he has received, has doubtless already
entered upon a discussion on this important matter
with the British Ministry. It will necessarily form
part of the general arrangement here sketched out,
and you will take care that it shall be suitably combined with the rest of the plan to be adopted.

A further point to be considered is the obligation
which would fall upon the two Powers after so costly
a struggle to obtain some advantages for themselves
to compensate them for their expenditure and to show
to the people that their own national interests have
not been forgotten. Russia especially will have the
right to demand that if her neighbours, such as
Austria, Prussia, and Sweden, obtain advantages
which it will be necessary to promise them in order
to induce them to act, she should have equivalent
ones. The peace of Europe could only be preserved
by means of a league, formed under the auspices of
Russia and England, which would be joined by all the

second class States and by all those who really wish to remain at peace. In order that such a league should effectually resist the disturbers of peace and be firmly established, it is necessary that the two protecting Powers should maintain a certain degree of preponderance in the affairs of Europe, for they are the only ones which by their position are always interested in order and justice being maintained, and which, by their union, would be able to maintain it.

Among the important points of which you will have to treat with the English Government the most difficult will be that of making it feel the propriety and necessity, at a moment when it would re-establish order and justice in Europe in concert with Russia, also to consent to make some change in its maritime code—the only matter as to which the British Cabinet is not free from reproach, and which enables its enemies to injure it by exasperating the neutral Powers. Some concessions on this point, not of a character to do any real damage to the commerce of England or to her preponderance on the sea, would destroy the fears and the mistrust of the neutral States and sincerely attach them to Great Britain. . . .

ST PETERSBURG,
September 11, 1804.

Signed :—ALEXANDER.

Countersigned :—PRINCE A. CZARTORYSKI.

CHAPTER V

1804

MEMORANDUM DRAWN UP BY PRINCE ADAM CZARTORYSKI IN 1804, SHOWING THE RUSSIAN PLAN FOR THE RE-ARRANGEMENT OF EUROPE IN THE EVENT OF THE COMBINATION WHICH WAS THEN BEING PROJECTED AGAINST NAPOLEON PROVING SUCCESSFUL.

AUSTRIA will obtain Bavaria and such frontier in Swabia and Franconia as may suit her ; also the Tyrol and a new frontier on the side of Venetia and Dalmatia.

The Archduke Charles and the late Grand-Duke of Tuscany will obtain principalities in Germany and Italy. Venetia would suit one of them.

Piedmont will be returned to the King of Sardinia with Genoa and part of Lombardy. This will form an intermediary and respectable Power which it is the interest of Russia to consolidate as much as possible ; the same interest exists as regards the kingdom of the two Sicilies, which will be returned to its legitimate sovereign.

Prussia will obtain in North Germany the States of the Grand-Duchy of Berg, the Duchy of Mecklenburg, Fulda, Anspach, etc. Sweden will obtain a new principality in Germany, according to her wish and convenience.

France will retain as a frontier the Alps and the Rhine up to a point to be specified.

Holland will again become a Republic, with a hereditary Stadtholder, and with part of the Austrian Netherlands returned to her. The independence of Switzerland will be guaranteed.

All the German States which will not be absorbed by Austria and Prussia will form the German Empire, a country intermediary between France, Austria, and Prussia, to be federated with Switzerland and Holland.

The Emperor of Russia, taking the title of King of Poland, will have all the territories that belonged to Poland before the first partition, together with the country called the Kingdom of Prussia, so that his new frontier would extend from Dantzig to the sources of the Vistula, and thence along the Carpathians as far as the source of the Dniester.

Note by Prince Adam Czartoryski

The compensations above granted to Austria and Prussia are sufficient to compensate those Powers for the cessions they would make to Russia. Nearly the whole of Germany can at this moment be made the subject of negotiations, in view of the conduct of her princes, which does not give them any claim to consideration. Italy also will, if necessary, serve to satisfy Austria ; but it would better suit the Court of Vienna to seek compensation in Germany, the

southern territories of which interest us less than any
other part of Europe, and where, moreover, a sort of
balance would always be kept up by the jealousy of
France and Prussia.

As to Prussia, she might, if such a course should
be absolutely necessary and England consented to it,
be also offered the Kingdom of Holland.

It is desirable, however, for the general good that
the proposals made above should if possible be
adhered to. If they were adopted, we should have
after the peace five great Powers in Europe : Russia,
England, France, Austria, and Prussia. Of these,
Russia and England, having the same interests and
views, would probably remain united ; the three
others could hardly make an alliance to disturb the
equilibrium that would thus be established, but their
policy would have to be watched and controlled.

Further, there would be three considerable masses
of intermediary counterpoises, each of which would
have its own particular federation, namely, Spain and
Portugal, Italy, and Germany proper. These three
masses would have the greatest interest in attaching
themselves to Russia and England, and sustaining
their influence, as it would also be the interest of
those two Powers to defend and strengthen them.
In such a European arrangement Russia would thus
have a marked preponderance, which would be the
more assured as France and England would then be
rivals for her friendship.

I have not mentioned Turkey, which it would
perhaps be best, after re-establishing her rights under

old treaties, to leave for the moment in her present condition, except as regards the proposed change in Servia, the reunion of Cattaro to Montenegro, and the Ionian Republic. If the question should ever arise of definitively settling the fate of the Ottoman Empire in Europe, the Powers which it would be necessary to satisfy should only obtain stations and rectifications of territory that might be suitable to them, but the mass of the Turkish territories in Europe should be divided into separate States, governed locally, and bound to each other by a federation, upon which Russia would be able to secure to herself a decisive and lawful influence by means of the title of Emperor or Protector of the Slavs of the East which would be accorded to his Imperial Majesty. In any case this influence would be established by the part the Russians will have taken in the liberation of these territories, by identity of religion and origin, and by a wise policy and a skilful selection of posts to be occupied by our troops.

If the consent of Austria should be necessary, she might be given Croatia, part of Bosnia and Wallachia, Belgrade, Ragusa, etc. Russia would have Moldavia, Cattaro, Corfu, and above all Constantinople and the Dardanelles, together with the neighbouring ports which would make us masters of the Straits. France and England could be offered some islands in the Archipelago or establishments in Asia or Africa.

CHAPTER VI

1804-5

FROM PRINCE ADAM CZARTORYSKI TO THE CHANCELLOR COUNT VORONTZOFF.

8th November, 1804.

I HASTEN to inform your Excellency that the concert* with the Court of Vienna was signed two days ago, and that the Russian and Austrian couriers bearing this news left yesterday evening. The drift of this instrument is already known to you ; the eventuality of an attack on the kingdom of Naples is provided for in it. The Austrian Ambassador insisted that a clause should be added to the effect that such an attack shall not be provoked by his Sicilian Majesty, and, in order to avoid any misunderstanding, we have endeavoured to state as precisely as possible in a separate article what is to be meant by the word ' provocation.' The point relative to the Court of Berlin is inserted in a separate and secret article, and

---

* This was a secret Convention pledging the two Empires to united action against France, with a view to preventing any encroachments by that power on Germany, Turkey, or Naples.

the Convention concludes by Austria promising reciprocity to Russia in the event of her being attacked by Prussia. The Austrian Ambassador had no instructions as to this, but he signed the article *sub spe rati.*

The article on the subsidies is the one that gave us most trouble. Austria asks two millions for the preliminary preparations and four millions a year. We had to promise our good offices with England in this respect, although we felt that the demand was exorbitant ; but we did so only on the understanding that if the Court of London should not supply the whole of that sum, the stipulations of the concert were to remain none the less valid. This indispensable condition was not signed by the Austrian Ambassador, as his instructions did not justify him in doing so. The matter was arranged subject to further declarations. Notwithstanding this, we thought it best to sign, as we thought it would be difficult for the Court of Vienna to refuse its ratification, which we must wait for before we can regard the matter as definitively settled. I forgot to say, with regard to the number of troops, that Austria is to give 235,000 men and we 115,000, which makes 350,000 in all.

The worthy Admiral Warren* has just left, full of gratitude for the friendship which has been shown him here and the kindness of the Emperor. The new Ambassador, Lord G. L. Gower, whom as yet I have only twice seen in my house, seems to me thoroughly

* Sir John Warren, British Ambassador at the Russian Court.

conversant with the matters with which he will have to deal. The Court of London is not quite satisfied with us, but I hope it will gradually become so, and I do not despair of matters taking a good turn. They complain in London of the mystery in which we shroud our negotiations with Austria. At Vienna they are very glad of it, and if the matter had not been kept an impenetrable secret, the pusillanimous Austrian Cabinet would not have gone so far with us as it has done. . . .

2nd December, 1804.

The Court of Vienna wishes to make advances to Berlin to try to draw Prussia into a concert with us, but I have little hope of success in this direction. Prussia wishes to preserve her neutrality with regard to France as well as with regard to ourselves ; that is I think her system, which at the moment of rupture might become very embarrassing. Altogether the problem of how to deal with Prussia is not an easy one.

We are now drawing up instructions for Italinsky relative to a new treaty of alliance with the Porte which will I think appease the alarms of Mr Pitt. So long ago as 1790 his system was based on the greatest jealousy of any new acquisition on the part of Russia.

CHAPTER VII

1805

I HAVE had preliminary conversations, first with Lord Harrowby, and afterwards, on two different occasions, with Mr Pitt, on the principles which, in the present state of Europe, any coalition which it might be possible to form would have to follow in order to have any reasonable prospect of establishing the balance of power, bringing back France into her old limits, and placing the general tranquillity of Europe on a solid and stable basis. These conversations have shown me that the opinions of the British Ministry entirely coincide with the intentions of his Majesty the Emperor, as regards the points which I had the opportunity of touching upon. Thus Mr Pitt, in a rapid statement of his point of view, said he was firmly persuaded that it was necessary to tear away from the French Government the mask with which it was always seeking to hide its offences against humanity in general and the independence of nations in particular, and that for this purpose no means should be neglected of undeceiving those sovereigns (if any) who, notwithstanding the experience of so many public misfortunes, still persist in not seeing that the great extension and enormous power which France has acquired, coupled with the unbridled ambition of Buonaparte, threaten Europe with total ruin.

Having seen, how much the ideas of the British Ministry with regard to public affairs approximate to those of his Majesty the Emperor, I thought it my duty, in my conference with Mr Pitt, to enter into the greatest detail, and take up the various matters in their proper order. I began by saying that it gave me very great pleasure to see from all that Mr Pitt had said that the benevolent views of his Imperial Majesty were so much in accordance with those of the British Cabinet; and that all the remaining subjects which I had to bring forward were, properly speaking, only a development of the same principles. Nevertheless, as the matter of which we were treating was in itself of such great importance that it cannot be dealt with too precisely, I requested him to permit me to resume my statement of it from the beginning, and to take up in their natural order all the various points which relate to it, so as the more easily to distinguish the principles as to which we are agreed from the subordinate matters which will have to be discussed and regulated afterwards.

Mr Pitt found that what I had said was perfectly just, and I accordingly entered upon my statement. I began by pointing out that what we had to agree about turned naturally on two principal points : one comprised the objects which the two nations would propose to attain by the convention which they would draw up; the other the means best calculated to ensure as complete a success as possible. There can be no doubt, I said, that the objects in question, taken collectively, should be reduced to a single one only— that of restoring the equilibrium of Europe and establishing its safety and tranquillity on more solid bases ; but as this object involves a great number of ideas, I thought it best, for the sake of order and pre-cision, to divide it into three distinct parts, which might be regarded as so many periods through which a coalition formed between Russia and Great Britain would have successively to pass in order to arrive at the ultimate object proposed.

The first object, in the opinion of his Imperial Majesty, is to bring back France into its ancient limits, or such other ones as might appear most suitable to the general tranquillity of Europe. The second is to place natural barriers to the ambition of Buonaparte, so as to prevent France from further aggressions in future ; and the third is to consolidate the order of things which would be established by an intimate and perpetual alliance between Russia and Great Britain, and by a compact between those Powers, the countries which they would liberate from the yoke of France, and any other States which might be disposed to join them for the maintenance of a condition of affairs indispensable for the balance of power.

Mr Pitt said that this view was entirely in conformity with his own ; and then I proceeded to the means which his Imperial Majesty thought would be best calculated to attain the three objects above stated.

With regard to the first, I remarked that the means for attaining it might be stated as follows :—

1. The employment of as large a force as possible against the common enemy.

2. The employment of it in the most advantageous manner.

3. The reduction of the enemy's strength to the utmost possible extent.

His Majesty the Emperor of Russia being practically unable to make effectual war upon France without the assistance of some of the great Continental Powers, it is evident that in order to bring against the enemy a force in proportion to the greatness of the enterprise, the two Powers, once they agree by a convention as to the principles on which they are to act, would turn all their attention to the task of binding Austria and Prussia, or, if it should be impossible to do this as regards both, at least one of these Powers, to form a coalition (which the Ottoman Porte, Sweden, and perhaps Denmark, would probably join) with Russia and Great Britain against the extension of France and the barbarous conduct of Buonaparte.

The *conditio sine quâ non* of this coalition would be that none of the members of it should in any case be able to make a separate peace on its own account. Great Britain would on her side engage to grant to these Powers such subsidies as the urgency of the case might render indispensable, to furnish transport ships, and to employ her own land forces in as great numbers as possible on every occasion where such assistance on her part might be useful to the common cause.

In this way there can be no doubt that the forces which might be used against France would be more than sufficient; the only question would be how to employ them in the most efficacious manner. In order to do this, I said, it is necessary that the two Cabinets should agree as to the points of attack, the best plan of military operations to be adopted, and the means to be employed for preserving among the combined armies a unity of aim and the greatest possible harmony in all the operations they might undertake. I added, in order to avoid any digression from my principal subject, that I would not fail afterwards to communicate to Mr Pitt all I knew of his Imperial Majesty's ideas on this matter.

I next passed to the means of reducing the enemy's strength. These, I said, would chiefly consist in the liberation of Holland, Switzerland, and Italy from their enslavement to France, and in the endeavour to employ them for their own defence as part of the coalition. I remarked at the same time that no means should be neglected which might prepare them for this purpose as soon as the coalition should begin to be formed. It was above all things necessary to gain their confidence by not leaving them any doubt that the two Powers which would be at the head of the coalition would not be actuated by personal views, and would only strive to recover and consolidate their political independence; that all the fortresses which would surrender to the armies of the coalition would be taken in the name of the nation to which they belong, and would be restored to it when it obtains a settled government after joining the coalition.

If the language and conduct of Russia and England are always in accord with these principles, they would not only produce the desired effect, but in all probability would prepare France herself for salutary changes in her government and render the task of the coalition much less difficult in other respects.

Mr Pitt answered that he entirely agreed to all I had said, and that he only wished to point out that no means should be neglected of bringing Prussia into the coalition. He suggested various inducements which might be held out to her with this object, and he also spoke of indemnities which might be promised to Austria. It seemed to me, however, that there were several other matters to be settled first, and I merely said that the principle which his Imperial Majesty thought should be followed in any overtures that might be made was to offer only what could not be refused; by so doing we should avoid the mistake which had been made recently, when all the efforts that were made were attributed solely to a wish of profiting by a general dismemberment. I added, however, that it was not very likely that we should be able entirely to avoid making some offers; his

Majesty had some ideas on the subject which would be communicated to him hereafter by our Ambassador.

As to the subsidies, Mr Pitt said that England would go as far as would be within the limits of possibility. 'We will give £5,000,000, perhaps a little more ; and this is all we can do, for if we wished to go further, besides the want of means, there would be the additional objection that our trade with the countries which would be subsidised would not admit of our sending them a larger sum. We will, however, fix the 1st of January as the date on which the subsidies will begin ; this would be three or four months before the troops can be sent into the field. The sum thus obtained would be pretty considerable, and might serve to cover part of the expense of preparations.'

I next represented to Mr Pitt that with regard to the second object—the imposition of natural barriers to the ambition of Buonaparte which would both keep France within her boundaries and prevent her future aggrandisement—his Majesty thinks the most trustworthy means, and the only one on which we could rely, would be to surround France with States which would be strong enough at least not to fear the first blows of an invasion, and which would thus be capable to a certain degree of making their independence respected. Starting from this principle, it is most necessary that at the close of a successful war the condition of Holland, Switzerland and Italy should be considerably improved, and their strength increased by suitable augmentations of territory. The old Germanic Confederation, divided into so many little States which have almost ceased to have any connection with each other, is in striking contrast to the object with which it was formed, and should also engage the serious attention of the two Courts. His Imperial Majesty's ideas on this subject would, I added, be stated to Mr Pitt by our Ambassador, to whom I had been charged to communicate them; and having no personal predilections, he would gladly receive any proposals that might be made to him by the British Cabinet. Being firmly persuaded that nothing can give more energy to a nation, and render it more respected abroad, than a good Government founded on just and equitable principles which attach people to their country and to its lawful authorities, his Majesty would wish to come to an understanding with the British Cabinet as to the form of Government to be introduced and encouraged in the countries which would recover their independence. . . .

Finally, in order to attain the third object—that of consolidating the new state of things by the beneficial influence which would be exercised through a permanent alliance between Russia and England, an alliance which nothing could dissolve but a total change of system and principles on either side—his Majesty thinks that the means of achieving this object would spontaneously present themselves as soon as an agreement is arrived at on the question of principle. The arrangements above indicated would be based on the interests and the security of the nations which would be liberated; and nothing would then remain but to fix on clear and precise principles the prescriptions of international law and ascertain how far they can be made predominant over the special laws of each State.

Mr Pitt listened to my statement with much attention, and when I had ended, he said : ' The principles on which his Imperial Majesty wishes to make a convention with Great Britain and to act against the usurpations of France are in all respects as analogous to the sentiments of his Britannic Majesty and of his Ministry as it is possible to desire, and they are at the same time so well adapted to the tendencies of the nation, and so much in conformity with the character and opinions of the individuals who compose it, that the Government could only maintain its popularity by literally following them. Moreover, the interests of England—the Sinking Fund, the National Debt, our trade, and the progress of our industry—all demand that in the policy we are to follow we should not neglect any measures which might bring about and solidly establish a general peace. The British Cabinet has always been so intimately penetrated with these sentiments that it has never ceased, either during war or peace, loudly to profess them and to give proofs of its disinterestedness by every sacrifice it has been capable of making.

Supplementary Memorandum handed to Mr Pitt as a development of the ideas expressed by him.

The Cabinets of St Petersburg and St James's will agree as to the above points and come to an understanding as to the individual and the family which should be called upon to reign in France. If the Bourbons, which of them, and at what moment he should be informed of his selection; what line of action he is to be required to adopt, and to what conditions he is to subscribe, the most essential one being that of submission to the constitution that might be adopted.

This selection is regarded by his Majesty the Emperor as a secondary matter, and he would not, so far as he is concerned, attach any importance to it except in so far as it might impede or facilitate operations.

Mr Pitt is of opinion that these points can only be determined upon as events occur.

(A confidential note in accordance with the above agreement was presented by Mr Pitt to the Russian Ambassador on the 19th of January, 1805. The text of this note will be found in Alison's History of Europe, vol. vi, p. 667).

CHAPTER VIII

1805

EXTRACTS FROM LETTERS ADDRESSED TO PRINCE ADAM CZARTORYSKI
BY COUNT VORONTZOFF, THE RUSSIAN AMBASSADOR IN LONDON,
RELATIVE TO THE FURTHER PHASES OF THE NEGOTIATIONS FOR AN
ALLIANCE WITH RUSSIA.—REFUSAL OF ENGLAND TO EVACUATE
MALTA OR ALTER THE MARITIME CODE.

LONDON, $\frac{7}{19}$th *January* (1805).

I saw Mr Pitt this morning with M. de Novosiltzoff. He told us that Buonaparte's letter,* and the answer here given to it, oblige him somewhat to change the plan which had been as good as agreed upon between us. It is necessary, he said, both in England and abroad to prove that what we desire is a sure and stable peace for the future independence and security of Europe. This being the case, pro-

---

* Proposing peace with England. This proposal was thus referred to in George III's speech from the throne on the 15th of January, 1805:

'I have received pacific overtures from the chief of the French Government, and have in consequence expressed my earnest desire to embrace the first opportunity of restoring the blessings of peace, on such grounds as may be consistent with the permanent interest and safety of my dominions; but these objects are closely connected with the general peace of Europe. I have, therefore, not thought it right to enter into any more particular explanation without previous communication with those Powers on the Continent with whom I am engaged in confidential intercourse and connection with a view to that important object, and especially the Emperor of Russia, who has given the strongest proofs of the wise and dignified sentiments with which he is animated, and of the warm interest which he takes in the safety and independence of Europe.'

posals must be made to Buonaparte that he should give up part of his possessions and abandon his interference in the affairs of the neighbouring Governments.   No one, Mr Pitt added, is better qualified to make such proposals than the Emperor of Russia, who is neither a neighbour nor an enemy of France, and who only desires to obtain a permanent peace for Europe ; the proposals should be clear, precise, and categorical, and made so as to exclude all negotiation, and to be either accepted or rejected.   If Buonaparte accepts them, he should be required to evacuate, within a brief specified period, the territories he has no right to possess ; if he rejects them, hostilities should be begun at once.   We should, he concluded, in order to be prepared for the latter contingency, work without intermission, and have everything ready for crossing the frontier.

LONDON, $\frac{9}{21}$ *January* 1805.

After many delays I am at length able to send this by courier.   The weight of business which falls upon Mr Pitt from all sides, and the quite recent entrance of Lord Mulgrave into the Cabinet,* are the chief cause of these delays.   Buonaparte's proposal of peace has also partly contributed to them.   It is not possible for an English Ministry to reject an offer of peace without a motive ; the country would not allow it to continue the war at its pleasure.   The Government must therefore show that it desires an honourable peace and one that would ensure the

* As Foreign Secretary.

safety of Europe. If Buonaparte rejects their conditions, the nation will support the Ministry in a
continuance of the war.

You will see from my official letter, and especially
from the draft Treaty which accompanies it, that
there is a talk of from four to five hundred thousand
men for acting against France. This arises from the
usual practice in time of war ; the enemy exaggerates
the number of his troops, and one's allies even surpass
this exaggeration ; and as some surprise is felt at the
little result which has been attained, it is thought
that the number of troops must be increased. It is a
known fact that during the terrible campaign at the
beginning of the last war, when Prussia received
subsidies from England for a great army which was to
take the offensive, she never had half of the effective
troops for which she was paid. Instead of having
80,000 men, she had less than 40,000, and she wasted
them during the whole campaign in besieging
Mayence, which could have been taken by 30,000
men in less than six weeks if the King of Prussia had
acted honestly. Austria, too, during the first two
campaigns, never had more than 40,000 men in Italy,
and during the last campaign 60,000, while the Vienna
Cabinet alleged that 60,000 were engaged in the first
campaigns and 100,000 in the subsequent ones. The
same happened in Swabia, in Switzerland, and on the
Upper Rhine. This is the reason of the obstinacy
with which the Government here insists on armies
being employed in such great numbers, though they
will find it difficult to obtain subsistence. . . .

I must here tell you that all you will find in the official despatches of the English Ministry as to arranging indemnities for Prussia and placing independent Powers between Holland and France and on the left bank of the Rhine are not really matters to which importance is attached here. Mr Pitt has often told me, and repeated to me yesterday, that these expedients are proposed because no better ones have been found, but that if any plan more likely to be effective for the purpose of keeping France in her ancient limits could be devised, the British Cabinet would gladly accept it, as it desired nothing more than the peace of Europe and the maintenance of a permanent friendship with Russia.

LONDON, 26 *January* (N.S.) 1805.

Russia and England should, and can, save Europe. England ardently wishes it, and will do her utmost to co-operate with Russia in this holy work; it only depends therefore upon the latter to employ the means with which England has decided to furnish her. The King, Mr Pitt, all that is great and enlightened in the country, and, which is more important, the whole nation (for this is the only country in the world where the people are not treated like a flock of sheep) desire a permanent alliance with Russia. . . .

Lord G. L. Gower, in a cipher despatch dated the 12th or 13th October (O.S.) says that Count Stadion,* after having received despatches from his Court, had stated to him that the Emperor, his master, had so

---

* The Austrian Ambassador at St Petersburg.

long hesitated as to the course he should adopt in present circumstances, because for two years he had seen an intimate alliance between Russia, Prussia, and France, the result of which was that these three Powers disposed of everything in Germany in a manner prejudicial to the power and even the security of Russia ; but that now Russia prefers to follow another system more in conformity with the welfare of Europe, being calculated to restore to it the independence of which France has deprived it, the Emperor, his master, no longer doubted the good-will of the Emperor of Russia, and was resolved to second his views, provided he be supported by Russian troops and English money.* This despatch, which Lord Mulgrave showed me, and which Mr Pitt afterwards showed our friend,† has given us all great pleasure. Here they are ready to do everything.

LONDON, 18 *April* 1805.

I am sending by to-day's courier a despatch to M. de Novosiltzoff announcing that the Court here acquiesces in the proposals he is to make to the Corsican, whom he will find in Italy. . . . I take this opportunity of repeating that I intend to leave this country next spring. Matters are tending towards a coalition or a peace, and this should be settled before the winter, after which my stay here will almost cease to be necessary. If they send in my place a man of frank and straightforward character, not given to

* The preliminary Convention for an alliance between Austria and Russia against France was signed on the 25th October 1804.
† M. de Novosiltzoff.

compliments, he will gain the confidence of the King, of the Ministry, and of English society in general. An intriguer and a flatterer would only inspire contempt.

LONDON, 10*th May* 1805.

(Written in sympathetic ink).

I am sorry to see our people do not understand the constitution of this country, which is very different from its theory, as stated in the works of Blackstone and his abbreviator Delolme. It rests with the nation to decide as to any point which it may deem absolutely necessary, and no administration, however strong, would dare to go against that decision : if it did, it would be overthrown, prosecuted, and punished, and what it had arranged against the public wish would be disavowed and annulled. Such a question is that of the restoration of Malta, the possession of which entails much expense on England, but which she feels it indispensable to keep at any cost, in order that the Mediterranean should not become a lake belonging to France, who would be mistress of all its shores, and thus be placed in a position to attack Sicily, the Ionian Islands, the Morea, Crete, and above all Egypt, whose possession by the French troops would induce them before long to attack the British possessions in India. If Lord G. L. Gower had agreed to the evacuation of Malta and the new maritime code which is again brought forward by our Government, his action would certainly not have been ratified here. He would have been recalled with disgrace, perhaps prosecuted, and would have lost all his reputation. . . . You tell me that if England will not yield Russia will not ratify the Convention. That being so, I can only regard the negotiations as broken off. The Continent will be enslaved, and this country will either make peace before Christmas and keep Malta, or will continue a defensive war which will cost it little money and which will preserve the rock which is the cause of all the existing difficulties.

London, $\frac{6}{18}$ *May* 1805.

. . . The English nation is quite decided not to give up Malta. I have been here twenty years ; I have done my best to make myself acquainted with the country, the Government, and the national character, and when I say it is not in the power of the Government to make this cession, I express not only the feeling of the Ministry and the most respectable members of the opposition, such as Earl Spencer and Lord Granville, but also the unanimous sentiment of all the most estimable and independent persons that influence public opinion. . . . I may be blamed for not having in my official reports stated that England would never consent to the evacuation of Malta, but I could not anticipate that such a demand would be made by our Government, as the matter was never mentioned to me, and in the conferences which M. de Novosiltzoff had with Mr Pitt, both alone and in my presence, there was no question of England abandoning Malta. . . . The proposed new code of maritime law is equally out of the question, and Lord Harrowby assured me that if Lord G. L. Gower had yielded on these two points he would have been recalled, and never again employed in the diplomatic service. The Government here would have preferred that he should have altogether refused to accept the note you addressed to him on the subject of the maritime code, and that he should have replied to you verbally that Great Britain simply adheres to her practice during the last two centuries in this matter, which is in accordance with her treaties with Russia, Sweden, Denmark, and Holland. The result of accepting the Russian proposal, added Lord Harrowby, would be to give France facilities for maintaining and augmenting her naval forces to the detriment of England; and this is a further reason why England will never accept it at any cost. France may obtain supplies for her navy from other countries in time of peace, but England will never allow her to obtain them in time of war.

I have done all that was humanly possible to mitigate the bad impression produced by my communication on the King, Mr Pitt, and Lord Harrowby, who, though still too unwell to take an active post in the administration, assists at the Cabinet Councils, where he possesses the influence given him by his great talents and the extreme deference paid to his advice by Mr Pitt. I begin to hope that some means may be found of avoiding a rupture of the negotiations, which during the first four days was almost decided upon. I endeavoured to gain time by persuading them not to send an unfavourable answer at once, and meanwhile I have had several conferences with Lord Mulgrave and Lord Harrowby. The latter seemed somewhat shaken on my pointing out that if the proposed alliance between Russia and England should fail by the absolute rejection of the Emperor's demands, the result would be the enslavement of the Continent. He said he would think about the matter further, but added that he had never seen his friend Mr Pitt, with whom he has been on intimate terms for more than twenty years, so deeply grieved as he was at the difference between the two Courts ; but he was unshakeable, and he never shrank from any danger when he saw it was necessary to incur it for the maintenance of the honour and the interests of his country. As to the King, I have employed the services of Count Münster, in whom his Majesty has the greatest confidence. He undertook the task with zeal, and spoke to the King some days ago in order to prevent a rupture between the two countries, and with some success, but as I knew the Ministry would have to be at the fêtes at Windsor, and the King, who is incessantly occupied with public business, would be sure to have private conferences with Mr Pitt and Lord Harrowby at which the question of the provisional treaty made at St Petersburg would probably be finally settled, I begged Count Münster to let me know how things are going on. Last night I received a note from him by express which gives me some hope. I shall probably see Lord Mulgrave to-morrow or the day after, when I will have the reply of the Government. . . .

P.S.—$\frac{15}{27}$ *May.*—The gleam of hope that some compromise might be arrived at here to satisfy our Government has disappeared. I learn that Mr Pitt has looked for one in vain, and that in order not to be disavowed and blamed by the nation he will be obliged to give up the co-operation of the Continental Powers, as our Court has peremptorily declared that it will not ratify the Treaty unless this country will abandon Malta. They have begun to prepare a long reply, which will be in great detail. I do not think it will be handed to me before five or six days hence.

[The Treaty of the 11th of April, 1805, was not ratified, owing to the difference between Russia and England as to Malta and the maritime code, until the month of July following, and the Russian Government only consented to ratify it after placing on record its opinion that the restoration of Malta and the alteration of the maritime code would be in conformity with 'the principles of equity and justice,' and would be 'the most efficacious means of securing the success of the cause.' (Despatch from Lord G. L. Gower to Lord Mulgrave of the 21st July 1805, and note from Prince Adam Czartoryski of the same date, both in the Record Office.)].

CHAPTER IX

1805

THE negotiations for bringing to a practical issue the convention of the 11th of April having been procrastinated through the refusal of England to give up Malta and alter the maritime code, Alexander, who had meanwhile begun to disregard the advice of his Ministers, and to take the government of Russia into his own hands, entered with Austria into a campaign against France, and made overtures to Prussia with a view to drawing her into the alliance. Prussia asked as the price of her co-operation that England should give up Hanover to her and provide her and her German allies with subsidies to enable them to carry on the war. Another special envoy, M. d'Oubril, was then sent by the Russian Government to London. The following extracts from a letter from Count Vorontzoff describe the interview which took place with Mr Pitt on this occasion :—

LONDON, $\frac{17}{29}$ *September* 1805.

I am very grateful to you for having sent M. d'Oubril to me. He has given me explanations as to the papers of which he is the bearer, and which have caused me inexpressible astonishment. But the thing is done, and nothing remains but to bow to the decrees of Providence, which seems still to protect the Corsican. I feared the Berlin interview, and my presentiment is verified. All the weapons of intrigue and sycophancy must have been employed against weakness and irresolution. I know too well your judgment and your elevation of mind to doubt for an instant that you have used all your efforts to prevent the evil that has been done, and I pity you very sincerely at not having been able to prevent it. As your private letter did not contain anything that I could not communicate to Mr Pitt, and it referred me for further explanations to M. d'Oubril, I sent it to Mr Pitt with a request that he should return it to me, and that he should defer his opinion on the papers I would communicate to him the same morning until after hearing the explanations which M. d'Oubril and myself would give him on all the points which might seem new to him. He returned me your letter with thanks, assuring me that it had not been communicated to anybody, and that he would be very glad to see M. d'Oubril. Though prepared to receive a disagreeable communication, and accustomed to master his countenance, one could see his emotion on reading the documents I gave him, which he handed to Lord Mulgrave after he had finished them. The proposal that the King should exchange a patrimony which his ancestors had enjoyed for more than a thousand years struck him deeply. He told me that, knowing his

Majesty's attachment for his German subjects and his
inflexible character, he would break off everything if
such a proposal were made to him; and what is
worse, being old, infirm, and extremely sensitive, it
might even place his life in danger. M. d'Oubril and
myself then pointed out that matters had arrived at
such a point that everything must be done to avoid
so perilous a contingency as Prussia remaining in-
active, or even turning to the side of France, after
the disasters suffered by the Austrian army through
the folly or the treason of Mack ;* that it was therefore
necessary to bring her over to our side at any cost
during the period of four weeks given to Buonaparte
to arrive at a decision; and that the demands on
which Prussia insists should not be flatly rejected.
Mr Pitt replied that though England would also have
reason to complain of the other articles of the proposed Convention, she will not object to them. ' All
the subsidies that Prussia asks for herself, for Saxony,
for Hesse, and for the Duke of Brunswick will be
given; we shall be delighted to agree to any other
indemnity that Prussia may wish to have, but as for
the exchange of Hanover, no Minister would be
imprudent enough to make such a proposal to the
King, and great care will be taken always to conceal
it from him.' He added that in all these proposals of
peace that are being made to Buonaparte there is a sort
of affectation not to speak of England, as if the Powers

---

* The Austrians under Mack, after occupying the line of the Iller from Ulm to
Memmingen, were outmanœuvred by Napoleon, who gained a position on the Danube
in the Austrian rear, upon which Mack surrendered at Ulm and the Austrian army
was broken up.

wanted to make him believe that they did not trouble themselves about her. This did not produce much effect upon the Ministry, as England does not fear France, but wishes to liberate the Continent ; but it will produce a bad effect in the country if Buonaparte publishes the proposals which have been made to him at the very time when Parliament has to be asked for enormous subsidies for Powers which ostentatiously affect complete indifference as regards England. I endeavoured to account for this omission by the urgent need of bringing over Prussia to the alliance, and d'Oubril justly remarked that if there had been any question of inserting a provision as to the interests of England, the limit of four weeks would not have been sufficient, as it would have been necessary to write to London and wait for an answer, which would depend on favourable winds, and might not come for months. This would have been playing into the hands of Prussia, who wishes to gain time and put off as long as possible her final decision. Mr Pitt afterwards admitted to me that this explanation was a valid one, but he added that it could not be produced in Parliament. He further objected to the passage in our official despatch in which occurs the following phrase : ' Moreover, the extraordinary defeats suffered by the Austrian armies might have given them a right to regard themselves as freed from this obligation,' i.e., that of not making peace except in concert with an ally. He remarked that if, instead of gaining a signal victory and depriving the enemy of nineteen ships of the line, the English fleet had been beaten

at the battle of Trafalgar, and England had then
negotiated a separate peace, thinking herself freed
from all engagements to the allies with whom she has
treaties stipulating that peace should not be made
except by common agreement, would such a course
have been thought right at St Petersburg and
Vienna? As to this point we fell back on the
necessity of pleasing Prussia, in order to draw her
into the war, as we were persuaded that Buonaparte
would reject the conditions of peace, and the Court of
Berlin would then be forced to show its hand. We
added that the crudity of the expressions to which he
objected was to be excused by the extraordinary
urgency of the case, as the Emperor was only a few
days at Berlin and Potsdam, during which there was
a constant struggle with the Prussian Minister, so
that there was really no time to weigh words. After
we had left Mr Pitt, M. d'Oubril suggested to me
that I should soften some of the expressions in
our official despatch which had shocked Mr Pitt, and
I accordingly went back to him to ask whether he
would agree to this being done. He replied that this
would make his task much easier with his colleagues
in the Cabinet. At length everything was pretty
well accepted here, though with evident repugnance,
except the exchange of the electorate, as to which Mr
Pitt spoke to me very strongly on various occasions
in several conversations which I had with him. He
repeated to me that such a proposal might either kill
the King or drive him mad, and that after losing a
sovereign so much esteemed and cherished, the country

would no longer consent to bear the enormous sacrifices of money it was making for continental wars. To provoke so fatal a crisis as the death or insanity of the King would therefore be most ruinous to the interests of Europe.

I conjure you to weigh well the considerations above stated, and I hope I shall be spared the pain of presenting the memorandum which is being prepared at Berlin and which will be rejected here. The weakness with which the Emperor has, in order to please Prussia, lent himself to a communication so offensive to the King of Great Britain, and so contrary even to the true interests of Russia, will be even more felt here when his Ambassador presents a detailed memorandum on the subject.

(Subsequently a despatch, dated $\frac{\text{23rd October}}{\text{4th November}}$ 1805, a copy of which is in the Record Office, was addressed to Count Vorontzoff by Prince Adam Czartoryski, urging that the cession of Hanover to Prussia was a *conditio sine quâ non* of obtaining the Prussian alliance; but England persisted in her refusal to consent to the cession. The result was that Prussia remained neutral during the war, and afterwards obtained Hanover from Napoleon as a bribe for her alliance.)

CHAPTER X

1805

IN order to understand the political movements of
that time and the animosity with which all Europe
wished to fight Napoleon, notwithstanding the defeats
he had inflicted upon her, it is necessary to recollect
what was the state of public opinion in Europe.
Those who had become enthusiastic at the outbreak
of the French Revolution had looked upon Buonaparte as the hero of liberalism; he seemed to them
destined by Providence to make the cause of justice
triumph and to remove by great actions and immense
successes the innumerable obstacles presented by facts
to the wishes of oppressed nations. When they saw
that Napoleon did not fulfil their expectations their
enthusiasm diminished. The French Republic and
the Directory had no doubt acted culpably and fool-
ishly, but though they were deceived as to the means,
they remained faithful to the end; they had done the
greatest harm to the cause of freedom, but had not

deserted it.   They might in course of time have
learnt the right means of doing justice and emancipat-
ing nations ; but no such illusions were possible when
Napoleon became the ruler of France.   Each of his
words and actions showed that he would act only by
the force of bayonets and of numbers.   By ceasing to
be the champion of justice and the hope of oppressed
peoples, he lost one of the strongest elements of the
power of the French Republic, and descended to the
class of ambitious tyrants, with immense talents it is
true, but with motives as mean as theirs.   This made
other Powers attack him without scruple, as a scourge
of humanity ; and the general opinion of Europe on
this subject spread to Russia, thereby drawing the
Cabinet of St Petersburg into a course of policy in
which it lost sight of the part Russia was really called
upon to play.

The peace of Amiens, which had been hailed with
equal enthusiasm on both sides of the channel, had
been broken by an act which Napoleon resisted with
his usual violence, but in which he had right on his
side.   He demanded the immediate evacuation of
Malta, which England had only occupied on the
express condition that she should withdraw from it
when peace was concluded.   It had been agreed on
all sides that the future destiny of this island was to
be regulated by the Powers in concert.   England
haughtily refused to execute this clause of the treaty,
and the war was at once resumed.   At this time
Lord G. L. Gower,* the British Ambassador appointed

---

* Father of the present Lord Granville.

by the new Ministry, arrived at St Petersburg. He was
then a young man, but he had much natural prudence,
and an instinct of propriety which manifested itself in
every word he uttered, and in the manner in which he
did business. He showed me entire confidence, and
even sincere friendship. He was accompanied by Sir
Charles Stewart, who had already had an opportunity
of acquiring diplomatic skill in various embassies
where he occupied the post of secretary. These two
personages were afterwards well known in Paris,
where they repeatedly succeeded each other. Lord
G. L. Gower, who afterwards became Earl Granville,
allied himself with the Whigs, while Sir Charles
Stewart, who became Lord Stewart,* remained with
the Tory party. Lord G. L. Gower arrived in
Russia with important despatches intended to draw
the Emperor into an alliance and active military co-
operation against France. The Austrian Government, whose leading Minister was at that time M. de
Cobentzel, at the same time sent another ambassador,
Count Stadion, to sound the real intentions of Russia.
The English representative spoke with as much decision as the Austrian one did with timidity and reticence. The latter was in constant alarm lest he
should compromise himself by his proceedings being
known too soon in London, and we had for some time
to conceal them from the English Government,
thereby incurring its reproaches, of which Count
Simon Vorontzoff made himself perhaps too devoted
an organ.

---

* Afterwards Marquis of Londonderry.

In descending into the arena Napoleon had cast aside everything that could have led people to believe that he had a high and generous mission. He was a Hercules abandoning his task of succouring the oppressed and thinking only how to employ his strength in order to subjugate the world for his own advantage. His sole idea was to re-establish absolute power everywhere, with its old forms and the greater part of its inconveniences. So long as he governed, his ambition and injustice eclipsed those of all other enemies of mankind; he seemed like a sinister and devouring flame rising above all Europe. In every country men who valued their national dignity, who were brave and high-principled, were unanimous in their opposition to him. He had no supporters anywhere except among those in whom fear was the strongest motive. As soon as this feeling began to subside, there was but one voice of opposition to the man who, after having made himself an ordinary despot, had everywhere wished to impose his yoke on the other European sovereigns.

The policy of Russia from the beginning of the reign of Alexander could, after what I have said of his opinions, only be one of conciliation between parties and Powers whose policy bore the character of mutual exasperation. It was with this object that the Emperor had allowed himself to be drawn by Prussia into taking part in the complicated question of indemnities in Germany. The parties interested in this matter showed a partiality and a disposition to give and accept bribes which did them little honour, and were not at all in accordance with the Emperor's pure intentions. While supporting the claims of princes who were related to him, and somewhat too partial to Prussia, his sole object was to rescue Germany with as little injustice as possible from the confusion into which she had been thrown by the Revolution and the French wars.

The spirit which at that time animated the Russian Cabinet rendered it eminently suited to speak to inflamed Europe in terms of peace and conciliation. The character of the sovereign and of his Ministers, which always has an influence on policy, must have added weight to the conduct which was then adopted by the Cabinet of St Petersburg, and its words would doubtless have been received with general readiness and confidence.

After the retirement of Count Panin, whose principles and manner might have inspired foreigners with distrust, Count Kotchouboy, who succeeded him, and especially the Chancellor Count Vorontzoff, possessed in a high degree the qualities necessary for ensuring their acceptance as mediators by the parties most hostile to each other. The Chancellor sincerely wished to remove difficulties, to tranquillise animosities, and to do justice while hearing both sides. His language was always calm, conciliatory, and dignified, never showing irritation at the obstacles he met with.

On each of the occasions which divided Europe and constantly fomented war, Russia had repeated the offer of her mediation; it was never, however, sincerely considered and was always rejected, especially by France.

The history of the Consulate and the Empire is the history of Europe up to the end of the reign of Napoleon. This work, which may be called immense, inspires an interest which is always sustained by the ability of the narrative; it is full of details calculated to interest and instruct the reader, who is lost in admiration before so much practical and profound information in the various branches of administration and policy. M. Thiers, in beginning his magnificent work, is enamoured of his hero, but this does not prevent him from being afterwards impartial and even severe towards him. He strives to be always unbiassed, and generally is so; but I may be permitted to point out that in some cases he has not done all that is demanded by a quality so important in a historian.

The somewhat disdainful way in which he speaks of the young men by whom the Emperor of Russia was surrounded does not seem to me quite just; these men were not all so very young. Count Kotchoubey, M. de Novosiltzoff, and the new Ministers, were of an age sufficient to protect them against such an epithet. In any case the assemblage of these men round the Emperor had the great merit of withdrawing Russia from a fatal groove. Disorder and corruption were succeeded by a regular and orderly régime, and the Empire could place itself on an equal footing with the other disciplined countries of Europe. As for foreign policy, the idea of making Russian ambition serve an honourable and just object does not seem to me to deserve the somewhat severe criticism which M. Thiers has applied to it. Napoleon was, I think, greatest during his consulate; a great administrator, great by the means he employed for the restoration of finance in France, great by his victories and his policy, which tended towards peace. But even then he allowed himself to be led into committing acts of useless severity and cruelty. He seems to me less great when I see him seduced by Imperial dignity, occupied with ceremonials, titles, and ancient etiquette, and with a crown on his head. All that looks like vanity diminishes true greatness. But the author of the 'History of the Consulate,' by the complaisant eloquence of his descriptions, proves that this did not lessen his admiration. Yet he perceives that Napoleon, once started on this course, will no longer deviate from it, and will be fatally drawn to the last goal of an unlimited vanity and ambition.

I ask which of these two policies was the more conscientious, the more moral, the wiser? Was it the one which was inspired by the mad longing for universal empire, or the one which took its origin in the dream—if it should be so thought—of peace and justice?

By dint of victories, Napoleon had raised up a new order of things; but its short duration and its total destruction have proved that its first idea was not more practical than other projects of his which M. Thiers calls chimerical dreams. The latter had at least the excuse of noble and ardent aspirations, while the plans of the conqueror were only a result

of passion and personal interest carried to the highest
point.

M. Thiers was acquainted with the part played by
the Abbé Piattoli in the negotiations which were
opened at this period. He acknowledges that the
Abbé was a man of some merit, but he does not seem
to me to have rendered him complete justice.

The Abbé Piattoli was invited to come to Poland
by the Princess Lubomirska, my aunt; she charged
him with the education of Prince Henry Lubomirski,
whom she had adopted. During my first visit to
Paris in 1776 and 1777, having entered into relations
with Prince Henry, I naturally found myself under
the influence of the Abbé Piattoli—an influence which
could only produce a very salutary effect. The Abbé,
like so many others who bear this title, was a layman.
He was a very learned man, had successively devoted
himself to various branches of science, and wrote with
great facility. He also had a warm heart, and was
capable of self-devotion. M. Thiers does not seem
quite to understand that people may devote themselves to an idea which has taken possession of their
souls, only from a feeling of generosity. This is
what happened to the Abbé Piattoli. No sooner
was he in a position to understand the condition of
Poland and her mode of government, than he conceived the idea of working at her deliverance, and
persisted in doing so as long as he could hope that
the idea might be realised.

The state of my country, before all the convulsions
through which it has passed since, was very different

from what it is now. It was a dead calm after the
storm. The recollections of the Confederation of Bar*
no doubt existed in the nation ; there was an anti-
Russian party, but it was weak, and its efforts were
powerless to produce any resistance to the arbitrary
acts of the Russian Embassy. The most famous
names in the country, those which were pronounced
with the greatest respect, had distinguished themselves during the Confederation of Bar. I wrote a
memorandum on this subject from the dictation of the
Abbé Piattoli. It was sent by a safe hand to my
parents, whose opinions were known to me, to Marshal
Ignatius Potocki, and to General Rzewuski, both of
whom were sons-in-law of the Princess Lubomirska.
It was hoped that this document would exercise a
salutary influence and bring about some practical
results. I recollect having passed a whole night in
copying it, and it was very well received. Piattoli
now became a steadfast adherent of the Poles and
their cause. He continued to occupy himself with
the education of Prince Henry, and accompanied the
Princess Lubomirska to England, Vienna, and Galicia.
When he came to Warsaw during the Great Diet he
was appointed Secretary to King Stanislas, after
the latter, having thrown off the Russian yoke, had
joined the national party. He contributed by his
influence and his councils to maintain the King in the
new course which he had sincerely adopted. Later
on, when this unfortunate sovereign, yielding to the
advice of the Chancellor Chreptowicz, his Foreign

* See note to page 31, vol. I.

Minister, submitted to the fatal decisions of the Confederation of Targowitza, the Abbé Piattoli resigned a
post in which he no longer had any hope of doing good.

Piattoli had much imagination, and this afforded
him the means of getting out of difficulties, but he
always showed remarkable disinterestedness and good
sense.   After the fall of Poland, he found a refuge in
the house of the Duchess of Courland, who had known
him at Warsaw.   This was at the time when she had
returned to claim from the Great Diet her rights over
Courland.   Her patriotic Polish sentiments were very
strong, and she never abandoned them.   The affairs
of Courland took her to St Petersburg, and Piattoli
accompanied her there.   We met again with mutual
pleasure ; he did not forget our former relations, and
sought to renew them, while I was delighted to have
the opportunity of using so trustworthy and able an
instrument.   A mere indication of the chief points of
a negotiation or of a political system was sufficient to
enable him to develop all its consequences.   He
generally did this in too much detail, but he readily
abridged or modified his statements in accordance with
the remarks that were made to him.

M. Thiers had seen the first draft of a statement
of this kind made after some conversations we had had
together as to our plans and the best means of executing them.   To form a judgment on so incomplete a
piece of work, written on the spur of the moment,
would be more than severe ; it would be unjust, and
this no doubt was far from M. Thiers' intention.   I
certainly was not under any illusion as to the numerous

difficulties which would arise, some of which were insurmountable. The possession of Gibraltar by the English was not based on any principle of justice ; on the contrary, it was a violation of international law. By giving it up England would have been able to detach Spain from France and bring her over to the general interests of Europe. Count Strogonoff, in proceeding to his post at Madrid, was to pass through London and to touch on this question with all possible reserve and with the consideration due to British susceptibilities. This was, so to say, an endeavour to begin a reform in the policy of the English Cabinet— an endeavour which did not produce any satisfactory results.

The plan was rejected as a whole, but it contained the points which reproduced themselves on every occasion when there was a question of reconstituting the map of Europe. They were repeatedly brought forward either by Germany, the Netherlands, or Italy, and they had occupied Carnot when he was a member of the Directory. It was, in fact, in the nature of things that they should come to the front on various occasions.

The proposals of Russia were of a nature to satisfy France ; but the cold reception which they encountered in England, and especially the peremptory refusal to evacuate Malta, gave Russia sufficient reason for withdrawing from the coalition. If this resolution had been firmly adhered to, it would have given the negotiations a different character, and would have produced different results.

The tendency of public opinion in Europe also
manifested itself in Russia, and carried along with it
the Emperor and his Privy Council. To oppose it
would have been regarded as showing an inclination
to yield to French promptings. Austria was already
arming; she insisted on the adoption of a general
plan of military operations with the object of guaranteeing her against the danger of foreign invasion. It
was necessary to think of preparing such a plan in
case hostilities should become inevitable. This was
done at St Petersburg with Austria on one side and
England on the other; the latter was to furnish the
necessary funds for arming Europe. The negotiations
lasted for some time, and presented great difficulties;
the exigencies of Austria seemed excessive to the
English negotiators. At length, however, by means
of reciprocal concessions, an agreement was arrived
at. Part of the subsidies was received for Prussia,
whom we incessantly spurred on and kept informed of
our movements by more and more urgent despatches.
I must admit that the improbability of Prussia entering into the concert of the Powers was not what I
most regretted. I did not neglect any argument
calculated to persuade her, but I foresaw with satisfaction the necessity of disregarding her interests in
the event of a refusal, for in that case Poland would
have been proclaimed a kingdom under the sceptre of
Alexander. He would have been received with
enthusiasm, for at that time this was the only possible
way of resuscitating Poland, which even France had
forgotten. Meanwhile Napoleon, as if he wished to

remove all possibility of a peaceful solution, had had himself crowned King of Italy,* without any reserve as to the rights of succession. By seizing the Genoese Republic, threatening Naples, and not leaving any prospect to the House of Savoy, he increased the general reprobation and also deprived Russia of all hope of obtaining the conditions which she had made it a point of honour not to abandon.

The only course now open was to prepare the means for a struggle which seemed inevitable. The great difficulty consisted in arriving at an arrangement by which England should agree to furnish subsidies of the amount demanded by Austria. This was not an easy matter; yet, thanks to our intervention, an agreement was arrived at. £3,000,000 were granted to the Court of Vienna, and a like sum was appropriated for overcoming the hesitations of Prussia. The military part of the arrangement was executed without delay. An army composed of Russian and Swedish troops assembled in the island of Rügen and at Stralsund; the Russian troops were commanded by General Tolstoï. Another Russian army corps, assembled at Corfu, was to set sail for Naples. An army under the orders of General Kutusoff moved towards the Austrian frontier in order to be available to assist General Mack, who was concentrating his forces at Ulm. Finally, General Michelsen advanced towards the Prussian frontier in order to put an end to the uncertainties of the Berlin Cabinet. All these various movements took place in

* On the 26th May, 1805.

accordance with a plan proposed by Austria and discussed between the two Powers. It seemed to meet
the exigencies of the situation ; if it failed, it would be
through the fault of the Austrians. Should Prussia
not consent to join us, we were to go on without her.

The time had come for the Emperor Alexander to
approach the theatre of events. But as the hour of
action drew near I perceived that his resolutions grew
weaker. We started, however, and during our journey
M. Alopeus' couriers brought us reports of the
anxiety produced in Berlin, both upon the King and
his generals, by the Russian advance. Alexander
decided to stop at Pulawy, at the house of my parents,
to whom he wished to pay a visit.

The plan of forcing a passage through Prussia was
not yet abandoned, and the Emperor also persisted
in his idea of declaring himself King of Poland. I
wrote to Count Razumovsky to prepare the Court of
Vienna for this idea. Austria did not show any
opposition to it, but she laid down as a condition that
the old frontier of Galicia should be maintained.

Lord G. L. Gower, on his return from a trip to
England, met us on our journey and informed us that
if we had to force a passage through Prussia, England
would pay Russia the subsidy originally intended for
the King of Prussia. He also said that if Poland
were to be restored, England would give her consent.

I left Brzesc so as to arrive at Pulawy four
and twenty hours after the Emperor. I found every
one in agitation, and making preparations for the
Emperor's reception. Major Orlowski was specially

charged with the preparations, and entered into communication with the Austrian authorities in the neighbourhood of Pulawy. Besides the Emperor and his suite, we were expecting the arrival of two army corps, those of General Michelsen and General Buxhoewden. Prince Poniatowski was warned of the Emperor's plan relative to the restoration of Poland; he was to place himself at the head of the movement and give it a national character. Immediately after my arrival at Pulawy, Polish agents went to Warsaw to announce the arrival of the Emperor, who was received by my parents on the following day. He spoke to them kind and friendly words, by which they were deeply touched. He seemed glad to find himself in a softer climate, and among people who were sincerely devoted to him. My mother, my sister, and my brother, tried to make the fortnight he passed at Pulawy as agreeable to him as possible.

Meanwhile the Emperor's resolution to force a passage through Prussia had been greatly shaken, and he sent Prince Dolgorouky,* who was glad to undertake a mission which seemed to be fatal to my hopes, to the King of Prussia to ask for an interview. It was just at this time that the Emperor Napoleon, who had not as much consideration as Alexander for circumstances which he regarded as of little importance, forced a passage through a Prussian province which was an obstacle to the execution of his plans.

---

* ' A young officer, full of presumption and ambition, an enemy of the coterie of clever young men who were governing the Empire. He sought to persuade the Emperor that these young men were betraying Russia in the interest of Poland. (Thiers' History of the Consulate and the Empire, Book xxii.) See also Vol. I of the present work, p. 331.

The King of Prussia, offended at this conduct, gave a free passage to the Russian troops, and Prince Dolgorouky, triumphant, came to ask the Emperor to go to Berlin to come to an arrangement with the King as to the ulterior measures. This resolution for the moment dissipated the hope of a restoration of Poland; but although the project was foiled, it proved to Napoleon that Poland had not ceased to exist, and that it was necessary to occupy himself with her future destiny—a necessity which he seemed to have forgotten since the Treaty of Lunéville and since the Imperial dignity had absorbed all his attention. The Emperor left Pulawy promising to return. We passed through Warsaw without stopping except at Vilanov, whose proprietor offered us a breakfast. Prince Poniatowski was there, with various other persons, who accompanied the Emperor on horseback up to a few leagues from Warsaw. They went back saddened at the disappearance of the first gleam of hope for the country.

In passing through Posen we met my eldest sister, who was returning to Pulawy with her two wards. The Emperor paid her a visit, and was amiable as usual. She afterwards told me that she was struck by the beauty of his features. He was indeed very attractive, and his charm of manner at once won the attachment of all with whom he came in contact.

Alexander was evidently much relieved on learning that the King of Prussia had given his consent to the passage of the Russian army. We arrived at Berlin,*

* On the 25th of October.

and our reception was most brilliant. The Queen
used all her fascinations to make the Emperor's stay
at Berlin agreeable to him and to remove the difficulties raised by M. de Haugwitz. Another Minister,
M. de Hardenberg, whose influence increased as
matters began to take their present turn, and who was
moreover supported by the Queen, succeeded in bringing the negotiations to a successful result. The
Treaty of Potsdam was signed on the 3rd of
November 1805. The union of the two princes was
confirmed by an oath of eternal friendship taken on
the tomb of Frederick the Great. A month was
allowed to Prussia for her war preparations, and the
day, even the hour, of the commencement of hostilities
was fixed in case the proposals to be presented by
Haugwitz should not be accepted. Meanwhile, the
Archduke Anthony came with the most disastrous
news as to the progress of Napoleon. The Emperor
and his suite hastily left Berlin to meet the Emperor
Francis, who was proceeding to the army corps commanded by General Kutusoff. The latter, in accordance with the plan sent him from Vienna, had
entered Austrian Silesia through Galicia.

It would be superfluous to recapitulate here the
events which are so admirably described by the author
of the ' History of the Consulate and the Empire.' I
will only cite some facts which could not have come to
M. Thiers' knowledge, and I will add an opinion which
does not in all respects coincide with his. I will not
do this without a certain feeling of regret. M. Thiers
has treated me with an indulgence, I might almost say

with a preference, which has deeply touched me, and I wish here to express my gratitude to him.

From Berlin the Emperor proceeded to Weimar, where he wished to pay his sister a visit. The old Grand-Duke still lived; though of advanced age, he was full of life and strength. He was an excellent horseman, and in former years had ridden the whole distance between Carlsbad and Weimar. He seemed desirous of reviving the memory of his ancestor, who had distinguished himself in the Thirty Years' War.

We were received with marks of true affection, and after making the acquaintance of several illustrious writers who were assembled at the Court of Weimar— such as Goethe, Schelling, Herder, and Wieland—we continued our journey. Alexander was anxious to arrive at Olmütz, where the Emperor Francis was waiting for him. This much tried and threatened prince strove to console his allies by telling them that it was not the first time that such disasters had befallen him.

The few days we passed at Olmütz were employed in coming to an understanding as to the operations we were to undertake. Colonel Weirother, who was to act as chief of the general staff, had already passed some time at Pulawy, and had obtained much influence over Alexander's mind. He was an officer of great bravery and military knowledge, but, like General Mack, he trusted too much in his combinations, which were often complicated, and did not admit that they might be foiled by the skill of the enemy. His presence at Olmütz and that of Dolgorouky, whose

impetuous ardour acted on the Emperor's mind, contributed not a little to reassure and animate him.   Just
at this moment arrived the Count de Cobentzel.*
He spoke some imprudent words as to its being
necessary for sovereigns to place themselves at the
head of armies in times of difficulty.   The Emperor
thought these words were meant as advice, perhaps as
a reproach.   He did not pay any attention to our
remonstrances, and would not believe what we continually repeated to him—that his presence would
prevent General Kutusoff from exercising any real
authority over the movements of the army.   This was
especially to be feared in view of the General's
timorous character and courtier-like habits.

The Emperor accordingly proceeded to the field,
while I was retained a few hours at Olmütz on
business.   When I had got through my work I
started also.   A few leagues from Olmütz I found
the Emperor Francis and his suite breakfasting on
the grass.   He invited me to join them, but I
refused, as I was anxious to see Alexander.   After
proceeding four leagues further, I arrived at Wischau,
which was occupied by Russian troops ; they had just
obtained a slight advantage over a French detachment
which left some prisoners behind in its retreat.   The
Emperor had gone to the front, and there was much
rejoicing at head-quarters.   The question now was
what steps to take in face of the French army.
Napoleon had advanced as far as Brünn, and his outposts were extended on a line parallel to ours.   I

* At that time Vice-Chancellor of the Austrian Empire.

found the Emperor Alexander almost at the outposts, very satisfied at the success obtained at Wischau, and surrounded by young officers.

They were discussing whether a movement should be made to the left so as to bring the army in touch with that of the Archdukes Charles and John, who had repulsed Prince Eugene in Italy, or whether it would be more advantageous to move to the right so as to join the Prussians who were, at a moment previously determined upon, to advance and take part in the operations of the combined armies. . The former alternative was adopted, thanks mainly to the influence of Weirother and other Austrian officers.

The best course would have been to abstain from any offensive movement, as such a movement would be likely to expose the army to danger. Time should have been given to the Archdukes to arrive, and it was above all necessary to wait till Prussia should declare herself and move her army, which was eager to fight.

It was not probable that Napoleon would leave Brünn and place himself at a distance from his reserves and his supplies; but even if he had made such a mistake, the Russian army should have declined to accept battle, and should have retired to meet the supports which were coming up. It was here that the Emperor Alexander and his advisers were in fault. They imagined that Napoleon was in a dangerous position, and that he was on the point of retreating. The French outposts had an appearance of hesitation and timidity which nourished these illusions, and reports came at every moment from our outposts announcing an imminent movement of the French army to the rear. Alexander forgot the extreme importance of the moment, and thought only of not allowing so good an opportunity to escape of destroying the French army, and dealing Napoleon a decisive and fatal blow.

During our flank movement we perceived, on the heights which concealed from us the French position, officers who came up one after the other to observe our march. Our movements were carried out in an orderly manner and placed the army in the position it was wished to take up. We were now so situated that we should have had no difficulty in approaching the Archdukes, in case—which did not seem probable —Napoleon should wish to follow us.

On the 1st of December, the day when Count Haugwitz arrived in Napoleon's camp with the ultimatum which, in the event of its rejection, was immediately to be followed by the co-operation of Prussia, the Emperor of Russia had since the morning received letters from Prince Dolgorouky, loading him with praises for having, as the Prince said, increased by his presence and his brilliant valour the courage of his troops.

Everything in the French army seemed to announce a resolution to attempt a retreat. It was therefore decided to advance, in order to take advantage of this disposition of the enemy. Although it was not expected that they would resist, the precaution was taken to fix the line of march of each army corps.

Colonel Weirother was entrusted with this task ; he thoroughly knew the ground, which he had several times gone over and even measured. I did not take part in the military council assembled to carry out this decision, as it was entirely opposed to my opinions. I do not know whether General Kutusoff was admitted to it ; but his advice was certainly not listened to.

The instructions which were to direct the movements of each General did not, I think, reach them till the morning of the 2nd of December. On the evening of the 1st it was cold and foggy, and the Emperor, surrounded by those who were more especially attached to his person, proceeded at a foot pace in the direction where the movements were to begin on the following morning. We met a detachment of Croatian Grenzers ;* they struck up one of their sad national songs. This song, combined with the temperature and the fog, produced a melancholy impression, and some one remarked that the following day was a Monday, a day regarded as unlucky in Russia. As the Emperor was passing over a grassy mound his horse slipped and fell, and he was thrown out of the saddle. Although the accident was not serious, it was regarded by some people as a bad omen.

At daybreak on the following day, about seven o'clock, the Emperor, surrounded by his friends, proceeded to the place which had in the general plan been fixed as the centre of operations. The united armies were composed of the corps of Buxhoewden,

---

* Soldiers raised in the Croatian province known as 'the Military Frontier.'

the vanguard commanded by Prince Bagration, the Guards corps under Miloradovitch, a reserve force which should have remained under the direct orders of General Kutusoff, and an Austrian corps under the command of Prince John of Liechtenstein, which was to take part in the battle should it come to fighting.

When we had arrived at this point, I looked round in every direction and saw a vast plain. A column of Austrian infantry which seemed to me rather loose in formation came to arrange itself in order of battle. Anxiety was impressed on the faces of the Austrian General, the officers, and even the soldiers. The artillery officers alone did not give way to the general depression, and expressed absolute confidence in the effect of their guns. Our wings did not seem to be in any way secured ; on the right were to be seen the Guards, who, following the plan traced out to them, were to move off to a greater distance, which would render it difficult to render any assistance on that side, while on our left it was impossible.

The outposts had from the early morning attacked the French at various points without gaining any advantage. Suddenly we perceived some French columns advancing rapidly and pushing back the corps opposed to them. When I saw the promptitude of the French troops, it seemed to me to augur ill for the result of the day ; the Emperor also was struck by the rapidity of this movement, which caused a real panic in the Austrian ranks. It is to be observed that there was no cavalry at this important point, which should have been the centre of operations.

A moment later there was an outcry for the Emperor's safety ; everyone turned his horse and galloped off. I did the same as the others, and reached a height from which I could see what was passing on the side of the Russian Guards corps, to which was attached nearly the whole of the cavalry. I saw very distinctly several charges executed in succession by the two lines of the enemy's cavalry, each of which took the offensive in turn, and was then withdrawn, passing some enclosures which seemed to embarrass their movements. These charges, which were frequently repeated, kept me for some time on the hill. A moment later, as I was advancing towards the scene of action on the right, between the Guards corps and the French, I met Prince Schwarzenberg. I urged him to restore order in the detachments near him, and to stop their retrograde movement. He seemed at first inclined to yield to my representations, but directly afterwards he told me he feared to interfere with plans which were already in full execution. Having met almost at the same moment a large battery of Russian artillery, which its commander, utterly disconcerted, was leading in an opposite direction to that of the battle field, I forced him to turn back and help the columns which were fighting in front. By a fortunate accident I constantly met the Emperor at the different points which he visited in succession : he often sent me forward to see what was passing, and sometimes I was left completely alone.

It was necessary to prepare for retreat, and the

Emperor proceeded to a point opposite Austerlitz, which was still occupied by the corps of Bagration, now the rear guard of the army. He was met there by his aides-de-camp—General Lieven, General Milo-radovitch, and Prince Michael Dolgorouky, the younger brother of Prince Peter and much wiser than he. He had been shot in the thigh, which did not prevent him from remaining on the field. I also saw the unfortunate Weirother, who had wandered from point to point and by bravely exposing his life strove to remedy the evil of which he had been one of the chief causes. He was tired out and in despair, and hastened away without making any attempt to excuse himself. Those of the officers who had been fortunate enough to make some prisoners presented them to the Emperor with many protestations of devotion, constantly repeating that they were ready to shed their blood for the glory and the safety of the Empire.

I do not know what had become of our friends, but none of them were present at this meeting. Being separated by the confusion which was everywhere prevalent, they did not succeed in finding the Emperor, and I think they lost all their baggage. While we were standing round the Emperor, General Milorado-vitch apostrophised me in somewhat singular fashion, saying, 'How is it you are so calm?' At the same time he indicated to me by a look the aide-de-camp General Lieven, whose countenance showed great anxiety and profound depression.

It was necessary at once to take measures for

sending orders to Bagration, who was quite alone in face of the victorious columns of Napoleon; for it was to be feared that disorder might also spread into his army corps. General Wintzingerode was directed to take orders to Bagration to retire into Austerlitz and maintain himself there as long as he could without exposing himself to a disaster.

Soon after we heard the cheers of the French soldiers; they announced the arrival of Napoleon in the midst of his troops. It was growing dark; the generals left us to return to their respective posts, and the Emperor, to ensure his safety, was obliged to take the road to Holitsch. Having advanced to see what was passing on our left, I met General Buxhoewden and his columns completely routed. The poor General had lost his hat, and his clothes were in disorder; when he perceived me at a distance he cried, 'They have abandoned me! They have sacrificed me!' He continued his retreat, and I hastened to join the Emperor.

Night came on, and we proceeded at a foot pace on the road that leads to Holitsch. The Emperor was extremely depressed; the violent emotion he had experienced affected his health, and I was the only one to bring him some relief. We thus passed two days and three nights before arriving at Holitsch. As we went through the villages we heard nothing but the confused exclamations of people who seek forgetfulness of their reverses in drink. The inhabitants suffered, and scenes of disorder were everywhere around us. After some hours we arrived at a village

somewhat larger than the others, and found a bedroom for the Emperor. We had a little rest, but our
horses were kept ready in case of pursuit. Indeed if
some French squadrons had been sent after us to complete our defeat, I do not know what would have
happened. There were no regiments nor army corps
left in the combined armies; there were only disorderly
bands of marauders increasing the general desolation
of the scene.

I should have liked to bring the two Emperors
together so as to ensure the safety of both, but I did
not succeed. The Emperor Francis went off in a
different direction, but he charged me from time to
time to communicate to Alexander some words of
consolation. These were always the same, assuring
us that he had already experienced similar disasters,
and that although the blow fell mainly upon himself,
he was far from losing hope. . . .

       *   *   *   *   *   *   *

[The Memoirs of Prince Adam Czartoryski here
come to an end. He was dictating them during his
last illness, and death interrupted his work; but he
left behind him a mass of letters, diaries, and other
documents relating to subsequent periods of his career,
a selection from which will be found in the following
chapters.]

CHAPTER XI

RUSSIA AND PRUSSIA AFTER THE BATTLE OF AUSTERLITZ.

THE battle of Austerlitz was fought on the 2nd of December 1805. On the 26th of that month, Napoleon signed a treaty of peace with Austria at Presburg, and meanwhile Alexander and his Ministers were consulting as to the best means of retrieving the humiliation that had been inflicted on the Russian Court. On the 17th of January, 1806, the following memorandum on the situation was presented by Prince Adam Czartoryski to the Czar :—

'The fate of the European Continent is for the present in the hands of three Powers—Russia, France, and Prussia. The relations which will be established between them—the system of policy which each will follow—the moderation, avidity, energy, or weakness, which will inspire its views and measures—will either bring about the enslavement of the smaller States, or secure to Europe at least a period of calm and tranquillity, if not of permanent independence and happiness.

'As I propose more especially to treat in this memorandum of the political relations of Russia with Prussia, I shall only speak of France in so far as she has an influence on those relations. I will first examine the principal features of the policy of each of the three Powers.

'Russia does not wish to acquire anything for herself, but she is not willing, and she ought not, to lose the place and character which a century of glorious achievements has assigned her. Satisfied with her advantages, her only ambition has been to preserve the weak against the attacks of the strong; her weapons have been appeals to right and justice, and she has only used force when those weapons have proved ineffectual. When the employment of force has also not been successful, the general confidence of mankind has been her reward, or has at least made her forget her temporary reverses.

'Between France and Russia, which, when Europe was in its normal condition, could hardly come in contact with each other, is Prussia : timid by system and by the necessity of economising her resources, she can do nothing alone either against Russia or against France. If these two Powers were equal in influence and in activity, Prussia would be entirely justified in keeping on good terms with both of them. But one is constantly encroaching on its neighbours, while the other seeks only to protect them against such encroachment ; and it is therefore both the duty and the interest of Prussia to join Russia in forming a barrier against France. This task devolves upon Prussia as

a first-class State.   Russia, on the other hand, should
not neglect anything that could enable Prussia to play
such a part with success, unless it were evident that
either from necessity or under the influence of
private interests, Prussia would refuse to undertake
the task, in which case Russia would have to seek
other combinations to protect the weaker Powers and
herself against attack. . . .

   ' It is to be remembered that during the recent
war Russia in vain exhausted all her means of per-
suasion to induce Prussia to take part in it.   The
latter Power drew a line of demarcation which im-
peded the operations of the belligerents, and while
affecting to be neutral, was really the ally of France,
receiving as her reward the great advantages she has
derived from the partition of Germany.

   ' When, after the treaties of Lunéville and Amiens,
Buonaparte began to make in the midst of peace
conquests more important than those which he had
achieved during the war—when by his arbitrary
conduct he violated the rights of nations and the
integrity of neutral States—Prussia was the first to
guarantee him in the possession of the territories he
had seized, to pardon, excuse, and justify his aggressions. . . .   When the danger became greater,
and Russia strove to bring about a combination of
the Powers to oppose Buonaparte's rapid progress,
Prussia was invited to take part in it, but she always
declined, at the same time making great professions
of impartiality and of attachment to the Emperor's
person.   Our wishes, she said, are for the success of

Russia's plans, but we have adopted a system of rigid neutrality, and moreover we are without resources, and to make preparations would place us in the greatest danger. So determined was the King of Prussia to reject Russia's proposals, that he punished General Zastrow for having communicated them to him. To put further pressure upon Prussia, Russian troops were sent to her frontier; but the only result was that Prussia protested against being thus threatened, and placed her army on a war footing. The Russian troops then withdrew; and this condescension was only followed by new disasters. While the negotiations were going on, the French defeated the Austrians and entered Prussian territory, arriving as far as Olmütz before the Russians could come to the assistance of their allies. This violation of Prussian territory on the part of France seemed at first to change Prussia's attitude towards that Power, but she never became an effective member of the coalition. She imposed the most onerous conditions on her acceptance of the Russian proposals, and although Russia was ready to accept them, the King was evidently unwilling to come to an understanding with us as to a plan of campaign, and his Government conducted the negotiations in such a dilatory manner that no practical result was arrived at.

'Prussia might in this have been influenced by her jealousy of Austria, her rival; but after Austria was beaten by Buonaparte and forced to sue for peace, the conduct of the Berlin Cabinet towards Russia was the same, though the Emperor offered it all the forces at his disposal if it would join him against France.

'The King of Prussia could at that time have brought an army of 299,000 men into the field, as will be seen from the following table :

Prussian troops, not including reserve battalions,			193,000 men
Saxon „		„	15,000 „
Hessian „		„	16,000 „
Hesse-Darmstadt troops		„	8,000 „
Brunswick „		„	3,000 „
English and Hanoverian troops,		„	24,000 „
Russian	„	„	40,000 „
Total of troops under the immediate orders of the King of Prussia,			299,000 men

'This enumeration was made by Baron Hardenberg after the battle of Austerlitz.

'Russia acted entirely in the spirit indicated at the beginning of this memorandum. She had a right to hope for a close union and perfect confidence and concert in the resolutions which were to be arrived at by mutual agreement, and expected no other reward for her cordiality.

'But from that moment there was an end of all frank intercourse, and only the appearances of friendship were retained. Prussia made an arrangement with France, not only without consulting Russia, but even without communicating to her the engagements into which she had entered. The Cabinet of Berlin received from Buonaparte the price of its complaisance. Whether through weakness or through fear, the King appears to have agreed to all that his counsellors wished; the only point he bore in mind was that the retreat of the Russians was the probable condition of the acquisition by Prussia of a country belonging to the Emperor of Russia's ally.* Thus Prussia, while reserving to herself up to the last moment the power of employing the forces of the allies, only took advantage of their being in the field to make an arrangement with France for her own benefit and to their detriment. Such conduct, pursued with such uniformity and perseverance, could only be the result of unavowed motives, which often constitute the secret springs of the policy of States and are to be inferred from their geographical position and the nature and degree of their resources.

'The power of Prussia is factitious; created by genius, it can only be sustained by a policy of greed and deception. In constantly adding to her territories she has absorbed into herself heterogeneous elements, and she keeps up an army quite out of proportion to her revenue and her population. To consolidate and extend her resources is the principal object of her policy; every other consideration, except that of fear, is subordinate to it. She consequently seeks her advantage everywhere, and interferes for this purpose in every European question; but knowing her weakness, she always avoids proceeding to extremes. She withdraws directly a question has to be dealt with by the sword, because she has not sufficient means in

---

* Hanover, then belonging to England, was ceded to Prussia by France by the Treaty of December 15, 1805.

herself to carry on a war. This want of power, combined with the wish to play a part and the necessity
of keeping it up, leads Prussian policy into combinations which are essentially opposed to the interests of
Europe and to any great or generous views with
regard to Russia. The latter Power seeks to protect
and strengthen the smaller States, while France
successfully pursues her system of aggression and
destruction ; and so long as this is the case Prussian
policy will take the side of France against Russia.
Though Buonaparte's ambition and greed are insatiable, Prussia will firmly believe, perhaps not without
reason, that by assisting France she can only gain,
while by opposing her she will be destroyed like her
neighbours.

'In striving to strengthen her dominions, Prussia
takes care to extend her influence as much as possible.
She wishes not only to be paramount in the north of
Germany, but also to remove all foreign influence from
it, especially that of Russia ; and with this object
she seeks every means of preventing and paralysing
all developments of Russian influence in that quarter.
Moreover, she is and always will be the rival of
Austria in German affairs, while our policy is to
support Austria in Germany in order that she should
not interfere with us in Turkey. France, on the
other hand, will always be the natural ally of Prussia
against Austria. Nor has Prussia so much to fear
from France as from Russia. We wish to be masters
of the Niemen and the Vistula ; these rivers are so
necessary to our trade, and so close at hand, that our

attention has frequently been directed to them, and they must become ours sooner or later. Prussia knows and fears this ; she will always endeavour to diminish our weight and our resources in Europe, in whatever direction we may attempt to extend them, but especially if we turn our eyes to Austrian Galicia, for if we possessed that country we could at any moment send troops into the very centre of the Prussian Monarchy. Prussia is the open rival of Austria, and does not conceal her jealousy and distrust of her ; but in secret she dislikes us perhaps even more, now that crippled Austria inspires her with less fear. . . . All these reflections lead to the conclusion that not only will Prussia never be the sincere ally of Russia, but that she will rather secretly incline to France, and ultimately perhaps revive the old coalition between France, Prussia, and Turkey.

'But though there is so little hope of sincerely attaching Prussia to Russia, it is none the less true that the union of these Powers can alone at this moment save Europe, and that nothing could be more injurious than an intimate *rapprochement* between Buonaparte and Prussia. The more the inclination of the latter to join France becomes manifest, the more should we strive to prevent such a tendency from becoming too predominant at Berlin, and take advantage, with the support of a powerful party in the Ministry and at Court, of every circumstance favourable to our interests in order to diminish its influence. . . . At the same time we should be most careful not to be led into taking mistaken steps. It would be most useful to bind Prussia by some precise engagement, and every means should be taken to attain this object. Berlin should become one of the chief pivots of Russian policy; our agents there should make themselves acquainted with every detail of the views and relations of the Prussian Court, so as to be capable of deciding on every proposal that might be made to them. In no case should they be authorised to confirm or guarantee the advantages Prussia might gain from her complaisance to France; on the contrary, they should be instructed to show Prussia that Russia cannot tolerate a system entirely opposed to her views, and inspire her with a fear of Russia almost, if not quite, as great as that of Buonaparte. . . . They should endeavour to point out to the King of Prussia that his interests coincide with those of Europe generally, and withdraw him from the influence of the members of his Cabinet, who are devoted to France either by principle or through corruption.

'The chief object of our negotiations at Berlin should be to make Prussia enter into defensive engagements, which would not be limited to the north of Germany, and which would especially include the preservation of the Ottoman Empire. These should, if possible, be accompanied by a guarantee of the order of things which would be established by a treaty of peace between France and Russia, and also between France and England, specifying among the territories to be guaranteed those of Turkey. A plan of military action should also be drawn up between

Russia and Prussia, for the eventuality of France attacking one of the guaranteed territories. . .

'It is possible that Napoleon's violent character may produce a renewal of the war in North Germany; in that case we should support Prussia with all the forces at our command, and we should at once give her an assurance to that effect. If the King sincerely wishes to join Russia and act as a buffer to Europe, facts will soon prove his sincerity. . . . But I must repeat to your Majesty that it is necessary to guard against too many concessions to the Berlin Court. The past has proved that Russia has nothing to gain from them. . . By trusting Prussia and blindly following her suggestions, Russia will run a great risk of disaster. Such suggestions can only be in the Prussian interest, which is nearly always opposed to that of Russia and of Europe; and by yielding to them we can only be led into taking steps which would deprive us of the respect of the world, and of the attachment and confidence of our true allies. Meanwhile Prussia would continue to enlarge her territory, and become a formidable Power, even to Russia herself. . . A war with Prussia is an event which circumstances must bring about sooner or later, and we should at once make our preparations for waging it with success.'

CHAPTER XII

1806

DISAGREEMENT BETWEEN THE CZAR AND PRINCE CZARTORYSKI AS TO
THE POLICY OF RUSSIA BEFORE THE BATTLE OF AUSTERLITZ.—
NEGOTIATIONS WITH ENGLAND.—THE LATTER PROPOSES TO GIVE
HOLLAND TO PRUSSIA AS AN EQUIVALENT FOR HANOVER.

IT will have been seen from the last part of Prince
Czartoryski's Memoirs (chapter x) that the Emperor
Alexander, who since the Memel interview* had always
been strongly inclined to an alliance with Prussia,
notwithstanding her treacherous policy, was on this
and other points at issue with his Foreign Minister
during the momentous year which closed with the
battle of Austerlitz. Prince Czartoryski, in a private
letter and memorandum addressed by him to the
Emperor in April 1806, gives the following details on
this subject and on the negotiations with England
during that period :—

'Your Imperial Majesty will appreciate my motives
in attaching to the enclosed memorandum on the
policy of your Cabinet. . . . some remarks

See Vol. I, pages 281 and 282.

addressed solely to yourself, and stating the whole truth without concealment or palliation. Sovereigns are so inseparable from the States which they govern that in speaking of their vicissitudes it is impossible to avoid dwelling on their personal conduct; which indeed often determines the success or the decline of Empires.

'Few reproaches have been made to the Russian Cabinet with so little justice as that of having allowed itself to be carried away by exaggerated ideas of self-sacrifice to the general good of Europe. Those who made such a reproach forgot that not only the reputation but the safety of Russia depended on the general good; and they were not aware of all the conversations with your Majesty during the past two years, in which ideas were repeatedly brought forward as to the combinations which might be advantageous to Russia—such as the possession of Moldavia and Wallachia, the Vistula as a frontier, the reunion of the Slavonic and Greek populations, etc.—as acquisitions of territory and securities for her trade. These ideas were always rejected by your Majesty, and it would consequently have been difficult to entertain the plan of a partition of Europe with Napoleon.

'But events were showing that the need of extending our influence and our territory might become more and more urgent either in order to maintain Russia in the place she ought to occupy or to establish a real and durable peace. It seemed, therefore, that the only course to be followed was one based on the purest and most disinterested sentiments. But I perceived, perhaps too late and with great pain, that your Majesty had no deep or decided conviction as to the subjects which engaged the attention of our Cabinet. The consequence was that after a plan of action of which you had approved had been partly carried out, you continually changed your mind, and we were obliged to reconsider the whole question as if no agreement had been arrived at.

'When the news of the death of the Duc d'Enghien came to St Petersburg, your Majesty will remember that though the despatches I prepared on the subject were very strongly worded, they were not intended to be made public, and that it was your Majesty alone that gave the impulse for further action. This energy gave me hope, for it seemed likely to develop in your Majesty that decided conviction which until then had not sufficiently shown itself in your actions.* War now seemed to me inevitable, but you thought otherwise. You thought up to the last moment that Austria would not dare to fight, and that this would serve as an excuse to Russia also to hold aloof. The consequence was that though the steps taken by the Cabinet by the express orders of your Majesty pointed directly to war, no preparations for war could be made in the interior of the Empire. . . . Your Majesty did

* 'Prince Czartoryski was the principal author of the system of European arbitration which had led Russia to take up arms against France. This system, which was used by Russian statesmen as a mask for their national ambition, was in Prince Czartoryski prompted by a sincere and frankly conceived idea. . . . He addressed to the young Emperor, formerly his friend, and now again becoming his master, noble and respectful remonstrances which would do honour to a Minister in a free country, and are far more creditable in a country where resistance to the sovereign is an act of rare devotion and remains unknown to the public.' (Thiers' History of the Consulate and the Empire, Book xxiv.)

not think proper to order a sufficient levy of recruits, though the necessity of such a measure was repeatedly pointed out to you. This indecision was most injurious and dangerous, as was strikingly shown in our conduct towards Prussia. The proposal to send Russian troops to act for Austria and against Prussia had been entirely approved by the most eminent personages in Europe. It was this that decided the Archduke Charles to declare himself for war, as he considered it a proof that Russia wished to make war in earnest. Pitt and Fox also agreed. " If hostilities take place with Prussia," said the latter, " they should be pushed on vigorously and without regard to other considerations."

'It is true that your Majesty afterwards told us that you had all along intended to regulate your conduct by the great probability that the King of Prussia would finally decide to join us. But who could answer for this ? The disastrous result of our operations is to be attributed to the Memel interview, which I look upon as one of the most unfortunate events that have ever happened for the interests of Russia, both through its immediate consequences and those which have followed upon it since and will in the future. The intimate friendship established at that interview, after a few days' acquaintance, between your Majesty and the King caused you to look upon Prussia not as a political State, but as an individual dear to you. This personal connection with the sovereign of a State whose interests are mostly opposed to those of Russia continually hampered the action of our Cabinet, and finally prevented the adoption of vigorous and decisive measures at the beginning of the campaign. In my opinion the suspension of the order to march the Russian troops into Prussia, and your Majesty's departure for the army, were the chief causes of all the misfortunes that have happened to us. I strove in vain to represent to you all the inconveniences which would result from your presence with the army, and my forebodings have unfortunately all been realised. Your presence transferred the responsibility of the generals to yourself, and you had neither the experience nor the knowledge necessary for taking the command. Meanwhile the order to send the troops into Prussia still remained suspended; yet each day of delay was a day lost for Russia and Europe, and gained for Buonaparte. He advanced and we remained stationary.

'Moreover, since your Majesty's departure from Pulawy your opinions and sentiments underwent a notorious change which necessarily exercised great influence on our operations. You sent away those in whom you had previously trusted, and although I accompanied you in your journey to Berlin, you rejected all my proposals and showed by your statements that your views and system of action had entirely changed. . . . The inference which was drawn from all this at Berlin was that your Majesty's policy was different from that of your Cabinet; this naturally encouraged the duplicity of the Prussian Government, and influenced the stipulations of the unfortunate Treaty of Potsdam,* at the foot of which I shall always regret that circumstances compelled me to place my name.

' If you had listened to the advice we were constantly giving you, at first not to go to the army, and afterwards not to remain with it, but to ask the King of Prussia for an interview in order to move him to decisive action, the battle of Austerlitz would not have been fought and lost, or, if lost, would not have had the results which followed upon it.† General Kutusoff, left to himself, would have avoided a battle until the Prussians should have joined his army. This would have obviously been the right course. Buonaparte's interest was not to lose time; ours was to gain it. He had every reason to risk a decisive battle and we to avoid one. Your Majesty will recollect that I repeatedly spoke to you in this sense, advising that the enemy should be harassed by partial combats and that the bulk of our army should march into Hungary to effect a junction with the Archduke. And if your Majesty had not been on the battlefield, you would have been able to issue your orders calmly and without precipitation. How could you do this in the midst of the confusion at Holitsch, where you were surrounded by people who loudly accused the Austrians of treachery and declared that the Russian army was absolutely incapable of fighting any longer?

* Signed on the 3rd of November 1805.

† 'The young Emperor refused to listen to any more advice, as he thought himself more clever than his advisers. Prince Adam Czartoryski—honest, grave, ardent under a cold exterior, who had become the inconvenient censor of the weakness and instability of his master—maintained an opinion which must have completely alienated him. He thought the Emperor's place was not with the army.' Thiers' History of the Consulate and the Empire, Book xxxiii.

'In the midst of this agitation and clamour it was impossible to say anything in favour of Austria or of the interests of Europe. People declared that your Majesty had done enough for others and that you must now think of yourself—as if your glory and your safety had nothing in common with the fall of Austria and your other allies. You thought fit to reply to me in this sense when I ventured to speak in favour of the King of Naples ; and you told the Emperor Francis that he could not reckon any longer upon your army. I was so deeply penetrated, however, with the great evil of such a complete abandonment of the cause which we had embraced that I took it upon myself to write to Berlin in another sense without being authorised to do so by your Majesty. But this step could have no result, since your Majesty thought it necessary to say to the Prussian Minister here that you would leave Prussia at liberty to come to an arrangement with France. . . .'

In the memorandum which accompanied Prince Czartoryski's letter he remarks, referring to the preliminaries of the battle of Austerlitz :—

'Prussia was a chief element in the plan that was about to be executed. It had been decided that she was to be brought into the coalition at any cost, and it was in every respect the interest of Russia especially to do so, as in sending a considerable force beyond her frontiers she could not leave behind her so suspicious a neighbour as Prussia. If the Court of Berlin had yielded, the success of the plan as a whole could not have been doubtful. If it had resisted, and our armies had been sent forward on the day agreed upon, they would have found the Prussians on a peace footing, and in no way prepared to receive us. . . . Our true policy was to make war upon Prussia : that would have been the safest, perhaps the only, means of success in our great undertaking. . . . The operation against Prussia was put off till the 16th of September, by which date it was calculated that Kutusoff's army would cover Bohemia and threaten Silesia, while the other armies entered southern and ducal Prussia ; and by that date the Prussians had had time to make preparations. But even then the Court of Berlin admitted that its troops would evacuate the districts up to the Vistula. We might at least have taken possession of those districts, and if we had gone further, our success would not have been doubtful. The Prussians may be good soldiers, but they are easier for the Russians to beat than the French. Moreover, we should have fought them in a country entirely devoted to our interests. The enthusiasm among the Poles was general ; all Poland was ready to rise *en masse,* and asked that the sovereign of Russia should add to his titles that of King of Poland. None of our allies could have objected to such a course, as they had all sanctioned the plan of marching into Prussia. England, who until then had, in accordance with her old principles of policy, been jealous of our exercising a preponderant influence over Prussia, now declared war upon her, destroying her trade in the North Sea while we

did the same in the Baltic; she even went so far as
to give us, for the purpose of acting against Prussia,
all the subsidies she had offered to that Power for
action against France. . . .

We lost all these advantages by our vacillation ;
our armies stopped on the Prussian frontier, and the
violation of Prussian territory by the French * made
Prussia more disposed to join the coalition. The
original plan of invading her territory was now abandoned, and your Majesty's Ministry did their best to
bring her over by conciliation, as she was no longer to
be made to yield by terror. . . Russia has been reproached for using her good offices in London to
negotiate the cession of Hanover to Prussia.† But
as to this point, we may appeal to people who were
then at Berlin and were aware of the negotiations, as
difficult as they were disagreeable, which led to the
Treaty of Potsdam. . . . Anyhow, we succeeded in
making England understand the urgent motives which
had led us to yield to the wishes of the Berlin Cabinet.
She agreed not to break off the negotiations, to sign
the treaty for the subsidies, and to assist in obtaining
some other acquisition for Prussia—even to assure
her the possession of Holland. Russia reserved to
herself equivalent acquisitions. . . .

Nothing was yet lost ; General Mack's defeat had
even established the preponderance of Russia over
Austria to such a degree that people looked upon
your Majesty as the future saviour of the Austrian

* See page 99.
† See Chapter IX.

Monarchy. . . But the next four weeks were wasted in mutual complaints, and ended in the battle of Austerlitz, in a feeling of extreme exasperation between Russia and Austria, in the retreat of the Russian army from Moravia, and in the abandonment of Europe to her fate.

CHAPTER XIII

1806

NEGOTIATIONS WITH MR FOX.—CORRESPONDENCE BETWEEN HIM AND
PRINCE CZARTORYSKI.—MR FOX'S PROPOSAL TO ATTACK PRUSSIA.

SHORTLY after the appointment of Mr Fox as Foreign
Minister in the administration of 'all the talents,'
formed by Lord Grenville after the death of Pitt,
the following correspondence took place between Mr
Fox and Prince Czartoryski :—

From Mr Fox

DOWNING STREET,
17th March 1806.

Relying on the confidence with which your
Excellency was so good as to honour me last year
as a private individual, I think I have almost a right
to ask for a continuance of your kindness in the
situation in which I am now placed. I would not,
however, have done this, notwithstanding all the value
I attach to the honour of your friendship, if I did not
entirely adhere to the opinion I expressed to M. de
Novosiltzoff that a full and reciprocal confidence between the two Courts is absolutely necessary both for

the good of them both and for that of the whole of
Europe. I was unfortunately not able to approve the
plan of last year, and I did not conceal my opinion on
the subject. Would to God that the last words I said
to M. de Novosiltzoff in the presence of the Prince of
Wales—whatever you do, take your time, piano, piano
—had made more impression! I beg you not to
think, Monsieur le Prince, that I remind your Excellency of all this in order to boast of my foresight. If
I look back on the past, it is only to obtain more
instruction as to the future. A proposal of peace
such as I wished to be made when I had the honour
of writing to your Excellency a year ago* would perhaps be out of place in present circumstances. Russia
has taken too prominent a part in the war now to
assume the office of a mediator. But since Buonaparte's last speech to his legislative assembly there are
many people who think he will send us some proposal
at least tending to a negotiation.† Might I venture
to ask your Excellency what would be your opinion as
to the course to be adopted in such a case? The first
answer would necessarily depend on the nature of the
overtures to be made to us. They might be made in
such a way that it would be necessary to reject them
without discussion; but let us suppose they will be too
plausible for us to do this. In that case it seems to
me that it would be well in the first instance to accept
the overtures, at the same time declaring that it will

---

* This letter cannot be traced in the Czartoryski Archives.

† The letters which passed between Talleyrand and Fox on this subject were laid
before Parliament in 1806. They are published in Lord Russell's *Memorials and Correspondence of Charles James Fox.*

be necessary that his Majesty the Emperor of Russia should take part both in the treaty and in the negotiations which may lead to it. I have not at this moment any reason to believe that any overtures whatever will be made to us : I speak only in accordance with the ideas of those who attach more weight to Buonaparte's language than it seems to me to deserve. Your Excellency will see that I speak to you frankly. If you will equally show confidence in me I will not misuse it.

Let us now consider the contingency—unfortunately the most probable one—that the war will continue even without matters coming to a negotiation. I must begin by saying to your Excellency plainly that I have in no way altered my old opinions, that offensive alliances are not at all to my taste, and that as they exist, our best course would now be to give them as far as possible a defensive character. A good opportunity now seems to present itself for attaining this object, and at the same time showing that we are resolved to oppose injustice and aggression. The King of Prussia has seized the electorate of Hanover ; his pretext is that he wishes to protect it by his troops, and under this pretext he deprives the King and the Regency even of the civil government of the country. He asserts that his occupation of the electorate is only to last until a peace shall settle its fate, but he has not distinctly stated that he will then restore it to the Elector. We have made representations to him on this subject, and Lord G. L. Gower has been instructed to communicate them to your Excellency. If the powerful support of your Court could induce Prussia to act nobly on this occasion, infinite good would be the result. In the first place, we would show Europe that the King of England still preserves his influence in Continental affairs, which is a great point, and further, that he employs this influence not to attack others, but to defend himself.

The King of Prussia has given up Anspach and Bayreuth; he should not be helped nor even encouraged to retake them, but he should be made to abandon the odious system of compensating himself with the property of others. In the event of Buonaparte retaliating on Prussia for such an honourable policy by making war upon her—which I do not think probable—she will have to be defended with all the forces at our disposal. Your Excellency has much more means than I have of conjecturing what the conduct of Austria would be under such circumstances. I am inclined to think that she would at least do no harm, if she is not able to do any good. It might perhaps be said that even with your support we would not be able to persuade his Prussian Majesty to abandon an object which it is reported that he has long coveted. But we would at least have shown him that he can never hope to have quiet and legitimate possession of it; and so far as our interests are concerned, we would remain in precisely the same situation as that which we now occupy. Moreover, I think one should in any case avoid the appearance of wishing to lay down the law to the King of

Prussia, or of provoking him to war against France.
Let him temporise as much as he thinks proper; I
would be the first to advise him to do so; but let him
not attack any other State, whether strong or weak.

As to Austria, I am very glad to hear that public
opinion thinks the friendship which has so long
existed between her and Russia has not been altered
as much as people thought some months ago.   A
friendly understanding, and if possible a perfect harmony, between all the countries which are not
dependent upon France is to be desired more than
ever.   Even with regard to those which are more or
less under her subjection it would I think be necessary
to avoid every kind of offence and not to show any feeling of revenge.   Opportunities might, for what we
know, arise in the course of time which two Cabinets
united as ours are, might by judicious conduct employ
to advantage.   The existing state of affairs, if we look
to the present or the future, is truly disheartening.
It cannot be remedied by a *coup de main* : a wise and
consistent course of conduct can alone enable us to do
so.   If we cannot reduce the enormous power of
France, it will always be something to stop its
progress.

I have thus entirely opened my heart to you, mon
Prince.   Let us seek to work together for the good of
our respective countries and for that of all Europe.
The more the two Courts and their Ministers understand each other, the better for our common cause.

Your Excellency will of course understand that this
letter, like the others which have passed between us,

is of a confidential nature, to be placed under the eyes of the Emperor or not, as your Excellency may think proper. Neither Lord G. L. Gower, in whom I have the greatest confidence, nor anyone else, knows the contents of it.

Accept, Monsieur le Prince, etc.

(Signed)   C. J. Fox.

Answer from Prince Czartoryski.

Your Excellency has anticipated me by the letter you were good enough to write to me on the 17th of March, as I was about to address one to you to express my joy and my congratulations on your entrance into the Ministry, and to ask for a continuance of your confidence. I now hasten to convey to you the expression of these feelings, and to add my sincere thanks for the frank and friendly manner in which your Excellency has expressed yourself in your letter. Pray believe me when I say that personally I attach very great value to the friendly and confidential relations which you are good enough to encourage me to maintain, and that no one can be more convinced than myself of the reciprocal advantage, I may say the necessity, of an intimate union and an invariable concert between our two Courts. It is to England and to Russia that the remains of Europe will cling, and their only hope of salvation is in the union of these Powers.

I know too well your Excellency's views not to be certain that you have seen with much pain that your forebodings as to the undertaking of the allied Courts should have been so completely realised. But you are at the same time too just not to agree that there was not after all any positive reason for supposing that our efforts would have such disastrous results. It was not the plan that was in fault. Its failure was due to circumstances which the Russian Cabinet had not the means either to foresee or to prevent.

But it is useless to look back upon the past except for drawing useful lessons from it ; what should occupy us is the present and the future. I will respond to your Excellency's frankness by also opening to you my mind on the subject. The communications which Count Vorontzoff lately made to you have partly done this already. We have explained our views with the greatest confidence and detail, and the British Government must have been satisfied with the principles which we developed. Several of the matters referred to in the first despatch rather required to be discussed confidentially and in much detail than to be treated officially, and as to this the two Cabinets will have to come to an understanding hereafter. The despatches which Count Strogonoff* will receive to-day will furnish him with new and very ample communications for your Excellency ; you will see that we do not wish to conceal from you any of our thoughts, and that our invariable principle is to do everything in common and in concert with England.

The aspect of affairs is indeed disheartening, and

The special envoy sent to London to negotiate with Mr Fox.

I entirely agree with your Excellency that the defensive principle should preferably be adopted in the transactions and the conduct of the European States. It is the principle held by the Powers which are opposed to the subversion of Europe, and never was there a more offensive policy than that of Buonaparte. Yet although a union for purposes of defence is always in principle the most useful one, there can be no doubt that when the time for action arrives it is indispensable, or at least more advantageous, to take the offensive if possible.

It may be that the circumstances of the moment and the nature of the elements with which it would be necessary to act are such that although a different policy would be more suitable, one is forced for the present to maintain a passive attitude on the Continent, and to avoid provoking new difficulties which might give rise to new disasters. If such bo the case —as your Excellency seems inclined to suppose — peace with France is only the more necessary, and it becomes the only course open to us. I confess that even if it were only a patched-up peace to last but a short time—if it were only a truce which would give us but a precarious and temporary security—it would still be better for the Continent than the present state of things, and it becomes clear that circumstances oblige us to see the danger increase and come nearer to us without our being able to prevent or meet it. On our side it may be said that peace is a necessity to us; we can neither reach the enemy nor do him any serious harm; it would therefore be better, as it seems to me, to bind him by some arrangement so as to arrest his advance if only for a short time, and make him believe and declare that he is also at peace with us. I must here remark that an attack on the part of the Turks, if we leave them the choice of the time when it is to be made, might also be inconvenient. It would begin on our frontiers, and at a time when the Turks would have completed their armaments, and the French been enabled to prepare all the means they could employ in favour of Turkey and against us. These various considerations lead me strongly to desire that the overtures which have been made by Your Excellency to M. de Talleyrand should produce some satisfactory result. Russia would certainly have awaited the consequence of these overtures, if the affair of Cattaro* and the dangers which threaten Austria had not obliged us to hasten a direct discussion with Buonaparte, as the only means of escape from the embarrassing position in which we find ourselves, between the necessity of giving up to the French an important post—the stepping-stone, so to say, from which they could easily proceed to the execution of their designs on Turkey—and the fear of exposing unhappy Austria to the resentment of Buonaparte and to complete ruin.

The explanations which I am giving here to Lord G. L. Gower on this subject, and those which Count Strogonoff is instructed to develop to your Excellency, will, I trust, be of a kind to satisfy you,

---

* After the battle of Austerlitz the Russian troops occupied Cattaro, in order to prevent its being taken by the French, to whom it had been ceded by the Treaty of Presburg.

and will prove to you that the fundamental maxim of our policy continues to be not to separate ourselves from England and to pay the greatest attention to her wishes and her advice.

It is not impossible that Buonaparte, after convincing himself that he cannot succeed in bringing either of us to an isolated negotiation, will at length agree to treat with the two Powers in concert. This would be a great point gained. Moreover, whatever might be the necessity and urgency for Europe of peace with France, it would not I think be inopportune to come to an early understanding as to the measures to be taken, if the continuation of the war should become inevitable ; for it must be anticipated that the more Buonaparte will perceive the great need of peace on the Continent, the less inclined will he be to accept reasonable conditions. Any overtures you may eventually make in this respect would be eagerly received here, and would be treated with the greatest possible consideration.

As regards Prussia, I do not lose the hope that the just and energetic conduct * of the British Cabinet with regard to her, will have a salutary influence on her policy. The more considerable the losses of Prussian trade will be, the more the general outcry of the Prussian people, who already lift up their voices against the action of their Government, will become threatening, the less will Prussia be in a position to

---

* *i.e.*, the blockade of the Prussian seaports, and the capture by the British fleet of Prussian merchant ships, after Prussia had seized Hanover and closed the Elbe and the Weser to British trade.

continue her present policy.   She will have to abandon
it in some way or other.   Our measures with regard
to her are fundamentally in accordance with your
wishes ; but our relations with her, and our situation
generally, are not the same.   We flatter ourselves
that we may yet be able to withdraw Prussia from
the shameful dependence to which she has submitted
herself ; the present moment of crisis, and the
extreme embarrassment in which she is plunged, are
perhaps even propitious for such an endeavour.   This
is the sole reason why we do not think we ought
entirely to reject the explanations and protests which
she is incessantly sending us, and we wish meanwhile
to stop her at least in the design which she might
have formed—if she had had nothing to care for or to
expect from us—of abandoning herself more and more
entirely to the will of Buonaparte and the execution
of the plans he is meditating.

I do not know if your Excellency will agree to all
the opinions I have expressed, but I flatter myself
that you will at any rate be satisfied with my extreme
frankness and unreserved confidence.

I have thought it right to show the Emperor the
letter you have done me the honour of writing to me.
His Imperial Majesty has expressly charged me to
express to you, sir, how charmed he is at the wisdom
and thoughtfulness of your views.   He desires that
his Cabinet should remain in intimate harmony with
that of his Britannic Majesty, and your entrance into
the Ministry has caused him much satisfaction.   This
disposition on his Majesty's part can only add to all

the motives of State which sincerely bind the Court of St Petersburg to that of London.

Count Strogonoff will have the honour of handing this letter to your Excellency, and I take the opportunity of particularly recommending him to you. I beg you to show him entire confidence (which you may do without the slightest fear); he will deserve it by the frankness and cordiality with which he will make his communications to you, and I flatter myself that at my request your Excellency will not on your part fail to encourage him in this conduct by acting towards him in a similar manner.

Your Excellency will not take it ill that I have shown your letter to Lord G. L. Gower. I did not think any harm could result from my doing so, and as he handed me your letter himself I could hardly have done otherwise in view of the intimate friendship which exists between us. It is with pain that we hear he wished to leave his post; I should infinitely regret it, and I will confess to your Excellency that I would much desire that Lord G. L. Gower should remain with us for some time longer, especially during the difficult circumstances of the present juncture. Your Excellency will pardon me if in this wholly private and confidential letter I have thought I might be permitted not to conceal this wish from you.

If M. d'Oubril should go so far as Paris, it is very possible that circumstances may cause him to go on to London, perhaps with some mission from the French Government. Should this be the case, I recommend him beforehand to your Excellency's kind-

ness.   Lord G. L. Gower will have given you good
accounts of the selection of M. d'Oubril ; he is a safe
man, on whose prudence and principles the two allied
Courts may wholly rely.*   This leads me to request
your Excellency to speak of him in the same terms to
the English Plenipotentiary who may proceed to
France, and to instruct him to have confidence in him.

P.S. of the 13*th of May* 1806.   My letter to your
Excellency was written long ago, but the despatch of
the courier who was to take it was put off from day to
day.   In the meantime we have received despatches
from London which inform us of the issue of your
pourparlers with France.   I open my letter to add
this postscript, as I cannot avoid expressing to your
Excellency how satisfied and enchanted we are here
at the wisdom, the loyalty, and the energy which your
Government has shown on this occasion.   The good
faith and the constant interest of which it gives proof
to Russia demand entire reciprocity on her part.   I
will not here multiply assurances and protestations on
this subject, for between us they seem to me entirely
superfluous.   Moreover, the communications which
you will receive, several of which are much in arrear,
can only refer to the state of affairs anterior to the
present moment.   I am glad to look upon the present
relations between the two countries (and surely your
Excellency will agree with me on this point) as those
of two parts of the same body.   There is no difference

---

* This estimate of M. d'Oubril's character was unfortunately not borne out by
his subsequent conduct in Paris (see Count Vorontzoff's letter of the 7/19 October,
1806, page 163).

in our objects, in our principles, in our intentions; and
our discussions can only turn on the most proper mode
and the most suitable means of realising our common
wishes according to circumstances.—Receive, etc.

(Signed)   A. CZARTORYSKI.

Count Strogonoff, the Russian special envoy,
arrived in London in March 1806, and Count Vorontzoff, the Russian Ambassador, in a letter to Prince
Adam Czartoryski dated the $\frac{19}{31}$ March, thus describes
his impressions of the interview which took place
between the two Russian diplomatists and Mr Fox :—

'I will add to my official reports, for your personal
information alone, that Fox wishes for peace at any
price, and that he would abandon all his allies to obtain it, but that he will not succeed, as the nation is
too strongly opposed to a shameful peace, and Buonaparte, flushed with victory, will not offer him any
other, especially as he knows Fox's immoderate desire
to end the war. Lord Grenville and the British
nation will oppose him, for they wish for a peace that
shall be honourable and arranged in concert with us.
Moreover, the great majority of people here are convinced that England will run less risk in continuing a
purely naval war than in making peace with the
Corsican, in whose good faith nobody trusts. The
Cabinet would not, however, be overthrown if it made
peace together with us.

You will see from my official despatches that Fox
has the strange idea of our troops quitting Sicily in
order to leave the English alone to defend it. He

could not support this proposal by any valid reason, and this confirmed my belief that with all his intellectual vivacity, which in his parliamentary speeches even rises to genius, he is not a man of judgment, and still less a statesman; that he is merely a party leader of great astuteness and a master of intrigue, and that he will never shine in the Ministry as he did in the Opposition.'

Prince Adam Czartoryski gives further particulars as to Mr Fox's Foreign Policy at this period in the following extracts from a memorandum presented by him to the Emperor in his capacity of Minister of Foreign Affairs :—

Memorandum of the 30th May 1806.

In the communications made to us by the Cabinet of St James's we are urged to bring the important questions pending between us to a definitive issue.

The British Ministry at one time thought there might be a means of opening negotiations with France. It took part in a correspondence started by Buonaparte himself; but the only preliminary point on which the Cabinet of London was bound to insist —that of not arriving at any definite conclusion except in concert with Russia—has just been rejected by the French Government. England now considers the negotiation broken off; she has arrived at the conclusion that Buonaparte evidently does not wish for peace, and that therefore she must make up her mind to war. At the same time England has been grievously insulted by the inexcusable conduct of

Prussia towards her, who has violated on this occasion all the obligations that were imposed upon her by the dictates of ordinary morality and by international law. The British Government has been obliged to take the most energetic measures against Prussia, and it must be admitted that it neither could nor should have done otherwise in reply to so direct an attack upon the interests and dignity of the King of England and so manifest a violation of international law.*

Strong in her rights against France and Prussia, and in her consciousness of the frank and loyal policy she has pursued towards Russia, England thinks herself entitled to regard us as an ally on whose co-operation she can reckon with perfect security. She rightly thinks that very energetic measures can alone bring about such a peace as is to be desired; her Government shows the necessity of striking a great blow on the Continent in order to restore the balance of Europe, and proposes that, as a matter both of convenience and of justice, this blow should be directed against Prussia.

To secure the success of such an undertaking, the British Government thinks it will be necessary to follow Buonaparte's plan, namely, the assemblage of considerable forces on a single point, so as to obtain a decisive result.

England recognises the inconveniences of our position between Turkey and Prussia, and asks what is the probability of our not being at war with those two Powers directly she attacks one of them. The

* The annexation by Prussia of Hanover.

British Cabinet thinks we might direct our efforts against either, and, in the event of our doing so, hopes we will push our conquests as far as possible, and offers us assistance and subsidies. But it would prefer that we should attack Prussia, so that she might suffer exemplary punishment for the duplicity she has shown during recent events. The example of a sovereign increasing his power and territory by a policy of servility towards France would encourage the other Powers and dissipate the hope of any States besides Russia and England uniting against Buonaparte.

At the same time the British Government still sincerely desires peace, and it would prefer a policy of conciliation to one of war, if by such means the desired object could be attained. Mr Fox even suggests a separate negotiation with France, Russia and England, each negotiating on its own account, but first coming to an understanding as to the essential conditions which are to be sought or rejected. Foreseeing that Russia, before stating any opinion on this suggestion, would desire to reconcile Prussia with England, Mr Fox states the conditions on which such a reconciliation might be brought about, namely, a raising of the blockade and a satisfactory arrangement as to Hanover.

Let us now consider our present position and the probable consequences of Russia deciding to maintain the passive position, midway between peace and war, in which she now stands.

The humiliation of Austria, the blind submission

of Prussia to Buonaparte's will, the occupation of the
greater part of Germany by French troops, and the
invasion of the whole of Italy, are not the only results
of importance to us which have followed from the
last campaign. Turkey, over whom our safety requires us to maintain exclusive influence, not only
strives to withdraw herself from it, but already begins
to defy us. M. d'Italinsky* reports that the Porte
has requested that the Dardanelles should be closed
to Russian war vessels and transports, that Turkey
permits flagrant outrages upon persons under our
protection, and that she will not refuse a passage to a
French army through the Herzegovina and Montenegro if Buonaparte should desire it.

Russia is thus in a critical position; but it will
become even more so if she persists in maintaining a
system of inaction. If England finds that we absolutely decline to join her either in a war or in arrangements for peace, she will find our alliance rather a
burthen than an advantage, and will seek other means
of attaining the objects of her policy. Turkey would
then entirely emancipate herself from our influence;
Sweden would become indifferent, if not hostile; and
the rest of Europe, not seeing any hope of Russian
support, would have no alternative but to attach herself
to Buonaparte's chariot. In that case the latter will
certainly not be idle. The Polish provinces have long
attracted his craving for glory and activity, and
already he is spreading a report that the Princess of
Saxony is to marry some member of the Buonaparte

* The Russian Ambassador at Constantinople.

family who will become King of Poland.   Another of
his objects is the regeneration of the Ottoman Empire;
and it is not to be denied that notwithstanding her
present decrepitude, Turkey could cause us great
difficulties if Buonaparte should make himself master
of all her resources and direct them against Russia.

It would appear from the above considerations
that the principal and essential thing for the safety of
Russia is to maintain, and even to draw tighter, the
bonds which unite her to England.   Russia is perhaps
more interested even than England in not abandoning
an intimate alliance which is now more necessary than
ever to save the remains of independence in Europe.
What would tend above all to make such an alliance
desirable to your Majesty is the composition of the
present English Ministry and the principles by which
it is actuated.   It shows in its policy as much
moderation and wisdom as energy and loyalty.   The
conduct of England with regard to neutral commerce
displays both the prudence and the liberality of her
Government; and the loyalty it showed to Russia
when France offered England an advantageous peace
demands entire reciprocity on our part.

Being deeply convinced of the truth of these
remarks, and considering the fatal results which would
follow from the ties which unite us to Great Britain
being loosened or broken, I do not hesitate to express
the opinion that the honour of Russia, her dearest
interests, and her safety, imperiously require her not
to separate her cause from that of England.

[Although, in consequence of the annexation by Prussia of Hanover and the closing of the Elbe and Weser to British trade, Mr Fox retaliated by blockading her harbours and seizing her merchant ships, neither England nor Russia sent any troops against her. Meanwhile the aggressive policy of Napoleon and the excesses of his soldiers caused an explosion of patriotic indignation in Prussia which her King found it impossible to resist. The Prussian Government demanded that the French troops should be recalled, and after some angry discussion Napoleon attacked the Prussian army and completely destroyed it at Jena (14th October 1806).]

CHAPTER XIV

1806

RESIGNATION BY PRINCE ADAM CZARTORYSKI OF THE POSITION OF
MINISTER OF FOREIGN AFFAIRS IN RUSSIA.—RETROSPECT OF HIS
POLICY IN THIS CAPACITY.—HIS OPPOSITION TO AN ALLIANCE WITH
FRANCE AT THE EXPENSE OF ENGLAND.

ON the 17th of June, 1806, Prince Adam Czartoryski,
after repeatedly requesting the Emperor Alexander
to relieve him of the duties of Foreign Minister,
finally retired from that post. He had, as will be
seen from the following letter, ample reason to justify
him in taking this step, but the chief cause of his
having done so was one that he could hardly state in
precise terms to the Emperor. He had only accepted
his position in the Ministry because he believed that
by so doing he might be of service to Poland. Alexander's persistence in seeking the alliance of Prussia
convinced him that this belief was a delusive one, and
his sole motive for remaining in the Russian Ministry
thus ceased to exist. Moreover, the hopes of the
Poles had been raised by the approach of Napoleon ;
if France were to make war again upon Russia, which
seemed more than probable, Napoleon would doubtless

strive to secure the support of the Poles by promising
to restore their independence, and in that case it would
be impossible for Prince Adam to continue to direct
the foreign policy of a State with which his countrymen might be at war.

Prince Adam Czartoryski to the Emperor.
22nd of March 1806.

It is not with the object of exaggerating to your
Imperial Majesty the dangers which threaten your
Empire, or of uselessly alarming you as to its position,
that I have prepared the memorandum which I now
submit to your consideration. It has been dictated by
sincere zeal, and after mature reflection. I have
thought it indispensable to point out to your Majesty
some of the dangers by which you are surrounded and
which you do not seem to perceive. Russia is really
in a very critical position. Her difficulties and yours,
Sire, may increase in a degree which I cannot contemplate without fear. I therefore think there is not a
moment to be lost in proposing to your Majesty the
only measure which can render possible all the others
which must be necessitated by circumstances—a
measure not sufficient to secure the safety of the
State, but without which it would become too precarious, if not quite unattainable.

Until the late war began there was a certain degree of uniformity in the action of the Government,
for your Majesty showed some confidence in the persons with whom you consulted, and usually discussed
affairs before deciding upon them. Even then, how-

ever, the necessity of introducing more unity among the various departments of Government constantly made itself felt. The disasters we have experienced must be partly attributed to the fact that such unity was not sufficiently established, and that afterwards it was totally destroyed at the moment when it became more necessary than ever to preserve it. . . .

Your Majesty will permit me here to observe that I have been greatly surprised to see that you assume the sole responsibility not only of every measure, but of every detail in its execution ; while the object of the establishment of your Ministry was to guarantee you against such responsibility. You possessed the means of calling any of your Ministers to account for any failure of Government policy ; but the fault of such failure must now fall upon you, as you wish to do everything alone, both in military and in civil matters. . . . If the passive policy of your Government should bring war into your frontiers—a by no means impossible case—I could not answer for the conduct of the Poles ; I would even fear the effect that such an example might produce on the Russians. Already the latter see with pain that the glory of the State is diminished and its pride humiliated. If our frontiers are crossed by the enemy, the fault will be thrown on your Imperial Majesty, and the talk on this subject in the two capitals is not reassuring. . . . But if you do not attach any belief or value to the opinions which I have taken the liberty of expressing, nothing will remain to me but to retire with the satisfaction of having done my duty. In that case your

Imperial Majesty will recognize the justice of my request that I should be allowed to quit my post at once. I will not remind you of all that has passed since my return here,* how little attention you have paid to my proposals ; . . . · and you are too considerate to wish to impose upon me any longer the painful obligation—I may say the martyrdom—of participating in an order of things and executing measures which in my opinion are directly opposed to the good of the Empire and your own.

Your Majesty thinks the system into which you have been led by your Cabinet is the source of all the disasters we have experienced. I could not conceal from you, on the other hand, that I am convinced that the true reason of our disasters is that you have not followed that system with frankness and decision ; that you have departed from the plan that was agreed upon ; and that you have withheld your confidence during its execution from those with whom it was formed, so that there was neither unity nor sequence in what has been done since. My opinion is that the principles which until then had regulated the conduct of the Russian Cabinet, should continue to direct it ; that they are the only ones which it can properly adopt ; and that the greatest energy and activity can alone rescue Russia from the difficult position in which she is placed. Your Imperial Majesty appears to be of quite a different opinion : you look upon the principles which have guided our action as noxious and dangerous, and you

* After the battle of Austerlitz.

seem especially to avoid any measure which would be consequent upon them. Whichever view may be correct, it is equally necessary either that you should require me to retire, or that I should ask permission to do so.

Such are my reasons for begging of your Imperial Majesty to allow me to retire. They are strengthened by the peculiar circumstances in which I am placed. . . Your Majesty will recollect that I was far from desiring my present post, and that I even long declined to accept it, foreseeing the unpleasantnesses I should have to suffer as a Pole. Since then, almost from the time when I took up the duties of my office, I have not ceased to look forward to the moment when you would permit me to resign it into your hands. . . .— I am, etc.   (Signed) A. CZARTORYSKI.

In a memorandum addressed to the Emperor on his retirement from office, Prince Adam thus describes the policy of Russia towards England and the other Powers during the time that he was Minister of Foreign Affairs :—

'. . . The new English Ministry* not having made any statement to us of its policy, this silence inspired us with some anxiety, notwithstanding the confidence we felt in the British Government. We had learnt that Mr Fox had made some overtures to M. de Talleyrand through the Prussian Minister Jacoby, and that negotiations had consequently taken place between England and France, which the British

---

* The Grenville Ministry, formed in January, 1806, after the death of Mr Pitt.

Cabinet had not communicated to us. This afforded us a reason for also entering into *pourparlers* with the Cabinet of the Tuileries in order not to remain isolated, or at least to place us in a position to do everything that the interests of the State might require.

'Meanwhile the British Cabinet informed us that Mr Fox had proposed to M. de Talleyrand a provisional arrangement between England and France, subject to the consent of Russia, such arrangement to be null and void in the event of Russia refusing to acquiesce in it. Mr Fox at the same time invited us to take part in the negotiations, and we had reason to believe that he wished to make peace at any price.

'Although it is certain that a war would be the only means of breaking the yoke which was oppressing a great part of Europe, yet, if through the weakness of some Powers, the ill-will of others, and the pusillanimity of all, there was no means of making a vigorous resistance to France, it was desirable that a state of hostilities which was only of advantage to Napoleon should cease.

'Such was the view we expressed in London; and Austria and Prussia equally desired peace. But it had yet to be ascertained whether peace was possible; if not, we should at least acquire the conviction that the only cause to be adopted was to enter on a vigorous and combined war. M. d'Oubril was accordingly sent to Vienna and Paris to sound the views of the French Government, and Lord G. L. Gower was fully informed as to this mission. . . .

'Shortly after M. d'Oubril's departure, an essential change occurred in the situation. From the moment that the British Cabinet became certain of the treachery of Prussia, a new turn was given to the opinions and views of the English Ministry, which now showed us the greatest confidence. France having repeatedly refused to treat with England and Russia together, the Cabinet of St James's at once broke off the negotiations, and declared that it would not resume them except in concert with its ally. It showed throughout equal loyalty and moderation.

'Having declared war against Prussia, England represented that it was necessary for the allies to strike a decisive blow on the Continent, so as to produce a strong impression of their energy and power, and thereby encourage the States under Buonaparte's influence, and at the same time to render him more moderate in his pretensions. In laying this plan before us, the British Ministry declared itself ready to enter into any other projects we might form either in the west or the south, and to support them with all the means at England's disposal.

'Though for various reasons your Majesty did not think fit to accept the English proposals,* you were deeply touched by this noble and loyal conduct, and you gave strict orders that no arrangement should be concluded with France except in concert with the British Cabinet. . . .

'Having now arrived at the period when the

---

* An allusion to one of the causes of Prince Czartoryski's resignation.

Ministry of Foreign Affairs has passed into other hands, I may be permitted, Sire, to submit to your Majesty a rapid survey of the system which has been followed under my direction, of its results, and of the state of affairs in Europe at the moment of my retirement.

'Since the rupture of the Peace of Amiens, Russia has had constantly to protest against the violation of treaties by the ruler of France, notwithstanding the most precise stipulations. She has constantly been threatened by the gigantic increase of a new Empire, which, by destroying and subjecting its neighbours, necessarily tended to fall with all its weight upon Russia, as the only Power capable of struggling with France for the Empire of the world. . . . There was but one mode of resisting Napoleon with any chance of success, namely, the creation of a system of general alliances. No European Power was capable of facing Napoleon alone; it was therefore necessary that all the greater Powers should unite to defend the existence of each of them. Russia especially was bound to support her neighbours in order to prevent their falling a prey to the conqueror, and affording him additional resources which he could use against her. This system, worthy of a great Empire, and conformable not only with its own interests and those of its allies, but with the good of humanity, was created by Russia.

'During the last two years Russia and her allies have four times made overtures of peace to Napoleon, and on each occasion the shameful conditions which he imposed and the outrageous pretensions which he put forward rendered peace impossible.

'Events which could hardly have been expected* have profoundly shaken the system, but have not destroyed it. Mutual confidence and the wish to bring together the threads of an indispensable union of which your Imperial Majesty would be the soul and the centre remained; the allies who were neither restrained by fear nor debased by discouragement continued their intimate relations with us.

'At the moment when your Imperial Majesty deigned to permit me to transfer to other hands the Ministry of Foreign Affairs, the situation was as follows :

'The successes of France over your Majesty's allies, however alarming their consequences may appear, only added new ruins to those of other States without adding any solidity to the fabric of the French Empire. A greater number of dismembered countries and humiliated nations increased the general confusion; Napoleon's power was increased, but not made any more secure.

'Austria was silently reorganising her forces, and was still turning her eyes to Russia. She gave us marks of confidence which we hastened to accept and cultivated with the object of renewing our old relations and securing her aid in case of need.

'Prussia, notwithstanding her disgraceful concessions to France, had not entirely bound herself to her, and sought by very secret and confidential negotiations with us to repair the faults of her policy.

---

* A further allusion to the disagreement between Alexander and Prince Czartoryski.

'Sweden, always faithful to her elevated and generous sentiments, defied the threats of the Berlin Cabinet and remained steadfast to her alliance with Russia and England. . . .

'The Porte, though led astray by the fatal suggestions of French agents, disguised its malevolent designs, and did not dare entirely to break the bonds which united it to Russia.

'Finally, England—the only Power which by her dominion over the seas can in combination with us still justify the hope of a possible equilibrium in Europe—always faithful to our alliance, always frank in her transactions with us and strict in fulfilling them, showed herself ready to second us everywhere, and was actually doing so most effectually in the Mediterranean and on the Adriatic.'

Sir A. Alison (Hist. of Europe, vol. vii. p. 155) suggests that Prince Czartoryski's retirement was caused by the Prince having been in favour of making an alliance with France at the expense of England, while his successor 'supported the English in opposition to the French alliance.' There is no foundation whatever for this suggestion. As will be seen from the papers here published, Prince Czartoryski was throughout a devoted adherent of the alliance with England and an uncompromising adversary of Napoleon. Moreover, when M. d'Oubril signed the treaty of alliance with France (July 20), Prince Czartoryski had already ceased to be Foreign Minister; and that he and his political friends strongly disapproved of M. d'Oubril's conduct is shown by the following extracts from letters addressed to the Prince by Count Vorontzoff, the Russian Ambassador in London :—

'SOUTHAMPTON, $\frac{12}{24}$ *July*, 1806.

'What I feared, and yet hoped would not happen, has come to pass. I have just learnt, to my great grief, that you have resigned your post, my dear Prince. I pity the Emperor and my country, and I cannot conceive how he could have been induced to accept your resignation.

I congratulate our mutual friends M. de Novosiltzoff and Count Kotchoubey on not having wished to separate from you. It is easy for those who know you as I do to understand that your resignation has been the consequence of a complete change in our political system, and that this change was opposed to your principles and views and to your high spirit. Your resignation does you honour ; I am proud to have such a friend. . . .'

'SOUTHAMPTON, 5*th August* (N.S.) 1806.

'I cannot blame you ; on the contrary, I can only approve your noble conduct on this occasion. Your counsels, which tended only to the glory and the good of the State, were not followed. The Government had fallen into the hands of intriguers, and you refused to soil your honourable name by lending it to their shameful transactions. It is only through d'Oubril's knowledge that your resignation was imminent and inevitable that he was able to cast eternal shame on Russia.

'WALCOT, ₁⁷₃ *October* 1806.

'Mr Battye has sent me here your letter of the 25th of August, which you gave him for me. The reasons you give for your resignation had been already anticipated by me, as I felt certain that a man of your judgment and character could not consent to carry out a policy contrary to his opinions and based on cowardly principles which could only bring danger and dishonour to the State and the sovereign who dictated them. . . .

'I am now staying at Lord Powis's estate in Shropshire, and Count Strogonoff came the day before yesterday to bid me good-bye. I showed him your letter, and he handed me the one he had received from you. The contents of these two letters prove to me that I had rightly guessed the motives of d'Oubril's infamous conduct. He knew that you were no longer in office; that Baron Budberg, like all Livonians, was attached to Prussia, whose interest is to keep Hanover and obtain other advantages from France, to promote dissensions between Russia and England, and to reconcile Russia with the Corsican, and that the Emperor is weak, pusillanimous, and also attached to Prussia. If he succeeded, he would be decorated and rewarded both by Alexander and Napoleon; if he failed, Budberg would see that he escaped punishment. I did not however guess that the Emperor had given instructions to a subordinate behind the back of the Minister who was his chief, and that the subordinate, though selected and protected by the Minister, concealed from him the instructions he had received. This passes belief, and would in itself have been a sufficient justification for your resignation. . . .

I can assure you positively that the King of England and his Ministry know and appreciate you, and that Fox alone is doubtless very glad to see your withdrawal from the Ministry of Foreign Affairs. Lord G. L. Gower speaks of you with the greatest respect, esteem and attachment.'

[See also Thiers' History of the Consulate and the Empire, Book xxiv : ' M. d'Oubril was strengthened in his idea of signing a treaty of peace with France by the fact that there had been a change in the Russian Ministry while he was on his way to Paris. Prince Czartoryski and his friends having wished to enter into more intimate engagements with England, not necessarily in order to continue the war, but to be in a more advantageous position to treat with France, Alexander, fatigued by their remonstrances, and fearing to be too closely bound to the British Cabinet, had at length accepted their resignations, which had been frequently submitted to him, and had replaced Prince Czartoryski by Baron Budberg. The Baron was formerly the Emperor's tutor and a friend of the Empress Dowager, and had neither strength nor inclination to resist his master.'*]

* The above views are further confirmed by a letter in the Record Office addressed by Mr Stuart, then Chargé d'Affaires at St Petersburg, to Lord Grenville on the 20th of August 1806, in which Mr Stuart says that he assured Prince Czartoryski ' that the high opinion his upright and honourable frankness had inspired in England would remain unsullied, and that although the real state of the case could not hitherto be perfectly known, his character was not implicated by the slightest suspicion to his disadvantage on the part of his Majesty's Ministers.'

CHAPTER XV

1806

THOUGH Prince Adam Czartoryski had ceased to be
Minister of Foreign Affairs, he remained for many
years after one of the most esteemed and valued of the
Emperor Alexander's counsellors, and there are
numerous memoranda on both internal and external
Russian policy in the Czartoryski archives which were
prepared for the Emperor by the Prince after his
resignation. Among these is the following paper,
dated the 5th of December 1806, 'On the necessity of
restoring Poland to forestall Buonaparte:'

'In the struggle which is to decide* on the fate of
Russia and of Europe, Poland has at this juncture of
affairs become a principal object of consideration with
the two Empires which are about to come into
immediate collision with each other; but she is looked
upon by each of them in an entirely different manner.
For the French she is a source of safety, an object

---

* It will be observed that this memorandum was written after Napoleon's
victory at Jena.

which animates their courage and strengthens their perseverance ; it is in Poland that Buonaparte sees his standpoint for fighting Russia and penetrating within her old frontiers. Though moving away from his centre of operations, Poland would furnish to his fertile genius and indefatigable activity the same resources as France—a population easily exercised in the profession of arms, brave and experienced officers, money, provisions, and an attachment to the existence, the honour, and the liberties of their country so deep that it will move them to the highest efforts. For Russia, on the other hand, the Poles are a motive of continual anxieties and suspicions ; they have frequently been used by Buonaparte as a bugbear to the partitioning Powers. Though Poland affords all the resources capable of supporting the war and powerfully contributing to the defence of the throne, the Russian Government fears to make use of the Poles lest they should turn against it. . . . Under these circumstances Poland diminishes the power of Russia in the same proportion as she augments that of France.

' It is obviously desirable, in the Russian interest, to reverse this state of things ; and to obtain such a result there is only one way : to proclaim Poland as a kingdom, the Emperor declaring himself King on behalf of himself and his successors for ever.

' The advantages of such a step—equally magnanimous and politic—would be incalculable. The general enthusiasm it would excite in all the Poles, the gratitude which would rally all Polish hearts and arms round the throne, would entirely change Russia's situation and that of her enemies. Instead of seeing her provinces exposed to Buonaparte's seductions, she would be able to raise their inhabitants against him ; and Russia, instead of having an immense frontier exposed to the colossal Empire of France, would, by re-establishing Poland, create an outpost behind which she would remain intact with all her forces at her command. Moreover, every cause of anxiety for Russia as to the conduct of the Poles, and every motive for speculating on such conduct on the part of her enemies, would be for ever removed—an inappreciable advantage for the internal happiness, tranquillity, and power of the Empire.

' If Poland is declared a separate State, with the Emperor as King, Buonaparte's difficulties in invading Russia will be immeasurably increased ; . . . . and should he succeed in overcoming them, he will have to pursue our armies into the interior of Russia, as they have very wisely been ordered to retire until they are sure of victory. He would then find himself cut off by the hostile Poles in his rear, and his defeat under such circumstances would mean nothing short of the absolute surrender of himself and his army. . . .

' It may be objected that to declare Poland a Kingdom would be to separate from the Empire one of its integral parts ; but this separation would only be apparent. The crown of Poland would be irrevocably attached to the throne of Russia ; and the Empire would at the same time gain the remainder of Poland. Imperious circumstances have forced Russia to commit the great political fault of allowing Poland to be partitioned instead of entirely possessing it. This fault has, to a great extent, been the cause of the misfortunes which have since overwhelmed Europe; should it not now be made good?

'No doubt, in order to produce the desired effect of inflaming the enthusiasm of the Poles, it would be necessary to give them a government in conformity with their wishes and their ancient laws. . . . But these benefits would render the bond between the Empire and the Polish nation stronger and more indissoluble. The more a nation is governed in accordance with its wishes, its character, and its habits, the more devoted it is to its rulers. The kingdom of Hungary, notwithstanding its special liberties and prerogatives, has for centuries been an example of fidelity and one of the firmest supports of Austria. Maria Theresa was saved by the Hungarians. The King of France was all-powerful in the provinces which had preserved their estates and privileges, and it was Brittany, Poitou, and Anjou which have up to the last moment been the defenders of the throne, of religion, and of the nobility.

'A further objection might be raised on the score that by reuniting Poland under her sceptre Russia would be despoiling her ally the King of Prussia. But the master of the Prussian monarchy is now Buonaparte; he exercises all the rights of a conqueror there, and is advancing towards Prussia's frontier provinces, which he proposes to disturb by a revolution that will threaten ours. The question at issue, therefore, is not the seizure of the property of an ally, but the forestalling of an active, inexorable, and aggressive enemy; the depriving him of a booty which if he obtains would cause a terrible conflagration in the Empire. This would indeed be the only means of saving Russia's ally; for otherwise she will perhaps not be able to continue the struggle and obtain some compensation for the House of Brandenburg in forcing the enemy to agree to an equitable peace.

'As to Austria, such an arrangement could not, of course, be made without frank and loyal negotiations with the Court of Vienna. But the basis of the arrangement is too just, and the House of Austria would be too sensible of the dangers it incurs, not to promise a speedy and successful result of these negotiations. . . .

' The only question which remains to be solved is whether, supposing the proclamation of Poland as a separate State is decided upon, Russia should act at once or wait until Napoleon makes overtures to the Poles. The first course would appear the preferable one. As soon as Russia enters into the fitting explanations with the Court of Vienna and the preliminary steps are taken in Poland to secure that the project shall be fully carried into effect, nothing should delay its immediate execution. On the contrary, the matter is urgent, and the slightest delay might weaken or destroy the results of this important operation. All the advantages of taking the initiative would be on Russia's side, and she would not have to combat the pride of a violent and self-willed man who has not hitherto known what it is to withdraw from a course of action after publicly proclaiming that he has decided to adopt it.

'The preliminary steps to be taken would be the issue of proclamations by the Russian generals, circular letters to influential personages in the country, and instructions to governors and commanding officers, to show a friendly attitude to the Poles, to ensure discipline in the troops, and to levy recruits ; and the despatch of intelligent and zealous agents to the Polish provinces.   The King of Prussia would be informed in the most considerate manner of the reasons and the necessity for the proposed measure, and would be given the hope of compensation as soon as the events of the war should permit, and preparations would be made immediately for the reorganisation of the new kingdom and for reconciling the inalienable rights of the sovereign with the institutions and customs most congenial to the Polish nation, a considerable part of which they have retained under the paternal Government of his Majesty the Emperor.'

The following was the Emperor's reply to the above memorandum and other similar proposals which were made to him by Prince Adam in conversation :—

The Emperor to Prince Adam Czartoryski
(Written in pencil and without date).

I have received the paper you have thought fit to address to me.   You wish for a discussion, and I am ready to grant it ; but I cannot help telling you that

I think it will be useless, as our fundamental principles are so diametrically opposed to each other.
After pointing out the critical position in which
Russia is placed and the evils she has to fear, the only
means you propose for meeting the danger may be
reduced to two :

1. That I should declare myself King of Poland.

2. That my Ministers of War and of Foreign
Affairs should be changed.

The discussion of the first of these points would be
too long, but I am ready to state my views and the
reasons which guide my conduct. As to the second
point, I am satisfied with the services which the
Ministers in question render me. Who is this perfect
Minister of whom everyone would approve ? Is it
General Suchtelen ? I tell you plainly that I do not
look upon him as possessing the qualities required of
a War Minister, and that of the two I do not hesitate
for a moment to give the preference to General
Viasnitinoff. Nor do I see anyone for the Foreign
Department. Would it be a Panin or a Markoff?
I must esteem those with whom I work ; it is only
on this condition that I can give them my confidence.
Clamour troubles me but little ; it is generally nothing
more than the effect of party spirit. Are not you
yourself an example of this ? Have you not been
exposed to the criticism and animosity of the whole
nation ? I must also remark that it would have been
better if the Committee * had not employed a stranger

---

* The 'Secret Council,' to which Prince Czartoryski still belonged. See Vol
I., p. 257.

to copy such a paper as the one I am answering. In order to bring us together again it will first be necessary for us to agree that, whatever may be said in the Committee, our individual and mutual relations shall remain intact, and that we should follow the example of English Members of Parliament, who, after saying the most bitter things to each other in the House in the heat of debate, are excellent friends when the debate is over.—Ever yours,

ALEXANDER.

The Emperor to Prince Czartoryski.

(Without date).

I was far from intending to give you pain. As I was speaking of such important matters, I was obliged to do so in accordance with my conviction, and I expressed myself accordingly. In the concluding part of your memorandum you offer to hand me a detailed and general plan of the measures to be taken in succession to those which you propose. If you like, we can meet in committee to-morrow, after dinner at six o'clock. We will make the plan together, and then discuss it.—Ever yours,

ALEXANDER.

[Prince Czartoryski's proposal was not accepted, and the result was that when Napoleon entered Warsaw (at that time belonging to Prussia), on the 18th of December, 1806, he was received by the

Poles with enthusiasm. Deputations came to him from all parts of Poland, a provisional Government was established, and volunteers presented themselves in great numbers to be enrolled in the French army.]

CHAPTER XVI

1806

PROPOSED PEACE BETWEEN RUSSIA AND NAPOLEON.

ON the 21st December 1806, Prince Czartoryski, who was still a member of the Imperial Council, addressed the following Letter and Memorandum to the Emperor Alexander proposing that he should treat for peace with Napoleon :

'Novosiltzoff and myself have of late several times had the opportunity of expressing to your Majesty our conviction that it is necessary to endeavour without delay to treat for peace with Buonaparte before our army can be attacked. I think we cannot at this moment give your Majesty a more real proof of our attachment, than to continue to press this advice upon you.

'Having heard that Lesseps was about to leave, I can no longer hesitate to lay before your Majesty the annexed memorandum which had been prepared on the subject.

'You will consider, Sire, the bad effect which would be produced by overtures of peace made only after a defeat, while at this moment, even if we gained some victories, such overtures could in no way be prejudicial to us. I would suggest that your Imperial Majesty should have the memorandum, which we take the liberty of presenting to you, discussed in your Cabinet Council. It would be only right that you should not take the sole responsibility for a step which might have decisive consequences.'

Memorandum on the Necessity of opening Negotiations of Peace with Napoleon.

Present State of Affairs.

Hardly a month has passed, and the disasters of Prussia, following each other with unexampled rapidity, have completely destroyed her. A considerable portion of Prussian Poland has been invaded, Warsaw is occupied by the French troops, large levies have been organised, and the inhabitants of the Polish provinces are fired with the hope of recovering their independence as a nation—a hope stimulated by Napoleon's numerous proclamations.

The Hanseatic towns, Mecklenburg, and Holstein, have been involved in the ruin of the German Empire ; Stralsund has been invested.

It is with all the forces and united resources of the French Empire, of Germany, and of Prussia, that Napoleon is approaching our frontiers.

While our enemy, as active as he is fortunate, is

making such terrible progress, we have only managed to reunite the various corps which compose our great western army, and are only beginning the preparations for the arming of the militia which have been ordered by your Imperial Majesty.

Notwithstanding the immense resources of this Empire, we must not lose sight of the fact that for the present we have only one army to oppose to the victorious armies of Buonaparte; that our recruits cannot be ready to fight till next spring; that our militia levies will come in slowly, and that time will be necessary to enable them to furnish corps capable of coming into line with the regular army and supplying our losses; further, that useful as they may be in combining the operations of a partisan war with those of a powerful regular army, they might be equally injurious, should that army be routed, by increasing the confusion and danger.

Under these circumstances every faithful subject of your Imperial Majesty—every good Russian— must be struck by the sad truth that the Russian Empire is nearly in the same situation as Prussia was last October.*   All the regular troops we can dispose of are on the frontier.   If these are beaten, an immense extent of country will be at the mercy of the French conqueror, and the elements of insurrection which he has doubtless spread in our western provinces lead one to fear that a lost battle would have incalculable consequences.

* Before the battle of Jena.

Necessity of Peace.

In presence of this alarming picture of the situation the want of peace becomes a universal sentiment, and should unite all hopes, wishes, and parties.

The enlightened politician and the determined soldier will both agree to ask themselves why pacific overtures should not be attempted rather than to persist in a struggle whose danger is imminent and directly menaces this Empire.

Objection.

How can we forget the maxims of energy, perseverance, and loyalty, which are the foundations of true greatness and a sure policy, and which have always guided the Russian Cabinet? Did we not on this principle refuse to ratify the Treaty of the $\frac{8}{20}$ July?* Would not an offer of peace compromise the national glory and show that we feel our weakness?

Reply.

Energy and perseverance have their limits, beyond which they become obstinacy or rashness. They should aim only at objects which are attainable, and whose pursuit is not accompanied by dangers out of all proportion to the advantages to be secured. These great qualities do not only manifest themselves in military operations; the latter have to be skilfully combined with political measures.

* The Treaty of Peace signed by M. d'Oubril at Paris. See page 161.

Difference of Circumstances.

The circumstances which have drawn Russia into this war, and which have made its prolongation indispensable, were essentially different from the present state of things.

Former Circumstances.

It will be remembered that in 1801 Russia was at peace with the French Government, whose friendship she cultivated.

The insults and provocations of all kinds, and violations of the most solemn treaties, which were perpetrated by the Cabinet of the Tuileries, forced your Imperial Majesty at first to complain, and then to make alliances to support common rights and share common dangers. The war which followed, becoming every day more fatal, also became every day more necessary.

Yet the enemy was far from having attained the point to which his astonishing successes have since brought him. Europe still afforded considerable means of opposing the overflow of his ambition.

Sacred engagements and those political considerations which constitute so essential a portion of the power of a State, did not permit Russia to abandon her allies or to sacrifice their hopes to her particular advantage.

The Cabinet of your Imperial Majesty was then obliged to develop all its forces to prevent or avert the fall of the neighbouring States, which served her as a barrier against the colossal Empire of Buonaparte, or through which it still had means of making a diversion.

So long as these motives and views existed, it was impossible to advise a peace which, owing to the complication of interests and the sacrifices that would be demanded by an enemy intoxicated with success, could only be a shameful one and could in no case reassure us as to the future.

Present Circumstances.

Now that by a succession of reverses, to which there is no parallel in history, all the countries that Russia has endeavoured to save are reduced to timid inaction, or have altogether disappeared from the ranks of the European States, there is no longer any question of protecting States on our borders; our borders themselves require to be protected. Our Empire is about to engage in a direct conflict with the French Empire, for the defence, not only of our integrity, but, if we may venture to say so, of our existence.

The war, so far as we are concerned, has changed its nature. The supreme interest of the State—the salvation of the Empire—must become the sole object of our policy at this new epoch of a struggle equally memorable and unfortunate for so many beaten nations.

Without ceasing to watch over the general good of Europe—without losing sight of the feeble hopes of our crushed allies—the indefeasible law of our own preservation is the only one that should guide us; all other duties and interests must give way to it.

Our policy thereby becomes independent, and if a tolerable peace, affording some elements of safety, could be concluded, there is nothing to prevent our entering into negotiations; on the contrary, every consideration should induce us to do so.

Even the safety of our allies makes such a course imperative; for if by a sentiment of false delicacy, by false principles of loyalty, or by personal feelings, we exposed ourselves to perish in order to save them, our fall would not alleviate their misfortune, but aggravate it by depriving them of the most distant hope of preserving what remains to them, or of some day repairing their disasters.

It is therefore evident that the changes which have occurred in our political relations, and in the situation of Europe, call upon us to seek peace as urgently as the position of affairs before the ruin of the Germanic Empire and the destruction of Prussia deterred us from doing so.

We should treat for peace without losing time.

If the necessity of this measure is agreed upon, it must equally be admitted that the negotiations should be opened as soon as possible, and that there is not a moment to be lost.

It is an incontestable principle in politics that peace should be offered at a time when one is in a position to insist upon it, or at least to accept it with dignity.

Our armies are intact; the enemy is no doubt aware of the formation of our reserves and the numerous levy of our militia. Soon he will hear of the patriotic offers which will be brought to the foot of the throne by all parts of the Empire; he will also be informed of our successes against the Persians, and the advantageous positions we have just occupied on the Dniester and the Danube. He is certainly not ignorant of the obstacles to his advance—the distance, the climate, the season of the year—in a war which would be equally long and dangerous. His first interest, therefore, will be again to astonish Europe by the rapidity of his combined movements, and to strike a decisive blow. He will hasten, therefore, directly he is able to do so, to fall on our great army with all the weight of his troops in order to force a battle; and our wise intention of evading one might perhaps yield to the vivacity of his pursuit, or to the thought of the pain it would give our generals to abandon the field to the enemy.

Such a situation cannot last long. Now or never is the time to talk of peace, if we do not want to wait till we are forced to beg for it after a reverse. And what peace could we hope for from a conqueror, whose pride would be swelled by his victory over the best troops in the world, and who would increase his claims and his demand for revenge according to the greatness of the vanquished?

Let us suppose—for it is prudent to anticipate the worst in our calculations—that our great army is dispersed, and our Western provinces are agitated by the hope of recovering their independence, or by the grant of liberty to the peasants. Shall we allow the conflagration to spread in these rich territories? Can we foresee where it would stop? Would we consent to the humiliation of offering territorial cessions to the conqueror? And if so, within what limits; or would we be entirely at his mercy?

These considerations, improbable as the supposition on which they are based may be, show that we ought to attempt to prevent such terrible extremities by concluding peace. The occasion naturally presents itself now that the war is assuming a new character. Before it begins between these two great nations, whose collision would shake the Continent, is it not natural that an effort should be made, even if only in the interests of humanity, to stop it?

Moreover, Buonaparte himself, in his address to the Senate, has declared that he is ready to make peace with Russia and England, and even with Prussia. Even more; he declares that the system of making separate peaces, hitherto followed by the French Cabinet, has only produced delusive truces and given rise to new coalitions, and that he will now only consent to a general peace with all the Powers concerned. He has thus, so to say, taken the first step, and it is for us to take the second, if we do not wish to leave him the advantage he is always claiming, of having professed peaceful sentiments in the midst of his success and yet never having been listened to.

This new phase in the policy of France, however

insidious may be its motive, offers Russia a plausible
pretext for proposing to open the negotiations, and
our Cabinet may take it the more frankly, as the
other belligerents are equally concerned in it.

On what basis can we treat?

The point here to be considered is on what basis
we can expect to get peace.

We must not forget that peace is, as has been
shown above, absolutely necessary to us ; that in
present circumstances the sole object of the negotiations should be the safety of the Empire, isolated as
it is at present from all that it had to preserve abroad;
that all interests not affecting that object, or only
indirectly affecting it, have become subordinate to it ;
and that we must be satisfied even with a tolerable
peace, provided it offers elements of security to
Russia.

All else that we could hope for as regards ourselves and our allies—whether in augmenting our
preparations and our efforts, or in gaining some
advantages, or through the support of other Powers,
or the skill of diplomatists, will always be an object
of our wishes and even of our action, but we should
not consider it essential to realise such hopes, or
regard their non-fulfilment as an insurmountable
obstacle to peace. We need be the less obstinate on
this point, that as our enemy is ready to accept
negotiation in common for a general pacification, our
allies, especially England and Prussia, will each look

after their own interests, and we shall relatively have greater latitude in working for ours.

The Treaty of $\frac{8}{20}$ July last* not to be revived.

Acting on the principle above indicated, it is unnecessary to observe that the Treaty of $\frac{8}{20}$ July last cannot be revived either by Russia or by France ; for, on the one hand, the evacuation of Germany by the French, as stipulated in that Treaty, can no longer be hoped for after the late immense conquests and aggressions of Buonaparte, and on the other, we now have what we did not have then—compensations to demand for the district which our safety compelled us to occupy in Turkey.

Bases of the Negotiation.

1. The greatest facilities would be given as to the arrangements Napoleon might be disposed to make either with England or Prussia or with any other Power as to the countries he has occupied since the renewal of the war.

The true and permanent interests of Russia are in no way opposed to the creation of new States of a moderate size near our frontiers, even if the enemy were to retain them under his protection.

2. We should, however, demand as a *conditio sine quâ non* that the French armies evacuate within a brief period the countries in question, and retire beyond the Weser, or at least behind the Elbe, so that

---

* This is the Treaty signed by M. d'Oubril, in Paris, but not ratified by his Government. See page 161.

their passing beyond those limits without our con-currence should be regarded as equivalent to a declar-ation of war.

3. Russia would restore all the fortresses and the territory she may occupy at the date of the treaty; she would consent not to keep Cattaro and even, if absolutely necessary, to evacuate the Seven Islands, on the express condition, however, that

4. France shall not keep that portion of Dalmatia which formerly belonged to Venice, and Cattaro at least shall not in any case be placed under her rule.

As the integrity and independence of the Ottoman Empire are of as great interest to Russia as to France, and the two Powers equally wish to guarantee it, it will only be just that there should be perfect reciprocity in this respect. Whatever guar-antee the Cabinet of the Tuileries may require from Russia on the north, the Cabinet of St. Petersburg will have a right to demand a similar guarantee in the south. The Porte has itself every interest in seconding us in this demand, and Austria and Eng-land will be called upon to take part in the arrange-ment.

5. The crown of Sicily would be retained in the possession of King Ferdinand. If Buonaparte were to demand that the title of King of the two Sicilies should be recognized in favour of Joseph his brother, one might grant it without any territorial or sovereign rights. Although this matter might seem of indirect importance to Russia, it affects her safety and pros-

perity too greatly not to form an essential object of the negotiations.

6. The kingdom of Sardinia will be maintained and guaranteed by all the Powers which have treaties with the King.

7. If England can make peace on the basis indicated by Buonaparte in his address to the Senate, *i.e.*, the retention of Malta, the island of Ceylon, the Cape of Good Hope, and her conquests in Mysore, Russia will accede to such an arrangement, without, however, interfering with regard to any difficulties which might ultimately be raised with regard to the negotiations between France and England.

8. If Sweden should accede to this peace, the two contracting Powers will guarantee her present possessions.

9. Indemnities could be afforded for the King of Sicily or Sardinia by the bay of Cattaro, the Seven Islands, or the part of Dalmatia which formerly belonged to Venice, should it be given up. Dalmatia might also be used for making useful exchanges of territory with Austria.

10. The happy idea of destroying the Barbary States having been formerly suggested by Buonaparte, would probably be now accepted by him, and these States would also afford a means of making arrangements whose results would be of general interest.

Similar negotiations will at once be opened in Austria, at Constantinople, in England, and at the other Courts, with a view to obtaining their concurrence or intervention as regards the objects of the proposed treaty.

[After the so-called ' Polish Campaign,' during the winter of 1806-7, Napoleon made peace with Russia at Tilsit (July 7, 1807). Although Prince Czartoryski had ceased to be Minister of Foreign Affairs at St Petersburg, he was present at the negotiations, and still exercised considerable influence over Alexander's mind, as will be seen from the following letter from the British Ambassador, Lord Granville Leveson Gower, urging him to use his good offices with the Emperor to prevent his concluding a one-sided peace with Napoleon :—

Mon Prince,

La confiance que vous m'avez toujours témoignée, et la conversation confidentielle que nous avons eue à Tilsitt, m'a fait espérer que vous ne le trouverez pas indiscret de ma part de m'addresser à Votre Excellence sur les bruits qui courent dans ce moment au sujet de l'armistice, et les négociations de paix qui la suivront. Les raisonnements sur la nécessité d'arrêter par la voie des négociations les armées Françaises sont trop bien fondés pour que je puisse en disputer la validité, mais il me semble que de consentir à une paix séparée après toutes les déclarations qu'a fait l'Empereur à cet égard, sera en effet avouer que la Russie se trouve au bout de ses moyens, et les ites fâcheuses qui en résulteront sont incalculables. Ce n'est pas l'Angleterre qui en souffrira le plus ; pour obtenir une paix générale solide et équitable je suis

persuadé que la cour de Londres fera de grands
sacrifices—et c'est bien l'intérêt de toutes les puissances
qu'on ne fasse pas la paix sans son consentement.
Tout ce qui tend à relâcher les liens qui unissent la
Russie et l'Angleterre doit être nuisible aux deux
Empires, et si jamais la France trouve le moyen de
séparer ces deux cours, c'en est fait de l'indépendance
de l'Europe. Je suis persuadé que votre influence,
quoique le portefeuille ne se trouve plus dans vos
mains, peut beaucoup faire dans ce moment si critique ;
usez-en pour le bien général, je vous conjure.
Pardonnez, mon Prince, la franchise avec laquelle je
vous ai écrit, et sera-ce trop abuser de votre bonté de
vous prier de me répondre avec confiance ? J'y ai
des droits, parceque personne ne vous est plus attaché.

Avec tous les sentiments que je vous ai voués, je
suis votre dévoué serviteur,   G. L. Gower.

A Memel, *ce* 23 *Juin* 1807.

One of the chief articles of the Treaty of Tilsit
was the creation of the Duchy of Warsaw, under the
rule of the King of Saxony, out of the Polish provinces annexed by Prussia in the various partitions.
This event produced some characteristic manifestations of Polish patriotism. Several persons gave
up the whole of their property for the maintenance of the Polish army ; others raised and equipped
entire regiments at their own expense. Six regiments
—one of artillery, two of cavalry, and three of
infantry—were raised and placed on a war footing
entirely by four individuals in a few weeks. Those

who were less rich supplied battalions, companies or smaller bodies of men. As the country was nearly ruined by the stagnation of trade and the constant passage of troops, those who thus came forward to increase the national forces had to sell their family plate, jewels, and even wedding-rings.]

CHAPTER XVII

1809-10

THE creation of the Duchy of Warsaw by Napoleon, and the augmentation of its territory by part of Galicia after the war between France and Austria in 1809, in which the Polish troops greatly distinguished themselves, had gradually restored in some degree to the Polish provinces south of the Vistula the powers of an independent State, though its sovereign, the King of Saxony, was practically the vassal of Napoleon. Under these circumstances Prince Adam Czartoryski gradually withdrew from the Imperial Council* at St Petersburg, and retained only the post of Curator of the University of Wilna, which had been conferred upon him by the Emperor Alexander together with the portfolio of Foreign Affairs. This post gave him extensive powers over the educational establishments in Lithuania, which he completely

.* The date of his last communication to the Council (on Russian Finance) is the 29th of January, 1810.

reorganised and developed in a national sense. He did not, however, lose sight of his favourite idea of reconstructing Poland as a separate kingdom under the sceptre of the Emperor of Russia ; and the following are notes, written by himself at the time, of his conversations with Alexander on this subject in 1809-10 :

12th November, 1809.

. . . Referring to Napoleon's letter to the Emperor and M. de Champagny's despatch on Poland, I said that I could only be pained at the knowledge that the Emperor is now made the chief enemy and persecutor of the Polish nation and name ; that it was only to please him that Poland had been abandoned and deprived of all hope ; and that he carried his animosity so far as even to wish the name of Poland to be effaced from history.

The Emperor at first defended himself against this charge. He said that his personal sentiments had not changed, that they had long been known to me, that he was bound by the duties of his position, and that every Russian Emperor would have done the same. I answered that I could not on this point separate the Emperor's personal inclinations from his political opinions ; that he had himself recognised that the restoration of Poland could be accomplished not only without injuring the interests of Russia, but on the contrary, to her great advantage, by uniting the two crowns on his Majesty's head. The Emperor replied that all this might be true, but that the thing was not practicable, and that it was therefore necessary to adopt another line of conduct. I at once rejoined that I could not understand this reasoning. If a certain policy was desirable in itself, it should not be adopted at one moment and dropped the next : if opportunities had been neglected or had not presented themselves, the proper course was to wait for new ones and in the meantime to prepare the ground, instead of alienating the nation by measures of undeserved rigour. Upon this the Emperor cast down his eyes and said : ' If at least one could expect some return on the part of the Poles ! '

I replied that I could not see what he had done to gain the affection of the Poles : ' Could anything be more revolting than the conduct of the three Powers with regard to Poland ? And is it surprising that the idea of seeing their country restored should fill the Poles with enthusiasm and bring them together ? It is thought that the peace will diminish this enthusiasm. I think otherwise, and the airs of triumph with which the papers here proclaim that the Poles have been deprived of all hope seem to me rather of a nature to serve Napoleon than to do him harm, as they will cast all the odium of his conduct on your Majesty. No one will now doubt that it was at the instance of your Majesty, and in order not to have war with Russia, that Napoleon yielded on a point which he would otherwise never have abandoned, and this can only embitter the Poles against you. . . .'

The Emperor replied that I knew his sentiments as to the partition of Poland, and that he still thought that all the evils from which Europe is now suffering date from that event. It could not, however, now be remedied. He did not see any means of executing the plan he had formerly contemplated with regard to Poland ; all that was possible was to grant a separate organisation to the provinces now under his rule, but even that would require much consideration, and would meet with much opposition in Russia. I said that knowing his liberal sentiments, which had been the origin of the connection with which he had honoured me, the only difficulty I could perceive would be the possibility of Napoleon opposing the scheme ; and that this made me anxious to know whether in the numerous conversations he had had with Napoleon he (the Emperor Alexander) had ever touched upon the subject. The Emperor replied rather vaguely that the matter had recently been in question during the Austrian war. Here he stopped short, and added that Napoleon would never consent to such a thing, as his sole idea was always to influence the Poles and use them as his tools.

I then remarked that the grant of a separate constitution to the Polish provinces now belonging to Russia would probably meet with more opposition in the Empire than the idea of uniting the whole of Poland to it. This I felt convinced was necessary for the security of Russia ; but I feared that when Russia would recognise that such is the case, it would be too late. The Emperor said that if he went to war with France it would certainly be advisable that he should declare himself King of Poland in order to gain over

the Poles to his side. I answered that it would then
be too late; and seeing that the conversation had lasted
too long, I did not wish to carry it any further.

December 26, 1809.

I had written to the Emperor to ask him for a short
interview, and in doing so I specially mentioned my
wish to speak to him about the continuation of my
leave, which was about to expire. Some days later,
after a dinner at my mother's, the Emperor came to
me and asked me to go to him on the following day,
as he wished to speak to me. I inferred from this
that he wished to speak about the contemplated
changes in the organisation of the Council which were
just then the talk of the town. Not knowing what
the Emperor's plan was or what he might propose to
me, I was a little anxious, for it is always disagreeable
to listen to a sovereign's proposals when one has
every reason to decline them.

Next day I went to the palace, and after waiting
for some time, I was admitted to the Emperor's
presence. He first asked me what I wanted. I
mentioned various private matters to him, and then
begged him to allow my leave to be prolonged. He
said he thought I had intended to stop longer at St
Petersburg, and that he had consequently believed it
might have suited me to have more active employment. He then informed me that the Council was to
assume a new shape, with more extensive functions
and an organisation for the formation of which that
of similar institutions in France and England had been

taken as an example ; that he had divided the Council into four sections—War, Home Affairs, Finance, Justice and Law—and that a place had been assigned to me in the fourth section. There was also to be a further discussion by the general body of the Council of the matters that had been dealt with in the sections ; but it was for the latter that good workers would be most required. I replied that I was extremely honoured by the confidence his Majesty was good enough to place in me, but that my reasons for soliciting a prolongation of my leave were already known to him—the advanced age of my parents, from whom I had been long separated ; the care of my health, with which the climate of St Petersburg did not at all agree ; and the habits and tastes which I had contracted during my prolonged absence from active service. The Emperor said he had no idea of disturbing my arrangements, adding that he had expected I should leave him, but had thought I would postpone my departure till the summer. I replied that I intended before the summer to pass some time at Wilna, where my presence was necessary in order to arrange the affairs of the university. . . .

The Emperor then told me that all the severe measures which had been taken with regard to the Poles would be revoked, that a decision to this effect had been arrived at, but that it would not be published for some weeks to come. He added that the motives which had impelled him to take these measures had ceased to exist, and that now he had reason to be tranquil as regards Poland. I thanked him, and asked what were the reasons for his tranquillity; was it only the passage in M. de Montalivet's speech,* or was there any other reason, such as an engagement no longer to contemplate the restoration of Poland? I knew from the conversations which I had had with the Chancellor, that there was some question of this between the two Cabinets, and I remarked to the Emperor that in that case he would himself be obliged to enter into a similar engagement, and would thus tie his hands. The Emperor made an evasive reply, merely saying that there was no question of what I was thinking about.

He then asked me as to the public feeling in Poland. 'Events,' I said, 'have revived the sentiments of fifteen years ago. The hope of the restoration of Poland seemed for a while to the Poles less possible; but now it is as if a half-cicatrised wound were accidentally reopened. It is thought that their hopes might have been diminished in consequence of the last peace with Austria, and certain letters and despatches from Napoleon which have been made public. Be this as it may, public feeling is nevertheless at the same stage as it was fifteen years ago. Moreover, there is the Duchy of Warsaw, which has

---

* The following was the passage here referred to. It occurs in the 'statement of the situation of the Empire,' presented by M. de Montalivet to the French legislative body on the 1st of December, 1809:

'The Duchy of Warsaw has been augmented by part of Galicia. It would have been easy for the Emperor to join the whole of Galicia to this State; but he did not wish to do anything which might have caused anxiety to his ally, the Emperor of Russia. Nearly the whole of the Galicia of the old partition has remained in the power of Austria. His Majesty has never had in view the restoration of Poland. What he has done for the new Galicia was prompted less by policy than by honour; he could not abandon to the vengeance of an implacable prince a population which had displayed so much ardour in the cause of France.'

been considerably augmented by the late war and which helps to strengthen and maintain the patriotic sentiment. It is a sort of phantom of ancient Poland which produces an infallible effect on all who regard that country as their real fatherland. It is as if, after you had lost a dear friend, his shade should come to assure you that he will soon be restored to you in person.

'Your Majesty must not be astonished at sentiments which I hold in common with all Poles. I do not speak to you as a sovereign : I beg you to lay aside that character and only to keep that which was the first cause of my attachment to you. . . . Your Majesty will remember that when I returned from Italy I had not the least idea of entering your service. When you wished to employ me, I repeatedly declined, and my chief reason was that being a Pole, my position might become delicate and difficult. I foresaw that circumstances might arise in which the interests of my country might be opposed to the duties of my office. Your Majesty replied that there was at that time no reason to anticipate such a thing, but that if there should be at some future period I would be at liberty to act as I thought proper. I must now say that the general impression produced on all my countrymen by circumstances, and by the existence of the Duchy of Warsaw, has also produced its effect upon me. I cannot help taking the strongest interest in my country.

'In my opinion a man who is not attached to his country is despicable. To disown one's religion, one's'

parents, one's country, is in my eyes equally odious.
These are feelings with which I was born, which education has strengthened, and which in me will never
change. Moreover, my brother, my sisters, and all my
family are in Poland, and I will confess to your Majesty
that this is one of the reasons which make me wish not
to mix myself up with any affairs here. It is not enough
for me to be clear, straightforward, and sincere in my
actions ; I also wish to be so in my sentiments and my
thoughts. I am therefore glad to have been able to
open my mind completely to your Majesty, and to
explain myself to you without any reserve. My first
object is to preserve my own esteem ; my second is to
preserve that of people whom I am accustomed to love
and respect. Should at any time your Majesty think
fit to confiscate my property and order me to be shot,
I will bear my fate with equanimity if you will do me
the justice to think that I was an honest man who
always spoke the truth and never deceived you.'

The Emperor seemed satisfied, and said that he
had never misunderstood me, and that the way I had
explained myself to him did me credit. For a moment
he was absorbed in thought ; then, as if suddenly
rousing himself, he said : ' There is no other means of
arranging all this than our old plan of giving a constitution and a separate existence to the kingdom of
Poland by attaching the title to the Russian crown.'
' We must wait,' he continued, ' until Austria commits
some blunder (fasse une bêtise) and provokes a new
rupture with France ; then we may find means to
come to an understanding with Napoleon, and give

compensation to the King of Saxony.' He added that in the meantime it would have been well to proceed in this sense with the provinces now belonging to the Empire, and to take the title of Grand-Duke of Lithuania; but that in presence of so skilful an antagonist as Napoleon, he had feared to awaken his suspicions and lead him to anticipate Russia by proclaiming the independence of Poland himself.

. . . As to this matter having ever been discussed in the Emperor's frequent conversations with Napoleon—a subject regarding which he had hitherto always avoided to give me any precise answer—Alexander stated positively that no mention had been made of it between the two Emperors. At Tilsit Napoleon had spoken with much levity about Poland and the Poles, and at Erfurth there was too much to do for them to touch upon that subject. I expressed my regret that his Majesty had not taken an opportunity of sounding Napoleon on the matter, and I added that notwithstanding the despatches and speeches of his Ministers, Napoleon had succeeded in spreading among the Poles a conviction that he not only had the interests of Poland at heart, but that he had a feeling of special affection for her. . .

His Majesty replied that Napoleon was a man who would not scruple to use any means whatever so long as he attained his object. As I had for some time heard various rumours in the society of St Petersburg as to Napoleon's fits of epilepsy and his being threatened with mental derangement, I asked the Emperor whether there was any truth in these

reports. ' Napoleon will never go mad,' he answered ;
' the thing is impossible, and those who believe it do
not know him.   He is a man who in the midst of the
greatest troubles keeps his head cool ; all his fits of
passion are only meant to intimidate, and are often
the fruit of calculation.   He does nothing without
thoroughly considering and foreseeing the consequences of his acts. . .   One of his favourite sayings
is that nothing should be undertaken without a plan.
In his opinion there is no difficulty that cannot be
overcome if you find the right mode of proceeding.
Once that is found, the rest is easy ; while if the
simplest matter possible is undertaken without finding the method of doing it, all is spoilt and no result
is obtained.   His health is excellent ; no one can
bear fatigue and hard work better than he does ; but
he requires eight hours' sleep a day, though he does
not keep regular hours.   He is not eloquent either in
speech or in writing ; I have heard him dictate letters
in an abrupt and unconnected style.' . . .

I remarked in the course of this conversation that
the Emperor still retained a sort of partiality for me,
but that he had no very strong desire to keep me. . . .
As for Napoleon, it is clear that Alexander under-
stands him thoroughly ; that Napoleon has preserved
a marked influence over his mind ; and that he greatly
fears him.

5th April 1810.
About three weeks ago the Emperor, whom I had
not seen for some time, suddenly sent for me.   After

talking about private matters and the grant of an
amnesty to those inhabitants of the Polish provinces
of Russia who had joined their countrymen of the
Grand-Duchy of Warsaw in the war against Austria,
the Emperor mentioned that he had a plan of uniting
the eight Polish provinces under a separate administration, and asked my opinion on the subject. I
requested to be given time for reflection. The problem
was a difficult one. How could I give the Emperor
any hope that the means to be adopted for producing
a reconciliation between him and the Poles would be
efficacious? And as regards my country, might not
the result be a civil war? Yet I thought it best to
reply, partly as a matter of courtesy, partly because
the future was so uncertain that I considered it
undesirable entirely to break a thread which under
different circumstances might become valuable.

After a few weeks I came back to the Emperor
and read to him a memorandum in which I stated my
views. . . . The Emperor interrupted me at the
beginning with the remark that it was not only for
the eventuality of a war, but to gain the affection of
the Poles in any case, that he thought of doing something for them. He then listened without saying a
word, but with much attention. It was only when I
stated that the most suitable time for doing something in favour of Poland was past, that he again
interrupted me. 'In writing that,' he said, 'you
were no doubt thinking of the year 1805 and my stay
at Pulawy.* I now see myself that that was a

* See page 99.

favourable moment—perhaps a unique one. We could then have done easily what can only be done now with great trouble ; but it must not be forgotten that we would have had the whole of the Prussian army against us.'

I answered that another very favourable opportunity occurred at the time of the last war with Austria, during which Russia could easily have demanded the restoration of Poland. 'That would have brought about the total ruin of Austria,' was the Emperor's reply. 'Any how,' I rejoined, 'the course which was followed was the worst, for it did not save Austria, whom it threw into the arms of France ; it annoyed Napoleon ; and it was of no material advantage to Russia.'

When I had finished reading, I apologised for not having arrived at any definite conclusion ; I could not say more, as I was imperfectly informed of what was going on, and I did not know what was the predominant feeling in the Polish provinces. 'Bah!' said the Emperor, 'it is not difficult to know what people think in the provinces and in the Grand-Duchy. The Poles would follow the devil himself if he would lead them to the restoration of their country. But I am satisfied at what you have written ; it will help me to reflect on a subject which has so long occupied my attention. I have sought all kinds of means of realising my wishes, but have not arrived at any satisfactory solution. The greatest difficulty is to find an indemnification for the King of Saxony ; this could only be done by still further dismembering that unfortunate King of Prussia.'

I remarked that the greatest difficulty was to obtain the consent of France, and that if this were obtained the rest would be easy. The Emperor agreed, saying that Napoleon's interest was not to change the present state of things, as he cared much less for the good of Poland than to use her as a tool in the event of his making war upon Russia. He at the same time admitted that it was natural that the inhabitants of the Grand-Duchy of Warsaw, in view of the respective forces of the two Powers, the talent and experience of the Polish generals and armies, and Napoleon's great chances of victory in any war, should not be inclined to throw themselves into the arms of Russia at the risk of losing the fruits of the efforts they had made for so many years. This was entirely my view of the case ; and the Emperor then told me some of his ideas for bringing about a restoration of Poland.

One of these was to enter on a sham war with the Grand-Duchy, so that by a preconcerted arrangement the Russian troops might occupy positions in which they would be joined by the Polish troops, and then fight the French together. Such a plan was obviously chimerical ; its difficulties were palpable, and it involved a war against Napoleon with very uncertain chances of success.

Another plan was to form a kingdom of Poland out of the Duchy and Galicia, and to allow the inhabitants of the Polish provinces of Russia to serve in the new kingdom as if it were their own country. This idea surprised me ; but the Emperor explained that the

Poles, being thus satisfied, would have no reason to oppose Russia ; that there would then be no longer any cause of dissension between Russia and France ; and that the evil would thus be got rid of by amputation instead of by cure. The Emperor's tone in saying this led me to believe that the idea might have been suggested to him by the French Ambassador, that it had been discussed between them, and that he might be disposed to adopt it as a convenient method of avoiding war with France.

The Emperor concluded by saying that he would consider all these ideas, and that he wished me also to seek a clue to the object he had in view. I replied that I was far from desiring to damp his Majesty's good intentions, but that so far as I could see there was nothing to be done immediately beyond taking the measures I proposed in my memorandum. I added that I thought the present year would not come to an end without producing events more serious and decisive than any that we had yet seen. The Emperor, interrupting me, said in an impressive tone that he thought it would not be this year, as Napoleon was entirely occupied with his marriage ; but that he expected there would be a crisis next year. ' We are now in April,' he continued ; ' it will be nine months hence.' * While saying these words, and indeed throughout the conversation, the Emperor had a severe and fixed look, which reminded me of his haggard gaze after Austerlitz.

* Napoleon's Campaign in Russia did not begin till more than two years afterwards (June 22, 1812).

CHAPTER XVIII

1810

FRIENDSHIP *versus* PATRIOTISM

ALEXANDER, notwithstanding his promises, did nothing for Poland, and Prince Czartoryski then determined to take no further part in Russian affairs, and to devote himself exclusively to his own country. This decision was only arrived at after a hard mental struggle, which he thus describes in a paper dated the 20th of June 1810 :—

In the difficult circumstances in which I am placed, and which are exposed on all sides to misunderstanding and misjudgment, I owe a sincere account of my actions to those who take an interest in me, in order to spare them as much as I can the pain of finding themselves deceived in their opinion of me. Seeing me as I am, their judgment may console me for the injustice of the majority, from which I shall perhaps not escape.

I seem continually to hear two voices which ring with equal force in my ears. One speaks as follows :—

'Your position is, no doubt, extremely difficult,

but your difficulties themselves trace out for you the course you should follow. . . You have played a part in Russia which for a time made you a prominent figure on the theatre of European politics. In doing so you acquired general esteem, and when you resigned office your withdrawal was regretted by the Governments and nations which were suffering under the devastating system of Napoleon. After your resignation, you maintained the opinions you had advocated when in office, and Cabinets and patriots still looked up to you as one of those by whom Europe could be saved.

'Will you now discard the principles you have proclaimed, attach yourself to the chariot of the tyrant, and become the tool of his projects, which in your opinion are fatal to the happiness both of present and future generations?

'You owe nothing to Russia or to the Emperor whom you have served well as long as you could. But do you owe nothing to yourself and to Europe? And to what would you sacrifice such grave considerations and precious advantages? Not to the evident good of your country, but to vague hopes and dreams. . . . Can you believe that Buonaparte sincerely wishes for the good of any country? All he wants is to make your countrymen his tools, and he will be ready to abandon them directly his interest requires him to do so.

'Would it be right for you to participate in such projects? Your country has nothing to reproach you with; you have been useful to your countrymen while you were in office; you have done your utmost to restore Poland. Under present circumstances it is difficult, if not impossible, for you to take an active part in Russian affairs; but on the other hand you should at least not mix yourself up with what is going on in your country. You should hold aloof, and remain neutral and passive as long as the present storm lasts.'

While I listen to these reasons and feel their force, the other voice says to me :—

' It is true that your position is different from that of the other Poles. They feel it, and they give you full credit for the conduct you have pursued hitherto.

' But your duties are changed. You passed under the rule of Russia together with the rest of your country. Circumstances placed you in the service of Russia, not as a Russian, but because you were a Pole. You belonged to Russia because Poland was destroyed; the cause having ceased, the effect as regards yourself should cease also. . . . It was solely your personal relations with the Emperor that led you to enter his service, notwithstanding the strong reasons to the contrary which you repeatedly urged to him. When he insisted upon your compliance, though still a Pole at heart, you honestly and zealously laboured in the interest of Russia. . . . There was an interval when all hope of restoring Poland had disappeared. Directly it revived, you strove to make the possibility of the restoration of Poland serve to glorify the Emperor, and to unite by the bonds of a common advantage the two interests which were most dear to you. But your counsels were not heard; your plans were not followed. The interests you wished to unite again parted from each other, and you retired in time to avoid a situation where you must have been guilty either on one side or the other. These interests have grown more and more divergent and will become entirely opposed to each other. You should leave a service and a State essentially hostile to your country, and bent on crushing out its existence and that of your countrymen. Nor is this all. A moment will come when you will have to take an active part—when Poland is declared independent and will be in arms to maintain her existence. This will probably be when France is at war with Russia, and every Pole who then holds aloof will be looked upon by his countrymen with contempt. . . .

'When people say Buonaparte should not be supported by the Poles because of his unjust and oppressive conduct towards other nations, they forget that there is not a single act of iniquity committed by Napoleon of which the Powers which partitioned Poland did not themselves set the example. It is not for them to become the champions of principles which they have trodden under foot. . . . A characteristic trait of the Polish nation is to love one's country above everything, and to be ready to sacrifice everything to recover it. Will you be more sensitive to what happens on the Tagus and the Adige than on the Vistula—be indignant at the acts of injustice committed with regard to other nations, and indifferent to those inflicted on your own ? . . .

'Buonaparte has never done any harm to Poland; he alone has held out his hand to her and has done all he could for her. The Poles condemn his policy as other nations do; they pity the Spaniards, and are ashamed to be obliged to fight against them; but no nation can be expected to commit suicide in order that other nations may be benefited. The Poles regret the necessity of their being attached to Napoleon's fortunes, but they cannot refuse benefits at his hands which are not offered them by any one else. They have done everything to prove their ardent wish to owe their national existence to the Emperor Alexander; but he has rejected all their overtures. On one side they find interest, support, and hope; on the other, animosity, persecution, and discouragement. The dearest interests of Poland, supported solely by France, have by the present conduct of the Cabinet of St Petersburg become diametrically opposed to those of Russia. Poland is ready to do the will of any Power that will help her. Buonaparte alone has hitherto done so, and she hopes through his assistance to recover her name and her existence as a nation. If she is wise, circumstances may perhaps enable her to come successfully out of the general cataclysm which is approaching, and she may by her efforts prove to the Russian Government and nation that it would be useful to bring her over to their side, and to unite the two nations by bonds of mutual advantage and interest.

'As to your position in the matter, it is quite clear. You have loyally served the Emperor, and you have always told him the truth : he knows better than anyone your sentiments with regard to Poland. You owe him a certain amount of consideration, which cannot, however, outweigh your duties to your country. The policy you proclaimed as a Russian Minister was in accordance with your duty and the state of Europe at the time. There was then a hope that resistance to Napoleon would be efficacious, and it was certainly right that Russia should attempt it. Circumstances are now entirely different, and as a Pole you can no longer advocate the same policy as when you were Minister of Russia, and Russia had not made a treaty of peace with France. Your principles, however, have always been the same; your period of office in Russia was merely an episode in your career.

'In Poland you cannot play a passive part. No family has more distinguished itself by its attachment to the country than yours, and though still young, you have already fought for Poland,* and your words as well as your deeds have been those of a patriot. Your countrymen have full confidence in you, and you cannot refuse them your assistance without dishonour.

'There is no question of your becoming a satellite of Buonaparte ; no one wishes you to do so. Nor is it necessary for you to decide too soon or without sufficient reflection. But you will have to come forward at the moment when the fate of Poland will

---

* At the battle of Granno, in 1792 (see Vol. I. page 53).

hang in the balance, when there will be no doubt as to the motives of those who declare themselves, or excuse for those who will withdraw at a time when your country will make decisive efforts to recover its existence.

'Will your relations of friendship with the Emperor excuse you? Those relations have almost. ceased; and your duty to your country is superior to any claims of friendship. Moreover, if you have sacrificed that friendship for the interests of a country which has been the cause of the ruin of Poland, how could you do less for your own country?'

Such are the two voices that speak to me one after the other, and the same arguments have been expressed to me with even more force by persons who are dear to me and whom I respect. Being thus placed between two such opposite opinions, I ought to decide for myself which I should follow; but I confess that I cannot yet clearly see any way of escape from the labyrinth in which I am enclosed.

My reason does not lead me to any result, for the arguments on both sides seem to me to have equal weight. But at the bottom of my heart the feelings and motives which speak for my country are paramount, and I would be happy were I able to follow them without constraint. I was born with these feelings; my education developed them; they are deeply graven in my heart. I think no one loves his country with more passion than I do. To keep the esteem of my countrymen and to do good to my country is the only glory that would give me pleasure ; and if her misfortunes continue and my reputation perishes with her existence, I shall at least have the consolation of knowing that I have never acted from any motive that is not just and honourable.

CHAPTER XIX

1810-12

AFTER Prince Czartoryski had returned to Poland he devoted himself entirely to his educational work as Curator of the University of Wilna; but finding that a Commission under a Russian Governor had been appointed to report on one of the colleges in his district and decide as to the future organisation of the college, he sent his resignation to the Emperor in a letter dated the $\frac{15}{27}$ November, 1810. The following correspondence then took place between Alexander and the Prince :—

THE EMPEROR ALEXANDER TO PRINCE CZARTORYSKI.

ST PETERSBURG,
25th December, 1810.

MY DEAR FRIEND,—I have received your letter, and

I will not conceal from you that it has given me much pain. You wish to break the only public connection which exists between us, and after an intimate friendship of more than fifteen years, which nothing has been able to alter, we are to become strangers to each other, if not by our sentiments, at least in our public relations. This is a thought which it is painful to me to dwell upon, the more so as I believed the moment had arrived when our intimate relations might be developed to their fullest extent. . . . As to that unfortunate affair of the college, I had not the slightest wish to cause you pain, and I did not intend to do anything after receiving the report of the Commission without first consulting you. . . .

But there is a more important subject which requires immediate consideration. It seems to me that the time has arrived to prove to the Poles that Russia is not their enemy, but, their true and natural friend; that although Russia is represented to them as the sole obstacle to the restoration of Poland, it is not improbable that Russia will be the Power to bring about that event. . . . This has always been my favourite idea; circumstances have twice compelled me to postpone its realisation, but it has none the less remained in my mind. There has never been a more propitious moment for realising it than the present; but before going any further I should like you to answer categorically and in the greatest detail the questions I must put to you before proceeding to the execution of my plan.

1. Have you sufficient *data* as to the feeling of

the inhabitants of the Duchy of Warsaw; and if so—

2. Have you a well-founded belief that they would seize with avidity any offer giving them the *certainty* (not probability, but *certainty*) of their regeneration?

3. Would they accept it from whatever quarter it might come, and would they join any Power, without distinction, that would espouse their interests sincerely and with attachment? It is self-evident that the proclamation of their restoration would have to precede any decision on their part, and would have to be such as to prove the sincerity of the conduct which would be adopted with regard to them.

4. Have you, on the other hand, reason to suppose that various parties exist in the country, and that consequently—

5. One cannot reckon on a unanimous resolution eagerly to take the opportunity of the first offer made for the regeneration of Poland?

6. What are these parties? Are they equal in importance, and who are the individuals that may be regarded as their leaders?

7. Do these parties also exist in the army, or should it be regarded as more united in opinion and feeling?

8. Who is the officer that has the greatest influence upon opinion in the army?

These are the most important questions I have to put to you at present. Directly I get your answers, I will give you further information as to my plans. . .

I must beg you to keep the contents of this letter

absolutely secret. I rely on your prudence, and I feel certain you will take care not to mar a work to which your country would owe its regeneration, Europe its deliverance, and you personally the glory and the pleasure of having co-operated in it, and having thereby proved that your conduct has throughout been consistent, and that those of your countrymen who relied upon you in the past have been justified in their expectations. If you second me, and lead me to hope that the Poles, and especially the Polish army, are practically unanimous in desiring the restoration of Poland from whatever quarter it may come, success, with the help of God, will not be doubtful, for it is based not on a hope of counterbalancing the genius of Napoleon, but solely on the diminution of his forces through the secession of the Duchy of Warsaw, and the general exasperation of the whole of Germany against him. I annex a short table of the auxiliary forces which would be at the disposal of each side.

This is what I had to say; consider it calmly. Such a moment presents itself only once; any other combination will only bring about a war to the death between Russia and France, with your country as the battlefield. The support on which the Poles can rely is limited to the person of Napoleon, who cannot live for ever. Should he disappear from the scene, the consequences to Poland would be disastrous; while if by joining Russia and the other Powers which would certainly follow her, the moral strength of France should be overthrown, and Europe delivered from her yoke, the existence of your country would be established with unshakeable solidity. . . .

I await your answer with the greatest impatience, and am always yours, heart and soul.

My best remembrances to your parents, your sisters, and your brother.

(Signed) ALEXANDER.

Note on the Forces which might be opposed to each other.

On one side—
> 100,000 Russians
> 50,000 Poles
> 50,000 Prussians
> 30,000 Danes
> ————

Total 230,000 men, who might at once be reinforced by 100,000 more Russians.

On the other side—
> 60,000 French (it is stated there are only
>   46,000 in Germany, but I
>   add those who might be
>   drawn from Holland and
>   the interior of France).
> 30,000 Saxons
> 30,000 Bavarians
> 20,000 Würtembergers
> 15,000 Westphalians and other German
>   troops
> ————

Total 155,000 men.

It is more than probable, however, that the example set by the Poles will be followed by the Germans, and then there will only remain the 60,000 French. And if Austria, in return for the advantages we shall offer her, should also enter the field against France, this will add 200,000 men to our side against Napoleon.

PRINCE CZARTORYSKI TO THE EMPEROR ALEXANDER.

$\frac{18}{30}$ *January* 1811.

SIRE,—Your Imperial Majesty will easily imagine with what attention and extreme interest I have read your letter of the 25th of December. . . . Allow me to express to you my deep gratitude for your benevolent intentions regarding my country, the favourable recollection you have retained of her in your political combinations, and the special proof of confidence which you are good enough to give me on this occasion, and which I will endeavour to deserve by carrying out your instructions with all the zeal and prudence at my command. . . . I will at once reply to your questions; but my replies, as you will have foreseen, can only be of a preliminary kind.

So far as I have been able to observe the public feeling in this country, I see a unanimity of intentions and objects both in the army and among the inhabitants of the Duchy of Warsaw. Their sole wish and object is the restoration of Poland—the reunion of all its parts into a single national body, under a national and constitutional régime. The differences of opinion which are observable as to the amount of

confidence to be placed in generals and other prominent personages, and as to their talents and patriotism,
cannot properly come under the designation of party
feeling, and these differences would either disappear or
have a quite subordinate influence if the higher
interests of the country were at stake. Unanimity,
therefore exists ; but it would be necessary to convince
everybody that the salvation of the country and the
realisation of greater and more solid advantages
demand a total change of policy and the abandonment of the only supporter that the Duchy has as yet
possessed.

The certainty of the regeneration of Poland would,
as it seems to me, be received with gratitude and
eagerness from anyone that could offer it, provided
that the manner in which it should be offered and
brought about inspired more confidence and greater
guarantees of success than the inhabitants of the
Duchy believe themselves to possess through their
union with France. The great difficulty in the
execution of your Majesty's plan would be at once
to produce such a conviction in the minds of the
Government, the army, and the inhabitants of the
Duchy.

This, indeed, is the gist of the whole question.
However just the grievances of the Poles against
Napoleon may be, he has yet persuaded them that it
was not want of good-will, but absolute want of power,
which prevented him from carrying the work of their
regeneration any farther, . . . and that at the first
rupture with Russia, Poland would be restored. To

this feeling is added gratitude for what Napoleon has already done, and repugnance at the idea of turning against him, just at the moment when he most reckoned upon its co-operation, the new Polish State which he has created. To all these considerations must be added the fact that the French and the Poles are brothers in arms, and the idea that while the French are the friends of Poland, the Russians are her bitter enemies—an idea which has been considerably strengthened by the events of the late war.

A further difficulty is created by the fact that there are 20,000 Polish troops in Spain, whom their friends and relatives in Poland would fear to sacrifice to the vengeance of Napoleon. Moreover, in the expectation of a war with Russia, many Poles have sent their children to be educated in Paris, as being at present the safest place in Europe; and these would be so many hostages in Napoleon's hands. Finally, Napoleon has hitherto been so uniformly successful, even in the most dangerous undertakings, that people think he will always conquer in the end, however much appearances may be against him. . . .

In order to meet these objections it would be necessary to make the Poles some offer so distinctly advantageous to their country as to overcome all personal considerations. They must be treated with magnanimity, for with all their faults they have the qualities which appeal to the heart and the imagination. The three following points would for such a purpose be indispensable : (1) The restoration of the constitution of the 3rd of May 1791, which is graven in ineffaceable characters on all Polish hearts; (2) The reunion of the whole of Poland under one sceptre, thereby putting an end to a state of things which separates members of the same family from their relations and estates merely because they are under a different government; (3) The re-establishment of outlets for trade, the closing of which has impoverished the country; and (4) A reasonable prospect of success in a war with Napoleon. . . . As to this last point, I can hardly believe that Napoleon could not get more than 15,000 men in Holland and France to come to the support of the 16,000 he has in North Germany. What has become of the new levy of 150,000 recruits? . . . And are you quite sure that you would have 100,000 men at your disposal at the beginning of the war? I have so often seen in Russia 100,000 men on paper represented only by 65,000 effectives. It would also be well to state precisely whether by the Power which will offer to restore Poland you mean Russia.

I have answered as well as I can your principal questions. As to the most influential man in the army, he is undoubtedly Prince Poniatowski, the Commander-in-Chief and Minister of War, whose personal character secures him an influence over his subordinates greater than that of any other chief.

In a few days I will go to Warsaw and sound the opinions of the leading personages there. . . . I regret your Majesty has not stated more precisely what you propose to do, and what you expect of the Poles, so that there should be no misunderstanding on either side. This alone could furnish sufficient arguments to influence the decision of those who will have to choose between the two alternatives. I forgot to ask if when developing this plan you do not intend to make an effort to bring about a general peace and gain your ends without war. I cannot tell you, Sire, with what hopes and fears I am continually agitated. What happiness it would be to labour for the deliverance of so many suffering nations, for the restoration of my country, and for your Majesty's glory! What happiness to see those different interests combined which fate seemed always to oppose to each other! But often I fancy that this is too magnificent a dream ever to be realised, and that the genius of evil, which seems always to be on the watch to break up combinations too fortunate for mankind, will also succeed in destroying this one. I am, with the profoundest respect, &c.

THE EMPEROR ALEXANDER TO PRINCE CZARTORYSKI.

ST PETERSBURG,

31*st January* 1811.

MY DEAR FRIEND,—I received your interesting letter of the $\frac{18}{30}$ January on the evening of the day before yesterday, and I hasten at once to answer it.

The difficulties which it points out are very great, I admit; but as I had foreseen most of them, and the results are of such supreme importance, the worst course to follow would be to stop half-way. . . .

I will begin by replying to the chief points in your letter—

(1) The Power to which I referred as willing

to take in hand the regeneration of Poland is *Russia.*

(2) By such regeneration I mean the reunion of everything that formerly constituted Poland, including the Russian provinces (except White Russia), so as to make the rivers Dvina, Beresina, and Dnieper the frontiers.

(3) The government officials, the established authorities, and the army, should be entirely of the Polish nationality.

(4) As I do not well remember the constitution of the 3rd of May, I cannot decide anything until I see it, and I shall be obliged if you will send it me. In any case a liberal constitution will be offered, such as to satisfy the wishes of the inhabitants.

(5) In order to convince them of the sincerity of my offer, the proclamations of the restoration of Poland must precede everything else, and it is by them that the execution of the plan is to commence.

(6) But the conditions *sine quâ non* on which I offer this are—

1st. That the kingdom of Poland shall for ever be united to Russia, whose Emperor shall in future bear the title of Emperor of Russia and King of Poland.

2nd. That a formal and positive assurance shall be given of a unanimity of disposition and feeling in favour of such a result among the inhabitants of the Duchy, to be guaranteed by the signature of the most prominent persons among them.

I will now endeavour to diminish your fears

as to the insufficiency of the military means at my disposal.

The army which is to support and fight by the side of the Poles is completely organised, and is composed of eight divisions of infantry, each comprising 10,000 men, and of four divisions of cavalry, each of 4,000 horses. This makes a total of 96,000 men, to which should be added fifteen Cossack regiments of 7,500 horse—106,500 in all. Non-combatants are not included.

This army will be supported by another of eleven divisions of infantry, a division of grenadiers, the Guards' division, four divisions of cavalry, and seventeen Cossack regiments—total, 134,000 men.

Finally, a third army, composed of reserve squadrons and battalions, supplies 44,000 combatants, reinforced by 80,000 recruits, all clothed and trained for some months in the depôts.

The army of Moldavia might in case of necessity also detach some divisions, without on that account being unable to maintain its defensive position, and the armies of Finland and Georgia, together with the corps in the Crimea, would remain entirely intact.

Two initial difficulties present themselves :

1st. The reunion of Galicia would create a difficulty as regards Austria. It is most necessary to treat her with consideration and avoid offending her in any respect. I have therefore decided to offer her Wallachia and Moldavia as far as the Sereth in exchange for Galicia. But it would be indispensable to postpone the reunion of Galicia until Austria gives her consent, so as to prove that we have no views that might be prejudicial to her.

The Kingdom of Poland would, therefore, in the first instance be formed of the Duchy of Warsaw and the Russian provinces.

2nd. The compensation to be given to the King of Saxony* presents a second difficulty which I find it not so easy to overcome. But I do not consider that I shall be bound to do so unless he comes over to my side.

Having thus stated the facts, I will enter upon a discussion of the subject generally.

It is beyond doubt that Napoleon is striving to provoke Russia to a rupture with him, hoping that I will make the mistake of being the aggressor. This would be a great blunder in present circumstances, and I am determined not to make it. But if the Poles were willing to join me, that would put an entirely new face on the matter. Being reinforced by the 50,000 men who constitute their army, by the 50,000 Prussians who could then also join me without risk, and by the moral revolution which would be the infallible result in Europe, I could advance to the Oder without striking a blow.

I agree with you that a proposal of peace might in that case be properly made. If it is not accepted, and war becomes inevitable, let us consider impartially the alternatives which are open to the Poles and the probable results of each of them.

First alternative, that of the Poles remaining on the side of France and co-operating with her.

This may be subdivided into two cases:

---

* The King of Saxony was Grand-Duke of the Duchy of Warsaw.

1st. Russia having decided not to take the offensive, it is possible that Napoleon will not do so either, at least so long as the affairs of Spain occupy him and the great mass of his troops are engaged there. In that case matters will remain as they are, and the regeneration of Poland will consequently be postponed to a more distant and very uncertain period.

2nd. If, on the other hand, Napoleon should attack Russia, and at the same time proclaim the regeneration of Poland, his proclamation could only have effect in the Duchy of Warsaw, for it would be necessary to deprive Russia of her Polish provinces by force of arms. Meanwhile the Duchy of Warsaw and the Polish provinces would become the theatre of war and of all possible devastation. It may thus be asserted with certainty that after such a war, whatever might be its result, Poland would be only a vast desert, and its inhabitants the greatest sufferers by the war.

Such is the probable result of the restoration of Poland being proclaimed by France.

Second alternative, that of the Poles joining Russia and co-operating with her.

The infallible results of this would be—

1st. That the regeneration of Poland, instead of being postponed, would precede any other event.

2nd, That this regeneration would comprise the Duchy of Warsaw and the Russian provinces, with a tolerably certain hope of its being extended to Galicia.

3rd, That the theatre of war, instead of being in the heart of Poland, would be transferred to the Oder.

Such are the *infallible* results, while the *probable* ones might be :

1*st*, A complete revolution of opinion in Europe.

2*nd*, A very marked diminution in the forces of Napoleon, increasing the chances of success ; for Napoleon would find it very difficult to withdraw his forces from Spain, being engaged with a nation bitterly hostile to him, and having 300,000 combatants in the field, which would not be satisfied with his retreat, but would take advantage of the new war Napoleon would have on his hands to invade France.

3*rd*, The deliverance of Europe from the yoke which oppresses her.

4*th*, The employment for the defence of Poland, as a kingdom annexed to a strong Empire, of the forces of that Empire.

5*th*, The revival of trade and prosperity, a liberal constitution, and a public revenue based on the real wants of the country, and not, as now, applied solely for the maintenance of a too large army destined to serve the ambitious plans of Napoleon.

Even the fears that you express as to the fate of the 20,000 Poles in Napoleon's service do not seem to me well founded, for the worst that could happen to them would be that for a time they would be regarded as prisoners of war . . . .

To resume : so long as I cannot be sure of the co-operation of the Poles I am decided not to begin a war with France. If such co-operation is to take place, I must receive *indubitable* assurances and proofs of it ; it is only then that I shall be able to act in the manner above stated. In that case you must send me all the necessary papers, such as proclamations, the constitution, and other indispensable documents. . . . . Our correspondence is an absolute secret, and even the Chancellor knows nothing of it, though I have often discussed the question with him. As to my military preparations, I have given them a defensive character, . . . and have sent a letter to Napoleon explaining that I am obliged to take precautionary measures, but that I am determined to adhere to my system of policy, and will certainly not take the offensive.   I must confess, however, that as rumours are being spread at St Petersburg that I am about to assume the title of King of Poland, I endeavour to put an end to them by declaring that the thing is impossible and cannot occur.   Such rumours are at present rather injurious than useful, though they prove that the plan would be highly approved by the Russians.

I must also warn you that I know from a good source that you are being watched by the French Minister of Police.   You must therefore double your precautions. . . .

I shall expect your answer with impatience. Yours for life, heart and soul.

Pray remember me most kindly to your parents, your brother, and your sisters.

The Emperor to Prince Czartoryski.

St Petersburg, 1*st April*, 1812.

I do not know, dear friend, whether you have guessed the cause of my silence.

Your previous letters had left me too little hope of success to authorise me to act, and I could not reasonably do so without some probability of success. I have therefore been obliged to resign myself to waiting for events, and not provoking, by any step on my part, a struggle whose importance and danger I thoroughly appreciate, though I do not believe I shall be able to avoid it. I also had certain information that you were being watched : and in order not to expose you to the least danger, I thought it best to allow a considerable time to elapse before resuming our correspondence. . . Finally, our projects have acquired a publicity which could only be very prejudicial to them, so much so, that they were talked about at Dresden and in Paris. . . .

A rupture with France seems inevitable. The object of Napoleon is to destroy, or at least to humiliate, the last Power in Europe which remains independent of him, and in order to attain this object, he puts forward pretensions which are inadmissible and incompatible with the honour of Russia.

He wishes all our trade with neutrals to be stopped ; .but this is the only trade which is left to us.

He also asks that, while deprived of every means of exporting our own productions, we should not raise any obstacle to the importation of French articles of luxury, which we have prohibited, not being rich enough to pay for them.

As I shall never be able to consent to such proposals, it is probable that war will follow,* not-

* It did, in the month of June following.

withstanding all that Russia had done to avoid it. Blood will flow, and poor humanity will again be sacrificed to the insatiable ambition of a man who seems to have been created as its scourge. You are too enlightened not to see how any liberal ideas with regard to your country are in his eyes out of the question. Napoleon has had confidential conversations on this subject with the envoys of Austria and Prussia, and the tone in which he has spoken to them, shows in its true light both his character and his indifference towards your countrymen, whom he looks upon only as the instruments of his hatred of Russia.

This war, which seems inevitable, frees me from all obligation to consider the interests of France, and leaves me unshackled in working out my favourite idea of regenerating your country.

All that remains to be done, therefore, is to decide upon the most advantageous course to be followed for securing the success of our plans; and in order that you may be better able to form a judgment upon them I think it useful to give you some indications as to the military operations I propose to undertake.

Although it is not impossible that we may push on with our forces to the Vistula, and even cross it so as to enter Warsaw, it is more prudent not to reckon on the resources and the prestige we should acquire from the possession of that city. We must therefore make the provinces the centre of our action.

Several very important questions will have to be settled in this connection.

Which is the most suitable moment for declaring the regeneration of Poland? Is it directly the rupture

takes place, or after our troops will have gained
some marked advantages? If the latter, would it be
useful for the success of our plans to organise the
Grand-Duchy of Lithuania as a preliminary measure
and give it one of the two constitutions of which I
send you drafts, or should the grant of a constitution
be postponed until the whole of Poland is restored?

It is on these vital questions that I invite your
candid opinion, and I would also wish you to state
which of the constitutions you think preferable.

I will not here discuss the chances of Russia in the
coming struggle. I will only remind you of the immense extent of territory which the Russian armies
have behind them and into which they can retire, while
Napoleon's difficulties would increase the further he
proceeds from his resources. Once the war begins we
are resolved not to lay down our arms. Our military
resources are very great, and the public feeling is
excellent—altogether different from that boastful
spirit which you witnessed during the two preceding
wars. . . . People think reverses are quite possible,
but for all that they are resolved to maintain the
honour of the Empire at any cost.

If under these circumstances the Poles should
join them, the effect would be immense, and the
Germans, forced by Napoleon to fight on his side,
would certainly follow the example of the Poles.

Sweden has concluded an offensive and defensive
alliance with us. The Crown Prince has a burning
desire to become the antagonist of Napoleon, against
whom he has an old personal grudge, and following
in the footsteps of Gustavus Adolphus, he only wishes

to be useful to a cause which is that of oppressed Europe.

Your idea of Napoleon consenting to a restoration of Poland, by placing her under the rule of a King who is also Emperor of Russia, is a chimerical one. He will never agree to a measure so advantageous to Russia, especially at a moment when he thinks only of destroying her. He will never attribute to complaisance on the part of Russia her inaction when he invaded Prussia, for it was impossible for us to interfere, in view of the absolute want of energy on the part of the King of Prussia, who thought only of saving Berlin and his palace.

Adieu, my dear friend, Providence alone knows what will be the issue of the great events which are preparing. It would have been a great pleasure to me to see you again, if only for a short time, at so interesting a crisis, at Wilna, for which town I shall leave in three days; but I dare not propose this to you, knowing the danger to which it would expose you. Be guided in all this only by your prudence, and believe me, etc.

[The further development of the plans referred to in the above correspondence was interrupted by the Russian Campaign of 1812. On the 26th of June in that year, immediately after Napoleon had crossed the Niemen, the Polish diet assembled at Warsaw under the presidency of Prince Adam Casimir Czartoryski, Prince Adam's father, and proclaimed the restoration of the whole of ancient Poland as an independent State. All the Poles in the Russian service were called upon to leave it, and Prince Adam, who still

held a post under the Russian government as Curator of the University of Wilna, repeatedly urged
the Emperor to accept the resignation which the Prince
had already tendered on several previous occasions.
Alexander took no notice of these letters, and directly
the campaign was over the correspondence between
him and the Prince as to the plan of a reconstruction
of Poland was resumed.]

LETTER FROM PRINCE ADAM CZARTORYSKI TO THE EMPEROR ALEXANDER.

$\frac{15}{27}$ *December* 1812.

. . . The events of the war having taken a turn
which seems to be decisive, I fear no one will now
plead to your Imperial Majesty for the interests
of my country, and I have accordingly sent Mr K.
with the accompanying papers, in the hope that they
may convince you.

I have no hope in the Continental Powers; they will
strive to divert you from an idea which will be offensive to them, and which is too noble for their Cabinets
to understand. What reassures me is that England,
in view of her clear interest, and of the opinions of the
Prince Regent, cannot fail to appreciate the plan. . . .

If your Imperial Majesty, at the moment when
the Polish nation is expecting the vengeance of a
conqueror, will hold out your hand and offer it that
which for her was the object of the war, the effect
would be magical.

If you would adopt the idea relative to the Grand
Duke Michael,* I would take it upon myself to get

* The Grand-Dukes Constantine and Michael were the Emperor's brothers.

everything signed without delay. I think it my duty not to conceal from your Majesty that a cause of incessant anxiety and terror to the Poles is the Grand-Duke Constantine, who is your heir-apparent; and this is the reason why they would prefer another branch. A King of Poland with 300,000 men under his orders would be able at any time to destroy what his predecessor may have established. It is this which makes the Poles so desirous of obtaining a regular constitution, though even that could not guarantee them against acts of arbitrary violence. But whatever arrangement you may prefer on the basis I have submitted to you, I do not think I am saying too much when I assure you that it would be settled to your entire satisfaction.

THE EMPEROR ALEXANDER TO PRINCE CZARTORYSKI

LEYPOUNY, 13*th January* 1813.

I received your interesting letter of the 15th of December 1812, with its enclosures, two days ago . . . , and to-day I have also received a document signed 'The Minister of the Interior, Mostowski,' and addressed to me. I do not lose a moment in answering you, and this letter will also serve as an answer to M. Mostowski.

The proposals in these papers, and the personal sentiments with regard to myself expressed in them, have touched me very deeply. The successes by which Providence has wished to bless my efforts and my perseverance have in no way changed either my sentiments or my intentions with regard to Poland. Your countrymen may therefore abandon any fears they may feel : vengeance is a sentiment unknown to me, and my greatest pleasure is to return good for evil. The strictest orders have been given to my generals to treat the Poles as friends and brothers.

To speak candidly, in order to realise my favourite ideas as to Poland I shall have to overcome some difficulties, notwithstanding the brilliancy of my present position.

In the first place, opinion in Russia would be against them. The sacking by the Polish troops of Smolensk and Moscow, and the devastation of the whole country, has revived old hatreds.

Next, if I were at this moment to publish my intentions with regard to Poland, the result would be to throw Austria and Prussia entirely into the arms of France; while it is essential to prevent such a result, especially as those Powers already show themselves very disposed to join me.

These difficulties will be conquered with a little wisdom and prudence. But for this it is necessary that you should second me, by justifying in the eyes of the Russians the predilection which I am known to feel for the Poles and their ideas. Trust me, my character, and my principles, and your hopes will not be deceived. As military events develop themselves, you will see how dear the interests of your country are to me, and how faithful I am to my old ideas. As to the form, you know I have always preferred liberal ones.

But I must plainly tell you that the idea of my brother Michael cannot be admitted. Do not forget that Lithuania, Podolia, and Volhynia are hitherto regarded as Russian provinces, and that no possible reasoning could persuade Russia to see them under the rule of another sovereign than the one that rules Russia. The name under which they would continue to form part of Russia is a difficulty that would be more easily overcome.

Pray communicate this letter to the persons whose co-operation you think necessary, and urge your countrymen to show good-will to Russia and the Russians, so as to wipe out the recollections of the campaign, and thereby facilitate my task. On my part, in order to give the Poles a proof of the sincerity of my intentions, I have given orders to my army not to occupy Warsaw; but for this it is necessary that no foreign troops should remain there, and Polish ones least of all, so as to deprive us of the anxiety of leaving a foreign garrison behind us. Pray urge the members of the confederation and the Government on my part, to remain quietly at Warsaw, and promise them that they will not regret their doing so.

As to the military operations, besides the armies now in the field, each regiment of the whole army has already in the rear a reserve of 1000 men per regiment of infantry and two squadrons per regiment of cavalry, completely equipped and mounted, and is also provided with reserve companies of artillery, to enter the ranks of the active army in the spring. Besides these reserves a levy of 180,000 men is at this moment taking place, which will serve to reconstitute the reserves of the regiments as soon as they are incorporated in the active army. Moreover, all the militia, foot, horse, and artillery, are on the march under Count Peter Tolstoï to form a corps of observation in Volhynia. The energy of the nation is beyond praise, and I am decided to push on the war not only during this winter, but until a general peace is established in a manner suitable to the security of Russia and of Europe. . . .

(Signed)   ALEXANDER.

KRASNOPOL,
3rd January 1813.

P.S. It has taken me two days to write this letter, as my time was taken up with the affairs of the army and other business.

As my letter bears a certain official character, I cannot allow it to go, my dear friend, without adding a friendly word for you.   Success has not changed me either in my ideas on your country or in my principles generally, and you will always find me such as you have known me.   Say many things from me to your parents and your sisters.

If, as a result of all these events, I should be able to stay for a moment with your family this would give me immense pleasure.   Yours heart and soul.

PRINCE CZARTORYSKI TO THE EMPEROR ALEXANDER.
WARSAW,
23rd April (*4th May*) 1813.

Sire,—. . . In returning from Kalisz, I met Prince Anthony Radziwill at Nieborow.   He gave me some details which it is well for your Imperial Majesty to know.   The King of Prussia is not at all opposed to the existence of Poland. He feels the necessity of satisfying the wishes of the Polish nation, and considers them just and reasonable. He was astonished at your Majesty not having as yet done anything definite for the Poles, and complained that whenever he wanted to touch upon the subject you seemed much embarrassed and talked about something else. He asked Prince Anthony to go to Warsaw to sound public opinion and confer with me. From all this it would seem that the King of Prussia would agree to any measure your Majesty might think fit to take in this sense. . . . There are, in fact, no difficulties in the way of your undertaking so far as the King of Prussia is concerned; on the contrary, he will himself contribute in a large degree to remove those presented by the Russian army, whose opinion will always be preponderant at St Petersburg. . . . I know that the Russian officers here mostly speak in this sense either by conviction or in order to flatter the inhabitants.

I hear with pain that an order has been given at head-quarters to confiscate the estates of all who serve in the Polish army. This order seems to me unjust and without an object ; people should not be punished for serving their country and obeying the orders of their sovereign, recognised as such by your Majesty. . . I confess that it gives me much sorrow to see measures so inconsistent with the policy of generous equity which you have adopted—the noblest and the most useful, even if only looked upon as a matter of interest.

PRINCE CZARTORYSKI TO THE EMPEROR ALEXANDER.

WARSAW, 27*th April* 1813.

. . . Those who know your Imperial Majesty cannot admit the slightest suspicion of the loyalty of your sentiments or fear that you do not intend to fulfil the hopes you are holding out to the Poles ; . . . yet those who have to carry out your policy are doing their utmost to defeat it.

The five Governments of Lithuania, instead of enjoying the benefits you wish to grant them, are suffering under an administration more unjust and arbitrary than any of those that have preceded it. No one's property, life, or honour is safe. Any official prompted by a desire of revenge or greed of gain may ruin the most innocent citizen and the whole of his family—. . . in a word, the Government and the authorities, instead of protecting the inhabitants placed under their care, seem to think it their duty to persecute and plunder them. You have no idea, Sire, of the evil that is being done in your name, for if you had you would put a stop to it. . . The inhabitants are in despair, and though hitherto they have been quiet, they may be driven to insurrection, not by a hope of success, but because they think it better to perish than to remain in their present condition.

CHAPTER XX

1813

AMONG the English friends of Prince Czartoryski was General Sir Robert Wilson. This officer had fought under Wellington at Talavera, was afterwards Military Attaché to the allied armies in Poland, and was tried for conniving at the escape of Count Lavalette, who had been condemned to death as an accomplice of Napoleon. When Sir Robert Wilson was asked at whose instigation he had assisted Lavalette, he replied: 'I was born and educated in a country in which the social virtues are considered as public virtues, and I have not trained my memory to a breach of friendship and confidence.'*

The following are some of his more characteristic letters to Prince Czartoryski :

' RUSSOPOL,
' *January* $\frac{3}{13}$, 1813.

'MY DEAR PRINCE—I received your letter with a transport of pleasure. Your absence had always been

---

* Diary of Henry Crabb Robinson, vol. ii. p. 6. Sir Robert Wilson was Member of Parliament for Southwark from 1818 to 1831, and then re-entered the army, ending his career as Governor and Commander-in-Chief of Gibraltar.

a matter of deep regret to me, and your vacancy in the circle could never be supplied. To hear from you, to know that I was preserved in your esteem, was a high gratification, but I became prouder when I found that you still considered me as a champion true to that most interesting cause, the re-establishment and happiness of your brave nation. I participate in all your feelings, and am in accord with all your sentiments. Your friend will tell you what I have done, and I pledge myself to you that everything which can be attempted to promote the object shall be put in execution with a zeal as ardent as your own. It is a matter in which, as an Englishman, I feel so much interest that I would sustain the plea with every personal sacrifice if it would tend to the desired accomplishment.

'There are many potent reasons why delay will prove detrimental to Russia (I cannot be more explicit on that subject, but you will discover my allusion, having so well judged of the past and speculated on the probable future), if fatal prejudices refuse the only security that offers for advantages obtained. The Emperor's firmness, the patriotism of the nation, and the courage of the army, cannot be too highly estimated or applauded, but Buonaparte's errors and the climate have assuredly brought his misfortunes to the degree that they have reached. If Buonaparte had been opposed by a chief who had only common military skill or energy he would indeed have perished altogether ; but as that, or rather *those* opportunities were lost, as the favours of the good genius of the world were scorned at Maloslavitz, Krasnow, and the

Beresina, Russia must not trifle with her interests.
Half measures—timid policy—will prove her ruin.
It is for the Council of the Empire to repair in some
degree the mischief which an inadequate direction of
the military powers has occasioned, for I consider the
escape of Buonaparte, even with his wreck, a serious
mischief that may cost her dear, and which certainly
entails great inconveniences. I use mild terms—
milder perhaps than I should if we conversed together.
I long to see you, and certainly I will. I have very
much to say to you on a variety of subjects, but if it
was only for the pleasure of seeing you half-an-hour.
I would go several hundred versts. . .

'England has been a little uneasy, and I do not
think the Government quite settled. Lord Wellesley
and Lord Grey must in my opinion be brought into
office. All will then be well, and *you* will have firm
friends. *Pars pro toto.* We only want to see the
operation performed by others than Buonaparte.
That Corsican never will attain the object so as to
receive our countenance, and I think the Poles themselves must be sensible that he takes no real interest
in their welfare—that he considers Poland but as a
stepping-stone to his ambition. His is such protection as vultures give to lambs, covering and
devouring. . . .

'I am obliged for a few days to be at the Imperial
head-quarters, but in general I rove about as usual,
and I have not been behind at the most interesting
turns of the chase. . . . I have escaped *sauf et sain.*
My nose only has been in danger, but it was in very
serious danger. For once in my life I shrank from

Glory's pursuit, or rather lamented I had been wooing a phantom who seemed resolved to wring off the noses of his votaries. Mine were only fears; but how many thousand poor wretches have suffered all the mutilating horrors of the angry climate. This campaign has certainly cost both armies very near half a million of men, and I calculate that more than 100,000 have perished with misery more terrible than any one heard except the Roman crucifixions of the Jews. I have seen sights of woe and could tales unfold—but, like Hamlet, I am forbid.

'Adieu, my very dear Prince. Keep me in your kind remembrance and believe me your gratefully attached friend, servant, and *colleague,*

'Rob^T. Wilson.'

'Kalisch,
'*February* 27, 1813.
'I have only this day, my ever dear Prince, received your letter from Dubnow. I am afraid your messenger will depart before I can communicate the result of some conversations that I expect on this interesting subject, which should engage every statesman's, of every country's, serious attention, and every honest man's affections.

'I have never been unfaithful to the *sacred pledges.* Co-operation in such a cause has ever been considered by me as a self-approving act, teeming with more joy and dignity of pride than all the distinctions which were conferred on those who originally resisted the appeals which your country made to justice and to honour.

'Poland has proved that the maxim is not infallible which recommends division to assure conquest. The spirit of independence has been unconquerable, although its efforts have not been undeviating. . .

'Head-quarters is not so cheerful as heretofore in our happy time. There are many good fellows in the army, but circumstances have been unfavourable to former good fellowship which prevailed anywhere and everywhere. The campaign has been one of great rudeness: toil and endurance with few social pleasures. The tone was *ab origine* discordant. Your return would, however, rally gaiety and concord. God grant it! Ever yours, with affectionate attachment,

'Rob^T. Wilson.'

'*September* 8, 1813.

'My Dear Friend,—You must not suppose me forgetful of you or of my engagements. There is no Lethe so potent as to erase these duties and affections from my remembrance. There is no centrifugal force so strong as to withdraw me from our united base. The distraction of affairs, the difficulty of communication, and the desire of seeing a person long expected, but who has arrived, prevented me from writing since I left Prague.

'I have now to urge your seizure of the *earliest* opportunity to make a journey to this part of the world. Approach the Emperor of Austria, and as soon as possible see Lord Aberdeen, our Ambassador to him. All is arranged for your visit, and he eagerly expects you. You will find him all you wish. I lost no time in introducing the subject to his notice.

He saw the moral and political advantages as I do, and on this and every other matter he will pursue the *honestum* as the most useful course of proceeding.

'Lord A. comes so fully aware of your value that he longs to make your acquaintance and converse on various matters. His society will not be indifferent to you. Come you must, and speedily, if you seek to found your fame on the foundation of patriotism. I have also procured high friends in other quarters. In good truth, I have devoted all my best efforts to the subject since we parted, and with very gratifying success. Come, and we shall triumph. If you come not, not only much but all may be lost. You will of course make a suitable pretext for this journey, and excite neither jealousy nor suspicion. As soon as I hear you are within tangible reach, I will go to you, as in all probability I shall be transferred to the Austrian Embassy, [where] I can act more independently. . . .

'We have had short but severe service. The worst spectacle which I beheld was the savage blow by which destiny struck down Moreau and so many national hopes. . .

'I do not enter into military or political details. All I can say is comprised in the statement of my belief that the events since the 17th of August* have increased the desire of peace in pacificators, disposed belligerents to negotiation, and that to the prejudice of war's amateurs peace will be made before the winter.

'Come, come, come, without loss of time. As an

---

* The date on which Austria joined the coalition against France.

inducement I will not be angry if you pass by Landeck and remain there forty-eight hours.

' Your ever affectionate friend,

' R. Wilson.'

' We were on march to assist Blücher, but B^{te}'s return to Dresden recalls us.'

CHAPTER XXI

1813-14

THE BIERNACKI MISSION TO LONDON.—CHASED BY A FRENCH MAN-OF-WAR.—LORD CASTLEREAGH.—CANNING.—BROUGHAM.—LEIGH HUNT.—'THE TIMES.'—TOM MOORE.—SIR SAMUEL ROMILLY.

THE policy of Austria towards Poland did not realise Sir Robert Wilson's sanguine anticipations, and the hostility shown to the Poles by the Russian authorities, notwithstanding the friendly professions of their Imperial master, made it improbable that Alexander would be alone able to carry out the restoration of Poland. As there was a talk of a Congress being assembled at which the Polish and other questions would be dealt with by the Powers collectively, Prince Adam Czartoryski sent his secretary, Biernacki, to London to sound the Government as to its intentions with regard to Poland and to bring the Polish question generally before the British public. During his stay in England M. Biernacki kept a diary which, though unfortunately incomplete, gives some curious details as to the leading men in the political and literary circles of London at that period.

He left Pulawy on the 12th of September 1813, and Warsaw on the 17th. Travelling was slow and

difficult, owing to the inundations and the crowds of
Russian soldiers on both banks of the Vistula, who
behaved as if they were the masters of the country.
On the 20th he arrived at Königsberg, where he
observed that the lower classes still spoke Polish,
though the province had so long been in the hands of
Prussia. He asked some educated Prussians the
reason of this, and they answered, with some surprise
at his putting such a question, that Polish is the
national language of the people, and that 'you cannot
make a whole nation speak a foreign language.'

On the 22nd he reached Pillau, and embarked on
board the 'Commonwealth,' Captain Hesketh, for
Carlscrona, in Sweden, where he arrived on the 28th
after a very rough passage. From this place he
drove for four days and five nights to Gothenburg,
which he calls 'the newest, cleanest, and most regularly built city in Europe.' He remarked that 'the
more wealthy merchants, chiefly Englishmen, had
beautiful country houses in the vicinity of the town,
with magnificent gardens and well-kept farm buildings.'

He left Gothenburg on the 6th of October in her
Majesty's Packet 'Lark,' Captain Sherlock commander. Among his companions were an Irishman,
'elegant, *bon vivant*, and a little feather brained,' 'a
romantic and polite Scotchman,' and 'a well-known
character who is convinced that he is John of Gaunt,
Duke of Lancaster. He amused us greatly, and
reminded me of Swift's saying that out of every
hundred of his countrymen five are mad.' The
'Lark' was a vessel of 16 guns ; there was plenty of
amusement on board, and the *cuisine* was excellent.

One day at noon M. Biernacki went down into the
cabin to dress for dinner, when as he was shaving he
heard cries of 'clear for action!' This, however, did not
disturb him, as he thought they were merely rejoicing
at having caught a turbot or some other fish ; but soon
after the captain called out to him, ' D— your razors !
It's no time for shaving. The French are coming!'
M. Biernacki then hurried on his clothes and went on
deck, where he found everything ready for action and
was ordered to take charge of a gun. The French
ship, which was much larger than the ' Lark,' advanced straight upon her, but seeing her guns and
crew, sheered off. ' I was very glad to see this,' he
says, ' and especially so when I was told that the
' Lark,' being a packet-boat, was forbidden to pursue
an enemy—which under the circumstances seemed to
me a very sensible rule.'

M. Biernacki arrived at Harwich on the 16th of
October. 'I have often heard and read,' he says,
that directly you set foot on English soil you
breathe more freely. My own impressions carried
me even further : not only are one's physical movements more free, but the first few days of one's stay
in England have an even greater influence on the
mind. It is a feeling like that of gratified ambition ;
you imagine yourself to be in a more dignified position than you were before you landed, and are
prompted to regulate your conduct accordingly. . . .
At St Petersburg, on the other hand, the visitor
breathes with difficulty, neglects himself and his
duties, and becomes less orderly and courteous than
usual.'

In London, M. Biernacki put up at the 'Spread Eagle,' Gracechurch Street, and he thus describes his first impressions of the city : 'Thousands of people from all parts of the world, of various complexions and costumes; thousands of carriages, carts, and cattle; the horns blown on the coaches, of which 2000 leave and arrive in London daily; the trumpets of the newsboys, the bells of the postmen; the street bands, the constant fights between thieves and their victims, and the crowds of beggars, make one deaf and produce a confusion of mind which lasts for several days, until one gets accustomed to this incessant turmoil.' On the third day after his arrival, M. Biernacki obtained an appointment with Lord Castlereagh at six in the afternoon in Downing Street. The interview lasted till a quarter to eight. He found Lord Castlereagh cold but frank in manner, speaking with much deliberation, full of preconceived notions to which he obstinately adhered, and imperfectly informed as to Polish affairs. He did not express himself with facility either in English or in French.

After M. Biernacki had fully developed the plan of a reconstruction of Poland, Lord Castlereagh objected that if Poland were restored the old anarchy would probably be revived, upon which M. Biernacki reminded him of the Constitution of the 3rd of May and the sittings of the diet of 1788-92, in which, notwithstanding the excitement produced by the French revolution, the debates were conducted with as much order and regularity as in the English Parliament, which the Polish Deputies took for their example. To this Lord Castlereagh made no reply,

but he said that it would be ungenerous on the part
of his Government to encourage the Poles by empty
promises to indulge in hopes or attempt enterprises
whose object it is not in the power of England to
promote. 'England,' he added with much emphasis,
'is, in fact, so placed that she must scrupulously avoid
everything that could give rise to distrust either
between her and her allies or between any two
Powers on the Continent belonging to the alliance.
It cannot be assumed that any of the partitioning
Powers will consent to return the provinces they have
taken from Poland, and I cannot think it possible
to effect the restoration of Poland by mere negotiation; the only means of doing so is by the sword.
If the Poles rose in arms for this purpose, England
might, under other circumstances than the present,
effectually assist them. But recent experience does
not incline me to wish for such an event, as the result
would not be worth the bloodshed and material ruin
which such a struggle would involve. In my opinion
the Poles should now submit to Russia and endeavour
to gain her favour. England is prevented by treaties
with her allies, and by her duties to the English
people—which must always be the first consideration
—from mixing herself up in such a matter; there
might, however, be means of bringing the Polish
question before the British public.' He then pledged
M. Biernacki to secrecy, and the latter asked for a
similar promise as to his mission, explaining that
Prince Czartoryski had purposely sent to London so
obscure an individual as himself in order to prevent
inconvenient reports or disclosures.

M. Biernacki next called upon Mr Canning, though from what 'he had heard of his character and political position,' he felt convinced 'that not the slightest assistance was to be expected of him.' 'Mr Canning,' he says, 'has much wit, but does not possess the ability which in England is necessary for dealing successfully with public affairs. He writes stanzas, elegies, and epigrams, and this rather does him harm with the serious public. The general opinion is that though he is the most fluent and attractive speaker in the House, he wants staying power ; that he has excellent ideas, but not sufficient industry or perseverance to carry them out. . . The affair which led to his duel with Lord Castlereagh, and in which Mr Canning played so shameful a part, has, though it took place eight years ago, not been forgotten by the British public, and has left an indelible stigma on his character. But what injures him most in public opinion as a politician, is his unscrupulous ambition ; there is a general feeling that he would even plunge the country into war, if by so doing he could please the Court and re-enter the Cabinet.' The following letter addressed by him to M. Biernacki after their first interview, shows that Mr Canning's French, like Lord Castlereagh's, was far from perfect :

'Oserois-je vous prier, Monsieur, de vouloir bien prendre la peine de me venir voir ou demain, ou l'après demain entre midi et une heure.

'Je suis bien fâché de vous donner cette peine-là. Mais je suis au lit, et fort incommodé d'une grosse rhume. Néanmoins, si vous préféreriez de revenir ici aujourdhui même entre une et deux heures, je serois prêt de vous recevoir.

'Aies la bonté de m'indiquer le jour qui vous conviendra.'

The impression derived by M. Biernacki from his interviews with Mr Canning was that he was 'more polite than is the case with Englishmen generally. He was eager for an opportunity of attacking the Ministry, and seemed better informed than Lord Castlereagh as to the affairs of Poland. He told me that since 1791, when the Opposition loudly advocated the Polish cause, Polish affairs had ceased to occupy the attention of the British Government and public. He expressed interest in our cause, but this was evidently not so much on account of the thing itself as of his own political objects, and he asked me with much curiosity about the people with whom I had talked and the views they had expressed. . . . He warned me against asking the Opposition to take up the cause of Poland. The Opposition, he said, is not only quite insignificant, but is despised on account of its impotence, as the Ministry defeats by means of its majority everything that the Opposition proposes. He did not think the Ministry could take up the question in Parliament, as they wanted money for subsidies to Austria, Prussia, and Russia. It was true that there was a great deal of talk in Parliament on behalf of Poland in the time of Pitt ; but this was not prompted by any partiality to the Poles or any feeling that their independence was necessary for the good of Europe ; Poland was simply made a stalking-horse for attacks on the Ministry. It was unfortunate for

the Poles that the Powers which partitioned them
were England's allies against Napoleon ; this was the
reason of her silence in presence of the iniquities committed by those Powers in Poland.   Moreover, those
who advocated the Polish cause were also supporters
of the French Revolution ; and this had led to a general
belief in England that the Poles are people of the
same type as the French Jacobins.   Under these circumstances the ground was not very favourable in
England for a movement on behalf of Poland ; and he
would advise that urgent representations should be
made to the Ministry, which has its hands free with
regard to the Duchy of Warsaw, and even if there
should be any secret conventions on the matter,
England might yet wish for and advise an alteration
of them.'

The following is a copy of the last communication
to M. Biernacki from Mr Canning, who on this
occasion wrote in English :—

'HINCKLEY,
'*December* 3, 1813.

'SIR,—I have received the honour of your letter
of the 27th, and have forwarded that which came
in it to Lord Granville Leveson Gower.

'I am very much concerned to hear of your indis-
position ; and particularly so, that it prevented me
from having the pleasure of seeing you again before I
left town.

'Any interest that I might take in the subject on
which you addressed yourself to me would, I am afraid,
be of little avail, if you find nothing but indifference
in other quarters.

' I am not without apprehension that you may have misunderstood something which passed between us respecting Lord Grenville. I expressed, what I feel, the highest respect for his Lordship's character and abilities; and gave it as my decided opinion that anything which *he* might say on behalf of your country would carry the greatest weight, and would be altogether free from any danger of misrepresentation. But I by no means intended to lead you to imagine that *I* could take the liberty of introducing you, or of stating the object of your mission to this country, to Lord Grenville. Although much acquainted with him some years ago, we are not now in those habits of intimacy either publick or private, which would at all warrant my taking such a step; and, I confess, I should also feel myself restrained not only with regard to Lord Grenville, but to anyone else, by certain expressions in Prince Czartoryski's letter to me, recommending a perfect silence on the subject of its contents.

' If you think it right to address yourself to Lord Grenville, and should find it necessary to refer his Lordship to me, merely for the fact of your having brought me a letter from the Prince Czartoryski, strongly recommending you to my good offices, I can have no difficulty in giving a satisfactory answer to such a reference; but I should not think myself justified in originating such a communication, or in entering with any other person into a correspondence on the object of your mission. Prince Czartoryski does not, in his letter to me, make any exception whatever to his general recommendation of secrecy.

' I have not had the opportunity of learning

whether Prince Czartoryski mentions your business here to Lord Granville Leveson Gower—or whether the letter to him be merely, as you suppose, a letter of introduction. I shall probably see Lord Granville Leveson Gower in the course of a few weeks. In the meantime I have not said anything to him of the nature of your business; nor shall I, unless I should find him informed of it.

'If there is anything in which I can be of service to you, a letter addressed to me at Gloucester Lodge will always be duly forwarded to me. I am, with great truth, Sir, your most obedient and faithful servant,   GEO. CANNING.'

'To M. BIERNACKI, at Mr DODD's, No. 12 Aldersgate Street.'

M. Biernacki's next interview was with Brougham, whom he was instructed to sound as to the best means of bringing the Polish question before the British public through the press. 'How am I to describe,' he says, 'this noble mind—what am I to say of him whose character, talents, eloquence, and knowledge, are celebrated in the whole of England, whose house is full of testimonials from towns and countries, and from families which he has saved? . . . I have observed that in other countries, and especially in Germany, a legal training narrows the mind. Here it has an opposite effect. As was formerly to some extent the case in Rome, the teaching of law is in England necessarily connected with that of the theory and practice of legislation, and is illustrated by frequent discussions both in Parliament and in the Law Courts on the objects for which laws were enacted. The learning and practice of the law evidently tends to make English judges and barristers large-minded, thoughtful, high-principled, and merciful. . . . Mr Brougham is cold and grave in manner, but it is impossible not to perceive that he has a fertile imagination which he has thoroughly under control, and with the help of which he gains some of his greatest successes. He is fond of pictures and music, is an accomplished *connaisseur*, and speaks French better than is generally the case with Englishmen.

'Directly I broached the subject of Poland he assured me that he had long taken an interest in that country, that he had the best opinion of it, that when a young man he had often thought of plans for its reconstruction, and that he was ready to do everything in his power to bring about such a result.

'I then mentioned to him the idea of appealing to public opinion on behalf of Poland through the English press. He promised me all possible assistance, asked for maps and books about Poland, and wrote down a series of questions as to religion in Poland, the national desire for independence, the results of the partition, the state of parties, etc., which I took home to answer in full. . . . He read my answers carefully, and we then agreed that the first thing to be done was to write a short appeal* to the English nation fully stating all the facts as to

* This pamphlet, the manuscript of which, in Brougham's handwriting, is in the Czartoryski Archives, was published in 1814, under the title of *An Appeal to the Allies and the English Nation on behalf of Poland.* London, J. Harding, St James's Street, 8vo. pp. 66.

Poland, of which they are at present profoundly ignorant. He promised to do this as speedily as possible. The next step would be to enlist the interest and sympathy of prominent journalists, poets, and other writers on behalf of Poland, so as to induce them to write in her favour; also to interest the Quakers, and the Irish Catholic party under the leadership of Mr Grattan—a very powerful party which is increasing in strength, has great influence, and will readily assist us. Another party which it would be very useful to enlist in the cause is that of Mr Wilberforce, which comprises many eminent politicians, such as Mr Vansittart, Chancellor of the Exchequer.

'As it would be impossible at present to obtain anything from the Ministry, which has its hands tied by the allies of England and matters of internal policy, and it would not be expedient to help the opposition to make Poland the occasion for a party attack on the Government, we decided to try the Burke party, which is not connected either with the Government or the Opposition, and has some of the ablest and most honest men in the House among its members, who are generally esteemed both in Parliament and in the country. At their head is the Right Hon. W. Elliot, formerly Secretary of State,* to whom Burke dedicated his works.

'As public discussion is most in fashion here, and it is very difficult to keep things secret, even in the Cabinet, we arranged that Mr Brougham should conduct the negotiations, I remaining in the background until it should become absolutely necessary

* Mr Elliot was not a Secretary of State, but Chief Secretary for Ireland in 1806.

for me to treat with such members of the party as might be most relied upon. Among these are Sir Samuel Romilly, a great favourite with the public, known as " the champion of British freedom and law ; " Sir Alexander Baring, a merchant prince who has made himself very popular by his patriotism, his talents, and his philanthropy ; and the young Marquis of Lansdowne, a man of great ability and weight in the House, with such a reputation for prudence that people say of him that "he was born in 1780, in the thirtieth year of his age." '

The following is a copy of the Right Hon. W. Elliot's reply to the letter written to him by Mr Brougham after the conversation described above :

'WELLS, 26*th December* 1813.

' MY DEAR SIR,—Owing to an accident, I did not receive your letter of the 18th inst. so soon as it ought to have reached me, which circumstance is the occasion of the lateness of my acknowledgment of it.

' No one, I assure you, can contemplate with more abhorrence than I do the various spoliations which Poland has undergone, and there is no one who could derive more joy and satisfaction from beholding her resume her due station amongst the nations of Europe. At the same time it is impossible for me to disguise from myself the many difficulties which stand in the way of the accomplishment of such a restoration. It obviously cannot be obtained without the concurrence of Austria and Russia (I may add Prussia), and it is but fair towards our Government to say, that even if

they were to take up the cause with all the zeal and
authority by which they could support it, their inter-
position could go little beyond exhortation, and means
very inadequate, I fear, to bring about an object that
must be attended with considerable sacrifices on the
part of these Powers.

'With regard to the course suggested by the
gentleman who has made to you the communication
you mention, I confess it appears to me perfectly hopeless.   If I understand it right, it is that the affairs of
Poland should in some form or other be brought under
the view of Parliament without his having made any
previous disclosure to the Government on the subject
of his mission.   Now I feel the clearest conviction
that this mode of agitating the matter could produce
no beneficial results whatever ; and that on the contrary much censure would be cast (I think not wholly
without reason) on the introduction of a topic which
had been withheld from the knowledge of the Ministers
of the Crown, although materially affecting the interests of his Majesty's allies, and of peculiar delicacy
at the present conjuncture because hazarding the harmony and cordiality amongst them necessary to the
continuance of that success which has of late accompanied their arms.   In truth, too, almost under any
circumstances, I should place little reliance on the
efficacy of the exertions of a few individuals in Parliament in a cause which, to ensure it any chance of
success, would require all the weight that the combined efforts of all the political parties in the country
could afford it.   Such a plan of proceeding would, at
least as it strikes me, be attended with no solid utility,

and it might (and this is an idea at which I shudder)
by exciting delusive expectations and even premature
movements in Poland, involve that unfortunate country in still more grievous calamities than those which
she has already incurred. These considerations will, I
acknowledge, render me very reluctant to share in the
management of the case ; and though I am unapprized
of the details of the extent of the views entertained, I
am anxious to give you immediately these my first and
hasty impressions (for I am writing under the fear of
losing the post) in order that the person who is
charged with the mission may not be prevented from
availing himself of any other means that may present
themselves to him for the furtherance of the business
committed to his care.

‘ Of course I shall strictly observe your injunction
of secrecy. On my way to London it is probable I
may call at Milton, in which event (I conclude from
the tenor of your letter) I may show it to Lord Fitz-
william and Lord Milton, unless I have an intimation
from you of your wish to the contrary.

‘ It was my intention to have been by this time on
my road, but I have been detained by the illness of
my servant, who is not yet able to travel, and I therefore propose to remain here for about a fortnight
longer.

‘ I have only a moment left to add, that I am
always—most faithfully yours,

‘ W. Elliot.

‘ H. Brougham, Esq.
‘ King's Bench Walk, Temple, London.’

Describing a visit to Madame de Staël, M. Biernacki says :

'Madame de Staël is immensely popular at the British Court and among the public. Her sentimentalism, her enthusiasm, her singular opinions as to morals and politics, have in no way prevented her from gaining the highest consideration among all classes; it was enough that as an enemy of Napoleon she had been banished from the Continent and had taken refuge in England. Her extraordinary eloquence and readiness in debate inspire universal admiration, and the highest personages in the country seek her acquaintance. Her influence is, in fact, so great that, in spite of her many indiscretions and her advocacy of Russia, I decided to seek her assistance. . . . She spoke, at a *soirée* given by her, with the greatest enthusiasm about Poland and loudly praised the Poles, and her remarks were most strongly supported by Sir Samuel Romilly and Mr Dumont, the editor of *Bentham*. We shall see if she will write in the same sense; but her *soirées* are so largely attended that even in conversation she might help us.'

M. Biernacki wrote her a long letter, urging her to advocate the cause of Poland, to which he received the following reply :

'Je n'ai jamais cessé de m'intéresser à la Pologne, et la noble persévérance de ses malheureux citoyens est respectable et touchante—mais qu'espérer pour elle en ce moment ! Si la personne qui m'a fait l'honneur de m'écrire une si belle lettre veut me voir, je la recevrai dans le secret le plus absolu, mais ce sera seulement pour lui exprimer l'admiration que m'inspire un sentiment national si courageusement conservé, si courageusement exprimé par les actions et les paroles.

'A. L. G. DE STAËL HOLSTEIN, née NECKER.'

Brougham* was very indignant at this smoothly worded refusal, and drafted the following characteristic rejoinder, which, however, M. Biernacki did not send to Madame de Staël, as he thought it was too polemical to be addressed to a woman; upon which Brougham drily observed : ' Perhaps you are right ; it would be best simply to tell her she knows nothing about the matter '—

'Je dois vous avouer très-franchement que votre réponse (signée pour comble d'inconséquence du nom de Necker), m'a donné une affliction sensible. Est-il possible que, toute clairvoyante que vous êtes, vous puissiez ne pas sentir que c'est précisément *dans ce moment* qu'il y aye quelquo chose à espérer pour la Pologne ? Y a-t-il la moindre probabilité que dans l'avenir elle verra un moment plus favorable ? Dites-le donc, avec la franchise que je vous crois propre, proclamez que notre état est pour jamais désespéré. Mais je vous supplie de ne pas voiler l'insouciance pour tout ce qui n'est pas Suédois, ou Russe, ou Allemand—l'indifférence pour tous les maux qui ne

---

* He thus states his opinion of Madame de Staël in a letter to Earl Grey, dated December 16, 1813, and published in Brougham's autobiography (Vol. II., p. 98) : ' This brings me to the said gentlewoman, Madame de Staël, whom I really think you all overrate. Her book seems terribly vague and general and inaccurate. She certainly follows old Lord Lansdowne's advice in avoiding details "as the more dignified line." Besides, her presumption is intolerable, and on all subjects, on many of which she *can* know nothing—as, for instance, the German metaphysics, except so far as she may have rubbed some of them off Schlegel. I never have seen her, and shun her as I would an evil of some kind, having heard her talked of as a grand bore, and being sickened by the concurring accounts of her fulsome flattery of the Prince, Ministers, etc., etc., and her profligate changes of principle. In women such things signify little ; but she must (as Talleyrand said) be considered a man.'

viennent pas de Bonaparte—sous le prétexte (prétexte qui ne manquera jamais quand vous auriez vécu, et l'admiration de l'Europe, encore une * demi-siècle) que ce n'est pas encore "*le moment.*"

'Je ne vous cacherai point que j'attribue ce que vous m'avez dit bien plus à la légèrcté d'un grand génie, qu'à la froideur d'un courtisan. Les lignes dont il est question ne vous seroient pas échappées si vous eussiez un peu réfléchi sur les intérêts gra\es et touchants que vous êtes dans le cas si puissament de servir. Si vous auriez senti aussi vivement que je le sache combien vous pourriez influer sur le bonheur de quelques millions en adoucissant leur sort, même quand il ne serait plus question de l'indépendance, j'ose vous croire incapable de vous refuser *à vous-même* un plaisir si vraiment inexprimable, pour toutes les tentations soit de l'espoir soit de la crainte que les cours dans leurs alternations de faiblesse et de cruauté puissent offrir. Encore réfléchissez—vous le devez à vous-même, au nom que vous avez tant illustré, à celui que vous héritez du meilleur des hommes.'

As will be seen from the following letters,† Brougham assisted M. Biernacki to enter into communication with some of the London newspapers:—

(*Postmark of January* 27, 1814).

'JEUDI.

'MONSIEUR,—Je crois que vous ferez bien de faire passer une note à

'Mons. Scott (l'éditeur du Champion) Catherine

---

* *Sic in orig.*

† These are exact copies from the originals in the Czartoryski Archives. It will be seen that Brougham's French, though fluent, was far from correct or elegant.

Street, Strand, Champion Office, pour le prier de faire
attention au sujet de la Pologne dans son numéro de
Dimanche.

'Vous pouvez l'envoyer *tout de suite* par la petite
poste, en anonyme, mais comme Polonois.—Je suis
toujours Votre fidèle ami, H. B.

'M. BIERNACKI, Mr DODD's, 22 Aldersgate Street.'

'VENDREDI.

'MONSIEUR,—Ayez la bonté de faire parvenir une
note à Mr Perry,* le renvoyant très-respectueusement
à la brochure pour les principes et les faits qui doivent
servir de bases pour la discussion. Vous pouvez lui
envoyer une exemplaire en même temps, et lui
marquer que rien de plus vrai que les détails qu'elle
renferme, mais que par menagement (à ce qu'il paroit)
pour les alliés, surtout la Russie, ces détails sont bien
au-dessous de la vérité! Aussi vous direz que les
horreurs pratiquées depuis la dernière invasion excè-
dent même celles des anciens partages, et qu'après
qu'il aura entamé la discussion vous lui indiquerez des
autres anecdotes. En attendant vous pouvez marquer
que probablement on va voir quelqu'unes des prédic-
tions remplies que la brochure a données, et notam-
ment sur la Russie, en le renvoyant aux pages où l'on
fait mention de la Suède et la Norvège. Vous ferez
bien de lui indiquer aussi les pages qui renferment
les détails des confiscations et des malheureux résultats
des partages à cause des changements de frontière,
en lui témoignant que tous ces détails sont de toute
vérité.

* Editor of the *Morning Chronicle*.

'Si vous envoyez une lettre dressée sur ce plan de bonne heure, rien ne l'empêchera de discuter le sujet demain matin. Je suis toujours, etc.,   H. B.

'Je serai chez moi entre 3 et 4 heures, mais vous devez envoyer votre lettre tout de suite.'

Among the journalists of the day with whom M. Biernacki corresponded was Leigh Hunt, who was at the time still confined in Horsemonger Lane gaol on account of his libel on the Prince Regent. M. Biernacki describes him as 'a young man full of talent and learning, romantic and ardent. His paper is one of the most popular in England; it has a sale of 8000 copies a day, which, according to the usual calculation in such cases, would mean that it is read by 40,000 people.' The following is a copy of Leigh Hunt's article on Poland in the *Examiner* of January 30, 1814, which also contains some remarkable extracts from Brougham's pamphlet :—

'The allies are now supposed, and with great appearance of probability, to be advancing to a point at which they will not only be able to secure present peace for Europe, but to act upon an improved scale the part which has hitherto been performed by the enemy, and settle the destinies of nations in their turn.

For this change in their prospects and power they are eminently indebted, as they themselves acknowledge, to the popular opinion that has gone with them ; and it is desirable, on every account, that they should preserve this best of friends and strongest of coadjutors by fulfilling in their prosperity what they undertook to perform when the strife was doubtful. Their enemy has found to his cost, that opinion in these times is not what it was even fifty years back, and that it cannot be put on and off at pleasure, without risking something worse than a chill.

'People's eyes, therefore, are fixed with no small anxiety on the diplomatic proceedings of the allies, and the more so, from some appearances of contradiction that have lately been witnessed in their military declarations. For our part, though we are among the most anxious, we confess we think little of these appearances. If the allies crossed the Rhine after their professions of moderation, and after their hint about not interfering with the natural boundaries of France, Buonaparte, by his own statement, seems to have attempted trifling with them on the subject of peace, and it would have been mere weakness on their part to lose more of their time.

'The proceeding does not compromise the sincerity of their professions;—it is at a peace the latter will be brought to the test. Again, there may be a difference of temper in the proclamations of the Austrian and Prussian Generals, without gainsaying the general spirit of the confederacy. If the Prussian has something of a vindictive tone, and taunts the French Emperor with some of his former boastings, he may be supposed to construe the natural feelings of his master, and to speak the language of his irritated countrymen, without involving the cooler feelings of ultimate negotiation. The Austrian Emperor has suffered less than the King of Prussia, and is besides connected with Buonaparte, so that his servant speaks in a more considerate manner. As to the Cossacks, of whom such a ridiculous noise has been made, it is well known that they enjoy a sort of mongrel independence, and that whatever antics they play are to be traced to themselves and not to the Russian Commanders : —their flags, therefore, with Paris on the one side and Moscow on the other, have as little to do with the temper of the allied sovereigns, as their beards and their brutality. If Napoleon had not played the part of a brother barbarian, he ought to have taken shame to himself for enabling such a tribe to come down and play the rawhead-and-bloody-bones among the people of Europe.

'It is not the sort of tone then that may be adopted here and there which is to settle our opinion of the allies and their principles ; but the sincerity they shall exhibit, when they come to conclude matters with Buonaparte, in acting up to their professions of universal justice, and in securing us all for the future, as far as they possibly can, against the irregular impulse of this or that man's ambition.

'To this end, it will not be enough that they shall compel sacrifices from Buonaparte ; they must make sacrifices themselves ; they must take away from him one of the most pernicious arms of his power against them,—the power of recrimination ; and prove to all the world that they have not been trifling with that awful force, those myriads of human beings, who have been fighting in their cause.

'These sacrifices are luckily not many, or of great moment, especially after the more humiliating ones which the allies have borne in their adversity. They only consist in doing that justice to their neighbours, for which they have been calling upon Buonaparte on their own account. Austria has said, for instance, "Do not attempt to force Germans to be Frenchmen :—it is a vain as well as inhuman effort : " Russia has said, " Do not insult all my native feelings :—do not come where you are not wanted, and lord it over my territory : " Prussia has said, " Do not take from me my strength and my spirit, do not garrison my fortresses, plunder my villages, and leave me only the shadow of an existence." Now there is a voice which says all this and more to these very Powers,—to Austria, to Russia, and to Prussia :—it is the voice of Poland—a voice crying from the ground, —the voice of a country declared no longer in existence !—Here let the proof of sincerity be given ; here let a proof be given, that the allied Princes have been taught lasting as well as momentary success, and that the men of the old school are prepared to give up these vices in themselves, which they have justly united to put down in the man of the new.

'This is a most important subject, and involves, with regard to the allies, or at least to their principles, the very same question that is now agitating against Buonaparte. We have never lost sight of it ; but we confess that we should have waited a little before we urged it again, had it not been for a publication that has lately appeared entitled,—" An Appeal to the Allies and the English Nation in behalf of Poland." It may be thought invidious by some persons to interrupt the allies at present by any representations, calculated to fall in with French misrepresentation ; and such a pamphlet may appear to them a little like casting a stone into the mouth of our advancing friends ; but a direct charge to this effect would only prove to us that such persons were afraid to meet their subject, and considered the allies as afraid also ; and it is perhaps better upon the whole to make the representation, however unpalatable for the moment, while the gratitude of the allies to popular feeling is yet warm, the policy of doing right yet fresh in their eyes, and their temptations to do wrong not yet excited by the final grasp of success.

The author of the pamphlet is evidently a true observer, who sees things in the gross as well as detail,—in their universal as well as their particular application. For a writer who can take so large a view as he does of the subject and its *principle*, we might be inclined to think that he takes rather too much pains to answer petty, Cabinet objections, and questions of interest ; but as politics go, and as questions of interest, by a proper reasoning, amount at last to the same thing as questions of principle, it may have been as well to show himself prepared at all points. What we like less, is an insidious way of occasionally putting his own apprehensions of the allies into the mouth of their enemies,— a kind of deprecating by proxy, and of imagining what other people might say of them, only to express his conviction that no such terrible want of principle can take place. It would have been better, we think, in a pamphlet on such a subject, to state at once what his own opinion of the allies would be, should they turn traitors to their profession,—and to state it too in the very broadest terms. If in the end they deserve it, he saves himself the pretence of a conviction to the contrary ; and if not, they can be the less offended with the plain speaking. But even the opportunities of humour which this underhand mode gives a writer, (and the one before us handles a pleasantry very easily), cannot compensate, we think, for the opportunities it gives to meaner understandings of doubting his good intention in general. Of this there cannot be the remotest suspicion. The writer may have his apprehensions with regard to the ultimate conduct of the allies, and we know some very excellent men who more than agree with him on that point ; but whoever he is, he is one that sees as clearly as any man the union of sound principle with policy, and who, notwithstanding his legal mode of occasionally putting his apprehensions, succeeds in convincing his reader that he feels as well as sees. The apostrophe to the "ill-fated Poniatowski" (p. 46) evinces cordiality of heart as well as justness of thinking.—But we are detaining the reader from a few extracts which it is our intention to give him, and which we shall give without any of these comments which the rest of the publication itself will abundantly supply.

' After stating that the subject of Poland need not be so painful to the allied Princes as some people may insinuate, since it was their immediate predecessors, not themselves, that made the partition, the author proceeds in a very successful manner to vindicate the Poles for having sided of late with the French, by putting a very strong and striking case, in which he supposes England to be lorded over by the latter, and suddenly visited by a Russian army, of which she takes advantage to try and shake off her yoke. He then enters into the subject historically, showing that " the great relaxation of public principles may be distinctly ascribed to the partition," and the Poles themselves, at the moment of their national annihilation, were removing the last flimsy pretext for the outrage by forming a new and free constitution. His next step is to prove, that the partition is not a thing gone by,—the discussion of which is no longer a

matter of connection with present events; and as this may appear
to some persons important to settle, and is settled by him very
completely, we shall make a good long extract on the subject.

'"I question if the time be even yet come, when the miserable
catastrophe can be adequately deplored that paralysed all those
noble efforts, and blighted the fair prospect unfolded by them to the
eyes of every friend of liberty. But one part of the calamity, that
which pressed the most sorely upon the interests of the European
community, will perhaps never be more deeply felt than at the
present hour. I speak of the peculiar moment chosen by the con-
federate courts. The new constitution was enveloped in a cloud of
foreign soldiery—the patriots were scattered abroad—the rudiments
of the national army were dissipated—the country was overwhelmed,
parcelled out, confiscated, jobbed, turned into money—blackened
with garrisons, prisons, gibbets, cemeteries, and the desolate abodes
of men who had perished for freedom—its separate existence finally
destroyed—its name blotted out from the map, and forbidden to
be any more uttered, as if it had been guilty of all the crimes
whereof it had been the scene and the victim—but why enumerate
particulars? Do they not all fall short of the deed itself?—The
partition of Poland was completed AFTER the French Revolution
had awakened slumbering royalty; had taught the force of France
to burst through its ancient bounds; and had made national independence tremble in every corner of Europe.

'"This is the fact upon which, at the present moment, it
imports us well to meditate. There is no getting over it. If Poland
had been left as she was when those great changes began which the
allies are now occupied in undoing, she would still have been one of
the greatest Powers on the Continent. She was seized when even
the pretences of 1772 no longer existed—when she was a safe,
orderly, and peaceable neighbour. But above all she was seized in
1793 and 1794, at the very time when France was seizing Savoy,
Belgium, and Holland. This is the matter which now presses itself
upon our attention. We are recurring to sound and ancient
principles. We are treading back our steps in order to get out
of the slough in which we have been since the French Revolution,
and to regain the eminence of a pure morality. We are endeavouring to undo as much as possible the recent changes of dominion, and
to place the affairs of Europe on their former ground, with all the
benefits of past experience. With what pretensions of consistency
—by what powers of face, marvellous even in this unblushing age,
can we meet either the enemy or the Polander, if the only change
on which we are obstinately silent is one of the most momentous

and least justifiable, and which our conscience tells us was effected in the very same month with the conquest of the Netherlands, admitted on every hand to be the fittest subject of restoration?

' " A pernicious but very flimsy heresy has been propagated on this question by some foreign politicians, the soundness of whose principles in other respects renders their mistakes the more dangerous. It has been said that the partition of Poland is now a mere matter of history, and that while the lapse of time exempts it from being again brought into discussion, the sanction of various treaties stops the parties to them from questioning it. This doctrine is so full of manifest absurdity, and so easily refuted by the whole system of those who adopt it, that one can scarcely imagine it to proceed from anything but a misplaced delicacy towards the partitioning Powers, and a determination to scare the enemy with big words and terms of law, from flinging at us a very favourite sarcasm in return for the many attacks of this kind to which we expose him. I would fain remind the very respectable persons to whom I am alluding, of the period at which they first treated this topic ; it was immediately after the Treaty of Lunéville, in 1801, not seven years after the final partition, the greatest in extent and the worst in all respects, except that it was not the earliest. Yet the advocates of this motley doctrine of a seven years' limitation of anti-Jacobin crimes, were the loudest against offences committed by France eight and nine years before the date of their invectives. Happily for Europe the same enlightened persons retain their influence over the popular opinions at the present day, and to it perhaps, next to the headlong rashness of the enemy and the temperate firmness of the allied chiefs, we owe the late successes. I hope their voice will be heard in the negotiations, and in the further prosecution of the war, should just terms be refused by France—I am sure they will spurn at the idea of considering the French conquests in the Revolution war as sacred ; and yet nearly twice seven years have elapsed since a treaty confirmed them ; so that both their doctrine of limitation and of *estoppel* by treaties, is much more applicable to these than to the last Polish partition. England too and France, I should think, may be reckoned something in a question of this sort, and they never by any treaty recognised directly or indirectly the dismemberment. Yet England as well as the allies themselves, by solemn treaties, recognised those French usurpations and new states created in the Revolution war, which all good men now hope to see restored to their ancient possessors. Even the Spanish usurpation was recognised by all the allies in succession, except England." pp. 22-25.

' The author then proceeds to exhibit the miserable state of
Poland after its partition, to calculate the little advantages the
partitioners have derived from their respective acquisitions of
territory, and to enumerate the frequent and striking disadvantages
they have experienced from the natural hatred of the Poles, in a
military point of view. The rest of the pamphlet is chiefly occupied
in answering objections on the score of Russian ascendency. We
shall make our other extract on the use which Bonaparte has made
of the Poles, as it brings the matter down to the time before us, and
refer our readers for the rest of the question to what will amply
repay their attention in the publication itself :—

' " The exact number of men drawn by the enemy from this quarter
it is neither very easy, nor very material to ascertain. Since 1806,
when he first held out hopes of restoring Poland, those numbers
have greatly increased ; and in the campaign of 1812, they did not
fall short of 100,000. The insecurity of the tenure by which the
country is held, may be seen from the events of the two Polish
campaigns. Immediately after the battle of Jena, the Prussian
troops were compelled to withdraw from Poland, as precipitately as
the French have lately done from Holland. No exertion was too
great for the country during that winter, notwithstanding the very
imperfect degree in which its wishes were met. Bonaparte, in
flattering them with the hopes of independence, had imposed one
very harsh condition, that the code Napoléon should be established.
Even on such terms, as if only anxious for existence, and careless of
the kind of being they should have, they accepted the offer. Let
us recollect that Emperors and Kings have in like manner received
their crowns, fettered by conditions that almost enslaved them to
their subjects or electors. So the Poles capitulated for national
existence, upon terms which could hardly be said to leave them a
separate people. But they amply performed their part of the contract. The enthusiasm excited by the mere semblance of restoration
was universal. Many persons sacrificed nearly their whole fortunes
to the State. Entire regiments of between two and three thousand
men each, were raised and fully equipped by individuals in a few
weeks. Others furnished single battalions, or companies, or only a
few men, according to their means ; and all this—not from the
superabundance of their wealth, not by the sale of their plate and
jewels only ; but by selling or pledging their estates, and part-
ing with everything that could raise a farthing, down to the marriage rings of village dames, or the single silver spoon of a poor
country curate. The peace of Tilsit closed the campaign which had
been so materially influenced by the exertions of Poland ; and upon

the first breaking out of the war two years afterwards, she evinced her sense of the benefits, unsubstantial as they were, which that treaty had conferred. The same extraordinary efforts were renewed, and the army of the Duchy rapidly over-ran the Polish provinces of Austria, where they met with allies in every corner. Indeed similar exertions were made in those districts themselves, and they were rewarded by the incorporation of their better half with the Duchy, at the peace of Vienna.—In 1812, a new attempt was made to soothe the Poles with the hope of real independence, although the alliance of Franco with Austria rendered it extremely difficult. The charm was again found all powerful; the people flocked from every quarter to join the invading army, and expended their utmost means to supply it. I question if an equal amount of contribution was ever raised upon the same extent of a country merely agricultural; and when we reflect that it had been exhausted by half a century of misfortune, the exertion seems scarcely credible. Besides the fixed war revenue of about five millions sterling, it furnished as much more in provisions and stores to the army on its passage, with a further sum of one million and a half in money. Such efforts, and the subsequent exhaustion of the country in 1813, may have drained it of wealth; but the people remain; iron is their gold; and if the allies prefer the neighbourhood of an unconquerable and friendly nation, to an uneasy rule over hostile subjects, they have only to speak the word. Let but the sound be heard which can really awaken Polish independence,—name to them the Constitution of the third of May, and every plain will be alive with horse—every thicket of their forests gleam with spears. All that Napoleon could do by offers, insignificant had they been sincere, will be forgotten in the exertions which a substantial restoration would call forth. So impregnable a bulwark never was raised against invasion, as Russia would present to all the rest of Europe, while Prussia and Austria would no longer touch upon that too powerful neighbour, and in a quarter where their security has been the most precarious." pp. 47-50.*

'We shall take a hasty farewell of this work by going somewhat farther than its author in our anticipations of what will be the consequences, should the allied monarchs not perform what is

* 'The eulogium of Mr Burke on the Polish Constitution of the third of May, is unbounded. It concludes with this passage :—"Happy people, if they know how to proceed as they have begun! Happy Prince, worthy to begin with splendour or to close with glory a race of patriots and of Kings. . . . To finish all—this great good, as in the instant it is, contains in it the seeds of all future improvement, and may be considered as in a regular progress, because founded on similar principles, towards the stable excellence of a British Constitution."—*Appeal from the new to the old Whigs.*—The passage in the former part of these reflections was printed, before I recollected the testimony of this great authority.' (*Note by Leigh Hunt*).

expected of them. In our opinion, they will not only be insecure from future attacks of the enemy, and from the intrigues which harass monarchs in general, but all that has happened in Europe for the last thirty years will not save them and their subjects from the danger of fresh revolutions; for if the times at present differ in any one feature from what they were eighty or a hundred years back, it is in the direct rank that understanding has taken in society, in the universal circulation of intelligence and good sense, and in the consequent and most formidable addition which has been made to the power, and conscious power too, of public opinion. The people have looked at their sovereigns, and the sovereigns, it is hoped, have now looked at their people, with eyes of mutual understanding. It is the interest of both to let this understanding be a good one.'

After seeing this article M. Biernacki wrote Leigh Hunt a letter of thanks, which the latter thus acknowledged in the *Examiner* of February 6, 1814:

'The letter written in French has been received, and has given the editor one of those enjoyments which he prizes almost above every other, and which will always be a sufficient reward to him for what little he may be able to do in a good cause.'

The Polish cause was also warmly taken up by Mr Perry in the *Morning Chronicle* and Dr Stoddart in the *Times*, which, according to M. Biernacki, was 'the only paper the Prince Regent allowed his daughter to read;' but Brougham did not succeed in getting any leading politicians except Earl Grey to advocate it in Parliament, though Sir Samuel Romilly, Wilberforce, Lord Lansdowne, Lord Holland, and Cobbett, 'le franc, le sauvage, le farouche,' expressed the greatest sympathy for it.

M. Biernacki, who, like most educated Poles of that time, was fond of quoting Latin, sent to some of his correspondents the following passage from Livy as a prophetic description of England's political mission :—Esse gentem in terris quæ suâ impensâ ac periculo bella gerat pro libertate aliorum, maria trajiciat, ne quod toto orbe terrarum injustum imperium sit, ubique jus, fas, lex potentissima sint;— they did not, however, accept the suggestion.

'Englishmen,' says M. Biernacki, 'only do one thing at a time. Just now they think only of the war with France. . . . It is impossible to see the Ministers : they fear the fate of Percival (his successor especially), and are overwhelmed with work; two messengers go to the Continent every day. Moreover, there is a split in the Cabinet. One party wishes to make peace at once on the French terms ; the other wishes to carry on the war in order to obtain further compensation for the sacrifices England has made. The Prince Regent favours the latter party, as he has made up his mind to bring back the Bourbons.' The only Englishman, in fact, who thoroughly identified himself with the Polish cause at that period was Brougham ; and he threw himself into the work heart and soul.

As stated at the beginning of this Chapter, M. Biernacki's diary is incomplete ; but it is accompanied by a collection of letters (besides those printed above), of which the following may be worth reproducing here :

From Tom Moore.
MAYFIELD COTTAGE, ASHBOURNE,
Thursday, Feby. 3rd.
SIR,—I believe I have to thank you for a very

able pamphlet, ' An Appeal to the Allies,' which I have just received under a blank cover. It had already been sent to me by a friend from town, but I am glad you have given me an opportunity of expressing my opinion of the book through a channel by which it has a chance of reaching the author himself; as I know that honest, sincere praise, even from so humble an individual as myself, is one of the rewards that such interesting labours look for. I have seldom seen anything better meant or better executed.

Your very obliged st.

THOMAS MOORE.

To Mr HARDING,
Bookseller, St James's.

From Brougham to Mr Vansittart, Chancellor of the Exchequer.

TEMPLE, *Feby.* 21, 1814.

DEAR SIR,—I am infinitely unwilling to give you the interruption of reading a letter in the midst of your manifold occupations at this singular juncture. Yet I cannot refrain from expressing my obligations to you for the patience with which you listened to my Polish friend. His situation is one of extreme delicacy—but as he is one of the most sincere and devoted patriots, so is he likewise a person of excellent sense and discretion in conduct. I am intimately acquainted with everything relating to him and his connections, and I can give you a most positive assurance of his being trustworthy.

He is very anxious lest he should have failed to convey his meaning with distinctness, and has begged

me to repeat several things for him; but I am quite
sure his fears are groundless, and I shall confine
myself to a single remark—viz., on the extreme importance of any, *even the smallest*, interest being shown
with respect to the unfortunate country in question.
Its possessors (especially Alexander) look to England
a vast deal more than they will always acknowledge
when they are treating with you. They regard the
publick opinion here almost as much as our own Government does, and it is a matter of fact that they are
influenced by it in the same way, though certainly they
are not very mindful of the publick opinion among their
own subjects. How much more, then, do they consider any expression of opinion or feeling on the part
of our Government! It is very certain that the mere
exhibition of some little interest (however little and
however privately) in favour of the Poles, could it be
made at the present time, would have great, immediate, and very practical effects on the happiness of
many millions of people. I suspect the Emperor
Alexander at least desires nothing more in that
quarter than the authority of our Government to back
him with his allies on the one hand, and his nobles on
the other, to adopt a more paternal system.

But all these things (as well as the larger view of
the subject) are undoubtedly familiar to you. I would
therefore only further suggest that there are one or
two topics on which you will derive some most curious
and interesting particulars from the Polish gentleman.
The commercial resources, yet unexplained, of his
country I pass over as an obvious point. But he is
possessed of some extremely singular circumstances

respecting Buonaparte and his proceedings both in
Poland and elsewhere, and if you remember to put
him on the subject (especially of Buonaparte's conferences after his return from Moscow) and he should
not be afraid of indicating the sources of his information, his account of it will greatly interest you.

I again beg your excuse for the interruption, and
wishing you all manner of success in your present
undertakings (which a person retired from politicks
may very conscientiously do at this time), I remain,
yours faithfully and sincerely,   H. B.

A single word addressed to me containing the time
you desire to see him, and without giving you the
trouble of writing a note, will at any moment bring
him to you.

Brougham to M. Biernacki.

LANCASTER, *ce* 7me *Mars* 1814.

MONSIEUR,—Je n'ai fini mon voyage que ce matin
et vous voyez que je profite de la première occasion
qui se m'est présentée pour écrire la lettre au P.—
Je l'ai envoyée ouverte afin que vous puissiez la lire
avant de la cacheter.

Le jour même de mon départ j'ai addressé une
lettre au Marquis de Lansdowne, en le renvoyant à M.
Baring et MM. Romilly et Elliot pour les détails.
Je l'ai remis entre les mains de M. Baring, qui ne
tardera pas (à) vous présenter au Marquis. Ce que
je lui ai dit doit l'intéresser autant qu'il est possible
dans la bonne cause. Après l'avoir vu (si ça vous
convient à vous et à M. B.) vous devez croire que la

semence est semée, et que l'on a fait tout ce qu'il vous a été permis de faire dans les circonstances actuelles. Je suis intimement persuadé que nous ne ferons que du mal en entamant des autres communications dans ce moment.

J'espère que votre santé est rétablie, et que vous êtes content de M. Tegart. Je me suis accusé bien de fois de votre maladie. Je crains que je ne vous ai fait trop travailler. Le repos et la maladie me sont presqu' inconnus, et j'avois dû menager votre santé un peu plus que je ne soigne la mienne. Faites moi le plaisir de m'écrire, et de me marquer votre rétablissement.

J'avais oublié de vous prier de m'écrire de la Hollande tout ce que vous aurez à remarquer, et de me faire venir de vos nouvelles régulierement. Après avoir quitté la Hollande, vous pouvez addresser vos lettres à Mons. Van H. à la Haye, en le priant de me les faire passer. Encore une chose—n'oubliez pas les moyens d'entretenir les liaisons entre les deux pays, par les voyages dont nous avons causé—et les avantages que procurera à vos grands une éducation Anglaise.

Adieu. Portez-vous bien, et croyez que je suis toujours, etc. H. B.

YORK, *ce* 24 *Mars* 1814.

MONSIEUR,—Je viens de recevoir votre dernière lettre, ayant il y a deux jours reçu celle qui m'avoit suivi de Brougham où (par contretems) on l'avoit envoyée.

Je vous remets la conclusion de la lettre de M. von H. qui regarde la Pologne, selon votre désire,*

---

* *Sic in orig.*

aussi ai-je ajouté un extrait de celle que je viens de recevoir de M. Van Grendown sur ce même sujet. Je me confie entièrement à votre discrétion (qui m'est si bien connue) que ces extraits ne parviennent à personne excepter * le P., et que vous me le fassiez parvenir quand vous en aurez l'occasion.

J'avais oublié de vous marquer une circonstance touchant la discussion des affaires Polonoises à Liverpool. Les essais qui y paraissent dans les journaux de mon parti viennent (à ce qu'on me dit) des personnes tout à fait inconnues des chefs du dit parti. Ça prouve au moins que la discussion commence à prendre. J'en ai vu des autres preuves.

J'ai engagé M. Jeffrey à écrire quelque chose pour vous dans son numéro qui doit paraître à la fin d'Avril.† La publication du dernier numéro a eu lieu ici, et à Edinbourg depuis la quinzaine.

Je crois que vous faites bien de partir le plutôt possible. Tout est préparé ici. La semence est semée, et je serai toujours sur le qui vive pour en recueillir les fruits. Avant la discussion des négotiations il n'y aura rien d'intéressant dans le parlement.

N'oubliez pas de me donner de vos nouvelles, avec tous les renseignements que vous pourrez de tems en tems.   H. B.

LONDRES, *ce* 27 *Avril* 1814.

MONSIEUR.—Ne sachant pas exactement si vous vous trouvez encore à la Haye, je n'entrerai pas dans les détails de notre sujet.

---

* *Sic in orig.*
† The articles appeared in the *Edinburgh Review* of September 1814.

Mais je crois que vous serez bien aise d'apprendre que Lord Grey (sans la moindre communication avec moi) a entamé la discussion sur la Pologne dans la Chambre Haute il y a dix jours. La mention qu'il en a faite a été très-bien reçue et applaudie de tout côté. Il l'a fait d'une manière très-imposante et avec beaucoup d'adresse et de ménagement pour l'Empereur de Russie. Comme je vis dans la société de Lord G. presque journellement, et que je jouis de son amitié et de sa confiance dans toutes les affaires publiques, je suis persuadé qu'il me soupçonne d'avoir commencé la discussion du sujet, et que j'ai quelque raison pour ne pas l'avoir entamé avec lui, car il ne m'a jamais dit un mot là-dessus.

Dans la société je vois assez clairement que l'intérêt va toujours en accroissant, et que nous pourrons espérer quelque bon résultat. Je ne vais presque jamais dans les cercles sans entendre prononcer le nom de la Pologne, et toujours dans le meilleur sens.

Écrivez-moi, et croyez que je suis toujours, etc.,

H. BROUGHAM.

Par une bêtise impardonnable quelques-uns des journaux, en publiant le discours de Lord G., ont mis ' Courland ' au lieu de ' Poland.' Ils l'ont corrigé après.

Les Quakers etc., dans leur journal (*The Philanthropist*) ont bien rempli leur devoir vis à vis de notre cause.

FROM SIR SAMUEL ROMILLY TO M. BIERNACKI.
RUSSELL SQUARE,
Mar. 22, 1814.

SIR,—I return you many thanks for a sight of the

enclosed papers, which I have read with very great interest. No person can be more sensible than I am of the wrongs which Poland has suffered, or more convinced of the bad policy as well as the injustice of the conduct of all the States of Europe towards her.—I remain, Sir, with great respect, Your most obedient and faithful servant,

SAML. ROMILLY.

CHAPTER XXII

1814-15

WHILE Prince Adam Czartoryski was endeavouring through his secretary to obtain the support for his country of public opinion in England, the allies pursued their campaign against Napoleon with undiminished success. The crushing defeat of Leipzig (October 18, 1813) was rapidly followed by the invasion of France, the occupation of Paris by the allied troops (March 31, 1814) and the abdication of Napoleon at Fontainebleau (April 4, 1814). The Emperor Alexander, who had granted an amnesty to all the Poles who had fought against him under Napoleon in the campaign of 1812, now reverted to his former plan of reconstructing Poland as a separate State under his sceptre, and invited his old friend and counsellor to assist him in executing it. Alexander was accompanied by Prince Adam in his visit to London before the Vienna Congress, and in a despatch preserved in the Record Office, dated 'Paris, May 23, 1814,' General Cathcart, then British Ambassador to the Russian Court, informs Lord Castlereagh that 'the Emperor has been pleased this day to add the name of Prince Adam Czartorisky (*sic*) to the list of persons who are to attend him to London.'

When the Congress met at Vienna in October 1814, Poland was the first object of its deliberations, and Prince Adam played so prominent a part in them that Lord Castlereagh wrote to Lord Liverpool that the Prince, 'although not in any official situation, appears now the actual Russian Minister, at least on Polish and Saxon questions.'* The chief objections to the Emperor's proposal to restore Poland were, strange to say, not made by Austria and Prussia, whose Polish possessions would under that proposal have been united to the new Polish kingdom, but by Lord Castlereagh, on the plea that the creation of such a kingdom under the sceptre of the Emperor of Russia would make Russia too strong. He would readily consent to the restoration of Poland as an independent State with a sovereign of her own ; but knowing that this was too great a sacrifice to be expected of Russia, he insisted on the maintenance of the partition.†

* Despatch of the 24th December, 1814 (in the Record Office). In another despatch, dated the 5th November, 1814, Lord Castlereagh says : 'The day but one after the return of the sovereigns from Buda, the enclosed communication was delivered to me by an aide-de-camp of the Emperor of Russia. It was prepared during his Imperial Majesty's absence by Prince Czartoryski, the memorandum being written in concert with him by M. Anstetem, a Conseiller d'Etat in the bureau. I have reason to believe that Count Nesselrode was not consulted. The Emperor has latterly, on the question of Poland, ceased to act through his regular servants. It is unfortunately his habit to be his own Minister, and to select as the instrument of his immediate purpose, the person who may happen to fall in most with his views. This has been particularly the case on the present question, all the Russians, I believe without an exception, being adverse to his projects, considering them both as dangerous to himself and injurious to his allies.'

† 'Up to the period of the Congress of Vienna, no British statesman had ever set his hand to an instrument acknowledging, as valid acts, the two partitions of Poland. Had the British Plenipotentiary founded his objections upon this principle —had he positively refused to commit his Government to any such acknowledgment, and had he insisted on the erection of an independent Polish State, he would, to use his own words, have been applauded by the whole of Europe, whilst Austria and

An angry correspondence followed between the British Plenipotentiary and the Emperor, and at length the attitude of the latter and his Prussian ally (who hoped to get Saxony as a compensation for the loss of his Polish possessions) became so threatening that England, France, and Austria, by a secret treaty signed on the 3rd of January 1815, entered into a defensive alliance binding themselves each to bring, if necessary, 150,000 men into the field.

Prussia would not only not have opposed it, but, on the contrary, would have acquiesced in it with pleasure.

'Backed by such powerful support, as well as by the voice of public opinion throughout Europe, it is more than probable that he might have been successful: but the moment he gave up this principle, and told the Emperor that he was not indisposed to witness, even with satisfaction, that his Imperial Majesty should receive a liberal and important aggrandizement on his Polish frontier, and that it was to the *degree* and the *mode* to which he alone objected, he threw away the only weapon which he could successfully wield. The greater point was attainable, but the abandonment of the greater was fatal to the attainment of the less. There was —there could be—no answer to the following argument of the Emperor as to the share of the spoil, considered as a matter of spoil, to which he was entitled : " Mais lorsque l'Autriche et la Prusse ont contribué, comme alliées de la France, à dépouiller la Russie de la plus grande partie des provinces Polonaises ; quand la Russie a été obligée de les réconquérir ; lorsque la conquête du Duché de Varsovie devient aujourd'hui une compensation pour d'énormes sacrifices : il s'agit effectivement d'un nouveau partage, et dans ce cas, les stipulations qui ont accompagné celui de 1797 n'existent plus."

'Had Lord Castlereagh denounced the original, as well as the proposed, *partage,* instead of making appeals ad misericordiam, his remonstrances might have been effectual. But it was of no avail to tell the Emperor that he was exacting from his neighbours and allies an arrangement incompatible with their political independence, and that the demand by Russia to retain so large a share of Poland as that to which the Emperor laid claim, was a source of consternation and alarm to Austria and Prussia and of general terror throughout all the States of Europe.

'His Imperial Majesty's Austrian and Prussian allies had no claim upon his forbearance, and it was impossible to defeat the Emperor's claims when, on the principle on which they were made, no one could deny their justice.

'The partition being admitted, the degree and the mode could only be decided by the will of that party whose claims were the strongest, and whose power was adequate to support the claims. The result was, that Great Britain accepted the partition as a fait accompli, and that Russia obtained almost all that she asked for.

'Mr Cook, a man of considerable ability and firmness, who was Under-Secretary in the Foreign Office, and who accompanied Lord Castlereagh to Vienna, endeavoured in vain to rouse his chief to an uncompromising condemnation of the two partitions. He urged him to fling the treaties on the table of Congress, and to declare that nothing should induce Great Britain to acknowledge the validity of those acts. He urged in vain ; but he set the seal on the sincerity of his own opinions, by resigning at once his post of Under-Secretary of State. He was succeeded in Vienna by Mr Planta.' (" George Canning and his Times," by Augustus Granville Stapleton, p. 354.)

Ultimately, however, concessions were made on both sides, and the result was that by the Treaty of Vienna (signed on the 25th of February 1815) Posen was given to Prussia, and Galicia (except Cracow, which was to be a free town) to Austria, and the remainder of the Duchy of Warsaw was made a kingdom 'irrevocably attached by its Constitution' to the Russian Empire, and with the Czar as its King. It was also stipulated that 'all parts of ancient Poland, as it existed before the year 1772,' should enjoy the right of free navigation and trade, and that all its inhabitants, whether subjects of Russia, Austria, or Prussia, shall obtain 'a representation' and 'institutions which shall ensure the preservation of their nationality.' Thus did Europe, while stipulating for the preservation of the Polish nationality over the whole of ancient Poland, give the sanction of public law to a partition which Prince Talleyrand described as 'the prelude, in part perhaps the cause, and even to a certain extent the excuse, of the disorders to which Europe had been a prey.'*

Lord Castlereagh's despatches on the subject will be found in the 'Correspondence relating to the negotiations of the years 1814 and 1815 respecting Poland' which was presented to Parliament in 1863. The following extracts from memoranda drawn up at

---

* 'De toutes les questions qui devaient être traitées au Congrès, le Roi aurait considéré comme la première, la plus grande, la plus éminemment Européenne, comme hors de comparaison avec toute autre, celle de Pologne, s'il lui eût été possible d'espérer autant qu'il le désirait, qu'un peuple si digne de l'intérêt de tous les autres par son ancienneté, sa valeur, les services qu'il rendit autre fois à l'Europe, et par son infortune, pût être rendu à son antique et complète indépendance. Le partage qui la raya du nombre des nations fut le prélude, en partie la cause, et peut-être jusqu'à un certain point l'excuse, des bouleversements auxquels l'Europe a été en proie.' (Note to Prince Metternich, dated 19th December 1814).

the time by Prince Czartoryski show some of the arguments on the Russian side of the question :—

'Hitherto experience has always proved that people who are unhappy and dissatisfied are usually restless, and that the surest way of keeping people quiet is to make them contented. There is no reason to believe that such a universal and infallible means of pacification would not succeed with the Poles, who have certainly shown themselves very active and stirring ; but all their energy has been directed to a single object, that of recovering their name, their Government, and their nationality. It is difficult to understand why people should when speaking of the Poles call that " levity " which in speaking of other nations they call " patriotism and perseverance." Such a misuse of words may lead to false conclusions, and there is not the slightest probability that the Poles, after obtaining the essence of their demands, should only become the more turbulent and disorderly. His Imperial Majesty is convinced, after many years' experience, that all classes in Poland have the same wish, and he has had a new proof of this in the addresses which have been sent him from all parts of the Duchy of Warsaw. . . .

'His Majesty, after much consideration, has arrived at the conclusion that the plan he proposes would be the best in the interest of Europe generally. By it he would keep acquisitions which he cannot give up, but he would so organise his possessions as to secure peace to his neighbours and to Europe.

'Suppose the name of the kingdom of Poland is restored, and part of the Duchy of Warsaw is reunited to

Russia. This could not in any sense be dangerous to
Austria or Prussia, for the Emperor would guarantee
to them the possession of their parts of Poland, and
the slightest attempt to recover them would be
opposed by Austria, Prussia, France, and England,
leaving Russia entirely isolated.... . It is not a little
more or less territory or fortresses that constitutes
the balance of power ; it is the parity of interests
which produces combinations in the hour of danger
that are far more formidable and effective than mere
arrangements of frontier.'

CHAPTER XXIII

1815

SIR JOHN BOWRING in his Memoirs of Jeremy Bentham (vol x, page 478, of the collected works) says that 'Bentham's hopes of being allowed to prepare a code for Russia were at this time (1815) strongly excited. His name and writings were very popular in that country. He had himself some—his brother, who had been so long in the Russian service, many—influential friends at the Court of the Czar. Dumont had lived long at St Petersburg, and his reputation and his labours were so associated with those of his master, that strong expectations were indulged that authority to prepare a Code would be communicated to him. The Emperor Alexander, who was fond of being considered the patron and protector of literary and learned men, sent to Bentham a diamond ring, which Bentham returned to the Imperial donor, with the seal of the box that contained it unbroken. His conduct has been deemed ungracious, but without reason. He cared nothing about diamond rings ; but he desired to legislate for the good of the Russian people. The Emperor would have had him communicate his observations—or rather reply to the questionings of a commission appointed to revise the Russian Codes. But Bentham knew that commission to be wholly incompetent to the work; and its President, upon whom everything depended, was peculiarly unfitted for his task, so that Bentham refused to take any share in a drama of feebleness and insincerity.'

The following letters were addressed by Bentham to the Czar and Prince Czartoryski on this subject :—

To the Emperor of all the Russias.

SIRE,—The object of this address is to submit to your Imperial Majesty an offer relative to the department of legislation.

My years are sixty-six. Without commission from any government, not much fewer than fifty of them have been occupied in that field. My ambition is to employ the remainder of them, as far as can be done in this country, in labouring towards the improvement of the state of that branch of government in your Majesty's vast Empire.

In the year 1802, a work extracted, as therein mentioned, from my papers, was by Mr Dumont of Geneva, published at Paris in nine vols. 8vo., under the title of ' Traité de Législation Civile et Pénale,' etc.

In the year 1805 a translation of it into the Russian language was published at St Petersburg, (by order, if I am rightly informed, of your Majesty's Government).

Since the publication of that work Europe has seen two extensive bodies of law promulgated within its limits : one by the French Emperor, the other by

the King of Bavaria. These two are the only bodies
of law of any such considerable extent that have made
their appearance within the last half-century. Of the
one promulgated by the French Emperor, a complete
penal code formed a part. In the preface to that
authoritative work, my unauthoritative one is mentioned with honour : among the *dead* Montesquieu,
Beccaria, and Blackstone; among *living* names (unless
it be for some matter of fact) none but *mine*. In the
Bavarian code drawn up by Mr Bexon, much more
particular as well as copious *mention* is made of that
work of mine, much more *eulogy* bestowed upon it.

In France under the immediate rod of Napoleon,
in Bavaria under the influence of Napoleon, the generosity displayed by the notice thus taken of the
work of a living Englishman could not but call forth
my admiration.

Approbation is one thing ; *adoption* is another.
With mine before them, both these modern works
took for their basis the jurisprudence of ancient Rome.
Russia at any rate needs not any such incumbrance.

In the texture of the human frame, some fibres
there are which are the same in all *places* and at all
times, others which vary with the *place* and with the
time. For those last it has been among my constant
and pointedly manifested cares to look out and provide.

Of the particularities of Russia I am not altogether
without experience. Two of the most observant years
of my life were passed within her limits.

Codes upon the French pattern are already in full
view. Speak the word, Sire,—Russia shall produce a
pattern of her own, and then let Europe judge.

To Russia, it is true, I am a foreigner, yet to this purpose scarcely more so than a Courlander, a Livonian, or a Finlander. In point of local knowledge to place me on a level with a native of Russia—to *me* as to *them*—information in various shapes could not but be necessary. Any such assistance no person could ever be more ready to supply than I should be solicitous to receive and profit by it.

In my above mentioned work a sample of a *penal code* is exhibited. In the first place what I should humbly propose is, to do what remains to be done for the completion of it. For this purpose not many months would, I hope, be necessary.

Sovereign and father—in this double character it is on all occasions your Majesty's wish and delight to show yourself to your people. In this same character, even on the rough and thorny ground of penal law—in this same happily compounded character, addressing them through my pen, your Majesty would still show yourself the sovereign by his *commands,* the father by his instructions; the sovereign not more intent on establishing the necessary obligations, than the father on rendering the necessity manifest, manifest to all men, and at every step he takes thus justifying himself in their sight.

Reasons.—Yet it is by reasons that a task at once so salutary and so arduous can be accomplished :— reasons connected and that by an indiscontinued chain of references, on the one hand with the *general principles* from which they have been deduced, on the other hand, with the several *clauses* and *words* in the text of the law, for the *justification,* and at the same time for the *elucidation* of which they have been respectively framed. An accompaniment of this kind would form one of the peculiarities of my *Code*: a sample is given in my above mentioned treatise.

This sample was a challenge to legislators: the well-intentioned but strictly shackled Frenchmen shrunk from it. How acutely sensible they were of the usefulness of such an accompaniment, how they wished and how they feared to expose their works to so searching a *test*—how they tasked themselves to produce a sort of substitute test—(I mean a mass of vague generalities left floating in the air, and destitute of all application to particulars)—how sadly inadequate is that substitute—what excuse is given for the deficiency, and how lame is that excuse—all this may be seen in their respective works.

All *comprehensiveness, conciseness, uniformity,* and *simplicity*—qualities the union of which is at once so desirable and so difficult—such, as far as concerns the choice of words, are the qualities for which the nature of the work seems to present a demand. To infuse them into it, each in the highest degree which the necessary regard to the rest admits of, would, on this as on all similar occasions it has been, be to my mind an object of unremitting solicitude. With what promise of success, let the above mentioned sample speak. Whoever sees that *one part*, sees to all such purposes the *whole*.

In the midst of war, and without interruption to the successes or to the evils of war, a line or two from your Majesty's hand would suffice to give commencement to the work, to this the greatest of all the works of peace.

As to *remuneration*, the honour of the proposed employ, joined to such satisfaction as would be inseparable from that honour, compose the only reward which my situation renders necessary—the only one which my way of thinking would allow me to accept.

With all the respect of which the nature of this address conveys so much fuller an assurance than can be conveyed by any customary form of words, my endeavour would be to approve myself, Sire, your Imperial Majesty's ever faithful servant,

(Signed)   JEREMY BENTHAM.

> *To Prince Czartoryski.*
> *Q ueen quare Place, Westminster,*
> *21st June* 1815.

DEAR SIR,—For one thing I must begin with casting myself upon the Emperor's forgiveness as well as yours ; that is the enormous length of time (upwards of a month), that has intervened between my receiving of the two letters, and the despatching of these my answers. Another thing for which, likewise, I must beg your indulgence, is—the rough state in which I am reduced to send a copy of mine to the Emperor, for your use.

Both trespasses have their source in an engagement under which the letter found me : viz. that of drawing up for this country, for the use of a voluntary association, a plan of National Education, in relation to which I may perhaps take the liberty of troubling you with a few words before the close of the present letter; or at any rate by the next messenger: the whole business was in danger of being put a stop to for an indefinite length of time had I not devoted myself exclusively to it. As to your copy (I mean of my letter to the Emperor) I hope you will find it legible, as consistently with my engagements, time could not be found for the copying and revisal of another fair one.

As to the original, you, as well as he, will (I fear) be sadly annoyed by it, were it only for the length of it. It was, however, absolutely necessary I should speak out, and I saw no hope of being able so to do, to any purpose, in any lesser compass. I hear it said everywhere that he is a good-natured man: by what you will find me saying to him, that quality will be put to the *test*. From me, if he has patience enough, he may thus *read*, what from a man in any other situation, it is not in the nature of things that he should either *read* or *hear*.

A bandage on his eyes—leading strings on his shoulders—on this part of the field of Government, such has hitherto been his costume. My aim is to rid him of those appendages: is it possible he should forgive me? Forgive me or not, that is not the point: that he should suffer himself to be rid of them, *that* is the one thing needful.

I hope this will not draw *you* into a scrape; a scrape on your part so perfectly undeserved: for no such thing as a *tale out of school* have I ever had from *you*.

If, by any thing I have said, an end should be put, not only to *that* correspondence, but to another which is so truly flattering to me, I shall be truly sorry; but it was necessary to run the risk, for I think you will agree with me that whether *with* it anything be done or no, without it nothing was at any rate to be done.

The letter addressed to his Majesty, I put into a separate packet.   I avoid purposely any such attempt as that of making it pass through *your* hands.   In relation to an official person there so frequently alluded to, it was absolutely necessary I should speak without reserve : and there seemed neither use nor necessity for *your* being involved in such business.

Even if it should be in the *constitutional* part of the field of law that my labours, such as they are, should be desired by you (though for reasons already given, *that* is the part in relation to which my hopes of being of use are least sanguine) I repeat my promise to put them under your command :

I. Because I do not absolutely despair of being able to do some good—here a little and there a little —even in relation to that branch.

II. Because (as I say to the Emperor) that is the branch which I imagine *you* had more particularly in view.   But my expectations are much more *extensive*, as well as sanguine, in relation to the *Penal* and *Civil* branches : including, in both cases (though so far as concerns the organisation of the *Judicial Establishment* it belongs to the *constitutional* branch) the *system of Procedure.*—Why ?—Because in the *Civil* branch there will be a good deal of matter, and in the *Penal* a good deal *more* applicable, with little or no difference, under *any form of Government.*   So far, therefore, I could myself *propose* matter, with a tolerable expectation of its being received, and thence with a proportionable degree of facility and alacrity : whereas in regard to *constitutional* law, in which is included the *form of Government*, it would be folly for me to pretend to originate anything considerable.— What is the monarch willing to *leave* or to *concede* to you nobles and the great body of the people, taken together? What are the monarch and you nobles, taken together, willing to *leave* or to *concede* to the great body of the people? What are the people at present in a condition to *receive*, if the powers, on which it depends, were willing to concede it to them? What more, within a moderate space of time, may they be *expected* to come of themselves to be *in*, or to be capable of being put *into* a condition to receive,— and by what means? All this, if known to anybody, is known to you:—not a particle of it to me.

When, near the close of the reign of poor King Stanislaus, a constitutional code for Poland was drawn up, *Bukati* * (I think it was he that was then resident here) sent me a copy of it. What is become of it I do not exactly know. But what I remember is—that people in general were here much pleased with it: myself among the rest, as far as I had looked at it; which was very slightly ; for being deeply embarked in other pursuits at the time, nothing called upon me to suspend them for any such purpose as the study of it.

On the present occasion, *that* paper, is it intended to form the *basis*? Here would be a field for experimenting in: and to a monarch with the whole Russian Empire under such entire command, what possible danger can there be from any such experiment?

* See Vol. I., p. 160.

Under the Great Turk was not Ragusa even a Republic? In such a case more real efficiency than what he would lose in the shape of *coercive power*, the Autocrat of Russia would gain in the shape of gentle *influence* : loss, were there any, would be all of it to the successor,—who, not having been the author of the *boon*, would not be a sharer in the gratitude :— But, even by him, he being used to the comparatively new state of things, the loss, if there were any, would not be felt.

It is now about forty years since I began to lift up my prayers for Poland. The most intimate friend I had was John Lind, privy counsellor to the King, and under his Majesty, original institutor, as well as director, of a school for 400 cadets at Warsaw, and Governor of Prince Stanislaus, nephew to the poor king, whose business at our Court he did for a number of years, writing a letter from London every other post day ; Bukati being all the while the resident kept for show, because our King would not see in that character one of his own subjects.

Lind's first appearance at Warsaw was in that of reader of English to your father or your uncle, I forget which it was. Oh, how he used to talk and talk of Poland! And how he used to curse the Fredericks— great as they were—not to mention other persons.

Being of all countries and of no party, I have just sent off to Paris a large packet of printed copies of a part of the educational scheme to leading men there, Bourbonnites, Napoleonites, and Republicans promiscuously,—some of them old friends of mine.

If you follow the camp, perhaps you may make

prize of them: yet I should be sorry you should; were it only because while you are at Paris, you would not be at *Warsaw;* and whether you are so or no, I am of the number—and that I believe not a small one—of those who are impatient for your being there.

Well, but about this education scheme: were it only to account for the delay, a few words I find I must trouble you with about it even here :—

An experiment of it is about to be made in a part of that garden of mine which you saw. It has for its object the applying to the higher branches of learning, and the higher as well as middling ranks of the community, that *new* system of instruction, of the success of which you can not but be more or less apprized.

Brougham, Sir James Macintosh—and if I can persuade him to lend his *name*—for that is all he can have *time* to lend—*Romilly*, will be at the head of it. For the *details* of the management there will be some very efficient men, with whose names you can scarcely be acquainted. For reasons not worth troubling you with, my fixed determination has been from the very first, not to be of the number. In the *Executive* department of it, I accordingly bear no part : but of the *Legislative* the *initiation* has fallen entirely to my share. My labours in that field had (I believe) already commenced, when I had the honour of receiving you : and, for want of their being completed, the business was at a stand, and by a few days more of delay, the season might have been lost—(I mean the time when the expected *contributors* are in town)—and the execution of the plan deferred for a whole twelvemonth ; and thereby perhaps finally defeated.

It is now in such advance, that everything which it is necessary to publish in the first instance, is either already in print or in the printers' hands. A copy or two will, I trust, be brought to you by the next messenger. On this field, at any rate, in doing what I have done, I consider myself as being at work not less for *Russia* and *Poland*, than for *London*. For the elementary branches, as taught upon the Bell and Lancaster system, *Paris* is already provided with a schoolmaster from hence. The son of a Protestant clergyman—Martin, I think, is his name—was in Louis XVIII's time sent from the south of France to a Lancasterian school for the express purpose of learning the method, and is now at Paris; and (I understand) much caressed there.

His business there is to *form* Instructors. The salary offered to him was £200 : for such a station, a very considerable salary at Paris. No, (says he) *that* would be too much. Success or failure depends upon the degree of economy. Such a sum (naming it, perhaps a quarter as much) is all that you need give. By this the price will be set to those who succeed me. If in my instance, in consideration of my being the first institutor, you see any claim to extraordinary remuneration, let *that* come by and by, when by experience you see what I have done. Just the same thing might the Emperor do for Petersburg and Warsaw. The expense—I mean the *necessary* expense—would be next to nothing ; and if this can not succeed with you, I am at a loss to think what else can.

For this purpose you will see how necessary it has

been for me to take a fresh peep into every nook and cranny of the whole field of art and science : my business having been to apply the new method of instruction to every part of that field that is deemed capable of receiving it. My endeavour has been to reduce the whole sketch into as narrow a compass as possible : and the narrower the compass the greater the quantity of time which it has cost me. Locke's Essay (so he tells us himself in his preface) is too long—Why? 'Because' (says he) 'I had not time to make it shorter.'

If upon the field of codification, it be in my power to throw any *light*, you see the terms upon which it is in the power of your Alexander to have it ? Exactly those upon which God Almighty had *His* : a couple of words the whole of the expense.

I hope the Emperor will not be angry with me for returning his ring ; if it had been a *brass* or a *glass* one, I would have kept it. If he will send the value of it, and no more, to my masters and employers, as above, for their *school*, I as well as they will be all gratitude. But of this in that ensuing letter with which this threatens you. Believe me ever, with the truest respect, dear sir, your most obedient servant,

JEREMY BENTHAM.

PRINCE ADAM CZARTORYSKI.

CHAPTER XXIV

1815-22

THE POLISH CONSTITUTION.—PROMISE AND PERFORMANCE.—RUSSIAN ATROCITIES.— REVOLUTION.

AFTER the negotiations at Vienna, the Emperor Alexander issued a proclamation to the Poles, dated $\frac{13}{25}$ May 1815, stating the chief points of the Constitution which was to be granted to the new kingdom of Poland in conformity with the treaty. A provisional government was formed at Warsaw, with Prince Adam Czartoryski as its head, and the following letter was addressed to him by Alexander on the same date as that of the proclamation :—

VIENNA, $\frac{13}{25}$ *May* 1815.

During the time you have passed here with me, you have had an opportunity of knowing my intentions as to the institutions which it is my will to establish in Poland, and the improvements I desire to introduce in that country. You will take care never to lose sight of them in the deliberations of the Council, and to draw the full attention of your colleagues to them, in order that the action of the Government and the reforms which it is bound to

carry out may be in accordance with my views. You
will not fail, if necessary, to take the initiative in this
respect, so as to hasten the progress of your task and
bring forward bills in conformity with the system
which has been adopted.

As you are equally acquainted with my ideas as
to the spirit in which I wish the selection of the
various officials to be made, you will not fail to
see that this is done in accordance with them. In a
country which has so long been tossed about by
disturbances and revolutions, it is of the highest
importance that a uniform and well combined course
should be pursued. This is what I wanted to recall
to your mind once more by this letter, which I allow
you even to show, so as to add confirmation to what
you will have to say in order to carry out my
intentions. ALEXANDER.

The new Constitution, which was promulgated on
the $\frac{15}{27}$ November, 1815, established a Parliament of
two Houses, which was to meet every two years, a
responsible Ministry, and liberty of the press, and it
stipulated that all the officials should be Poles, and
that Polish should be the official language. It will
be seen, however, from the following letters addressed
to the Emperor by Prince Czartoryski, that, owing
mainly to the arbitrary proceedings of the Grand-
Duke Constantine, the military governor of the
country, this Constitution gradually became a dead
letter :

' 1815.

' As the bases of the Constitution provide for a

Ministry of War among the branches of the administration which, reunited under the same central control, make up the whole body of government, we think it our duty to seek the decision of your Imperial and Royal Majesty on the subject.

'The presence of the Grand-Duke Constantine in this country, and the special powers with which he is invested, have precluded all relations between the provisional government and the military administration, which is placed under a separate committee. This total separation between the civil and military administrations gives rise to the gravest difficulties. It has made it impossible for the Government to present to your Majesty a general report on the situation and the probable requirements of the State, as the army constitutes one of its principal elements. So long as the most considerable and expensive part of the administration remains entirely independent and isolated it cannot be subject to any control, and the expenditure of the country cannot be restricted in proportion to its resources.

' The Government, being constantly brought to a standstill in every measure which has any bearing whatever on military affairs, often finds itself obliged to give up useful reforms whose execution is only possible with the regular and zealous co-operation of the military administration.

' The savings we have endeavoured to introduce in the whole expenditure of the country, and especially in the civil administration, by reducing to the lowest possible point the number and salaries of the officials, will not produce any effect, and cannot be maintained, if the same spirit of rigid economy is not applied to the administration of the army, and if a certain proportion is not established between military and civil emoluments.

'Moreover, the administration of the army touches at so many points on the civil administration that they can neither be properly organised nor governed except on a uniform system.

'The above considerations, the certainty that the Polish army will immediately have to be paid out of the treasury of the Kingdom, and the fact that its revenues will not be sufficient for that purpose, have decided the provisional government to submit to your Imperial and Royal Majesty whether you will not think fit to order the creation of a Ministry of War to take the place of the military committee, and to be organised on the same principle as the two other Ministries. The first duty of this Ministry would be to present a plan for its internal organisation, and the Government, subject to your Majesty's approval, reserves to itself the duty of afterwards submitting to you its observations on the plan in question and the savings which might be introduced in the establishment of the army.'

'WARSAW, *June* 1815.

'. . . The general impression at the promulgation of the new Constitution has been as favourable as could be desired . . . . Its principles have attached the people to your Majesty, and after the long period of waiting, and the conduct of the Grand-Duke, the grant of the Constitution was necessary to produce such a result. The change in the Polish arms and the interference of the Russians with the Government have caused some pain, but the bases of the Constitution have made the people forget everything.'

'WARSAW, $\frac{17}{29}$ *July*, 1815.

'The organisation of the Ministries of the Interior and of Finance, and of the Courts of Justice, is about to be completed ; the result will be a pretty considerable saving. Our first care was not to stop the course of government ; the second is to introduce without delay all possible order and economy from the beginning. . . . I do not doubt that the result would be most satisfactory if it were not for the existence of an independent military authority with which the Government is not in a condition to struggle. I would not have ventured to touch on this delicate point if the urgency of the case did not oblige me to do so. . . .

'His Highness the Grand-Duke is not to be moved by any zeal or submission. He seems to have taken a dislike to the country which is increasing in alarming progression, and is the subject of his daily conversation. Neither the army, the nation, nor individuals find any favour in his eyes. The Constitution especially is made by him a subject of incessant sarcasm ; everything that is matter of law or regulation he scorns and covers with ridicule, and unhappily his words have already been followed by deeds. He does not even adhere to the military laws which he has himself confirmed. He insists upon introducing flogging in the army, and he ordered some men to be flogged yesterday without paying any attention to the unanimous representations of the committee. Desertion is increasing, and will become general, and most of the officers arc about to resign.

'It looks as if a plan had been formed for rendering your Majesty's benefits illusory and making your scheme fail from the beginning. In that case the Grand-Duke is, without knowing it, the blind tool of certain persons in his confidence who encourage his sombre and passionate temper. I fear the most lamentable results if he should remain here.'

'31st July 1815.

'The position of the Government of your Imperial and Royal Majesty in this country has for some time become extremely painful and difficult, and I feel it my duty to bring to your knowledge details of which I would have wished never to be obliged to speak.

'His Highness the Grand-Duke has several times intimated to the Government that civil officials, magistrates, mayors, etc., should be brought before him, and the other day he placed the President of the town of Warsaw under arrest. Some days ago, too, his Highness issued a decree by means of which he will have the power of trying any citizen by court-martial.

'The provisional government cannot but recognise that such proceedings are contrary to the rules established in all countries for the public peace and security, and that they are especially in direct opposition to the Constitution which your Majesty has just granted to the country. . . Under these circumstances all the members of the Government are unanimously of opinion that the above facts should be laid before you with a view to your Majesty placing your Government in a position to carry out your will.'

'WARSAW, $\frac{16}{28}$ *January* 1816.

'. . . Your Imperial Majesty are alone capable of maintaining the edifice you have raised. If you abandon it from the beginning to the attacks of those who are hostile to it, it must fall to pieces. What else can be the fate of a Constitution granted by you with so much solemnity and violated almost immediately after it was proclaimed? If we obtain the support which we have a right to ask of your Majesty, all will go well. I have observed with joy that so far as the Poles are concerned, more importance is attached to measures than to individuals. Our institutions, though as yet in the process of formation, are sufficient to work the Government machine, and since the establishment of Constitutional Government perfect harmony exists among all the Ministers. . . . Your Majesty's Lieutenant Governor,* however, though zealous, persevering, and enlightened, seems to consider that every wish expressed by the Grand-Duke Constantine must be regarded as that of your Majesty. He is ready to violate the Constitution at any moment if his Highness should require him to do so, and he has even plainly expressed himself to the Council in this sense. . . . Such a degree of submission in the highest official of the realm would make your Consti-

---

* General Zajonczek, a veteran who had lost both his legs in the Napoleonic wars.

tution a farce. If you will inform him that you wish
to respect your own work and cause it to be respected,
and that his duties to his sovereign and his country
may be combined with, but should never be subordi-
nated to, his obligations to the Grand-Duke, he will no
doubt carry out your will. This, however, is an
essential condition of preventing the ruin of the
country. . . You, Sire, are our destiny; our only
resources and hopes are bound up with your Majesty,
and you alone can give permanent solidity to the
institutions which you have created.'

'17*th* *April* 1816.
'Suicides have for some time been very frequent in
the Polish army. The annexed letter, the original of
which is in the Grand-Duke's hands, shows the cause
of most of these unhappy occurrences. Its writer
was a distinguished officer, aide-de-camp to General
Krasinski, and a great favourite in Polish society.
His example was followed by a sub-officer who killed
himself because, as is stated, he could not survive the
shame of the disgraceful punishments inflicted upon
himself and his colleagues. It is absolutely necessary
that the army should be given a code of laws and
regulations. At present it is administered solely by
caprice. It suffers not from too much severity, but
from constant humiliations and acts of arbitrary
power.'

(*Enclosure.*)
'My Dear Sister, . . . I can no longer bear what
I see daily—my brothers-in-arms and my fellow-

citizens dishonoured, the glory of our fathers trodden under foot, the laws of the best of sovereigns violated. I leave my poor country helplessly delivered up to the caprices of one man.

'How often have I nearly become an assassin! What a blow that would have been for you, dear sister! I wished to sacrifice myself in order to free us from these shameful chains, but feeling that the result might not realise my hopes, I prefer to deprive myself of an existence which might become fatal to my country. . . . I know that I shall be accused of weakness; I would have done this deed long ago if our holy religion and my attachment for you had not prevented me. But being now quite convinced that I can no longer be of use to my country, I and several of my friends have determined to leave this world. . .

'Give my sword to your son. Let him wear it, as I did, for his country and his friends.'

'SIENIAWA, 21*st August* 1821.

'I feel it my duty to submit to your Imperial and Royal Majesty some observations on the present condition of Poland. I do not often trouble you with letters, and I beg to be permitted on this occasion to write to you at greater length than usual. I have given a heading to each paragraph, so that your Majesty need only read those which may seem to you most worthy of attention.

'*State of Public Feeling.*—People's minds are in a state of extreme uncertainty and total discouragement. Everything seems unsettled; every institution is in danger, and the most lamentable changes of system are expected. Nothing can be more pernicious than such a state of affairs, which stifles noble aspirations and leads weak people to look only after their own interests, in the belief that public considerations are disregarded by their Government.

'*Causes of Alarm.*—It is feared, from certain phrases which have been uttered by those who are supposed to be the confidential interpreters of your views, that you regard the Constitution as impracticable, useless, and involving too much expenditure, that the independence of Courts of Justice is to cease, that public education is to be restricted, that the diets are inconvenient obstacles which should be abolished, and that the Kingdom is to be governed like the other Polish dominions of the Empire. I do not know how much truth there may be in these discouraging rumours, but it is asserted that your opinions have of late undergone a complete change, and are totally opposed to those you held before. I can hardly believe this, and I appeal with confidence against those who wish to injure my country and its Constitution to principles and traits of character which should be above all passing circumstances.

'*Expense of the Army.*—It would be unjust to make a nation suffer for faults which it has not committed. You have been led, Sire, by motives whose force I am far from disputing, to decide that the expense of the Polish army shall not be diminished. But it is a fact that this expense is greater than the Kingdom of Poland within its present limits is capable of bearing, and that it is relatively greater than that borne for similar objects by various independent kingdoms, such as Sweden, Saxony, Würtemberg, and Piedmont, where, with greater resources, the military system is less costly.

' Limits of the Kingdom.—When the fate of this country was decided your Majesty will remember that you magnanimously promised to reunite all the Polish provinces under your sceptre and under a national régime. You yourself thought the regeneration of Poland should be carried out on a more extended scale ; the present Kingdom, smaller by a third than the Duchy whose place it occupies, was in your eyes to be a merely provisional creation. Reasons of prudence have led your Majesty to suspend the execution of this promise ; but would it not be obviously unjust to punish the Kingdom for the restricted limits imposed upon it, the extension of which the nation would make the greatest sacrifices to procure ?

' The Constitution.—The Constitution granted by your Majesty has been subjected to much unjust criticism. It cannot be made responsible for the ill-directed or superfluous expenditure of the administration, for this expenditure has occurred because the Constitution was not sufficiently obeyed. The army is too large, the taxes are levied with extreme rigour, justice would be impartial if it were not influenced by persons above the law, and the system of police is sometimes inquisitorial and vexatious. The Constitution prevents nothing that is necessary ; unfortunately it does not prevent that which is superfluous and injurious to the state. The introduction of measures of the latter class depends entirely on your Majesty's will, and the Diet should not be blamed for rendering it difficult to introduce them. It is one of the advantages of Constitutional Government that it tends to stability ; the rejection of a bill simply leaves things as they are.'

The above letter was, as will be seen from its date, written shortly after the formation of the Holy Alliance, the Congresses of Troppau and Laybach, and the revolutionary movements at Naples, in Spain, and in Piedmont. Alexander now gradually abandoned his liberal tendencies and gave up Poland entirely to the cruel and arbitrary rule of his brother Constantine. Prince Adam Czartoryski, seeing that any further intervention with the Emperor on behalf of Poland was hopeless, ceased all further correspondence with him on the subject, and in 1823 he gave up his post of curator of the Wilna University, which he had held for twenty years, the atrocious persecution of the students by the Russian authorities rendering it impossible for him any longer usefully to conduct the affairs of the University, which had under his care risen to the position of the first educational institution in the Empire.

In 1825 Alexander I died and was succeeded by Nicholas. Among the persons arrested in connection with the outbreak at St Petersburg which preceded Nicholas's accession were several Poles, who were brought up for trial before the Senate at Warsaw. Prince Adam, who was then in Italy, hurried to Warsaw to take part in this trial as a member of the Senate. After a careful inquiry, which lasted more than a year, it was found that the accused had not taken any part

whatever in the rebellion, and had merely protested
in a legal manner against the repeated violations of
the Constitution. Prince Adam, as the father, so to
say, of the Constitution and the chief adviser of the
late Emperor in all matters relating to Poland, was
naturally called upon to take a prominent part in the
deliberations of the Senate on this matter, and his
view of the innocence of the accused was accepted by
the whole of the Senate with the exception of one
member. The verdict was reversed by the Emperor,
who ordered the Senators to be retained at Warsaw
under the surveillance of the military authorities,
and the accused to be taken to St Petersburg and
imprisoned in the casemates of the fortress.

This outrageous measure was the beginning of the
events which led to the Polish insurrection of 1830.
The savage cruelties of the Grand-Duke Constantine, and the endless violations of the Constitution
and deportations of distinguished citizens, are well
known, and need not be recapitulated here. The
Poles had for years been subjected to indignities
which no high-spirited nation, with a patriotic and
warlike army, could long tolerate. Revolutions were
breaking out in France, Belgium, and Germany;
Nicholas had ordered the Russian and Polish armies
to march against the insurgents in those countries;
and the Poles could no longer delay the outbreak
which had for some time been in preparation. The
whole nation—not only in the Kingdom of Poland,
but in Lithuania, Volhynia, Podolia, and the Ukraine
—rose against its oppressors. Constantine left the
country with the Russian troops, the Polish throne

was declared vacant, and Prince Adam Czartoryski was unanimously elected President of the National Government. A Russian army invaded Poland in February 1831, but it was repeatedly defeated by the Poles, though they were inferior in numbers. The Russians, reinforced by 20,000 grenadiers, were again beaten in the vicinity of Warsaw, and were forced to retire to Lublin for winter quarters. In April the Poles gained further victories, and the Russian army, dispersed in a marshy country, was almost annihilated, but new Russian troops constantly poured in from all parts of the Empire, while the forces at the disposal of the Poles were limited and they had great difficulty in procuring provisions and ammunition in consequence of Austria and Prussia having closed their frontiers to them. By degrees the Russian army retrieved its defeats; on the 7th of September, 1831, Warsaw was taken, after a sanguinary battle in which the Russians lost one-fourth of their troops, and the remains of the Polish army, including Prince Adam Czartoryski, who had fought in its ranks, were driven into Austria and Prussia.

CHAPTER XXV

1831-2.

AFTER the collapse of the Polish Revolution of 1830-1
Prince Adam Czartoryski proceeded to London, where
he arrived on the 22nd of December 1831. The
revolution which had just taken place in France made
Paris an unsuitable starting-point for a European
intervention in Poland, as the other Powers on the
Continent looked upon the new French Government
with suspicion as representing the aggressive and
revolutionary tendencies of the year 1792, which it
was hoped had been finally crushed by the coalition of
1815. In London, however, a Liberal Cabinet had
come into power almost simultaneously with the outbreak of the Polish Revolution. This seemed a good
omen for the Polish cause, and the more sanguine of
the Poles already looked forward to an Anglo-French

coalition in their behalf and in that of the other oppressed nationalities. But as usual Ministers in office held very different language from that which they had used in opposition. The envoys in London of the Polish national Government, Marquis Wielopolski and Count Walewski (afterwards Minister under Napoleon III), reported that the Liberal Government, alarmed at the excitement in France and the cries of revenge for Waterloo, had come to the conclusion that the policy of England should be 'not to weaken Russia, as Europe might soon again require her services in the cause of order,' and to prevent Poland, whom it regarded as the natural ally of France, from becoming 'a French province on the Vistula.'* The Reform Bill and the Belgian Question, too, absorbed the attention of the Government and rendered it indisposed to take up so delicate and dangerous a question as that of Poland. Accordingly, although at the beginning of the Polish Revolution the British Cabinet had represented at St Petersburg that England, as a party to the Treaty of Vienna, could not consent to any violation of its provisions, it afterwards rejected the proposal of the French Government of July for a combined intervention with the object of stopping further bloodshed in Poland.

'London,' says M. de Gadon in his manuscript account of the Polish mission, 'was at that time the head-quarters of European diplomacy, as the Conference on the Belgian question, which presented many difficulties and dangers, was being held there. The

* Despatch of the 19th March 1831, from Marquis Wielopolski to the Polish mission in Paris, and of the 29th March and 8th April 1831, from Count Walewski to the Minister of Foreign Affairs in Warsaw (MSS. in the Polish Library in Paris).

chief men of mark in the political world were Earl Grey and Lords Palmerston, Brougham, Holland, Melbourne, Lansdowne, and Althorp, while among the diplomatists at the Belgian Conference were Talleyrand, Lieven, and Esterhazy. The feminine influence in politics, which at that time was not inconsiderable, was represented by Lady Holland, the Princess Dino-Talleyrand, and the Princess Lieven. The first of these, still bearing the traces of great beauty—proud, witty, and imposing 'as a Czarina—' assembled at her famous receptions at Holland House all that was most brilliant by position, merit, or talent. The Princess Dino, daughter of the last Duchess of Courland and wife of the nephew * of Prince Talleyrand, had lived with the Prince for many years, and was his constant companion. She had great influence over him, and used to preside at the magnificent receptions in the French Embassy while Talleyrand was Ambassador. The rooms of the Embassy at Hanover Square were fitted up with all the splendour of the great French aristocratic *salons* of the eighteenth century ; the *cuisine* was perfection ; and the inexhaustible wit of the host, notwithstanding his seventy-eight years, and the amiability of the hostess, made these receptions the most brilliant and the most sought after in London. Even the Court was so anxious to please

---

* When Prince Talleyrand, at that time Napoleon's Foreign Minister, sought a wife for his nephew, ' Napoleon appropriated all the heiresses of France for his aides-de-camp,' and the Prince accordingly arranged, through the intervention of Alexander I, a marriage for his nephew with the youngest daughter of the widow of the last Duke of Courland, who was the friend of King Stanislaus Augustus and many other Poles. The marriage took place in 1808, and Talleyrand afterwards gave up to his nephew the title of Prince Dino. The latter was, however, so addicted to riotous living that his wife obtained a divorce from him and took up her residence with Talleyrand.

Talleyrand, that the Princess Dino, although not his
wife, was admitted, in contravention of all the rules
of etiquette, to the position and privileges of an
Ambassadress.*

'As for the Princess Lieven, the wife of the
Russian Ambassador, everyone has heard of this
consummate type of a Russian political agent in
petticoats.† The poet Niemcewicz, who was at that
time Polish envoy in London, and who did not spare
people whom he did not like, expressed surprise that
this 'old and ugly woman, with a red nose, should
possess such influence and make everybody submit to
her decrees ;' but this is explained by her rare intellectual qualities, her dialectic skill, and her extraordinary pliancy in social intercourse. She had been
in London for eighteen years, and having in this long
period made many friends and acquaintances, she was
not only an agreeable companion but a political force.
More than once she influenced not only the decisions
but the fate of Cabinets, even in England. The most
distinguished English statesmen—Lords Liverpool,
Castlereagh, and Aberdeen, the Duke of Wellington,
Canning, Peel, and Lord Harrowby—were her confidential friends, and although by disposition and
training she was an ultra-Tory, this did not prevent
her from being on the best terms with Liberal

* One of Talleyrand's greatest admirers and pupils in the art of diplomacy was
Lord Palmerston, and a comic paper published a caricature representing them walking together, with the inscription, 'the lame leading the blind' (an allusion to the
fact that one of Talleyrand's feet was deformed).

† The Princess Lieven, a descendant of the Esthonian family of von Benkendorff,
was the sister of General Alexander von Benkendorff, the confidant of the Emperor
Nicholas, and the creator of that mysterious and all-powerful institution, the Secret
Police, known in Russia by the modest appellation of 'the third section of the
Imperial Chancellery'.

Ministers, " for the advantage and glory of the policy of the Czar." The only prominent statesman with whom she could never agree was Palmerston ; she used to call him " un très-petit esprit, lourd, obstiné," and she cordially detested him. He, on the other hand, used to say that he had been in a Tory Cabinet, and knew what her services cost. Of Earl Grey it was reported that every morning before he got out of bed he used to write her a note on paper scented with musk, in which he mingled gallantry with politics.

' Being a zealous servant and admirer of the Czar, Madame Lieven showed bitter hostility to the Poles and their cause. She would not allow any Polish sympathies to be expressed in her presence, and she carried her animosity so far that when one of the secretaries of the French Embassy said something in favour of the Polish revolution, she went to Talleyrand and insisted on his dismissing the culprit from his post.

Such was the position of affairs in London when Prince Adam Czartoryski, eager as ever to serve the cause of his unhappy country, came to advocate it before the members of the Government and the continental statesmen who had assembled from all parts of Europe for the Belgian Conference. He was received in London by the poet Niemcewicz, who still remained there after the close of his functions as envoy of the Polish National Government. His venerable appearance, his perfect knowledge of the English language and English customs, and his reputation as a companion of Kosciuszko,* had made him generally liked

* He was Kosciuszko's aide-de-camp, and afterwards accompanied him to the United States, where they remained together for several years.

and respected. Niemcewicz was too plain-spoken and hot-tempered, however, for a diplomatist : 'Palmerston,' he says in his Memoirs, 'found me too hot, and I found him colder than ice.' But his unflagging industry and perseverance made up for this defect, and Prince Adam, in his life of Niemcewicz,* says that 'perhaps he never showed more boundless attachment to his country than in this last and difficult public service. . . Notwithstanding his age and growing infirmities, he thinks of everything, and I saw him day and night working solely for his country's cause.'

After narrowly escaping capture by the Russian army at Cracow, Prince Adam had travelled with a passport given him by Metternich in the name of 'George Hoffman.' This was a necessary precaution, considering the power at that time exercised by Russia throughout the German States. 'He arrived,' says Niemcewicz in his Memoirs, 'without a servant, deprived of all property, and his whole luggage represented by a small trunk. . . What a freak of fortune ! I well recollect when I was his father's aide-de-camp fifty years ago, and when during an inspection of the Lithuanian army the tents of his suite were carried by 300 horses and fourteen camels. His son is now destitute ; but he feels the misfortunes of his country more than his own.'

Prince Adam's first visit was to the French Embassy. The Princess Dino was an old acquaintance of his, and in 1808 the Abbé Piattoli, who was a friend both of the Prince and of the Duchess of Coburg,

* Published at Berlin and Posen in 1860.

had endeavoured to arrange a marriage between him and the Duchess's youngest daughter. Although nothing came of this project, the young Duchess, even after her marriage, remained on the most friendly terms with Prince Adam, and Talleyrand had also for many years been well acquainted with him. In 1807 the French Minister was opposed to the Poles, saying : 'avec les Polonais on ne fait que du désordre ;' but he afterwards changed his opinion on this and other subjects, and showed some favour to Poland at the Vienna Congress. So much, indeed, was he regarded as hostile to Russia that when he was appointed French Ambassador in London, the Emperor Nicholas is said by M. Louis Blanc* to have considered this appointment 'as a sort of declaration of war ;' and Count Walewski described him as 'one of those who were least indifferent to the Polish cause.'

Talleyrand and the Princess Dino received Prince Adam in the most friendly manner, and repeatedly urged him to take up his residence in their château of Valençay. Talleyrand added that in view of the general desire for peace, the only means of raising the Polish question would be to appeal to the Treaty of Vienna, which, he thought, all the Cabinets would insist on maintaining. Prince Czartoryski would, he said, be especially qualified to carry on the negotiations on this subject, as he had acted during the Vienna Congress as a sort of mediator between the Poles and the Emperor Alexander.

The Christmas of 1831 was a melancholy one for

---

* *Histoire de Dix Ans*, vol. ii, p. 101. Guizot, however, says that Talleyrand's Polish sympathies were purely historical, and that he was then entirely absorbed with the Belgian question (Hist. vol. ii, p. 229).

Poles in all parts of the world, and Prince Czartoryski and his few Polish friends in London spent it in sad reminiscences of the terrible struggle through which their country had passed. Most of the Prince's English friends and acquaintances were out of town, but on the 29th of December he obtained an interview with Lord Palmerston, then Secretary of State for Foreign Affairs, which he thus describes in a letter written by him shortly after :

'Lord Palmerston struck me as a man of very cold temperament, who, having made up his mind on the Polish question, only thought of rebutting our arguments on the other side. I began by saying that although England had not given the Poles any help, they owe her gratitude for her good wishes. To this Palmerston rejoined that if the fate of the Poles had depended on his personal wishes and those of Englishmen generally, their struggle for independence would not have had such an unfortunate result; but that circumstances and treaties often prevent States from following their most just impulses. I here remarked that if treaties prevented the Powers from interfering in behalf of Poland, they should at least see that the treaties are carried out. The Emperor Nicholas had appealed to the Treaty of Vienna during the progress of the Revolution, and he could not repudiate the Treaty now that the Revolution was over. . . . We Poles have nothing to ask for or to expect from him, and we only refer to the Treaty of Vienna as a means of diminishing our sufferings. The maintenance of the treaties which relate to Poland is a matter which specially concerns the Powers that signed those treaties. Lord Palmerston made no reply to this remark, but said that it is a principle among States not to interfere between a Government and its subjects except in cases where a State has a direct interest in so interfering, or is distinctly authorised to do so by treaty. The stipulations of the Treaty of Vienna with regard to Poland were not clear, and might be variously interpreted. " It provides, for instance, that the kingdom of Poland is to be united to Russia by its Constitution, but it does not say what the Constitution is to be, or that the Emperor is not to have the power to alter it. The Powers are not therefore bound to resist any modifications the Czar might deem fit to introduce in the Constitution ; and Austria and Prussia, which are the Powers most interested in the question, concur in this view. . . ." I answered that it was not to be wondered at that the article about Poland is not clear and precise, seeing that it was hastily put together, after much opposition, at the moment when the news arrived of the return of Napoleon from the island of Elba, and those who drew it up, even on the Russian side, did not agree with the Emperor Alexander on the matter. It was evident, however, that the word ' Constitution' was not inserted in the Treaty as an expression without any real meaning. By that word was meant the Constitution which Alexander had designed for Poland, and in using it Alexander spoke in the name of his successors, and bound himself never to alter it. Moreover, all the members of the Congress had specially expressed a wish to maintain the Polish nationality, and any change of the Constitution

tending to weaken that nationality must be opposed
to the spirit of the Treaty. As to the allegation of
Austria and Prussia that a separate Polish State under
the Russian sceptre does not afford more security to
its neighbours than a Poland annexed to Russia as
part of the Empire, it was thoroughly understood by
the Congress that although a contented Poland would
increase the Czar's defensive forces, a Poland with a
Constitution and a separate army of its own would
diminish the force of Russia for purposes of aggression.
Lord Palmerston seemed to admit the justice of these
remarks, and after some questions as to the Poles in
Austria . . . he looked at his watch, and as we took
our leave he told me that whenever I should wish to
see him I would find him at the office every afternoon.'

On the following day Prince Czartoryski saw Earl
Grey. He said that the Ministry would be glad to
interpret the Treaty of Vienna as much as possible in
favour of Poland, but that in his opinion this must
depend on Austria and Prussia, who were directly
interested. The Treaty would be maintained, but the
question was how it was to be interpreted. Prince
Lieven, Earl Grey added, had communicated to him a
memorandum in which Austria holds that the Treaty
does not demand adherence to the Constitution, that
the Powers cannot prevent Nicholas from altering it at
his pleasure, and that no more can be required than
that the Kingdom of Poland should have a provincial
diet like Posen and Galicia. ' Prince Lieven,' Lord
Grey continued, ' was not at all satisfied with my
answer. I told him that we could not accept this
interpretation of the Treaty of Vienna, and that in

our opinion the Constitution should be maintained in the shape in which it was granted. But what can we do when Austria and Prussia are of a different opinion ? If those two Powers, the neighbours of Russia, are not convinced of the necessity of limiting Russian power by maintaining the concessions made to the Poles, how can we insist on their being maintained ? ' Prince Czartoryski having here remarked that the Poles did not look to their oppressors Austria and Prussia, but to England and France, to decide their fate, Earl Grey continued : ' Ah, but things in France are so unsettled. The preservation of peace depends there upon a single man, M. Périer. If he falls, God knows what will happen. But I will do my best to maintain the Anglo-French Alliance, for I agree with you that it is necessary for the good of the two countries and of the whole of Europe.' This conversation produced a bad impression on the Prince. ' The Ministry,' he says, ' does not seem to feel strong, or to be conscious that it stands at the head of a great nation capable of exercising a powerful influence on the destinies of Europe. All this leaves a free field to our enemies in the north.' The two friends dined together next day at Earl Grey's house at East Sheen, and after dinner the latter admitted that England's policy had been ' too timid with regard to Poland ' and that ' England and France had not been sufficiently conscious of the means at their command.'*

The high social position of Prince Adam Czartoryski, the prominent part which he had taken in the

* See also a letter from Earl Grey to Brougham in Brougham's Autobiography, vol. iii., p. 164.

Polish Revolution, and the savage ukases issued
against him by the Emperor Nicholas, made him a
remarkable and interesting figure in London society,
where he was received with an esteem almost amounting to veneration. This feeling was not confined to
aristocratic circles, where he was personally known;
it also spread to the middle classes, and on the 2nd of
January 1832, the 'Literary Union' club gave him a
dinner, at which the poet Campbell made an enthusiastic speech. The Prince's popularity was still further
increased when it became known that Prince Lieven,
the Russian Ambassador, had complained to Lord
Palmerston of Earl Grey's having invited 'the
President of the rebel government' to his house, and
that the Princess had at the same time addressed a
letter full of bitter reproaches to Earl Grey.

Some days later the Prince had an interview with
Brougham, who had now risen to the position of
Lord Chancellor, and whose official position and
advancing years had greatly calmed the fervid enthusiasm with which he had taken up the cause of the
Poles eighteen years before (see Chapter XXI).
'Your Highness will understand,' he said, 'the
difference between the feelings of a private individual
and the duties of a Minister. The opinions of Lord
Grey and myself as to Poland are well known to you;
but we were obliged to adapt our policy to the condition of England, who was absolutely incapable (*sic*) of
making war.' 'But,' said the Prince, 'why did you
refuse to join France in diplomatic representations at
St Petersburg?' 'Such a step,' answered Brougham,
'would have been of doubtful efficacy. . . . The fate

of Poland will always interest us, but unfortunately
the Polish cause is opposed to the wishes of all the
other Powers.   They all want peace, while to take up
the cause of Poland means war.'

Though discouraged, Prince Adam did not lose
heart, but prepared a memorandum, entering fully
into the rights of Poland under the Treaty of Vienna.
After showing it to Talleyrand, who highly approved
it, he handed it to Palmerston.   The latter said he
would do all he could for the Poles, but that nothing
could have been done by England during the Revolution, as the proclamation of the deposition of Nicholas
by the Poles had deprived her of the only ground on
which she could interfere in their behalf. . . 'Now
that the struggle is over, however,' he added, ' we
have forwarded our representations and remarks as to
the maintenance of the Treaty of Vienna.   We recognise that Russia has not fulfilled it, for she has
done nothing in the provinces, and after granting a
Constitution to the kingdom, has violated its provisions.   We adhere firmly to this view, although
Austria and Prussia dissent from it.   We hold that
the Constitution granted by the Emperor Alexander
should be maintained, and can only be altered by the
Diet ; also that the Polish provinces of Russia should
have a representative assembly and a provincial
administration.'

The Russian answer to the representations referred
to by Lord Palmerston came at the end of January.
It was very courteous in tone, but it decisively
rejected the English view of the Treaty, pointing out
that Russia had a majority in her favour of three to

two, as Russia, Austria, and Prussia were on one side
and only England and France on the other. 'Russia
is quite wrong,' said Palmerston to Prince Adam,
'but how can we force her to accept our view? We
cannot send an army to Poland, and the burning of
the Russian fleet would be about as effectual as the
burning of Moscow.' The Ministry did not, however,
even attempt to pursue the subject diplomatically.
France was beginning to strive for the favour of the
Emperor Nicholas, and England, wishing above all
things for the settlement of the Belgian question,
also found it her interest to remain on good terms
with him. Under these circumstances it was not
surprising that not only Russia but Prussia repudiated
their obligations towards Europe. Ancillon, the
Prussian Foreign Minister, cynically advocated the
complete annihilation of Poland 'so as to have done
with her once for all,' * and when the British Ambassador at Berlin appealed to the Treaty of Vienna, he
sharply replied that 'every one can do as he likes in
his own house.' † In Austria, too, Metternich,
terrified at the re-appearance of the revolutionary
spectre in France and Germany, although he had
admitted that 'he would rather have a friendly and
peaceful Poland for a neighbour than an aggressive
Russia,' ‡ began to talk of a renewal of the Holy
Alliance, and of the two evils—Russia and revolution
—preferred the former as the least.

Although it has often been shown that the cases

* Conversation with General Flahaut, the French Ambassador, reported by
Count Walewski in a letter preserved in the Polish Library in Paris.

† Letter from Prince Adam Czartoryski, dated the 24th of January, 1832.

‡ Despatch of the 25th September, 1830 (*Memoirs of Prince Metternich*, vol. v.
p. 77).

of Poland and Ireland bear no resemblance to each other, it is still the constant practice of Russian writers and their sympathisers in the English press to compare them. Earl Grey, in a conversation with Prince Czartoryski on the 8th of March, 1832, told the Prince that this comparison had been used as a *tu quoque* argument by the Russian Ambassador. ' The Czar,' he said, ' will not allow anyone to interfere in the affairs of Poland.' ' Le Prince et la Princesse de Lieven ont répété plusieurs fois que l'Empereur ne permettra jamais que d'autres puissances se mêlent dans les affaires de la Pologne, de même que l'Angleterre ne permettrait pas qu'on se mêle des affaires de l'Irlande. . . .' Lord Palmerston, referring to this remark two days later, said to the Prince : ' There is not the smallest similarity between the two cases. Ireland has belonged to us for centuries ; it speaks the same language as England and is the same nation.'— ' Moreover,' observed the Prince ' the union of England and Ireland was not the result of a European Treaty.'

In the conversation above referred to Earl Grey added some interesting particulars on Continental and English politics. ' Russia,' he said, ' is backed up by Austria and Prussia, and we cannot rely on France ; her position is too unsettled. . . As for England, public opinion is certainly interested in Poland ; but it is much more interested in various internal questions, and in the maintenance of peace. Moreover, we have other questions pending with Russia, which demand mutual concessions. . . . We have financial difficulties, but if public opinion were in favour of war, means would be found of raising the necessary

funds. What most troubles us is the uncertain state
of Europe. Some want to maintain everything
by force, others to upset everything by force. . . .
Party feeling, too, runs very high here. Wellington is
opposed to all liberal plans, and force is his only policy;
this pleases the other Cabinets. He thinks he will
yet return to office; he had never been beaten before,
and will not believe that he is beaten now. I did not
seek office; my advanced age did not allow me to do
so. The King himself called upon me to form a
Cabinet, as the Duke after his declaration could not
remain in office.' In reporting this conversation the
Prince adds that Earl Grey asked him several times
if he had seen Lord Palmerston, 'as if he feared to say
anything which might not be in accordance with
Palmerston's views,' and that he 'looked very
anxious.'

The priceless collections of Pulawy, the relics of
his fortune that had survived the confiscations of
Nicholas, and his duties to his family, now urgently
claimed Prince Adam's attention, but the interests of
his country were in his eyes paramount over all
private considerations, and he stuck manfully to his
post so long as a spark of hope remained. In a letter
written about this time to one of his friends he says:
'I am glad, at any rate, that I have, though in a
somewhat violent and expensive way, liberated myself
from the chains that bound me. I will certainly not
resume them even at the price of my whole fortune.
. . . Every Pole should all his life be prepared for
oppression or exile. You have experienced it already.
My turn has come, at too advanced an age it is true,

but I feel strong enough to bear it even with good humour.'

All through his long life his proudest boast was that he was the servant of his country; while he was Foreign Minister of Russia he did not draw the salary of the appointment, and repeatedly refused the decorations and other dignities which the Emperor Alexander pressed upon him. In one of his speeches to the Polish Historical Society he said he would like to add to the family motto of the Czartoryskis— 'Come what may'—that of the Black Prince, 'Ich dien.'

Although it was evident that neither England nor France would do anything for Poland, Prince Adam was anxious at least to bring into prominence the fact that international engagements had been broken, and that a wrong had been done which, if not protested against, might be given the appearance of a lawful proceeding, and be accepted as such by public opinion. The state of the Continent, too, was then so unsettled that a conflict might at any moment arise in which the Polish question, if kept alive before Europe, might play a prominent part. The Prince accordingly did his utmost to keep both the Government and the public fully informed as to the position of affairs in Poland. The whole of the London press—notably the *Times*, the *Morning Herald*, and the *Morning Chronicle*—advocated the Polish cause, and the Foreign Office readily accepted the information communicated by the Prince on the subject, especially as Lord Heytesbury, in his despatches from St Petersburg, was completely silent as to the persecutions and cruelties of the Russian

Government in Poland, the destruction of the national collections,* and the suppression of the university and schools. 'These,' said Lord Palmerston to the Prince 'are the results of animosity after a sanguinary war.' 'But,' observed the latter, 'victory should produce leniency.' 'True,' Palmerston rejoined, 'in civilised countries; in half-savage ones victory only produces increased severities.' Among the documents which reached the Foreign Office in this way were two letters from a Pole named Borowski, who was taken in his childhood to South America, fought there for the independence of the Spanish republics, and afterwards went to Arabia. Here he heard the news of the Polish Revolution, upon which he at once proceeded to Persia, where he was well received by the heir-apparent Abbas Mirza and attempted to induce him to take active steps against Russia. His last plan of helping his country was to equip two cruisers on the Black Sea for the capture of Russian ships, and he asked that letters of marque should be granted by England for this purpose.

With a view to spreading information as to Polish affairs, Prince Czartoryski, assisted by several English political writers, founded a monthly Magazine, 'Polonia,' afterwards expanded into the 'British and Foreign Review,' containing articles on Polish history and other subjects connected with that country. He also collected for the use of English writers a number of historical works about Poland, some of which had

* The total number of books (most of which have been destroyed) taken by the Russians from the great Polish libraries is about 700,000. Of these 17,000 belonged to the Radzivill Library, 400,000 to the famous Zaluski Library, 200,000 to the University of Warsaw, 30,000 to the Society of the Friends of Science, 20,000 to the University of Wilna, and 15,000 to the Czartoryski Library at Pulawy.

already been sent to London in 1814 by his secretary Biernacki, and he presented some of the latest works published in various countries on Polish affairs to the British Museum Library. On the 25th of November, 1832, 'The Literary Association of the Friends of Poland,' a society which has ever since continued to be the head-quarters of all English action on behalf of the Poles, was founded. A Polish Committee' for the relief of Polish refugees had already been formed by Messrs Bach, Hunter Gordon, Arthur White, and Kirwan, but, thanks to the influence and efforts of Prince Czartoryski, the scope and importance of this committee was considerably enlarged, and it became the association above described, which consisted entirely of Englishmen. Its first President was the poet Campbell, and among his most distinguished successors were Lord Dudley Stuart—the most devoted, zealous, and indefatigable of the English friends of Poland—and Lords Harrowby, Houghton, and Lytton. The Association took up its quarters at No. 10 Duke Street, St James's, where Oliver Cromwell and Milton once lived ; and there it still remains, relieving out of its scanty funds the helpless survivors of the Polish Revolutions of the last sixty years.

Another matter to which the Prince devoted much attention was the introduction of the Polish question in Parliament. Neither the adherents of the Ministry nor the members of the Opposition were inclined to take such a course, the former because they feared it would embarrass the Government, and the latter because they looked upon the Poles as revolutionists. At length Mr Cutlar Fergusson, M.P., an independent member with a good position in the House and considerable talent as a speaker, consented, after consulting Lord Palmerston and Sir James Mackintosh, to undertake the task. As his motion would necessarily have to be based on the Treaty of Vienna, he had to be supplied with as much information as possible on the subject; unfortunately the Prince no longer had his papers relating to the Vienna Congress, including despatches from Pozzo di Borgo, Stein, and Castlereagh, as they had been taken out of his wife's carriage by the Austrian customs' authorities. Ample material, was, however, collected by the Prince and his untiring companion and friend Niemcewicz for the proposed debate, but the Belgian Question and the Reform Bill prevented its coming on so soon as was hoped, and finding that for the present there was nothing to be done, and that his slender resources were being exhausted by the expense of living in London, the Prince left in March, 1832, for Clifton, where he could live more cheaply and have more quiet for his political and literary work. He also wanted to become more closely acquainted with rural life in England, that being the country which he liked better than any other, and where he hoped ultimately to settle with his family. He returned to London at the end of March for the Polish debate in the House of Commons, which took place on the 18th of April.

In June the Prince's family* also came to London,

---

* The Prince married on the 25th of September 1817, the Princess Anna, daughter of Prince Alexander Sapieha-Kodenski. He had three children : Prince Witold, who died on the 14th of November 1865, Princess Isa, and Prince Ladislas, the present head of the family.

but the English climate acted so injuriously on his
wife's health that he was obliged to give up his
plan of settling in England, and at the end of
August he took up his residence in Paris. During
the interval two more interesting debates on Poland
occurred in the House of Commons. The first
was on the 28th of June; the subject was again
introduced by Mr Cutlar Fergusson, who was seconded
by Lord Sandon (afterwards the Earl of Harrowby).
As on the previous occasion, the condemnation of
Russia's proceedings in Poland was unanimous. Lord
Morpeth spoke of ' the immortal memory of the land
that first resisted the torrent of Mahommedan invasion and secured the liberties and the religion of
Europe,' and O'Connell even went so far as to call the
Emperor Nicholas ' a miscreant.' This elicited an
expression of regret from Lord Palmerston at the use
of such language in the House, upon which Mr
Beaumont declared he was delighted at the appellation which had been given to the Emperor, and
entirely concurred in it; and Mr Hume said he would
not only call the Emperor a miscreant, but a monster
in human form. But nothing was to be done by
denunciation, however eloquent. Poland was in the
iron grasp of three of the strongest States in Europe,
and England had no power to help her.

CHAPTER XXVI

1834

THERE is a curious note in Prince Czartoryski's diary, dated the 12th November 1834, on the relations between Talleyrand and Lord Palmerston. 'Talleyrand,' he says, 'formerly in strict friendship with Palmerston, has now had a little quarrel with him because, when the latter complained that France did not respond to the overtures of England in the Eastern question, Talleyrand replied that France was only following the example of England when she was asked to act with France on behalf of Poland during the Revolution of 1831.' In a subsequent conversation with Lord Brougham (14th December 1834) the latter said of Talleyrand—' I think he does not just now know what he is talking about. Imaginez qu'il m'a parlé de la nécessité de rassembler un Congrès Européen qui aurait pour but de garantir les institutions existantes, et pour calmer les esprits, et qu'à ce Congrès la France et l'Angleterre déclareraient qu'ils mettraient des limites à la licence de la presse. C'est de la démence.'

During the same conversation Brougham said that

the reason why the English Government had refused
to join in a demonstration in favour of Poland in 1832
together with France, and with the concurrence of
Austria, was that it would have been necessary to
arm, and the Ministry was uncertain of its existence
in consequence of the Reform bill.   He called Thiers
'un petit littérateur,' and said that even Lord Durham
had not been able to say a word at St Petersburg.
Prince Czartoryski here remarked that Lord Durham
had told him he had spoken very strongly on the
subject of Poland at St Petersburg.   'Oui bien,'
answered Brougham, 'à M. de Nesselrode; mais à
l'Empereur lui-même il n'a pas osé dire un seul mot,
parcequ'il lui ferait la cour pour obtenir un cordon.
C'est l'homme le plus vain, le plus aristocrate, qui
existe.   Il a tourmenté pendant dix-huit mois Lord
Grey parcequ'il ne l'a pas fait de suite comte.   Il a
été contre Lord Grey pendant le Ministère Canning,
qui l'a fait entrer à la chambre des pairs.   Ce qui a
été mal calculé, parceque dans la chambre des com-
munes il avait quelque influence, au lieu que dans la
chambre haute il n'en a aucune.   C'est mon ami, et
cependant je ne puis m'empêcher de le dire.   On a
voulu nous brouiller, je n'ai rien dit de ce que m'on a
attribué; ce sont les journaux qui ont fait ce pâté.'
He afterwards proposed to the Prince to go to Italy
with him.   'If you do,' he added, 'people will say we
are plotting for Poland, and I shall be delighted.'

CHAPTER XXVII

1839

CONVERSATION WITH LORD PALMERSTON.—CIRCASSIA.—PROPOSAL TO SEND THE BRITISH FLEET INTO THE BLACK SEA.—RUSSIAN DESIGNS ON INDIA.—PERSIA.—AFGHANISTAN.—PALMERSTON'S OPINION OF METTERNICH.—TURKEY AND RUSSIA.

ON the 13th of February and the 10th of March 1839 Prince Czartoryski had conversations with Lord Palmerston on English Foreign Policy generally, and about Circassia, which had been invaded and nearly conquered, after a heroic resistance, by the Russian troops. The following is the Prince's report of these conversations:—

PRINCE CZARTORYSKI.—You have lost Persia , you are engaged in a costly war in India; Turkey is vacillating, and Circassia will fall if she does not obtain help. Why not send a British fleet into the Black Sea, or even only before Constantinople ? This would produce a great effect upon the entire East and restore your influence with the Porte.

LORD PALMERSTON.—The war in India is not very expensive, and Russia has been obliged to give up her plans as to Herat. Persia, it is true, is lost to us for the moment, but the movement at Candahar and Cabul, and the restoration of the old legitimate sovereign in these united Kingdoms, will secure the independence of Afghanistan and serve as a barrier against Persia and Russia. A British fleet cannot under the Treaty of 1809 enter the Dardanelles without the permission of the Sultan, and I am not at all sure he would give it. And what would the fleet do once it had got there? It would have either to blockade the coast of Circassia—which belongs to Russia, or at least was ceded to her by the Treaty of Adrianople, which has been recognised by England— or it would have to attack the Russian fleet, harbours, and arsenals. In either case this would be war. Now the English nation is able to make war, but it will only do so where its own interests are concerned. We are a simple and practical nation, a commercial nation; we do not go in for chivalrous enterprises or fight for others as the French do. Even supposing, as you seem to think, that Russia would not make war upon us if our fleet were to appear in the Black Sea, she would bitterly complain of our conduct, and we would have to explain it to Parliament, which would certainly not be satisfied with our arguments. We have a strong majority against us in the House of Lords; in the House of Commons we have an uncertain majority of thirty votes, which we would lose, and then we would be driven from office.

PRINCE CZARTORYSKI.—You might act without compromising yourselves officially. In Russia everything is done by the Government; in England much is left to the initiative of individuals acting in a private capacity. You might help the Circassians by private effort without open Government intervention.

LORD PALMERSTON.—Possibly ; but we have no secret funds which we could employ for such a purpose. Besides, it would soon be known ; nothing can long remain a secret in our country.

PRINCE CZARTORYSKI.—But then you are not on equal terms with Russia. She does not scruple to use every possible means of injuring you.

LORD PALMERSTON.—That is an advantage enjoyed by despotic States. Free States have other advantages.

PRINCE CZARTORYSKI.—By leaving Russia to act as she pleases you expose to tne greatest dangers the independence of the Asiatic States, and your own dominions in India.

LORD PALMERSTON.—True ; but John Bull will not go to war to save Circassia.

PRINCE CZARTORYSKI.—It is not only the fate of Circassia that is in question. You are losing all your influence over the Sultan ; already he has accepted the demands of Russia as to Wallachia, and if you continue your policy of non-intervention he may abandon you altogether.

LORD PALMERSTON.—I do not believe it. Our influence is like the tide, which, though it advances and then recedes, yet steadily gains ground. . . . Mehemet Ali is an animal that Russia is fattening before she sacrifices him. . . . Russia is unfortunately surrounded by weak neighbours like Turkey and Sweden, and by others attached to her either by an alliance of fear (Austria) or an alliance of relationship (Prussia).

PRINCE CZARTORYSKI.—So long as Poland remains

divided between the three Northern Powers, you cannot rely upon Austria.

LORD PALMERSTON.—No doubt; but how are we to induce her to change her policy? Prince Metternich is undoubtedly a man of great talent, but he is timid and prejudiced; he fears revolution more than anything else. He is accustomed to the admiration and incense of his *coterie*, who are offended if he is only praised in ordinary language. He cannot be persuaded that anything he thinks or does is not right. Besides, if there were an independent Poland, do you think Bohemia and Hungary would not claim independence too? Poland would no doubt want a representative Government, which implies a parliament, freedom of speech, and a free press. The very idea of these institutions would make Metternich's hair stand on end, he is so accustomed to be adored without the slightest opposition in his drawing-room. He said once that he would rather be a convict than a Minister in a free country. I do not think he would ever consent to the restoration of Poland unless there were a war, in which case Austria might find the Poles useful for defence or aggression.

PRINCE CZARTORYSKI.—The new French Ministry is strongly inclined to go hand-in-hand with England; and this would add weight to your representations at Vienna.

LORD PALMERSTON.—It would no doubt facilitate our action, but France must first reassure Austria as to Italy. She must be disabused of the idea that we are revolutionists, and she must be able to rely upon our support in the event of a war with Russia; but she does not trust us. I know that many people whose opinions I respect are in favour of sending our fleet into the Black Sea, but I have fully considered the matter and I do not see how such a course would be either desirable or practicable. . . . Besides, it would be a bad plan to try to secure the Sultan's independence by forcing his hand.

PRINCE CZARTORYSKI.—You have often done such a thing, as at Naples and Copenhagen.

LORD PALMERSTON.—At Constantinople, more than anywhere else, good can be done and evil prevented by an increase of *moral* influence. Our influence, joined to that of France and Austria, would produce an effect upon Russia which might be attained without a war. She will not be allowed to make any more victims.

PRINCE CZARTORYSKI.—Yes, but how about those she has made already? Your policy ought to satisfy Russia entirely if she is reasonable. She has taken so much that she can wish for little more. She is allowed to tear up and devour at her leisure all she has unjustly appropriated, and the sufferings of her victims are not even recognised.

LORD PALMERSTON.—I know that fresh horrors have been perpetrated in Poland of which people have no idea ; but this can only be remedied by a war. Yet who knows ? If we could only inspire Austria with full confidence in us and detach her from Russia, I am convinced that her moral influence might have a good effect on the fate of Poland.

PRINCE CZARTORYSKI.—The Opposition seems very warlike, and it would probably support you in a warlike policy.

LORD PALMERSTON.—Yes, they want us to augment the army and the fleet; but when the money will have to be found they will oppose every new tax and leave us in the lurch. These are the usual tactics of the party, and we are not going to be duped by them.

CHAPTER XXVIII

ONE of the most ardent supporters and patrons of the Literary Association of the Friends of Poland was H.R.H. the Duke of Sussex, who used to say that he once wore the Polish crown, as that of the latest Polish King, Stanislas Augustus, was put on his head by the guardian of the crown jewels at Berlin when he visited that city. The following letter is in reply to one from Prince Czartoryski thanking him for a speech he made at a meeting of the Association :—

MON CHER PRINCE,—Une multiplicité d'occupations auxquelles j'ai dû faire attention m'a empêché de répondre plus tôt à votre aimable lettre. Aujourd'hui, me trouvant plus en liberté, je m'empresse de vous remercier pour toutes les expressions obligeantes que vous avez bien voulu me marquer au sujet de notre réunion en faveur de la cause de la Pologne, à quelle occasion j'ai eu la satisfaction de présider.

Mes opinions en faveur d'une liberté réelle et constitutionelle ayant pour base et guide des lois sages, explicites, et definitives, sont trop connues pour

que j'aie besoin de vous les exposer ici, encore moins
de les répéter dans cette occasion. Ce sont des
principes que j'ai adoptés après une reflexion la plus
sérieuse ainsi que d'après une longue expérience.
C'est une matière de conscience la plus sacrée pour
moi, la considérant comme formant partie de ma
religion. Je n'ai donc fait que remplir mon devoir en
élevant ma voix contre des actes que je crois injustes
et contraires aux lois divines et humaines.

Dans un gouvernement constitutionnel comme
celui de l'Angleterre, où les ministres sont respons-
ables à la nation pour les conseils qu'ils soumettent
à leur maître, *le Roi n'a jamais tort*, mais dans un
gouvernement despotique le souverain ne jouit pas
d'un pareil avantage ; chaque acte de l'exécutive
est attribué à sa personne, comme émanant de sa
volonté immédiate, sans qu'on réfléchit qu'il peut y
avoir été poussé par des factions qui dirigent souvent
les affaires de l'Etat en secret, ou que dans certaines
occasions sa raison peut être ou avoir été surprise
par la misréprésentation de quelque ministre ainsi
que de quelque autre individu qui est irresponsable,
puisque la loi ignore son existence, et qui n'a en vue
que ses propres intérêts en flattant l'ambition du Prince
sans consulter aussi peu le bien être de sa patrie que
le bonheur général du genre humain.

Si mes remonstrances pouvaient parvenir aux
oreilles de l'Autocrate, comme les opinions désinteressées
ainsi que comme les expressions d'un cosmopolite qui
ne cherche que le bonheur de son voisin et qui travaille
incessamment pour établir une harmonie universelle
dans ce bas monde, et qu'elles puissent lui faire peur

pour quelques moments, je m'estimerai bien heureux ! ! !
Ce n'est pas seulement par des conquêtes qu'un
souverain se rend célèbre, ou qu'il gagne l'admiration
du monde, encore moins se fait-il aimer par de tels
procedés, mais c'est par des actes de justice et de
bienveillance qu'il contribue au bonheur, à la sécurité,
à la tranquillité de ses sujets. C'est en réprimant les
vues d'ambition et d'accroissement dans les autres, en
maintenant la paix, en encourageant les arts et les
sciences, ainsi qu'une bonne intelligence entre les
nations voisines et la sienne, qu'il acquiert l'estime des
hommes sages, justes, et loyaux, et qu'il laisse son nom
et sa renommée comme un héritage ainsi qu'un souvenir
précieux à la postérité. Voilà mes idées, mon cher
Prince, que je vous communique franchement, vous
priant en même temps d'être l'interprète de mes sentiments connus auprès de ces Messieurs qui avec vous
sont à la tête des différents bureaux pour conduire les
interêts des Polonais et qui se sont unis à vous pour
m'adresser une lettre à laquelle je mets le plus haut
prix, la regardant comme un témoignage public et
précieux de leur approbation de ces principes que je
me fais, et que je me ferai toujours, une gloire de
professer et de plaider dans toutes les occasions, quand
ils pourront produire du bien.—

Agréez, mon cher Prince, les assurances de mon
sincère estime et de ma haute considération, aussi de
mon amitié, avec lesquelles j'ai le plaisir de me dire
Votre dévoué et sincère ami,

(signed) FREDERIC, DUC DE SUSSEX.
AU PALAIS DE KENSINGTON,
ce 16 *de Juillet*, 1839.

CHAPTER XXIX

1853-5

ALTHOUGH Lord Palmerston did not conceal from Prince Czartoryski his conviction that in the state of affairs which then prevailed on the Continent nothing could be done for Poland, the noble character of the Prince, his devoted patriotism, and his wide knowledge and experience of European politics, made him a welcome visitor at the Foreign Office, and Lord Palmerston repeatedly took occasion to express his admiration and sympathy for the Polish nation and its venerable chief. After the last spark of Polish independence had been extinguished by the absorption of the Republic of Cracow into the Austrian State, notwithstanding the protests of England and France—which as usual remained fruitless in presence of the alliance of the three spoilers of Poland—Lord Palmerston made some appreciative remarks in a speech at the Mansion House on the devotion of Lord Dudley Stuart to the Polish cause, and a deputation from the Polish Historical Society took the opportunity of presenting him, in recognition of his sympathy for the

Poles, with a medal of Prince Czartoryski, on which was the inscription: ' H. T. P. Vice Comiti Palmerston quia memor exstat fandi atque nefandi. Societas Historica Polona grata offert.'

In 1853, when the Prince came to London to sound the disposition of the Ministry in view of the crisis in the East, he records in his diary (June 27) that he found Lord Aberdeen ' abaissé ; il a l'air de succomber sous le poids de la responsabilité.' A few days after he saw Lord Clarendon, Palmerston and Disraeli. The former gave him an impression of ' indécision—désir de conserver la paix.' His description of Palmerston is ' visage de bois, regard impassible, bouche close, pas un mot de réponse à tous mes arguments,' and of Disraeli, ' excellent pour la bonne cause ; nous causons en parfaite amitié sur la Pologne.' Lord Malmesbury called upon him and expressed ' excellentes intentions.'

In Paris Prince Adam Czartoryski was one of Napoleon III's most trusted counsellors, and he sent numerous memoranda to the Emperor on the conduct of the Russian campaign which, though the Prince was then eighty-three years of age, entered minutely into every detail and showed an extraordinary power of remembering past events and adapting the knowledge derived from them to existing circumstances. He was a warm advocate of an Anglo-French alliance, and in a memorandum* addressed to the French Minister of Foreign Affairs on the 10th of February 1853, he pointed out that such an alliance would be the only means of preventing the encroachments of

---

* The drafts of the memoranda and notes drawn up on this occasion are in the Prince's own handwriting.

Russia in the East. 'The conduct of Russia and Austria towards Turkey,' says this document, 'resembles in all respects that pursued by those Powers with regard to Poland, and undoubtedly tends to a similar result. Turkey and the peoples forming that country can only be saved by the simultaneous and united action of France and England. They alone, acting with the same object, can neutralise the deleterious influence and the immense weight of the two former Powers. . . . Such an alliance, though evidently necessary for the good of Europe, yet presents many difficulties. Under the Restoration the French Government was alienated from England and sympathised with Russia. The policy of Louis Philippe, though more friendly to England, was too vacillating and timorous to inspire British statesmen with confidence ; and the recent talk of French officers about an invasion of England has naturally increased the distrust towards France on the other side of the Channel. The subordinate British agents in the East, on the other hand, show an extreme jealousy of their French colleagues, and instead of acting hand in hand with them in matters where the two countries have a common interest, they often foil them at the risk of injuring the interests of their own country. The struggle which has begun between the Protestant propaganda and Roman Catholicism in the East may add to these difficulties. Yet they must be overcome in view of the supreme interest of justice, of the common good, of the security of all Europe, and of the dignity of the two Powers which are its true guardians. A sincere, decided, and persevering line of conduct will remove many obstacles, and if frank communications and friendly overtures do not prove sufficient, France should prove her sincerity by at once offering to act in concert with England in any warlike step she might propose to take. Russia and Austria should not be allowed any longer to pose as the protectors of the Christian subjects of the Porte. It should be pointed out to the Sultan that if in his relations with his Christian subjects he acts at the dictation of his two enemies, he will only humiliate himself in the eyes of the peoples under his rule, while if he listens to the counsels of his allies, he will gain both in security and in strength. To put a stop to the abuses of the Turks with regard to the Christians would be to render a signal service to the Ottoman Empire and furnish it with the most efficacious guarantee against its early dissolution.'

In a further note, dated the 28th of March 1854 (the date of the declaration of war against Russia), Prince Czartoryski gave some valuable hints as to the best means of carrying on a war against Russia by England and France. 'Russia,' he says, 'is defended on the west by the two German Powers, and cannot be reached from that side so long as their neutrality is maintained and respected. But her frontier may be attacked at other points with advantage. The first of these is the Crimea and the adjacent territories. The second is the Lower Danube and the Polish Ukraine on the borders of the Black Sea. The third is the coast of Lithuania on the Baltic. These three points, if attacked simultaneously, would all have the advantage of being in territories inhabited by populations which wish to throw off the Russian yoke. It would first be necessary to conquer the Crimea and Sebastopol, which would entail the destruction of the enemy's fleet; next, and if possible at the same time, to occupy with an expeditionary force the country between Batoum and Anaklea. The Russian part of the coast, being undefended on the side of the sea, could be easily captured in a few hours. The country is surrounded by mountains which cannot be crossed by an army with artillery, so that the expeditionary corps, being master of the sea, would be perfectly safe, and would be able, together with the Turkish troops in Armenia, to march on Tiflis by way of Kutais and Gori. The people of the Caucasus, who would be supplied with arms and ammunition, would rise *en masse* from the Caspian to the Black Sea; while the Georgians and Imeritians, who also are far from satisfied with the methods of Russian Government, would ask to be allowed to con- stitute a separate State as formerly. As the Russian army in these districts contains a great many Poles, it would be desirable to attract them to the armies of the allies by displaying the Polish flag. At the second point of attack—the Lower Danube and the Polish Ukraine—the allied armies would find themselves in a country rich in grain and with a numerous and friendly population and large towns. The Cossack legion,* if raised to 10,000 men, with a corresponding proportion of infantry and artillery, would here render important services. The people would regard them as their brothers and co-religionists, and would join

* Formed of Poles who had taken service with the Sultan.

them under the national (Polish) standard. Finally, while the English and French fleets would threaten Riga, Revel, and Cronstadt, thereby forcing Russia to keep a large force at those places, an expeditionary corps landed in Lithuania would produce most decisive results, for it would penetrate into the very heart, so to say, of European Russia. It will be for experienced naval officers to determine at which point of the coast of Lithuania, or the adjoining coast of Courland, the landing could most easily be effected. The corps should consist of from 30,000 to 40,000 men. It would find itself in a wooded country surrounded by marshes and lakes, well suited to a guerilla war, and lying across the chief line of communication between the capital and the western frontier. This country is inhabited by a Roman Catholic people who are thoroughly Polish in sentiment, and would at once join the national standard. The combined force, after securing its communications with the sea, could then either assist the fleet in an attack upon Riga, or march upon Wilna, supplying the people with arms, destroying the military magazines of the Russians, and cutting off the Russian forces in the north from those in the west and south.'

Prince Czartoryski's scheme, it will be seen, aimed at striking Russia where she is most vulnerable—in Poland. But the allies, fearing to raise Austria and Prussia against them, only adopted that part of it which relates to the Crimea and the Baltic. Moreover—as was said by Lord Palmerston to General Zamoyski when the latter proposed that the Polish legion, which formed part of the Turkish Contingent during the war, and was paid by England, should be allowed to carry the Polish flag—the allies did not wish 'to make an enemy of Russia.' It was not to be a war 'à outrance,' but a mere trial of strength; Russia was not to be crippled, but only to be forced to abandon (for a time) her designs on Turkey and the Black Sea. Under these circumstances it is not surprising, though surprise has been expressed on the subject by some English writers, that the Poles should during the war have maintained a passive attitude. There were 100,000 Russian troops in their country; the Poles were without arms or war material of any kind; and they were not willing to be massacred *pour les beaux yeux* of England and France. The following passages from a letter addressed by Prince Czartoryski to his countrymen on the 26th of August 1854, throw an interesting light on the views of the leading Poles at this period :—

'It has been said that you have everywhere entered into a conspiracy of calmness and wisdom. Let us strive to justify this charge. Receive advances and offers from whatever side they may come, but before taking action insist upon substantial guarantees for your future. Such guarantees would be afforded by the creation of a Polish force under Polish leaders, to serve as a nucleus for an army to be formed out of those whose ranks are filled by our countrymen ; by the recognition of independent Polish authorities ; and by a declaration on the part of the Powers, or any one of them with the consent of its allies, that Poland has a right to an independent existence. . . . We have been too often deceived by promises, and been made the victims of our too adventurous and trusting spirit. My advice and that of all the sincere friends of Poland is that you should keep quiet and wait events. This is not, as some suppose, a proof of apathy, but of wisdom and prudence; of the strength of a nation which knows how to restrain itself, and which will only show the more energy when the time of action arrives.'

What his own course would be in such an event he had already stated in an address to the Polish Historical Society. 'When,' he said, 'the decisive moment comes, I will go with my sons where duty calls me, and will not hesitate to give up to my country, which I have served all my life, the last remnants of my strength and my abilities.'

CHAPTER XXIX

1855-61

THE following are extracts from letters sent by the Prince to London during the Crimean War :—

'16th May 1854.

'Sweden is ready for everything, and wishes to act with considerable forces. She asks and offers to join the allies. What folly if they refuse ! Clarendon knows all about it, and I hear would like to accept. The negotiation is being conducted through his brother Charles Villiers. Here (in Paris) all is for peace. Persigny now declares that the naval superiority of the Powers is sufficient.'

'19th May 1854.

'The allies can only expect a fruitful result from the war in the alliance of Sweden, who is ready and willing to act at once, and of Poland, who only waits to be called upon and armed. These are the only real allies of the Western Powers. The Roumanians also should not be neglected. . . . If peace is impossible, can the Powers refuse the overtures of Sweden,

who would probably be followed by Austria? I
cannot believe that the British Cabinet would neglect
such an opportunity or not use every means at its
disposal to induce France also to take advantage of it.'

'18*th December* 1854.

'If the Polish question should be raised by the
war, and Austria be unwilling to mix up Galicia in it,
Russian Poland alone would rise if it were declared
independent, and this would be a decisive force on the
side of the allies. Galicia and Posen will remain
quiet; for that I will vouch.'

'20*th December* 1854.

'On nous reprochait jadis que nous étions prompts
à nous jeter en avant de toutes les aventures; à
présent nous sommes plus réfléchis, moins audacieux,
moins imprudents, et on nous reproche aussi. Je
crois que nous avons raison d'être sages et de demander
des garanties, avant d'offrir un dévouement sans bornes.
Telle est l'opinion positive du pays, et telle est celle de
l'émigration, avec les modifications que sa position
comporte.'

'23*rd April* 1855.

'Lord Stratford est un terrible homme; son
ambassade et les grandes affaires qui lui ont passé par
les mains, et les événements, qui ne furent pas
toujours heureux, l'ont rendu je crois encore plus
nerveux, plus irascible et difficile à vivre, qu'il ne
l'était naturellement.'

* * * * *

Prince Adam Czartoryski's long life was now drawing to a close. The Treaty of Paris, which closed the Crimean War, was a great disappointment to him; but he did not abandon all hope. At the time, says M. de Mazade in his introduction to the French edition of the Memoirs, when the negotiations of the Paris Congress were still going on, the Prince was preparing a fresh memorandum on the Polish question, when a friend informed him that the bases of the Treaty had been agreed upon, and that Poland was not mentioned in it. An expression of pain passed across his face; he stopped writing for a moment, but soon proceeded with his manuscript, saying : ' It will do for another time.' The accession of Alexander II, notwithstanding his brusque speech to the Polish nobles—' Point de rêveries ! tout ce que mon père a fait est bien fait,'—seemed to offer some prospect of a change of system in Poland,* and after the conclusion of the Treaty of Paris, Prince Adam drew up an elaborate paper, fully describing the rights and grievances of his country, for the use of M. de Morny, the French Ambassador at the Russian Court, on his proceeding to Moscow to take part in the ceremony of the coronation. During the first few years of his reign, the new Emperor seemed almost as well disposed to the Poles as his uncle, Alexander I, had been. But, like him, he admired liberty in theory and abhorred it in practice. He gave the Poles some liberal and national institutions, and persecuted them directly they made use of

---

* In May 1836, Prince Orloff told Lord Clarendon that the Emperor was well disposed towards the Poles, but would do nothing if any of the Powers should nterfere. (M.S. Diary of Prince Czartoryski.)

their newly acquired liberties. The result was the national movement of 1861-2,* in which the Poles opposed a passive resistance to the oppressive measures of the Government, until the Wielopolski decree for drafting the youth of the country into the Russian army drove them into insurrection. Prince Czartoryski admired and praised the movement, but did not live to see its sanguinary consequence. In a letter written to Count Andrew Zamoyski in his own hand, at the age of ninety-one, a few months before his death, he says (20 March 1861) :—

'For the last fortnight we have been full of anxiety, emotion, admiration, and inexpressible joy, as if we had been present during those days with you in Warsaw. One may well say that God has manifested a great deed in you. In one day he has raised the nation to such a height of moral power as no other nation has ever reached ; it can only be compared to the inspiration of the first Christians, who conquered the world armed only with the palm of martyrdom. God forbid that you should descend from that position ; for if Poland remains there, she will attain her great object.

* It is known that after the Crimean War Austria began to show herself favourable to the Poles. This change of policy became more evident during the insurrection of 1863, and the Poles in Austria now have free institutions and a national self-government which make them the envy of their countrymen in Russia and Prussia. The following extract from a letter addressed to Prince Adam Czartoryski on the 15th of May 1860, by a personage holding a high position at Vienna, may be quoted in this connection : —

'On m'a indiqué comme candidat proposé (pour le trône de la Pologne) le second fils de la Reine d'Angleterre. On envisage ce choix comme un moyen pour calmer les inquiétudes jalouses de la Grande Bretagne. Le Cabinet d'ici ne voit pas d'un mauvais œil cette question. Il lui sera même favorable du jour où il saura ce qui lui reviendra en échange pour la Galicie. Le besoin d'un intermédiaire entre l'Autriche et la Russie se fait sentir tous les jours davantage. L'Empereur F. J. (François Joseph) reconnaît toute l'infamie du partage de la Pologne et toutes les difficultés qu'il a amenées à l'Autriche. Il s'est exprimé plusieurs fois très-clairement à ce sujet. Ces jours-ci cette question sera portée au Conseil des Ministres afin de formuler les instructions à donner au réprésentant de la cour de Vienne à Saint-Pétersbourg.'

'So long as the news which arrived here only spoke of street disturbances and broken windows, the Emperor said this ought to stop, as the movement was an untimely one and would injure the cause instead of helping it. But now, after the important events which have occurred at Warsaw, showing how strong is the national spirit, he thinks otherwise. The Western Powers, at first not believing the news, and then astonished at them, cannot as yet understand what is going on and fear that the only result will be an exacerbation of Russian severity. No one thinks of giving us any official help ; do not therefore in any way reckon upon it ; but be convinced that if you adhere to your present line of conduct, public opinion in Europe will be on your side and will insist on a more moderate policy on the part of Russia. The present friendly understanding between that Power and France, has enabled Napoleon III already to make confidential representations on the subject at St Petersburg.

'In conclusion I must again urge you not to descend from the position which is your strength and moral support. Let all good citizens unite to strengthen the conviction among our countrymen that if they allow themselves to be drawn into an armed struggle, they will only bring upon their country fruitless defeats, while by an unarmed resistance to unjustifiable and wicked oppression, they will avert it and gain a moral victory.'

In the same spirit the Prince addressed his countrymen in a speech made on the 3rd of May, 1861.

'Do not descend,' he said, 'from the elevation

where nations and sovereigns must respect you. By firmly remaining there you will be safer and more certain in seeing your goal and continually approaching it. Though racked by bitter suffering, though driven to despair by treason and violence, resist the temptation to fight your oppressors by meaner weapons. You shine above them by your virtue and goodness : these are the indomitable forces of Poland, and in them lie her hopes for the future.'

He died at Montfermeil, near Meaux, on the 15th of November 1861. Like his great contemporary Pitt—Prime Minister of England when he was Foreign Minister of Russia—Prince Adam's last words were of his country. Pitt, with the sudden despair of baffled genius, lamented the misfortunes which he thought were about to fall on England ; Czartoryski's tender and hopeful spirit pictured to him a new Poland rising chastened and invigorated by her long martyrdom. There was as little ground for despondency in the one case as for hope in the other. The disappointment of Austerlitz was soon brilliantly retrieved by the British victories in the Peninsula and at Waterloo ; the hopes raised by the noble self-sacrifice of the Polish nation perished in the midst of blood and ruin.

THE END

ALPHABETICAL INDEX

ERRATA

In pages 18 and 19, *for* Woloczyn, *read* Wolczyn.

In the footnote to page 73, *for* 1795, *read* 1794.

In the footnote to page 74, *for* 1434, *read* 1595.

In page 151, line 11, *for* Wiszniowiec, *read* Wisniowiec ; and in line 13, *for* Wiszniowiecki, *read* Wisniowiecki.

In page 152, line 5, and the footnote, *for* Wiszniowiecki, *read* Wisniowiecki.

In the footnote to page 152, *for* 1675, *read* 1673.

In page 170, line 27, *for* 1793, *read* 1798.

In the footnote to page 183, *introduce the words* and at Narva *after* where.